AF508052

Impressions of Lucia Richard: Literature, Art and Society in the Chile of the Fifties

Daniel Piedrabuena Ruiz-Tagle

Booksideals

ASTURIAS, SPAIN

To my sons, heirs of this great life story.
To my uncle Guillermo Piedrabuena Richard and
my brother Juan Enrique for all their affection.
To my great-uncles, Carlos and Roberto Humeres Solar,
large promoters of Chilean art and intellectuality

"Works are loves and not good reasons"

—LOPE DE VEGA CARPIO (1562-1635)

INDEX

hrough the pages of *Impressions of Lucia Richard*, we enter the literary and artistic lifework of the poet, writer, storyteller, essayist, columnist, lecturer, biographer, and radio speaker Lucia Richard. This is an engaging work, which addresses the creation and activities of the so-called Cenacle of Poetry of the Conservatory of Declamation, making a pleasant follow-up not only of Lucia Richard but of all her companions. In particular, it focuses on the study of a group of women in the forties and fifties, shedding light on events until now hardly evoked.

Among them, it is the founding of the House of America in Santiago and all the initiatives and projects of these people. It is an unprecedented work in its class that revives endearingly the personality of Vera Zouroff and her entire group. Through recitals and lectures, Latin American congresses and publications, these women joined their voices to express their truth, pursuing an ideal that has endured to this day. The involvement and recognition of these groups by such outstanding people as Samuel Lillo, Gabriela Mistral, Miguel Rocuant, Ines Echeverria, Jorge Gustavo Silva, and many others, gives a seal of quality and transcendence to their committed work.

We are faced with the powerful emotional strength of a group that actively struggled to find its place in history, to restore the dignity of women, and ultimately, to create a brotherhood among the peoples of The Americas. Their aspiration for universality led them to try to build a transnational project that would survive the passage of time and spread a message as inspired as altruistic that gave meaning to their lives through the renewing of their cultural heritage in search of a fairer and free world.

They fought against the intransigence of Santiago's society. To achieve it, they confronted the same bourgeois society they belonged but were nevertheless trying to transform. On their journey, these women found light in the shadows. But on the horizon, there was always a glimpse of their diamond ideals: love, truth, and spirit worship. These were for them the only forces that made the mountains roar, freeing man from his maliciousness. In their endeavor, they envisioned a world in which they could raise the culture, the identity, the far-looking, of the essential human being. Thus they forged the greatness of their dreams, showing us how the most beautiful things in life can be within everyone's reach.

Daniel Piedrabuena Ruiz-Tagle

May 13, 2016

INTRODUCCTION

Under the halo of mystery with which all poets perish, Lucia Richard, my grandmother, left this world on August 14, 1969. After her death, it only remained the disbelief of her loved ones at the impact of the sudden loss and some scattered writings. There also persisted the riddle of a person who had devoted her whole life to cultivating immateriality. At the time of her disappearance, I was only five years old. I scarcely have a few fleeting memories of her in Conchali's farm, a photo, and little else.

However, something of her transcended time and settled in the far corners of my subconscious: a look that moved me, a natural grace, or a way of expressing beauty. Once and again, I see her in the long line of trees that led to the entrance of the farm. There she appears before me with an aura of goodness and purity. I can still feel her pale, sweet face, full of tenderness, and sensitivity. Then she enters my childish world, telling me affectionate words that today I cannot decipher.

Like those falling leaves, which she so often evoked in her poetry, time passed. The autumn of life came. The people who left and were so important by then are now barely remembered. In 1973 my father, looking for new professional horizons, moved with his family to Spain. New events covered as snow the remembrances of yesterday, and little by little, our Chilean past was fading away from our memory.

A new but routine life came to replace that other one full of emotions. Despite this, an idealized feeling attracted me again and again with increasing strength. Something imprecise and persistent remained in my consciousness, crying out for expression. It was that luminous childhood manifested in me irresistibly. Beyond the unfathomable oceans, the unfortunate times, and the storms of life, Lucia came to me like the spores roaming in the vastness, looking for a promising place to germinate.

I was about 13 when I discovered my grandmother's poems. At that time, there were only two of her books in my house. Their covers, faded by time, were not luxurious. One was published in 1925 and was entitled, *Sursum Corda*. On the first page, you could barely see her profile in a sketch by Jorge Delano. Its prologue spoke of humility and affection. The other book appeared in 1938 and was simply entitled *Poetry*. This second book had neither prologue nor images. The first poem told us to always remember her with the naïve smile of the Mona Lisa.

As I read them, I perceived her love for life, her high sensitivity to world beauties, a soft melancholy tempered by moments of happiness, and a way of giving and sharing that mesmerized me. Time and again, I went back to those pages that became my particular book of faith. Since then, I began to write my poems and writings, perhaps trying to emulate my grandmother's virtues. Later I was captivated by the reading of her *Travel Memories* of 1934 and then her 1946 stories *The Enigma*.

Thus I grew up dazzled by these beautiful expressions of spirituality that, over the years, gave meaning to my existence. Around 1995, I took a trip to Italy, visiting the cities where my grandmother had been in the 1930s. During this tour, I had the opportunity to experience that wonderful Renaissance she cherished so much. Year after year, I continued to enjoy in Spain the subtle verses of my grandmother Lucia. Meanwhile, my aunt Carmen Piedrabuena Richard, on the other side of the ocean, patiently collected her mother's works.

Around 1997, my sister Maria de la Luz brought me from Chile a shipment from my aunt, Carmen. It contained several articles by my grandmother, reviews of her work, as well as her essay entitled *Mrs. Marina Ortiz de Gaete*. I kept in touch with my aunt, and thanks to the development of the internet, I soon got her radio auditions, her philosophical studies, her plays, her poetry *Blue Smoke*, and other unpublished essays and works. In this way, I obtained most of Lucia's literary production.

During these years, journeys of my brothers and relatives to Spain followed one another, bringing me news from my homeland. In April 2002, I traveled to Chile and met my uncles and cousins. I also took the time to visit all the museums in the capital, soaking up the Chilean culture. An exciting moment occurred on Christmas 2004. My uncle Guillermo Piedrabuena Richard, despite his many responsibilities as Attorney General, found time to pay tribute to his mother, Lucia, by presenting her *Complete Works* to the public. Along with moving speeches, the newspaper *El Mercurio* published several articles about her, and copies of the book were distributed. We also had the honor of seeing the piece with a preface by Hugo Montes, a member of the Chilean Academy of Language.

This new impulse represented an immense effort, this time much more formalized, to bring together all Lucia Richard's works. For the first time, a linguist, an academic, recognized Lucia Richard as part of her generation. For the first time, we had an overview of her writings. However, due to formatting constraints, the work was limited, leaving some unpublished works aside from the complete compilation. Still, it became a great achievement that paved the way for others to expand that vision.

Later, small findings made me realize that we were not having a comprehensive approach to her figure. Therefore, it was possible that underneath the tip of the iceberg, an imposing personality remained hidden. It is also true that Lucia's work was not universally recognized. Yet, she was acclaimed in her time, even beyond the boundaries of Chilean culture. Many have speculated that her countless family duties and concerns - despite the help of maids - did not leave her enough room to consolidate a professional career in literature. However, it also distorts reality not to recognize Lucia's leading role and her contributions to a whole generation of intellectuals. Among her many achievements, we must mention her active support for Chilean feminism.

Therefore, my first intention was to complement the *Complete Works*. I did so by correcting small errors and omissions, highlighting those unpublished works not included in the compilation, and finally, enhancing all unknown about Lucia Richard. Thanks to detailed research, I have found four new articles written by the author: "To Gabriela Mistral" 1922; "The Women of Don

Quixote" 1946 (*Revista SECH*); "Who is Gonzalez Vera?" 1950 *(La Hora)*; "The Book of the Hours" 1957 (*El Mercurio*), and an interview in the *newspaper Opinion.* Also, it appeared many literary reviews and bios on the writer unheard by the family.

Moreover, it was interesting to study several works of literature that mentioned Lucia. These publications placed her amid a maelstrom of cultural initiatives and in contact with many artists and intellectuals of her generation. In this same regard, it was useful to examine the newsletters of the Cenacle of Poetry. Now we could understand in greater depth the goals of these groups, their activities, and purposes. To my surprise, their members stood out among the most prominent scholars of that time.

It also became essential to enter into the dynamic personality of Vera Zouroff, the main mentor of Lucia's intellectual career. She was the cyclone that fostered an entire generation of artists and promoted many cultural projects. Thanks to the study of the poetic recitals organized in Santiago by the feminist, it was possible to learn about Lucia's participation in these events and the great reviews they had in the continental press.

Other exciting facts about Lucia include the discovery of new radio programs run by her, which until now were totally unknown to her family. These programs allow us to understand the true scope of the lectures given by the poet. It was also essential to know in greater detail all the ins and outs of Chilean feminism and the real involvement of our protagonist in these events. Likewise, it enriched this work by getting to know its main participants and the objectives of the Pan American Women's Round Table of Chile, among many other themes.

Equally important was the study of Vera Zouroff's book entitled *The Cenacle of Poetry to its Poets*. The work included Lucia as a prominent figure among the most significant personalities of the time. It was also very informative to explore Vera's bi-monthly publication entitled *Women of America*. This gazette collected news of these groups and showed Lucia in direct contact with many of her Cenacle colleagues.

The primary pursuit of the publication was to divulge the achievements of Americanism, bringing together intellectuals from all over the continent. It also publicized the great undertakings of the recently created House of America in Santiago, a decisive moment in which Lucia actively took part. Along with this periodical, the *Bulletin of the House of America* turned a useful resource to recover many facts.

Another matter to consider is the many members of the Cenacle who were in constant communication with Gabriela Mistral. The greatest literary figure of the time was very aware of the activities of her companions in Chile. Recently a valuable letter from Vera Zouroff has been found. It shows her at the head of the House of America's Steering Committee, welcoming Gabriela Mistral upon her arrival in Chile in 1954. Besides, the entire committee signed the letter, including Lucia Richard. No less exciting was discovering Lucia's collaboration with the famous musicologist Rene Amengual. Together they wrote Christmas songs, in which he composed the music, and our artist collaborated with the texts. Hopefully, one day they will be played again.

Another important aspect of this book has been the literary analysis of Lucia Richard's work. This examination has become the most complex and challenging task. Some say that she was progressive, that pantheism underlies her work, as we can also perceive a mystical halo in her writings. But what were her aesthetic conceptions? What was her position on modernism? What did Lucia think of surrealism, cubism, impressionism, and existentialism? What affinity did she have with Pablo Neruda and Gabriela Mistral? What was the canon of beauty that the artist was pursuing? What was her judgment of new scientific trends in the art such as Psychoanalysis? What ideology did her writings convey?

In 2004, Andonie Dracos, a journalist from *El Mercurio*, wrote an article defining her as: *"The writer who transgressed the canons without breaking them."* (2004). Reflecting on this article, I got interested in knowing the canons she transgressed and the ones she did not break. Was Lucia Richard an advanced woman for her time, or a regressive woman? Was she a representative of bourgeois literature or an exponent of popular literature? And finally, was she a romantic, criollist, costumbrist, or naturalist writer?

In her article, Ms. Dracos says that Lucia was undoubtedly: *"an outpost in her time, feminist and multi-faceted."* (2004). The renowned journalist Pedro

Pablo Guerrero had a different opinion in his article "Reviving Lucia Richard." For him, *"She was not a militant feminist, but the writer showed sympathy for women's demands."* (2015).

In contrast to this, Toto Romero, in her article in *Caras magazine* entitled "Très chic revolutionaries," places Lucia Richard among the first feminist leaders to promote poetry, music, and various cultural initiatives between 1940 and 1960 (ca 2006). Finally, the acclaimed scholar Hugo Montes, in the prologue to *Lucia Richard's Complete Works*, portrayed her as a lyrical poet, pointing out the great difficulties of women of her generation (2004).

All these questions have intrigued me, and I have tried to answer them all. Lucia Richard was a woman of the time, a country, a continent, and her social group. In her personality, you can see very advanced aspects along with more conservative ones. She was a woman who had a place within the intellectuals of the time, especially among feminists. This space should be duly recognized.

Although Lucia Richard wrote, published, and carried out cultural activities from the 30s to the 60s, she rather belonged to the generation of the forties. However, her most outstanding achievements took place from the end of the forties to the mid-fifties. We must not forget that she led a radio program between 1949 to 1951, inaugurated The House of America in Santiago in 1950, published important articles in *El Mercurio* in the fifties, concluded *Blue Smoke* in 1957, and even wrote excellent essays in the 60s. For all these reasons, I thought it more appropriate to include in the title the borderline period of the 1950s to describe most of her activities.

In conclusion, I hope to have contributed with this work to enhance the figure of Lucia Richard, or at least to value her role in Chilean letters. Now we can see her not only as an author of works of greater or lesser importance but as a dynamic writer of her generation who was in contact with the intellectual pleiade of the forties and fifties, contributing unequivocally to the advancement of national thinking.

From this point of view, it is no longer so important to respond to the fact that Lucia published some works and yet left others unpublished. Neither is it necessary to consider her greater or minor literary transcendence. But we must realize that in one way or another, she helped to channel the spiritual progress of a beautiful country. It will not be the first time in the history of art that an exceptional talent dissipates ignored in the twilight of one era to be appreciated in another. I would venture to predict that this will be the case for Lucia Richard and her precious work.

Daniel Piedrabuena Ruiz-Tagle
El Casar, Guadalajara, July 14, 2010

CHAPTER I

OVERVIEW OF HER LIFE AND WORK

An Intellectual Committed to Art and Beauty

Lucia Richard Barnard was born in Santiago on December 13, 1900, in a prosperous family, being the daughter of Enrique Richard Fontecilla and Delia Barnard Ramirez. She died in Viña del Mar on August 14, 1969. What a brief epitaph for a woman who loved life with overwhelming intensity! She was descended from two English families and inherited from them those feelings of cold overseas countries, evocations of distant druid lands, foreboding, and legends. In those lands, writers like John Keats, Percy Shelley, or Lord Byron were born. From her ancestors, the author received a gentle melancholy, along with deep psychological introspection.

Her great-grandfather had been Henry Richard, an Englishman from the Isle of Guernsey. This island locates in the middle of the Channel, which successively had English and French sovereignty. Educated in his youth in London, he later, in 1819, settled in Chile, becoming a great educator. His contemporaries praised him for having introduced new methods of teaching. He also achieved considerable notoriety like a teacher of English and French.

He was one of the first teachers of the National Institute. In 1847 he taught at the Minvielle School in Santiago. He was a man of extraordinary accuracy in all his deeds. He died in Santiago after half a century, dedicated to teaching the youth. The educators Jose Bernardo Suarez and Jose Antonio Perez appreciated him. They called him the most original and admirable man for his righteous conduct and the discipline of his correct and exemplary customs (Figueroa, 1900).

Another of her ancestors was John James Barnard, a member of an illustrious family of merchants from Boston, Lincolnshire. In his youth, in 1805, he attended at the Normanstone School. In this establishment, he regularly read the book of Adam Smith, *The Wealth of Nations*, work that preserves his annotations. He migrated to Chile before 1810, where he became the leader of the English community in Valparaíso. In his new country, he developed important commercial activities. He collaborated with O'Higgins and San Martin in pursuit of Chile's independence, providing intelligence and resources, fighting for the freedom of trade. He was the brother of Robert Barnard, founder of a distinguished family in the USA. So well positioned he was, that exchanged letters with Thomas Jefferson, president of that country[1].

Lucia Richard wanted to be remembered with the smile of Mona Lisa and found a resemblance to her personality in the portrait of the Sphinx. Thus, with the apparent simplicity of these two fleeting perceptions, she appears before us as an enigmatic woman. And so she built a world of beauty and truth, in a time and a place, where the woman did not find space to express herself. The young girl received a traditional and religious education at the College of the Nuns of the Sacred Heart of Santiago. In its classrooms, she was

---

[1] From these ancestors of hers, Lucia must have had many references, and it is not surprising that she inherited many of their tastes. Both the Historical Society of Washington and George Washington University hold a great deal of documentation about the Barnard family (Robert, William, Samuel, John James, Theodosia, Mary, Crosbie, etc.). They not only have information about their earlier settlements in England or their pedigree. They also have records of their many activities in the USA. Everything suggests that John James, the youngest son of this wealthy saga of bankers-merchants, received a less attractive destination like that of Chile, farther away from England. His older brothers instead established major commercial networks and operational bases in the United States. This American branch of the family is behind the founding of IBM Company.

a companion of Juana Fernandez, later canonized by the Pope, with the name of Saint Theresa of the Andes.

Nothing presaged then, the depth of her thought, or the diversity of her many interests, which in time would make her a great writer. At this moment, she outlines only a few family epigrams. At eleven, she lost her father for whom she felt true worship. This loss leaves a deep vacuum in her sensitive spirit. Shortly afterward, she began to write her first poems as "Avenue of the Pines," where we can guess her early love for nature. Her world was that of abstractions, which by then could reflect almost a mys-tical immanence for everything created.

In her writing in prose, *The Path of the Kangaroo*, she describes her first experiences in her father's beau-tiful country house in Ñuñoa. Immersed in that garden, she slipped away, giving free rein to her first thoughts. The poet experienced, for the first time, what would be in her later life a perpetual evasion. Lucia felt an urgent need to express herself. She tried with music, which she loved powerfully. But then she could not play well, nor did she consider gifted enough for composition.

Lucia Richard
in her twenties

She then rehearsed with painting, but she made it worse. At fifteen, she became interested in astronomy, tried to draw, at-tempted with acting, continued with the dance, but nothing materialized. Afterward, she devoted herself to writing. *"Devote yourself ... these are mere words without meaning when you refer to a woman!"* (Richard, 2004, pp. 27-35). At that point, with the limitations that the social environment imposed on her sex, Lucia had discovered her interest in all manifestations of art, culture, and the human heart. The impediments were considerable, but she would not give up. Lucia would be a *savant* for the rest of her life.

After these first sketches, she channeled her nascent intellectual vocation in a first attempt to conquer the public sphere. She did so with her article enti-tled "To Gabriela Mistral," which appeared in the press on April 16, 1922 (Richard, 1922). The young author had just married in 1920 with the lawyer Guillermo Piedrabuena Bories and signed adding the surname of her husband.

In a tone of humility and tenderness, she thanks the universal poet for her poems *Songs of the Cradle*. With its deep meanings, she claims to comfort her first child.

We can also contemplate these first columnist abilities in her "Letter to the Women of The Americas." It appeared on the 31 of December 1926 in a Viña del Mar publication. In her writing, she returns to the subject of the "Song of Cradle," this time creation of the Spanish author Martinez Sierra (Richard, 2004, page 456).

At the early age of twenty-four, she published her first work, *Sursum Corda*, which had remarkable success in Santiago's circles. Very soon, it captivated her readers with the beautiful and delicate craft of her verses. *Sursum Corda* is a Latin term meaning "above the hearts"! This expression was used in liturgical services to incite fervor. It is also defined as a call to elevate the mind and heart towards the best: intelligence headed to its rational use and the spirit towards courage and hope (Richard, 1925).

The book was edited by Jorge Delano, a renowned cartoonist and political caricaturist. It contained simple but suggestive illustrations of his, and glamorous poems like "Pray." Here, Lucia manifests an ethical code, a Decalogue of behaviors, of a man who wants to achieve great goals in life. In her verses, she depicts the greatness idolized towards her father, in a work that directs to her newborn son. The author glorifies a superior man, but not as an oppressor of the weak. Instead, he is an individual gifted with exemplary virtues that make him prostrate before the miseries of this world. It is an indisputable moral legacy that years later deeply impressed the Brazilian poet Jesu de Miranda. So stunned he was that soon after he translated it into his language[2].

---

[2] Recently a first notebook of the poetry of Lucia has been found, dated January 3, 1921. It anticipates much poetry that later she included in *Sursum Corda*. It also incorporated other unpublished ones: "To my Mother," "Who Will Never Find a Strong Woman," "Excelsior," "Contemplation," "Spring Song," "The Swallows Come," "The Birds Sing in the Cornfields," "The Souls' Love," and "Landscapes." "The Avenue of the Pines" was not part of this notebook, and its exact date is unknown. Some believed she wrote it in Ñuñoa Country House. She created some of these early poems when she was between 12 and 15 years old.

This first collection of poems received generous reviews. There are so many sublime verses in it that it's hard to choose any of them. Its themes are simple and inspired by nature. The summits, the rivers, the sunsets are the cosmogonies that captives her. In "The Mountain," she describes the ascent as a kind of mystical experience. Here, we may see a clear metaphor of the evolution of life itself and its stages: birth, expansion, and decay.

In themes such as "The Soul of the Landscape," "The Wild Rose," "The Old Tree," "Melancholy,".. she raises a lyrical ode, full of colorful feeling. Not without some sadness, nature floods the sanctuary of her dreams, evoking the dreamlike beauty of Ruben Dario. In "Life of Fishers," it is not the costumbrist landscape that interests her, but the emotion that contrasts with a tragic feeling of life. It is the man subverted by the fatality, dragged by the unpredictability of destiny.

In "Forgive me, O Lord," she radiates a deep pantheism. Enthroned on the altar of her visions, it will dispute the rest of her life with her religious convictions. Therefore, from this first stage, stand out their motifs plagued by remoteness and longing, reminiscence and mystery, loneliness and melancholy, serenity, and placidness. All of them are concepts full of omens that touch those who read them.

But if this was not enough, the work includes a prose article entitled "Art." In it, the author consecrates not only as a poetess who portrays the world that surrounds her but as an accomplished intellectual. Thanks to her many readings, she began to get a degree of culture, an understanding of the human spirit, of history, which might well qualify her as visionary.

In 1925, Mariano Latorre knew how to capture the tranquility emanated from the work of a young writer. At first sight, he viewed in her opera prima the intensity of her fragrance:

"Mrs. Richard of Piedrabuena is a poetess whose lyre has not entangled in the artificiality of modernism. She does not seem to care much about the prevailing currents. Even more, the desire for originality does not torment her. She has a placid soul without intricacies and a quiet and uncomplicated style. There is something about her of the idyllic tranquility of bucolic poetry..." (Richard, 2004, p. 131).

Shortly after, the *Athenea Magazine* published about her:

"Mrs. Lucia Richard de Piedrabuena–Mariano Latorre points out referring to *Sursum Corda*–pleases to cultivate, like the poets of the School of Good Taste in the Gongorist period, her well-kept classic garden. "(La Torre, 1926)[3].

In *La Estrella newspaper*, on July 20, 1928, a columnist drunken of beauty compliments the young author:

"Bright sincerity of pure water and inspiration, and a glass of cordial essences, form the aesthetic duality of this distinguished lady who has expressed each attribute in the smooth verse of this volume of poetry ... It is a marvelous piece of literature that has no clumsy concepts, nor twisted sensations. It shines anointed of abundant grace. For all this, we admire the author of *Sursum Corda*." (Richard, 2004, pp. 351-353).

Virgilio Figueroa gathers in his *Biographical Dictionary* the exultant words that Omer Emeth dedicated to the young artist:

<u>Virgilio Figueroa:</u>

Omer Emeth was very selfish in his criticism of authors, except when it came to French intellectual hegemony. But when he referred to *Sursum Corda*, a collection of poetry by Mrs. Lucia Richard that appeared in 1925, he thought otherwise. For the first time in twenty years, he had met a poet who confessed to being happy. And to prove it, he transcribed some verses, imbued with the honey of sweetness and the elixir of happiness.

---

[3] Mariano Latorre (1886-1955) was the President of the PEN Club of Chile, novelist, and pedagogue. In 1931 he taught Spanish, Chilean, and Latin American Literature at the Pedagogical Institute. Later, in 1945, he was the principal of this teaching institution. He got the National Prize of Literature in 1944.

<u>Omer Emeth:</u>

Few disciples of Apollo sing psalms of joy and offer on the altar of conformity. Almost all of them cross the valleys full of tears and distill the juice of their sorrows, which are fictitious and imaginary most of the time. In *Sursum Corda*, Mrs. Richard ignores the pathetic voices and sings joyful songs. In "Dim Light," unlike the legion of the sad, she does not seek the pain or sorrow of the gray days. In "Forgive Me, O Lord," she admits to being happy and asks for forgiveness (Figueroa V., 1974).

Note the reader that Omer Emeth (1860-1935) was not one critic more but one of the most exceptional educational talent Chile has ever had. Due to his profound humanistic knowledge, he has been compared to that other portent that was Andres Bello. Many qualified him as the father of literary criticism in Chile. For this reason, libraries cataloged his many articles for the advantage of future generations. His real name was Emilio Vaisse and was born on December 31, 1860, in Castres-sur-L'Agout de Tarn, a small town of the Languedoc in the South of France.

He entered as a young man in the seminaries of Castres and Albi and later in the Lazarist Fathers of Paris. There he ordained as a priest in 1884. In these institutions, he learned Greek, mastered Latin, and penetrated the arcana of philosophy and theology. Between 1884 and 1886, his many studies enabled him to attend the chair of Philosophy in the seminary of Chalons sur Mer. His superiors from the Lazarist community later sent him as a missionary to Chile.

In Chile, he studied the Castilian language that got to speak and write with the mastery of the best national writers. Little by little, he absorbed the national culture until he knew it as well as the greatest scholars of the country. He was for some time in Chillan preaching on missions. In 1888 he traveled to Peru, where he became a professor of Theology at the Trujillo seminary. Returning to Chile, he collaborated with the parish of Valparaiso, where he was a priest. In San Pedro de Atacama, he deepened in the classics, becoming interested in modern literature, and the secret of dead languages.

He wrote a Latin-Hebrew dictionary, to ease the learning of the biblical language. After that, Omer focused on the popularization of the Gospel. In March 1893, he served in the parish of Calama. On his return to Valparaiso, he exerted as a second priest. Then, the energetic theologian became a chaplain in Pirque. Next, he returned to Santiago to take over the chaplaincy of the Brothers of the Christian Schools in Providencia. He was also a chaplain at the Hospital of St. Vincent Paul. His companions remembered him as a vibrant conversationalist, rich in brief and resourceful expressions. All these abilities revealed the intellectual power of his elegant speech.

But the turning point of his intellectual career took place when Dr. Carlos Fernandez Peña, invited him to attend an event at the Athenaeum of Santiago, in a session presided over by Carlos Silva Vildosola. On that occasion, Mr. Emilio gave a lecture on the Bible and science. From 1906 on, he practiced literary criticism in *El Mercurio newspaper*, where he adopted the pseudonym of *Omer Emeth*. The pen name means in the Hebrew language, "I am the one who speaks the truth." From its columns, he spread the word of God. During the years 1907-1908, he was in charge of a Sunday commentary called "Religious Week" or "Religious Day."

He also had a section called "The Universal Finder," which first appeared on August 2, 1922. In *Zig-Zag Magazine*, he held another one named "Questions and Answers," which began in January 1909. Yet one of his most encouraging initiatives was the creation together with Mr. Carlos Silva Vildosola of the section titled "Weekly bibliographic chronicle." In it, he exerted a constant and responsible journalistic criticism for thirty consecutive years (1906-1935).

Along with this initiative came others, like creating the "Literary and Scientific Supplement" and founding the Library. In *El Mercurio newspaper*, he left an unforgettable memory of the exemplary, methodical, correct worker. No intelligence activity was unknown to him, among which was his journalistic gift. In March 1912, thanks to his many aptitudes, Mr. Carlos Silva Cruz, director of the National Library, offered him to join the noble institution.

There, he served as head of the Information Section, where he outstood in the management and classification of subjects. From his initiative was born the *Chilean and Foreign Bibliography Magazine* (1913) and the *General Bibliography of Chile* (1915). He achieved to publish the first volume of this later work. It included a dictionary of authors and works, a dictionary of books, a bibliography of journalism and Chilean reporting, and topo and systematic bibliography.

Along with the preceding, he developed a brilliant teaching activity. First, in 1910, he worked as a teacher of Logic at the Lyceum of Girls number 4 in Santiago. Later he held the chair of Latin at the National Institute for ten years (1911-1921), receiving by the government a "prize of constancy." He was also responsible for conducting religious studies at the Normal School number 3. Between 1923 and 1926, he collaborated with the Catholic University, teaching courses and lecturing.

He was one of the most prestigious professors of the Faculty of Humanities and the Academy of Fine Arts, and his Chair of Contemporary Literature had great applause and recognition. He also collaborated with *El Peneca Magazine* (1911-1921) and founded in 1929 the magazine *Le Courrier du Pacifique*. He retired in 1928 with full salary for special concession in recognition of his many years of services. In 1930 the Supreme Government granted him the decoration of the Order of Merit, and the Minister of France, Mr. des Longchamps instituted him, by cable order of his government, Knight of the Legion of Honor (Yutronic Cruz, Año CXIII, tercer trimestre de 1955)[4].

Knowing the profile of the Colossus, one wonders why such an analytical and rigorous spirit, and a staunch Francophile, gave his support to a beginner writer. Although this is not historical truth but speculation, we may conjecture that there were strong reasons for this. Mr. Vaisse, a man of religion and vir-

---

[4] The original article by *Omer Ometh* on *Sursum Corda* poetry by Lucia Richard has the catalog number 1878 of the articles published by the author. He put it to press in "Literary Movement" which was a weekly bibliographic chronicle of *El Mercurio* that appeared in the front pages of the newspaper on Monday, where *Omer Emeth* commented on a new book. This one specifically came out on December 28, 1925, on p. 3. From this first collection, some news showed up in the *Album of the National Institute*, p. 115, December 28, 1925.

tues, was born in 1860 and was a contemporary of Mr. Enrique Richard Fontecilla, father of Lucia. Mr. Richard was an eminent man, a public figure, and a fervent believer. He cared throughout his life for the afflicted and needy and belonged to many religious institutions.

Among them, he held the position of President of the Conference of St. Vincent Paul. He also led the chair of Civil Law at the Catholic University. Mr. Vaisse, as we have seen above, was a chaplain of the Hospital of St. Vincent Paul. Besides, he actively collaborated with the Catholic University, presiding over several chairs. Therefore, it is more than likely that he was acquainted with Mr. Richard. There is also the fact he taught at the National Institute where he could meet Lucia Richard.

When on December 28, 1925, he is before the poetry of *Sursum Corda*, this religious spirit, endowed with a robust classical formation, must have felt perfectly identified with a collection of poems, not only pleasing but also alluring of mysticism and classicism. The memory towards the father by then disappeared could also have exerted its influence in getting the support of Mr. Vaisse.

Anyway, a critic so severe to other authors knew that day to praise and recognize the talent of the young author. That's worthy of commendation, as well as being part of our literary history. A tiny fact perhaps, but it belongs to the life of a man too great. Without further ado, here are the generous words of Mr. Vaisse:

LITERARY MOVEMENT BY OMER EMETH

SURSUM CORDA. Poems by Lucia Richard de Piedrabuena. Illustrations by J. Delano. Santiago. Universo Publisher, 1925.

When opening this book, we notice from the first poem that we enter in a garden of delights where a fresh breeze blows, and everything speaks of health, vigor, hope, and joy of life. Even if the verses were bad (and I hasten to say they are not), the author of *Sursum Corda* would deserve my most sincere congratulations and all my gratitude for that breeze and that joy...

I do not know if, in this, my readers share my way of feeling, but I confess: I am tired of reading pessimistic verses that seem written in prison, in a hospital, in a land that in no case is a happy copy of Eden and where life has become purgatory or hell.

It disgusts me as much for the lack of art as for the absence of sincerity. Some of those tearful poets whose laments distill so much sadness are actually cheerful people who take good advantage of their youth. "The rest is literature," as one French poet used to say.

Mrs. Lucia Richard of Piedrabuena confesses her happiness and sings it:

Up hearts! / Life is joy! / Who dares to cry / when the sun smiles? / Look, it has come out / and the day is radiant / without winds and without rains / or clouds or glow.

Let us not think, however, the author of this stanza is incapable of perceiving the melancholy of certain landscapes at special hours:

I adore the imprecise landscapes / that are sketched in the light of the afternoon / when everything is mystery and gloom / in the sad environment.

I seek the quiet solitudes / where vague melodies are heard / and the quiet voices of things / evoke memories.

And the quiet and gloomy woods / where some fountain murmurs uneasy / and through the thick foliage / I discern the stars.

But these moments of melancholy are very brief: the joy of living overcomes even to the point of engendering scruples. And so the poetess, feeling too happy, asks God for forgiveness:

Forgive me, Lord, if I love the earth / and put my loves in things, / You sowed my way with flowers, / of fragrant flowers.

I have felt perfume on the path / and I have seen the light of the day behind the mountain / I wait it dawns and I look for flowers... / Lord, you send them!

Forgive me, Lord, if sometimes I look / at the earth with affection and tenderness / here, you created it and well you know it! / There are also pure things!

For the first time in twenty years, I stumbled upon a poet who confesses to being happy. This is one of those days that the Roman poet marked with white stone... Praise God! (Omer, 1925).

Another great testimony of this first work by Lucia Richard we may find it in a book published in 1928, titled *Women's Activities in Chile*. Its authorship belongs to Mrs. Sara Guerin de Elgueta, who expresses the following:

"Without great patrons, a volume of poetry by Mrs. Lucia Richard de Piedrabuena, entitled *Sursum Corda*, recently came to light.

Her subjects are tender, absolutely poetic, so to speak, because the author does not versify but delicate and spiritual motives. We can see this in her way of feeling and interpreting nature, as in "Country Quietude." It is also visible in the simple and sweet expression of her maternal love, and her Christian piety, as in her "Prayer to the Nazarene." All these features predispose from the first moment in her favor.

She is inspired, correct, and her well-formed phrase springs up easily. Making no effort to gain a place in the ranks of the women who write, Mrs. Richard de Piedrabuena stands out among our best poets. The reader can judge our claim by reading some stanzas of her most beautiful poem "Prayer," which we cannot resist transcribing." (The text continues with the most representative passages of "Prayer"). (1928).

Since the publication of her first book until the year 1937, she had already married the lawyer Guillermo Piedrabuena Bories, and her eight children had been born. In such a situation, any writer would have abandoned his literary career. At that time, women did not go to college. Nor could a woman expect to have any social role, much less harbor ideas of her own or have a critical spirit. The only function of women was to consecrate themselves to marriage and to fulfill the ends of procreation.

We also know Lucia was suffering from the encroachment of her social milieu, which kept her quiet when her voice gave signs of nascent talent. She was the victim of a too dominant mother-in-law, who dosed her access to the piano, her great escape. Put her aside by temperaments less timid than her own, she turned on her verses where she found her vast universe. So Lucia did not intimidate herself from difficulties and persevered in conveying her message. Seeking new intellectual horizons, in 1933, she left on a journey to Europe joining a diplomatic mission.

The Chilean group makes stops in Barcelona, then in Madrid, continues to Paris and keeps on to cities like Milan, Venice, Rome, Florence ... Our author is enthusiastic. She makes as *chroniqueur*, writing about events as she is living them, assiduously informing her compatriots in Chile, who anxiously await the news that were published periodically in the newspaper *La Union de Valparaiso*. In 1934, because of all these experiences, she put out a work titled *Memories of Travel*. It is a piece that transmits all the passion of a woman who has freed herself from the prudery of her Santiago enclosure to open herself to a world of infinite possibilities.

She visits the Sagrada Familia, the Escorial, the Prado Museum, Toledo, Notre Dame, and many Italian locations. The group theoretically goes on pilgrimage, but Lucia Richard caught much more. The greatness of Rome surpasses her. Pope Pius XI receives the group. In St. Peter's Square, she feels—*Urbi et Orbe*—the telluric vibrations of being in the center of Christendom. The transcendence of ecumenism and the splendor of the universal Church move her. She also feels overwhelmed by the grandeur of other Christian manifestations, such as the Sistine Chapel and Michelangelo's art.

But all this did not prevent our artist from contemplating fascinated the Greco-Latin or pagan culture. This movement is the wonderful Renaissance world, which, as we know, it was a return to classical antiquity. It is no longer just virgins, saints, cathedrals, or mysticism. Instead, her pupil opens to mythology, history, art, sculpture, painting, and all kinds of architectural works. They are prints that leave an enduring impression on her spirit and to which she will come back in her later work.

On another note, we may compare Lucia Richard to Madame de Staël. She was a famous eighteenth-century writer, daughter of Jacques Necker, a powerful minister of Louis XVI. In the highlights moments of the French Revolution, she had to flee to Switzerland for being a realist. Bridging the gap, Lucia Richard was the daughter of Enrique Richard Fontecilla, an eminent Chilean political figure. Her father stood out as a high lawyer, dean of the Pontifical Catholic University, leader, and speaker of the Conservative Party. Furthermore, he was elected several times deputy and member of the Council of State. For all this, he became a respected and admired eminence in the Santiago Congress.

In this context, it is necessary to say Lucia has a bourgeois extract, an intellectual refinement, a sweetness of images, which, like Madame de Staël, reflects in her beautiful work. Vera Zouroff, in her book *The Cenacle of Poetry to its Poets,* alludes;

> "... to her exquisite femininity, her vitality of a strong woman, sweetened by the pallor of her countenance, her good manners, her birth in an aristocratic home, her education according to her lineage, from which emanate verses like richly carved gems..." (Zenteno de León, 1947).

Unlike Pablo Neruda or Gabriela Mistral, our lady is not a populist writer. Nor is she interested in a first stage, in social, political, or biased disquisitions. She does not want to get into class-struggle issues. Only at the end of her life and in her philosophical essays can we glimpse her concern for women, the youth, the equality of the races, the horror of the war, etc. At that moment, the influx of new currents of thought and political tendencies were appearing. In due time, these movements would make up the government of Allende.

But most of all, Lucia wants to make herself understood. In her article entitled "Neruda and the Chilean Poets" appeared in *La Hora* on July 2, 1950, Lucia rebels against this Attila of culture, which she defines in this way:

> "He was a Prometheus of modern times who fought against the consecrated gods, destroying the venerable statues of the metric, grammar, and dictionary, putting instead the products of his fantasy." (Richard, 2004, pág. 495).

This iconoclastic furor stuns her. Neruda is a son of surrealism, cubism, disorder, chaos, and she is perhaps a diffuse but clairvoyant image of neoclassicism. In her work, there is nothing obscure, neither pretentious nor complex. Her constructions are neat, refined, well-shaped, and above all, understandable. It seems that Chopin, which she so often played at the piano, led the tempo and the melancholic harmony of her poetic compositions. Her palette, her chromaticism of emotions, after its apparent simplicity, houses in its interior messages full of symbolism.

But these evocations, whether visionary, avant-garde, or metaphorical, never disturb her mood. In other words, she never gets to the point of breaking the balance of her loved vision of life. Our writer crumbles before the literary mess of Neruda, who breaks with her harmonic perspective of the universe. Neruda was a genius or perhaps a "fool" (as he defined himself) and that only God and woman know.

Lucia Richard was a very intuitive intellectual. Even though she did not dare to break the molds of her education, she harbored many progressive ideas. It is also well known her pantheism, her concupiscence, or worship of the earthly beauty. All this brought her to admire the Renaissance, which must have led her to more than one crisis of conscience.

Her sons allude to the fact Lucia Richard did not bear contemptuous comments to other people in her presence. She was a good-natured, kindly person who radiated condescension. She never spoke of her achievements, but cared about the needs of others. Artist incapable of condemning or prejudicing, she respected the religious beliefs of others. The poet had a marked conciliatory character. This melancholy goodness, a sensitive woman's countenance, is the one she conveys to her verses. Her literary work is plenty of transparent, beautiful stanzas. They float in her imaginary world, with the winged rhythm of a Pegasus. Her numen is exquisite and delicate, like a slight butterfly.

Her daughter Carmen describes her mother's character this way:

"Our mum Lucia was the intellectual of the family, very deep, of truly good feelings, delicate sensitivity, and great conditions as a poet and woman of letters. She was our admiration and awakened in us desires to overcome. Also, very prudent, she never spoke ill of anyone, and everyone sympathized with her. She was not sociable, and she found it hard to follow in the foot-steps of her husband, who liked to play cards, go to the club, and attend parties..." (Piedrabuena Richard, 1995).

She begins her literary career in her father's country house in Ñuñoa and continues in that of her husband in Conchali. The latter was an Eden full of greenery, which we may well compare it to Monet's garden in Giverny. There, the poet finds all the leitmotifs that invade her thoughts. She unleashes her imagination among avenues of trees, many vines where copious grapes ripen. There are also figs and other fruit trees. Flowers and more flowers envelop her. There she sees the seasons passing. She contemplates the rain, the first shoots of spring, and the fall of the ochre leaves in autumn.

In all these manifestations, she perceives parallels with the yearnings, evo-lutions, and sufferings of the human soul. Those are the elements that make up her worldview, along with a personality, especially sensitive to those reali-ties. Thanks to the testimony of her daughter Carmen—which I also have some memories—we can reconstruct how it was that idyllic place of Conchali, today turned into the municipality of Huechuraba:

"The country house was beautiful, with parks, well-manicured gardens, and huge and varied trees. It also had a large vine with pink, a white, and black grape that gave so many grapes we could not eat them. There was too an enormous avocado tree with very large and rich avocados. We had to our disposal all kinds of fruit trees: peaches, apples, sour cherry, figs, almonds, pears, loquats, plums, walnuts, chestnuts ..."

"It also had two roundabouts with grapes: one at the end of the vine and another near the house, next to the park. In a boulevard of enormous Linden trees, my mother sat in a hammock to write."

Carmen also gifts us with traits of Lucia Richard's personality:

"In those years, and already a little bigger, we loved to go with our mother, on moonlit nights, to walk the vine. We were slightly frightened by the dark-ness of the night but excited by the adventure. We were carrying guitars and singing. Mum told us stories, talked about her family, the stars, and the uni-verse, awakening our imagination."(Piedrabuena Richard, 1995).

Lucia Richard has read, traveled around Europe, had children, and matured. In 1938, she publishes a new work that carries the modest title of *Poems* that compiles her poetry of the last decade. The book receives praise from critics of the main newspapers in the capital: *"She is young and from her we much expect, forward!"* writes Santiago Cruz Guzman. Even the prolific historian Domingo Amunategui Solar congratulates her: *"No wonder you are the author–he says–because I knew your father and I appreciated his talent. Whoever inherits it does not steal it." (Richard, 2004, 358).*

In "Motionless Silence," our author slowly takes us to a mental climax, to a shuddering intimism. Its scenes are naked confidences whispered to a close ear, memories of a past that will never return; yearnings for childhood. They are also remembrances of a better time, whose evocation clouds the understanding. In the "Romance of the Golden Thread," she conveys all her optimism, of the wanderer that at dusk goes on a hunt for adventures walking by the brightness the sun leaves on the sea. She captures that moment of twilight, in which sailing a sea of fable, her soul of a girl lives a thousand adventures with her imagination.

On "Moon Night," our Sibyl delves into the mystery of the first love and the inscrutable feeling that underlies in the feminine heart:

> "We all had the love of a man / and even if the years and life pass, / at the bottom of the soul is hidden / a tomb and in it is his name." (Richard, 2004, pag. 82).

In "Farewell," she makes us partakers of her anguish at the idea of death, of being forgotten, considering whether at least the heart could triumph. Here death is the end to which through lapidary sentences, she faces defenseless and frightened. In "Expansion," she feels unhappy with a crowd only interested in gold and ambition. That provokes in her a feeling of solitude, reducing her to a misunderstood ascetic. In "By the Stubble," she is disrupted by people who are not able to see the beauty of things. They pass through them with ignorant indifference.

In "Jasmines," she envelops us in a world of sensations, colors, perfumes, and illusion. In "Medal," she builds an interesting antinomy between those triumphant and defeated. They are the obverse and reverse of the same humanity that goes suffering. Thus she continues in dozens of poems in which condenses all her affront and curiosity before life. Among them, we cannot forget "The Convent." It is a charming poem, that with a lightness of a dream it disintegrates us in purity, abandonment, placidness, silence, evaporation of the soul. The convent is a pure enclosure where the evil and malice of this world do not penetrate.

Beyond the titles with which our Pythoness letters her verses, it emanates from her way of feeling an entire original construction. It is a new scale of values, which seems an innovative philosophical system. Under a scenario much more Apollonian than Dionysian, she is concerned to unmask men from their lies and miseries. She cares about the best words that were not said, the feigned feelings, the inability to resign to the idea of death that terrifies her. She needs to transcend, to leave something of worth that survives the passage of time, that death does not surprise her like the hunter to the bird entrusted. These are ideas that confuse her, abominations that at times reach esoteric levels.

In "Poem of Water," "Spring Symphony," "Dawn," among others, we contemplate a joyful spirit. She is ecstatic and exultant before all the manifestations of life. These are scenes that open their way under the haste of events that crowded. She maintains a true fixation with pools. Not only because they are a mirror of the heavens but also an allegory of life, a receptacle of all human subjectivity. Skies, reflections, sprouts, the fecundity of fields, water drops, streams, everything serves the polychrome watercolor of her dreams.

CHAPTER II

THE POETRY CENACLE OF THE CONSERVATORY OF DECLAMATION

Its Foundation, Members and Activities

After publishing this second collection of poems, the author makes further incursions into the cultural environments of the capital. It is a time when, after having had many children, she resumes her intellectual activities with great enthusiasm. She felt the impulse to express herself and found the channel for her word and his art by entering the Cenacle of Poetry around 1942. There she became friends with Vera Zouroff, president of that noble site of Apollo's cultivators. She also met many other companions, members, and collaborators of the fraternal institution.

But to talk about the Cenacle of Poetry, it is necessary to mention before the Conservatory of Declamation. From it, it brings its precedent and the basis of its truest inspiration. It was the year 1937, and Vera Zouroff, who had already had several successes abroad, intended to create this Conservatory in Chile. We say "intended" because the noble initiative was not alien to enormous obstacles. Its culmination represents the spiritual effort of a woman. With limited material means, but with unwavering dedication and will, she concentrated all the energies of her soul and her great moral faculties to realize a long-cherished dream.

At first, she tried to get the support of the Faculty of Fine Arts. But not getting the interest of the official artistic spheres, she went and found an answer to his wishes at the Catholic Conservatory of Music and Declamation. This was created and maintained by the artist priest, the presbyter Pedro Valencia Curbis. From the beginning, he understood the selfless ambition that emanated from that reciter. So, one day, she introduced herself to him carrying a scrapbook of printed material as a testimony to her intense work.

For three years, Vera Zouroff directed a declamation course at this Conservatory. About thirty young ladies and some gentlemen attended it. Very different reasons seduced them. But soon, many were discouraged by the difficulty of learning this art, leaving their studies soon after starting them. Those who quitted left their teacher sad to see her efforts in the education of her students fail. Despite this, one day the possibility arrived to introduce four of her reciters to the public. In the opinion of their teacher, they had already achieved enough preparation to stand themselves to the critic.

Thanks to the courtesy of Mr. Benito del Villar, they could have a sober and elegant stage in the Royal Theater, with no requirements. The debutants Teresa Bustamante, Olga Nasthas, Cristina Figueroa, and Estela Sepulveda performed before the audience. After the performance, both Lautaro Garcia from the *Diario Ilustrado* and Daniel de la Vega from *El Mercurio* praised them in each other's journalistic articles. They emphasized with grateful comments on their proper technical preparation, proficient diction, and Castilian accent. They also underlined their acute ear, the pleasant tone of their voice, the perfect knowledge of the breath, and the excellent taste in choosing the lyrics.

After this ephemeral enthusiasm, those students disappeared. They shone brightly like stars that crossed the Chilean scenic horizon. But like one-day flowers, they were unable to make the art of recitation their livelihood, and soon migrated to other professions. Anguished by the departure of her students, the teacher locked herself in her house. She gave up a course that was causing her infinite discomfort and from which she did not benefit.

Despite the logical setbacks of a developing enterprise that involved many difficulties, the blind faith that the founder placed in her mission was paying off, and little by little things began to change. A small group of about six or eight young people, who had begun their studies at the Catholic Conservatory and others who were requesting her teachings, went to her home. There they met, studied, and spent the afternoons chatting amicably around their teacher, imbued with an atmosphere of spirituality and art.

From this group emerged a young and charming reciter named Ines Moreno. Mrs. Zouroff successfully introduced her in a brilliant evening at the Municipal Theatre. At only twenty years old, full of grace and temperament, she immediately captured the sympathy of the audience. Full of emotion, they responded with warm applause to that beautiful voice. It vibrated like a silver cord, sounding splendidly in the magnificent acoustics of our first Coliseum. Many compared her mastery to the incomparable Argentinean reciter Berta Singerman.

With the backing of these first successes, in early 1938, the University of Chile asked Vera Zouroff to create a collective recitation course. She put all her enthusiasm into it, and more than a hundred students signed up. Her excellent work was soon rewarded. At the end of the course, and before leaving for a season in Argentina, things were going well for her. The teacher was able to send to the Municipal Theater a new group of ten reciters of both sexes. The day arrived, and these young people received a warm welcome. Thus, the prestige of these recitals spread to the public. This generous audience often came to the theater to cheer the first signs of this divine art with their applause. It was an art that until then had been caricatured by unprepared amateurs.

From this university group, emerged a young woman of only 18 years old, named Maria Maluenda. She was a charming doll, gifted with a voice rich in sonorities. She achieved continental fame by taking Chilean verses to countries such as Ecuador and Colombia. There, the local newspapers dedicated entire pages to her talent. Intelligent and modest, her many triumphs did not make her vain. At this moment, a second stage in the master's activities begins. In March 1939, upon her return from Buenos Aires, she suffered a car accident that left her recovering for several months. Convalescing, she cannot teach.

Annunziata Caputti was a very gifted Ecuadorian girl. The government of her country had granted her a scholarship to study under Vera. But due to the accident, she had to return to her country with only a few lessons. In August 1939, Vera Zouroff was able to resume her recitation classes at the University of Chile. By this time, a large group of students was eagerly awaiting her recovery. Mr. Manuel Avila, Secretary-General of the Department of Cultural Extension, told them that they should be grateful. Their professor, still delicate, returned to direct her chair at the University. She did it for the benefit of the youth, besides the fact that the courses were totally free.

It was then that Vera Zouroff planned to create a Conservatory of Declamation and Dramatic Art. The following year of 1940, the new center had an intense work, finishing the season with two great recitals in the Cervantes Hall. After these performances, there were many more in the following years. Complementing these, she also had various activities and meetings in his home.

Also, in 1940, the beginning of a recitation course took place at the Catholic University. The Faculty of Philosophy and Letters directed the course, to which a growing number of students enrolled. The event culminated with a recital of mystic-profane poetry, held in the University's Hall of Honor. On that occasion, fourteen students recited, receiving much applause. In early 1941, the students offered a new recital of Spanish poetry to the newly appointed ambassador of Spain, Marquis de Luca de Tena, and his wife. Both Vera Zouroff and the rector of the University of Chile, Monsignor Carlos Casanueva, attended the performance (Zenteno de León E., 1942, págs. 30-40).

Thanks to the gathering of a good number of followers, the Conservatory of Declamation achieved its ends. It attracted the interest of the critics, spread its activities, and took root in the two most famous universities of the capital. Therefore, once the Conservatory was established, Vera Zouroff created the Cenacle of Poetry. The new institution was the result of the previous one, to which Lucia Richard was linked for many years. The purpose of this Cenacle was not only the recitation of poetry -the main goal of the Conservatory- but the intense and conscious study of poetry and poets. Furthermore, it promoted Latin America's most important spiritual values through Inter-American cultural exchange.

The Cenacle of Poetry was born one winter afternoon in an event held at the National Library. It took place on July 28, 1940, sponsored by the prestigious poet Dr. Antonio Orrego Barros. The great man was also a professor, journalist, and parliamentarian, belonging to an illustrious family of intellectuals. For that memorable occasion, he read a magnificent work of poetry. After him, some ladies reciters of the Conservatory, recited poems by Gabriela Mistral, Amado Nervo, Delmira Agustini, and Santos Chocano (Zenteno de León E., 1941).

The Cenacle's beginnings were timid, like every nascent institution. But from the start, its promoters showed high conviction in what they were building. Neither journalistic apathy, nor the lack of material resources, nor the lack of adequate premises, nor the incomprehension of the theater entrepreneurs discouraged them. After its consecration, that afternoon in 1940, the Cenacle of Poetry began its activities on the initiative of Mr. Francisco Barra Vasquez, its most enthusiastic maintainer. That year, the board of directors was composed by Mrs. Esmeralda Zenteno de Leon (Vera Zouroff), General Director, Mrs. Maria Cristina Menares de Gongora, Secretary, and Mrs. Berta Ernst de Rochefort, Treasurer.

There were also twenty-four adherents who contributed financially to support the institution: the chaplain Bernardino Abarzua, Pedro Galvez Galvez, Washington Espejo, Patricia Morgan, Francisco Figueroa, Samuel Lillo, Ines Araya de Salas, Carlos Núñez, Sara Prats Gutierrez, Marta Grez, Mahomed Mathat , Victoria Barrios, Rosalia v. Of Ruiz, Juan de la C. Vial, Jorge Gustavo Silva, Juan Rochefort, Berta Porter, Enrique Astorga, Hilda C. de Guzmán, Oscar Jara Azocar, Alfredo Sanhueza Oliva, Ofelia G. de Cortez Manroy, Laura de Carrasco and Mr. Hermelo Arabena Williams. This number of participants will skyrocket as we shall see in 1944. At thath time, Lucia was not yet a member of the board, but she was actively involved in its projects (Zenteno de León E. 1942, pág. 1) (Zenteno de León E. 1942, pág. 1).

The Cenacle had its headquarters at 15 Central Street, being its name changed two years later to Phillips, keeping the same number. The previous year was one of intense activity. Many recitals and conferences were given. They had a sincere and cordial welcome by the Superior Direction of the National Theater. Willing to support them, it gave them its elegant auditorium. At the same time, the members of the Cenacle intensified the exchange of books and correspondence with other countries. But above all, they were proud to have gained the sympathy of an audience in which the taste for properly recited poetry had been awakened.

However, all this could not be possible without the support of many entities. This is the case of the Italian-Chilean company and, in particular, of Mr. Manuel Troni, president of the film company of the same name. In addition, the administration of the Cervantes Hall was generous enough to host their poetry recitals. The beginnings were not easy. The Cenacle had to fight for the theater companies to make room for them in their halls. They were suspicious of poetic auditions offered by people with little training. And so they were firmly opposed to providing their theaters.

But either by female persuasion or by the immense will of Mrs. Zouroff and her group, the fact is that they prevailed. In the end, they convince these businessmen of the mastery of their reciters. In their opinion, they represented the voices of Latin American poetic inspiration. They assured that the girls had an unsurpassed artistic quality, always maintaining the flame of art in their Cenacle. In that holy place, young, graceful, and intelligent priestesses took care of the sacred fire. All of them were very grateful to the Troni Company, owner of many theaters in the city of Santiago. It had provided them with the beautiful Sala Cervantes, which had been built especially for concerts (Zenteno de León E., 1942).

To understand Vera Zouroff's personality and the spirit that emanated from that purity enclosure, we have an inaugural bulletin of the Cenacle published precisely in 1940. On its cover, we can contemplate a young and beautiful Vera, who looks at the sky with her precious and big blue eyes. In that look beyond, she seems to be seeking answers to her many questions. It is a face that radiates commitment to its art, sensitivity, and melancholy, but also strength.

After seeing an image that moves us because of its message of dedication and generosity, we can read: "Mrs. Esmeralda Zenteno de León (Vera Zouroff), founder of the Cenacle of Poetry, professor of recitation at the Catholic University of Chile, a former professor at the State University, exclusive reciter of the Columbia Phonograph Company, New York." Then, in its interior pages as an introduction, Vera transmits the ideals that inspired that great congregation of select spirits that was the Cenacle of Poetry:

"To speak of poetry and of a Cenacle to officiate it as a religious rite seems crazy in this age of materialism, hatred, ideological struggles, and human disturbances (an ironic and compassionate smile emerges to the skeptical lip). However, this is a reality; a Cenacle where poetry is a cult and verse a prayer. The thought of the Latin American poets can now reach the temple of art. There it suspends its flame on youthful fronts, animated by a noble yearning for artistic excellence.

I am thirsty, said the Man-God expiring on the cross of human incomprehension, complaining about his physical suffering. In the soul, there is endless thirst, and what the mundane world offers is only vinegar and gall. Let this cenacle of poetry be the miraculous fountain where the spirit thirsty for beauty can commune with art in its highest manifestation: verse.

Shortly after announcing the creation of the Cenacle, poets and cultural institutions throughout Latin America cooperated with the initiative. Soon their verses will be fervently performed in recitals where the sounds will take them all over the American continent. Last year it was Rosario Sansores, the inspired Mexican poet, and Daniel de la Vega, the Chilean bard of the golden lyre, who enlivened our artistic evenings. For this year, we have a vast program in which we will deal with the poets who have honored us with the gift of their verses."

VERA ZOUROFF

On the next page, the *Blue Hour Radio Siam* radio transmission is published. In it, the director of the radio, Mr. Juan de Rosas, spoke:

"Today, as promised, we introduce to our listeners another praiseworthy figure, the internationally acclaimed writer Esmeralda Zenteno de Leon, better known by the pseudonym Vera Zouroff.

A few days ago, when talking about another great poet, I referred to these bohemians of fertile inspiration. They always have an inexhaustible source of wonders, subtle mirages, and dreams. They have chests that contain at their bottom a treasure of grace and emotion. Their spark is the crystalline source where those who dream of a better life drink.

Vera Zouroff, thanks to her talent, has in honorary titles what many diplomats need. The press and personalities of all Latin American countries have paid tribute to this lyrical ambassador, as many other European countries have done as well. And so Vera Zouroff is leaving a trail of unforgettable memories. The verses of all the poets emerge like the song of the flutes, modulated in the arpeggios of their crystal voice. In every port and every city, she has lit the white rose of her art, like dewdrops on an autumn afternoon. And so Vera Zouroff, in a gesture of intimate comfort, reflects: They have torn the darkness from my solitude, leaving a trail of comforting light."

On the same page, Vera defines with great feeling what in her understanding poetry is:

What is poetry? What is a poet? Why do they possess that divine gift of creating beauty, harmony, and feeling? How do they transform words into musical notes that rhyme with thoughts? Without a doubt, the poet is a being different from the rest of humanity. He is an intermediary between God and man. He is closer to God because he has received from the Supreme Creator the holy spark of inspiration as a spiritual origin.

The poet lives in the daily bustle of human vulgarity. Like a traveler, he has to cross a dusty path to reach his destination. He continues to walk without paying attention to everything around him. He goes with his eyes fixed on the ideal. His verses leave behind a trail of light. They are fragments of emotion, pointing to the stars the way to infinity.

Who is it that goes through life, stumbling over other walkers as if he did not see them and who looks more like an enlightened man than a miserable mortal? The crowd asks as they rush after an interest that sums up the price of a day. But in the end, a day comes without having drunk at the miraculous fountain. That is a place that quenches the thirst of the burning heart. Who is that? He is a poet anointed by God with the holy oil of the chosen. He is the one who goes alone like an orphan, alienated from all understanding. But he carries the sun within himself, a sun that shows his poetry in golden rays. Everything that surrounds him and touches him at once becomes incomparable beauty.

Penetrating the life of poets is a difficult task. It is hard to understand their intimacies, the bitterness of their gray days, or the luminosity of their happy hours when they vibrate like a lute. To get into this realm is like entering an idyllic jungle. There you can see the whole Nature animated in a triumphant hymn. If you want to access the poet's private sanctuary, the miraculous source of his inspiration, you must approach it with your bare feet and your forehead smeared with ashes. It is like entering an isolated temple where a mysterious rite of love and harmony is performed.

Man's first intellectual expression was poetry or verse. They were rough, perhaps, as rough as all archaic beginnings. But already in the first manifestations of thought through language, the ancient man sought the rhythm to give verbal form to his idea. The Koran and the Holy Bible are written on verses that already looked for the harmonious beauty of words.

And from then until today, poetry has crossed the stormy seas of materialism, indifference, misunderstanding, and even people contempt. The majority of those who belong to the human conglomerate only listen to what reach their physical ears. They only see what reflects in their blue or black eyes, but they are souls completely closed to harmony. As Carrere said, 'only those who go dazzled by a miraculous spark are capable of hearing and seeing that infinite landscape.'

Getting close to them, listening to their melodies, repeating their verses, is a gift from heaven that we will never thank enough. When the aesthetic sense of the poem comes to us, we possess a science that doctors us with a priesthood of exceptional excellence. This understanding allows us to officiate in the temple of art, the divine art of poetry. Some say -and it seems incredible that the art of reciting has detractors- that the poetic expression of the verses is a second class art.

This interpretation is a mistake or malice. And if not, let's see where other artistic manifestations head. Painting copies the splendors of nature, the color of the landscape, the light of the sky, the fury of the sea, the beauty of a face. But it always copies nature, the trees, the birds, the animals, everything material that we look at.

The engraver, with his chisel, looks for the human form in the marble. But he always copies something material. In the case of music, we try to find and spread the harmonic sound through instruments that evoke the voice of nature. This is the case of noises, the elements, the wind, the scream, the waves, etc. Always imitate something. But poetry or recitation is the word expressed in the human voice. It is the only distinction that God placed in man as a seal of his divinity. It gives form to the immateriality of mind and the vibration of feeling.

Showing the superiority of this art over others is easy. The world is full of musicians, singers, painters, and artists of all kinds. There are good ones, bad ones, and medium ones. But we will find few reciters. That is because this art does not admit mediocrity. You must be brilliant.

VERA ZOUROFF (Zenteno de León E., 1940a)

Note to the reader that this inaugural bulletin is important because it gives us the exact date of the creation of the Cenacle. In these words of Vera, there is a conviction that borders on fervor, nourished by passionate assurance in her mission. This perseverance to achieve a goal gives us a first glimpse of the ideals of these worshippers of immaterialism. They were dreamers of beauty, cultivators of naked truth, and tireless seekers of all that is genuine. Lucia's father, Mr. Enrique Richard Fontecilla, had been Dean of Civil Law at the Catholic University. It is possible that under those precedents and influential groups, both artists met at the Conservatory of Declamation of that university. Or they met at the University of Chile, where years later Lucia would give several lectures.

After the first bulletin, of a defining and informative character, in 1941, they published a new one. It included all the activities of the Cenacle of the previous year and those of that year. Thus, it announces the arrival in Chile of the Argentine poet Servio Quiros Mouzo. The Cenacle of Poetry received him at its headquarters by all its members. They portrayed him saying: "Not all are poets because they versify, and instead, sometimes there are some who do not write verses." In this way, they praised his beautiful book Words of the Earth, where each poem in prose was a triumphant hymn of Nature. They also said that he had come to Chile to bring the "Illustrated Poem Exhibition," which had been very successful.

The passage through Chile of the distinguished artist Manuel de Gongora did not go unnoticed either. He had two great qualities: that of an inspired poet and that of a reciter with impeccable technique. Accompanied by his wife, the fragile and exquisitely feminine Leonor, he gave a series of recitals at the Royal Theater. These performances brought together the most cultured and refined members of Santiago society. His voice, appearance, and expression, as well as his sober and precise gestures, earned him the sincere, unanimous, and audible applause of the audience.

Also, the figure of Patricia Morgan is enhanced as a distinguished member of the Cenacle. By then, she had published two books and had just made two trips, one to Buenos Aires and the other to Rio de Janeiro. There she fulfilled a mission entrusted to her by the Department of Educational Outreach. The Academy of Letters of Rio received her in solemn session. In the event, its president invited her to recite some of her verses. She also gave a recital at a press institution called ABI. There, she was heard and acclaimed by a large audience and invited as an honorary member to a meal at the Pen Club. Gabriela Mistral, who at that time was Consul of Petropolis, received Patricia Morgan with fine courtesy, not only as a diplomat but especially as a friend.

On another occasion, Mrs. Lina Muda Sandoval, a student at the Conservatory of Declamation, gave an excellent lecture on the poetry of Guatemala to a wide audience. Among them was the Consul of Guatemala in Chile, Mr. Gaspar Mora, who on September 10, 1940, addressed a letter of thanks to the Director of the Conservatory, Mrs. Esmeralda Zenteno de Leon. In it, he communicated to her the articles that had appeared in the *Liberal Progressive newspaper,* which contained favorable comments to her work of educational outreach.

In a similar vein, a journalist named Orozimbo wrote in the *Últimas Noticias newspaper.* Instead of reporting, he described with emotion the day he spent with the Cenacle of Poetry in the Auditorium of the National Theater. Thus he spoke of a compact, tight and respectful hall that vibrated at the winged cadence of the verses recited. The praise extended to the figure of Vera Zouroff, whom he described as a great and enthusiastic woman. In his opinion, she had worked in silence, knowing how to convince with her silky voice. To these blessings, he added her excellent qualities as an organizer and producer.

Another highlight of that year of 1940 was the reception offered by the Cenacle of Poetry to Carmen de Lys, pseudonym of Manuela Penna, Countess of Hibouville. The Cenacle invited her as an honorary member of the institution. At the meeting, the Chilean poet Oscar Jara Azocar offered her one of his poems:"The offering of his voice." Then, she presented her new book, *From Life to Life*. Carmen de Lys was portrayed as a cultured lady of diplomacy. A fine and exquisite woman, noble of soul and pure of heart, her verses reflected a crystalline inspiration. Established in Uruguay and France, she had taken advantage of the many trips and environments in which she had lived. All these experiences had shaped her sparkling personality. Her verses were full of sweetness, love, and rapport with nature.

Cenacle members outline Washington Espejo as "a poet friend very admired by us." In his book *Lost Song*, he had turned life into a luminous poem, singing the intimate joy of home. The poet was the product of a clean mind, a healthy soul, a generous heart. He focused on all that rests warm and eternal, as well as on deep and true affection. Despite being a painter, Dora Puelma is noted as a poet of the brush. She did not paint to please but to make the landscape speak, showing us its naked authenticity.

On a tour by Rio de Janeiro, she honored Chile, exhibiting her penetrating and sympathetic intelligence, her neatness of feeling and thought. Samuel Lillo was then considered the most acclaimed poet in Chile. A member of the Royal Academy of Language, he had been honored many times. Despite his many merits, the humility of his gaze prevailed. Classic and impeccable in his versification, he made the mountains of Araucania thunder with his ardent inspiration.

In the writings of Javier Vergara Huneeus, the central theme of the Colombian poet Maruja Jaramillo was love in its most genuine representation. For her, love was the only useful science. In her way of feeling, it acquired a feminine tenderness and softness. That same love blew in the work *Wind in the Rigging* by the same Javier Vergara. He was a sensual and delicate poet, diligent in the details and harmonious in the verification. His companions saw his creation as "a small jewel of precious gems." Maria Letelier, once Queen of the Floral Games, collected in her book *Nostalgia*, the essence of the exquisite perfume of her soul.

The publication recognized Teresa de Bustamante's inspiration and originality in her work *Under the Temple of the Sun*. However, it criticized her modernism. It also praised Amanda Amunategui in her work *Mirrors of Ecstasy*. It highlighted her sensitivity and emotionality but condemned her ultra-modern style. Other books announced in the Gazette were *Remoteness* by Torcuato Luca de Tena, a young Spanish poet, and *Footprint of the Days* by Roberto Sanchez Bolaños. In the critic's opinion, his verses resounded like music on the lips when recited (Zenteno de Leon E., 1941).

The next bulletin that appeared in 1942 also contained countless news items about these groups. It celebrated the achievements of the delicate and cultured Spanish reciter Myrtia de Osuna. She had passed through Chile, giving an excellent poetry recital at the Royal Theater. Later, she traveled to Lima, where she had a great reception. The University of San Marcos invited her to give a series of lectures. The capital's newspapers gave extensive coverage to these events. In Chile, the members of the Cenacle pointed out that this fine poet could recite in Spanish, Catalan (her mother tongue), French and Italian.

They also boasted that Myrtia was their delegate and a correspondent for poets in other countries. Unfortunately, fate cruelly shortened the life of this admirable reciter who died tragically two years later in Buenos Aires. By this year of 1942, these young women were full of projects. They intended to publish a complete anthology of Chilean poetry. Another of their plans was to intensify the exchange of poetic books with various universities and cultural centers, both in Latin America and Spain. They also convened poets and artists of the brush and pencil to create in Chile what they called "the illustrated poem." (Zenteno de Leon E., 1942, page 4).

Cenacle members also celebrated the great success of Maria Cristina Menares in Peru. Like Myrtia, she gave a brilliant performance in Lima. All the newspapers in the capital collected fervent praise, exalting her talent, grace, and sympathy. In particular, they reported on the beauty of the verses she recited there. The Peruvian-Chilean Culture Institute sponsored the event, in which she received many applauses, flowers, and congratulations. As Secretary of the Cenacle of Poetry and a student of the Conservatory of Declamation, she became a magnificent herald of these two institutions. She was considered an enthusiastic collaborator. The publication also showed the affable humor of these women:

"While in circles of high diplomacy, ambassadors rush to imagine suspicion, intelligent and graceful women represent the embassy of sympathy and affection. Even if they do not sign international policy treaties, they bring hearts closer. Only armed with smiles, these ladies create the invisible but strong bond of friendship and spiritual understanding between peoples." (Zenteno de Leon E., 1942, page 5).

Another highlight of the bulletin is the conferences and recitals that Cenacle members had offered that year in Chile. The 1942 season was inaugurated in the Cenacle of Poetry by the writer Gustavo Loyola Acuña. He was an astrologer, meteorologist, General Secretary of the Scientific Society of Chile, and a romantic poet. Author of many books, at that moment he went to the Cenacle to give a talk about the woman. This speech was an advance of his book *Evolution of the Woman* that he was about to publish. There he developed his subject with erudition and gallantry in the word. The audience listened to him attentively, receiving enthusiastic applause.

Lucia was not left behind in these activities. So much so that on May 28, 1942, she was giving a lecture on the death of Stefan Zweig at the Cenacle of Poetry. As for this conference, we have an exciting testimony. It was published as the previous one in the Cenacle Bulletin of that year, which reminds us of how warm the evening was:

Stefan Sweig

"On the personality of this wonderful Jewish writer, there was a brilliant lecture given in the Cenacle of Poetry by the writer and poetess, Mrs. Lucia Richard de Piedrabuena.

The speaker is a prominent figure of the Chilean feminine intelligentsia, who treated the subject with extreme ease and amenity. The ill-fated suicidal writer revived in the speech of the cultured lady. She depicted him with all the outstanding lines of his intellectual silhouette.

The select audience that filled the Auditorium listened in fervent recollection to the enlightened words of Lucia Richard de Piedrabuena, who was much applauded and congratulated, being forced, by the demands of her admirers to recite some of her original poems. "(Zenteno de León E., 1942, page 6).

On another occasion, the aforementioned Spanish poet, Mr. Torcuato Luca de Tena, also recited at the Cenacle. He was the son of His Excellency, the Ambassador of Spain in Chile, Juan Ignacio Luca de Tena. With his eloquence, he amazed everyone in a brilliant evening, knowing how to conquer his audience. Some of his beautiful poems were unpublished, and others belonged to his book *Albor*. Being only twenty years old, he already had the inspiration of a mature poet, treasuring harmonious verses with profound themes. Among them was the poem "Isis," with which he ended the recital. The audience filled the auditorium, warmly encouraging him in an inspiring evening.

Of ancient ancestry, he was talented, inspired, handsome, and of a manly figure. As a poet, he was destined to be a great reciter. But life and his social status led him to other paths. In 1942 he studied Law at the Catholic University where he was an outstanding student (Zenteno de Leon E., 1942, page 7)[5].

---

[5] Mr. Torcuato Luca de Tena y Brunet belonged to a very prestigious Spanish family. His grandfather, Torcuato Luca de Tena y Alvarez Ossorio, was a lawyer from a wealthy industrial family in Seville, linked to the liberal spirit of the city. He stood out as a great journalist who came to revolutionize the Spanish press. He created the magazine *Blanco y Negro*, the influential newspaper *ABC*, and the publishing house *Prensa Española SA*, from which many publications emerged. He was the founder of a dynasty of journalists and thrived in diplomacy, opinion, and even in the parliamentary world.

For all these reasons, Alfonso XIII granted him the title of Marquis of Luca de Tena for himself and his descendants. Son of the previous one was Juan Ignacio Luca de Tena, II Marquis of the same title, lawyer, writer, and journalist. A member of the Court of Seville, he was for many years the director of the newspaper ABC and was closely linked in his ideas to the Monarchy. Between 1941 and 43, he was the ambassador of Spain in Chile and of Greece in 1962. He was elected to the Court and the Academy of the Language in 1944, receiving much recognition for his work.

Two of his sons were the continuators of the family traditions: Torcuato and Guillermo. Torcuato, born in 1923, inherited the title of Third Marquis of Luca de Tena and stood out as a playwright, diplomat, and member of the Royal Spanish Academy between 1946 and 1974. He spent some years of his youth in Chile, where his father was an ambassador, studying law for three years. Upon his return to Spain, he graduated and began his career in journalism. He founded the air edition of the newspaper *ABC*, of which he was director for some time.

Another conference held in 1942 was entitled "Aesthetics in Artistic Creation." This time, the Cenacle of Poetry invited Carlos Yañez Bravo. He was a professor of Aesthetics at the Palacio de Bellas Artes in Viña del Mar. Before a large audience, which included personalities from the plastic arts, the distinguished intellectual and artist gave a suggestive lecture. The lecture, divided into several attractive points, deeply interested the audience. In the absence of time to develop them all, and at the request of the attendees, the organizers asked the professor to continue in a second talk.

Another interesting talk was about the famous Uruguayan poet Delmira Agustini. At the time, she was considered a brilliant flash of Latin American poetry. Edelmira Muñoz, as an outstanding reciter of the Cenacle of Poetry, gave the lecture with charm and imagination. Before a large and distinguished audience, the speaker presented her work with great naturalness. She immediately found the sensibility of the audience. They listened in pleasant and attentive silence, rewarding her recitations with enthusiastic and sincere applause.

Edelmira evoked with feeling, delicacy, and truth all the captivating and brief existence of the unfortunate Uruguayan poet. Even when she had the sheets in her hands, she addressed her audience, speaking to them with affec-

---

Torcuato was also a correspondent for the newspaper in London, Washington, the Middle East, and Mexico. Like his elders, he was a lawyer at Court and showed great loyalty to Juan de Borbon. A member of the Spanish Academy in 1973, he wrote many works of poetry and literature for which he received honorary distinctions. His brother Guillermo, born in 1927, was a lawyer and journalist, polyglot, director of *ABC*, and editorial chief executive officer. He also served as president of the Board of Directors and the Executive Committee of the company *Prensa Española*, as well as director of the weekly newspaper *Blanco y Negro*.

He belonged to the Private Council of the Count of Barcelona, the Board of Trustees of the Royal Alcazars of Seville, and the Prince of Asturias Foundation. He became a Royal Senator of the Constituent Courts. In 2003, King Juan Carlos I named him Marquis of the Valley of Tena with the grandeur of Spain. He received this title because of his unique dedication to the world of communication. During his lifetime, he won many awards and distinctions. It is interesting to note that Lucia's eldest son, Enrique Piedrabuena Richard, graduated as a lawyer from the Pontifical Catholic University of Chile. In 1973, he emigrated to Spain, where he always felt proud to have been in Chile, a university classmate of Torcuato, with whom he shared many affinities.

tion, with a well-toned voice and clear diction. Her emotionality and the sobriety of her attitude, elegantly dressed in a simple long ruby dress, immediately conquered the will of all who listened and applauded on this occasion (Zenteno de Leon E., 1942, page 8).

It should be noted that all these reciters were Lucia's companions in the Cenacle. They had also been students at the Conservatory of Declamation. Lucia knew many of them from the Conservatory. So it is very likely that she went to all these Cenacle conferences and activities, which she was joining.

Also, the bulletin added news and commentary on books received by the Cenacle in the first half of 1942. Among them, *Golden Sunrise*, by Maria de la Cruz; *Poetry*, by Rafael Maya; *The Violet and its Vertigo*, by Olga Acevedo; *Full Moon*, by Elena Osuna de Mutis; *Rumor of the World*, by Julio Barrenechea; *Aspects*, by Teresa Vidal; *Faded Mansion*, by Daniel de la Vega; *Transparency*, by Carmen Lys (Countess of H'yvouville, wife of the Minister of France in Chile); *Eternal Root*, by Maria Cristina Menares; *Dreamy Orbit*, by Gemma of Tharsis, among many others. The Cenacle dedicated generous words to all of them.

As for the poet, Marta Goycolea de Boizard, better known as Gema de Tharsis, was on the cover of the 1943 Cenacle of Poetry Bulletin. Young, beautiful, and distinguished, the publication enhances her figure as a lady of high social standing. She had broken into the Chilean artistic environment with a book of original verses. This piece was robust in its creation, rich in the lexicon, sonorous in its vibrations of harmony. Another work announced on the cover that had already reached the Cenacle was *The Letter Charlotte Did Not Write to Werther*. It was an extension of the original novel that Goethe believed would end with the disappearance of the protagonist. Only a woman of exquisite sensibility could perform the prodigy of adding one more chapter. She did so without desecrating the immortal work of the great German writer.

From a sentimental and transcendental perspective, the poet Maria Cristina Menares builds clamorous praise to the great patron of art who was Vera Zouroff. According to her, Vera was a person who did not need to be introduced either inside or outside of Chile. Her way of speaking was very cordial; her pen was precise; her heart was always open to everything that meant art, emotion, and sensitivity. All these qualities were living credentials, which placed her among those who were born for the final destination.

Through her initiative, the Cenacle of Poetry had grown. Under her watch, the only Conservatory of Declamation that existed in Santiago flourished. She could be satisfied with all her achievements. Anyone who did not remain impassive before a night full of stars, a petal, a note that ripped the air; anyone who palpitated before a pure emotion, would understand the meaning of the noble work that Vera Zouroff had done in Chile.

In turn, Vera Zouroff writes a subtle article entitled: "The literary personality of Lucia Richard de Piedrabuena." This year of 1943, Lucia enjoys the position of secretary of the Cenacle of Poetry. This promotion denotes the rapid incursion she had in the institution, as one of its most recognized members. Vera's retina captures for the first time the facade, the corporeal entity, of a lady of high social status. She was elegant and exquisite, of great intelligence and culture. The poet came from an illustrious house, trained in a school of ancestral virtues, being heir to qualities of the soul and heart. Also, she had enriched her education through the monuments and corners of old Europe.

But behind the discretion of a talented lady who silenced her merits, avoiding showing herself to her audience, a delicate, refined, and sentimental woman emerged. The writer had many emotions and possessed a rich artistic temperament. There was something transparent and crystalline about her. She knew how to write with elegance, with an absolute command of language and classic correctness of speech. In her craft, she combined feeling and thought. This blend produced a brilliant style, sober and diaphanous, of admirable versatility. For Vera, Lucia had a robust intellectual personality, which could not hide behind the veil of a superfluous social life. As she tells us: "The values of the spirit or death when they are legitimate refuse to be proclaimed and seek penumbra. But they always glow, like the diamond with its shining facets."

On April 15, 1943, a ceremony took place in the Honor Hall of the University of Chile, which demonstrated the great acceptance Lucia Richard had among these groups. On that occasion, as secretary of the Cenacle of Poetry, she offered a tribute to the famous poet Samuel Lillo. In a large room full of people, the audience greeted him with resounding applause. The writer Tomas Gatica Martinez, in a magnificent speech, entered his work. Through his words, the personality of the singer from Arauco shone in his most outstanding profiles. Reciters Fide Alessandrini, Olga de Falconi, Guacolda Ponce, Edelmira Muñoz, and Alma Montiel, recited poems by the acclaimed poet for the occasion.

Vera Zouroff, General Director of the Cenacle, thanked the audience for their presence. She also highlighted some spiritual features of the poet, whom she knew through a long and close friendship. Overwhelmed by the strong ovation, he found it difficult at first to stand up and thank the audience for their sincere recognition. When he was able to do so, he enlivened the evening with an interesting talk. In it, there was no lack of humorous turns, sweetened with the tenderness of the best memories of the past. Lillo, because of his high intellectuality, his vast culture, and his poetic and literary work, was undoubtedly considered the first figure of the time in the Chilean Parnassus (Zenteno de León E., 1943, pp. 1-5).

The old titan of Chilean letters, in his 1947 work *Mirror of the Past*, did not forget these women who had honored him greatly. Thus he tells in his work that at that time, several apostles of recitation were meeting in Santiago. Because of these gatherings, a true rebirth of the art of the word was taking place in the most cultured spheres of society. Vera Zouroff, whose true name was Esmeralda Zenteno de Leon, was more than an ambitious poet. In her early days, she was a journalist, traveled around the United States, collaborated with New York magazines, and even participated in Hollywood movies.

These groups of poets interested in recitation assembled in places like the Ateneo de San Bernardo. Poets such as Manuel Magallanes, Enrique Nercasseau, and Washington Espejo attended. Vera spoke of Spanish romantic poetry, especially Espronceda. She was able to wrap her assistants in a warm and artistic communion, to which they corresponded with unanimous applause. Vera also organized theater companies that performed beautiful pieces of modern theater. Several of the best-known poets attended her literary gatherings, becoming the genesis of the first professorship of declamation.

Lillo tells us about Mrs. Zouroff's incredible activity. With great personal sacrifice and selfless devotion, she had dedicated a great effort to the recitation chair at the University of Chile. This energetic woman had also written a treatise on the art of recitation. She also founded a Conservatory of Declamation with a Poetry Cenacle. From it emerged figures such as Ines Moreno, Maria Maluenda, and the wonderful Pochita Nuñez. To this Center of Declamation and its Poetry Cenacle came soon after people like Lucia Richard, Washington Espejo, Oscar Azocar, Guillermo KoenenKampf, David Perry, or-Samuel Lillo himself, National Literature Award in 1947 (Lillo, 1947, pp. 289 - 298).

That year of 1943 was a year of great vitality for the Cenacle. The Chilean poet Oscar Jara Azocar became very dear and integrated into the institution. He knew its members well and was very involved in its activities. Jara Azocar was not only a poet but a complete artist, open to any manifestation of art and beauty. At that time, he was returning from Montevideo, where he had developed an important book exchange. The poet propagated the immense entity of the Cenacle of Poetry in all those educational forums where he spoke. Ronald's prestigious pen collected all this enthusiasm in an article entitled: "A reflection of the continent's intellectual restlessness."

In it, he described Jara Azocar as a young man, with a brief, gently melancholic smile, cordial in his handshake, close in conversation. This detached man had dedicated himself intensely to cultural exchange. His business was that of intelligence and commerce of the spirit. With this purpose in mind, he had traveled through countries such as Peru, Bolivia, Brazil, arriving now in Uruguay and its capital, Montevideo. There he spoke of his favorite subject: the Cenacle of Poetry, to which he belonged. It embodied a cultural organization that stood out for its extraordinary character and its crucial Americanist mission.

In his opinion, the Cenacle was an institution of artistic culture, whose primary aim was the exaltation of poetic art. It housed some representative figures of Chilean lyric art. One of its most cherished postulates was the exchange of thought with the continent's poets. Besides, their compositions always integrated the programs of its recitals. Through lectures, radio broadcasts, meetings, recitals in private auditoriums, and theaters, they created the so-called "staged poem." With great effort, they achieved the feat of gathering an enthusiastic audience around them. These sympathizers followed their performances regularly.

To carry out these ends, the Cenacle gathered an excellent group of reciters. It was composed of talented men and beautiful, gifted women. Thanks to them, Vera Zouroff promoted the creation of a Conservatory of Declamation. She was a bold and visionary woman, gifted with an extraordinary personality, as we know the founder and director of the Cenacle. These recitals had been perfected to a remarkable extent, through the selection of appropriate stage design. Also, the careful choice of skilled reciters was important. Through this method, Vera harmonized voice, temperament, sensibility, and art.

These institutions had a strong Americanist vocation. For example, they exchanged books with many universities and cultural centers. They also published an anthology of Chilean poets. Their initiatives also incorporated a call for poets and painters to create the so-called "illustrated poem" in Chile. They even attended congresses or traveled abroad. That was the case of Patricia Morgan, who went to the UN, representing the rights of Chilean women.

The idea of the "Illustrated Poem" sought to bring together different aspects of artistic expression in the same inspiration of art. It aimed to unite poets and visual artists in an exhibition of a poem that fused colors, sounds, rhythms, and movements. In other words, the initiative pursued to blend the landscape with the poet's inspiration. The commented anthology of Chilean poets was a kind of almanac or encyclopedia. It was an ambitious project to make Chilean poetry known abroad in all its rich nuances. To achieve this goal, its organizers strove to strike a balance -not an easy one- between classicists and modernists.

The objective was to summarize quantity and quality in a proportional way. But as expressed in the Bulletin of the Cenacle of 1943, not all people had in the poetic panorama of the country the place they deserved. While some were making their way to popularity by ignoble means that undercut true merit, others kept their talents in a kind of arcane. The latter occurred for the modesty of some seeing mixed in the literary mud their sacred treasure. Certainly, they preferred to preserve it hidden from the worldly noise (Zenteno de Leon E., 1943, pp. 12-30).

As Lucia herself said in the introduction to her poetry, *Blue Smoke*, some wrote poems that made them famous. Then, they fell into a tedious spiral, in which they had to continue writing to prolong their fame. The light kept coming, but the star became already extinguished. In her opinion, the first condition of the poet was naive admiration. When we get used to the landscape, we stop being surprised by its wonders. When we take up the pen, we have to do it as if we were writing for the first time. True poetry, like true music, does not begin on paper, but in the heart. The rest, well, it's just wit, intellect, cerebral lucubration, fireworks (Richard, 2004, p 177).

Recitals and Performances

here is no doubt that at that time, Lucia Richard was not only writing but perfecting her ability to declaim publicly. Proof of this is a series of seven poetic recitals that took place in the Cervantes Hall from 1940 to 1944. However, Lucia did not take part in these performances until two years after the Cenacle's debut before the Santiago society. Here we always refer to "published" recitals. There were many others, whether in universities, private houses, or the Municipal Theater, which were not divulged.

For example, there is a record of a recital that took place in the Cervantes Hall on Tuesday, July 27, 1943, at 6:30 p.m. of which there is no news. These recitals emerged as an oasis of understanding at the height of World War II. They represent "a balm in an age of irrationality." The first one came about on November 29, 1940, announced under the title "Great Poetic Festival in the Cervantes Hall."

In it, Vera Zouroff made her debut through five of her students: Olga Falconi, Virginia Contardo, Marta Valenzuela, Lila Wolnitzky, and Fide Alessandrini. The show included an introduction, "The Language of Flowers," and two parts. The reciters put their excited voices and their entire stage ardor at the service of an expectant audience. In a vibrant tone full of sincere modulations, they released their feelings, reciting the works of the most renowned Spanish and Latin American authors.

Thus, for example, in the first part, Marta Valenzuela put her warm voice to the work "Frivolity" by the Chilean Maria Letelier. Virginia Contardo shared her sensitivity with the poetry entitled "To a Moorish Poet" by the Argentinean Eloisa Ferrerias. Lila Wolnitzky gave herself completely to the composition entitled "Spiritual" by the Brazilian Gilka Machado. Fide Alessandrini, audacious and sublime, treated "The Anger" by the Uruguayan Raquel Sáenz. Olga Falconi showed her talent through the verses of "You Had Me" by the Chilean Gabriela Mistral.

In the second part, the illusion emerged again, now expanded. The reciters showed their most polished inspiration and femininity in works such as "The Fountains of Granada" by the Spaniard Francisco de Villaespesa; "The Sadness of the Inca" by Jose Santos Chocano; "Song of Death" by the Spaniard Jose de Espronceda; "Psalm to Life" by the Panamanian Enrique Greenzier and "The Bells" by the American Edgar Alan Poe, among others.

The newspapers *El Mercurio, El Imparcial, and El Diario Ilustrado* collected effusive comments on the performance of these young artists. They looked like vestals of chaste purity, who knew how to interpret the dreams of famous poets like flapping wings' swans. The intuitive Samuel Lillo followed the development of these groups. Before the show, he had already expressed in *La Nación* all his enthusiasm for some debutants who would reveal their best qualities of temperament:

> "Virginia Contardo, Fide Alessandrini, Marta Valenzuela, and Lila Wolnitzky, whom we have applauded in several private auditions, will respond with dignity this afternoon to the teachings of their teacher and write a consecrated page with their names in the young annals of our national recitation."

Maruja Jaramillo, Colombian writer, referring to "The Bells" wrote in *El Mercurio*:

"When I saw these four reciters, dressed in white, almost immaterial, I felt a great admiration for all that atmosphere of sublimity. At that moment, my soul joined the poets whose poems fell on us, like dewdrops on our hearts. We all empathized with the reciters. They were gracious interpreters of the beautiful art of recitation. We gave them a well-deserved and happy welcome."

A journalist from *El Mercurio* described the performance with heady words:

"A large crowd enjoyed a brilliant evening. The four young reciters were loudly applauded, as they performed each poem with admirable vigor and color. The way they recited "The Bells of Poe" received a standing ovation." (Zenteno de Leon E., 1940b).

Before the end of 1940, another recital took place. Again four disciples of the Conservatory of Declamation directed by Vera Zouroff performed in the Cervantes Hall. These were Lila Wolnitzky, Marta Valenzuela, Fide Alessandrini, and Virginia Contardo. The performance had an introduction, a first part, and a second part. In it, the artists put their emotional voice at the service of the works of the best Spanish and Latin American authors. Among them, they recited "The Bells" by Edgard Allan Poe. Martha reclaimed "The Silver Bell" (the sleigh), Lila, "The Golden One" (the wedding), Virginia, "The Bronze" (the fire), and finally, Fide, "The Iron" (the funeral). The Argentine poet Carlos Obligado translated the work.

The Colombian Maruja Jaramillo wrote an excellent article on a play from the first part, "The night." Written by her compatriot Jose Asuncion Silva, Marta Valenzuela recited it for the occasion. In Maruja's opinion, never before had the harmonious and painful verses of this night been recited with such emotion, purity, and perfection as in that enigmatic evening. It caused a complicit silence, a mixture of admiration and restlessness that flooded the whole room. It was like a question mark launched into the consciousness of the people. Looking for something transcendent, they saw in it a perfect refuge. The theme of love fascinated Maruja Jaramillo. She soon learned to recognize the peculiar eroticism that underlies Asuncion's work.

When we look at the faces of these women on the cover of the copy preserved at the University of Texas, it is hard to believe that the event took place seventy years ago. Their pure, penetrating gazes bare our souls. Beyond death, they appear volatile in the intangible. Their faces seem to defy the space-time, going to the conquest of immortality, by the simple majesty of their features. Their expressions are much more than emanations of a mortal body. They incarnate a revealing dream of incorruptible beings. The intensity of their looks blinds us with their frankness, generosity, and feeling.

The third of these recitals also took place in the Sala Cervantes, on October 30, 1941. On this occasion, five female reciters performed. Among them were Josefina Silvan, Teresa Marquez, Edelmira Muñoz, Elba Mathat, and Nelida Rigoletti, all disciples of Vera Zouroff. Most of them recited beautiful poems by Latin American authors. The profound poetess Cristina Menares recited her verses.

The show had three parts. The first one was in charge of the five reciters who put their tender voice to poems like "Maria Luisa's Report," by the Spanish Cavestany; "Power Equal Goodness" by the French Victor Hugo; "Spring High Tide" by Brazilian Gilka Machado; "Whistling" by the Argentine Miguel Camino; "Fallen in the Desert" by the Chilean Oscar Castro; "Blaze" by the Bolivian Virginia Estenssoro, among many other excellent creations.

The audition comprised the declamations of Chilean, Peruvian, Argentine, Brazilian, Bolivian, and Spanish authors. It also included a Frenchman, Victor Hugo, whose work was translated into Spanish, and another in Galician "Son de Muñeira" recited in its original language. We may appreciate the same diversity in the third part, where the five reciters put their warm voice to *Black Dance*. They also showed the best of their art in the staging of the symbolic poem *The Feather Dress* by the Japanese Ha. Goromo, translated into Spanish.

The public highly applauded this third part. *Black Dance*, an original play by Palos Matos, received a special follow-up by a chronicler of the newspaper *La Nación*. He emphasized the flexibility and understanding of the play by Josefina Silvan. She smoothly went from the dramatic to the frivolous, without losing control of her voice, or gestures. He portrayed Teresa Marquez as a reciter of exceptional temperament. She had absolute mastery of herself, having a beautiful voice, and elegance in the gestures. Edelmira Muñoz had, in his opinion, a lively, flexible, and deep voice. He described Elba Mathat as an artist with a great capacity to convey emotion to the audience. Nelida Rigoletti was a woman who had an exquisite ability to move from the dramatic to the folkloric.

The Feather Dress was a beautiful poem versed in Sapphic rhyme by the Japanese Ha Goromo. It was carefully adapted to be staged in its entire splendor that glorious Thursday in the Cervantes Hall. With it came a symbolic piece, full of grace and sentimentality. It combined the delights of oriental culture, impregnated with all sorts of superstitions, refinements, and traditions. Jose Reyes Martin, a chronicler from the newspaper *El Imparcial*, beautifully depicted the play in his glamorous article: "The impression of the perfect."

In it, he highlighted that the keenest ear could not have grasped the slightest fault in the diction or the tone of voice of the reciters. Not either the most severe critic could have objected anything in the gestures or performance of these ladies. They gave a marvelous insight into the poems, seeking in each one its precise meaning.

Radio Pacífico hired Marta Valenzuela, who admirably performed "The Fairy," embodying the ethereal fragility. Julio Muller, endowed with a rich and masculine voice, incarnated the "Japanese prince." Lucia Porter, dressed in the Oriental way, stood out for her interpretive ability, beautiful voice, and sense of expression. This entire stage prodigy was possible thanks to the powerful spiritual force that encouraged Vera Zouroff. Her main lesson was to awaken a sense of beauty in the young spirits that requested her teachings. She taught them feelings of kindness and companionship, moving away from them all ideas of rivalry, vanity or pride (Zenteno de Leon E., 1941).

But the main attraction of the gala was the renowned Chilean poet Cristina Menares. She was a member of the Cenacle of Poetry and the companion of Lucia Richard. In the later publication issued after the great poetic festival, we can see her announced with great splendor, monopolizing the whole cover. There she came forth with a gaze as deep as the infinite space. Her semblance showed her wide eyebrows and the robust features of a great matron. Along with them, it appeared the face of a mature woman, thoughtful in a world of shadows. She had her hair gathered like a Greek goddess and wore a beautiful white dress from which hung a broad skirt up to the feet.

In a friendly gathering, Cristina shared her innermost emotions, reciting her most evocative works. The immense sentimental trance displayed in the event stunned the audience. Among them, she recited "The Star in the Water," "Words to the Girl Who Has Died in Love," "Nocturnal of the White Horse," "Poem of What Does Not Return," and finally, "Lullaby."

Very eloquent and sincere comments surfaced in the leading presses of the capital and abroad. Carlos Rene Correa, a renowned literary critic and author of many works of literature wrote:

> "What we could only guess in her first book, it is a reality in The *Star in the Water* as it announces her future maturity as a poet. Maria Cristina Menares has found the naked beauty in her polished art. She has met her path and will not lose it."

Manuel Arellano Marin, outstanding Chilean dramatic author, university professor, and diplomat, also had encouraging words for the profound poet:

> "We believe Maria Cristina Menares is beautifully gifted for poetry. Her poems have extraordinary artistic value. They have originality, freshness, and passion, qualities that define this young writer. It surprises the novelty and the vigor of her images. All her poems are touching and forceful to the point of tragedy."

The newspaper, *El Comercio de Lima* published praiseworthy words:

> "Maria Cristina Menares is one of the newest talents of Chilean poetry. She is a vitalist in her life and work. Her sensibility is not eager for complex nuances. Her strong personality, inside and outside the literary environment, makes us foresee her as one of the most important values of the Latin American lyric. Maria Cristina Menares does not reach literature, but literature comes to her." (Zenteno de Leon E., 1941).

The fourth of these poetic festivals in the Cervantes Hall took place on December 10, 1942. The disciples of the Conservatory of Declamation were no longer mentioned in this recital. In the show, they were going to declaim the reciters of the newly created Cenacle of Poetry. That meant that now the audition had gained in status and gravity, being in charge of professional reciters.

On its front page appeared a portentous Silvia Rochefort, enveloped in an air of assurance and self-confidence. The photograph showed her with her left hand resting delicately on her waist. Her right one softly spread out over her long dress, holding a bouquet. Next to her shined in all her youthful freshness, Alma Montiel. She wore a beautiful diadem interlaced in the hair while reading lively "The Feast of Love."

The Cenacle's bulletin portrayed Alma Montiel with particular acuteness. She was by then a girl who later on would become an internationally renowned dancer and actress. From an early age, her talent and artistic feeling predisposed her to any manifestation of art. Too tender, her somewhat serious and melancholy countenance soon alarmed her relatives. The dance was her first way of expression. But she better found her vocation in the Conservatory of Declamation. From there she went to acting, having in a Chilean film called *The Old Tree*, her first opportunity in front of the camera.

Henry de Bronteaux, from the newspaper *El Imparcial*, commented with special grace "The Feast of Love" in an excellent article titled: "The Art of Vera Zouroff." He emphasized the role of Vera, who was creating drama school in Chile. With this new theatrical fantasy came to the Chilean proscenium a work rich in contrasts. In the performance, the great protagonist "Love" confronted with "Envy," "Reason," etc. In his regard, if Molière had been there that Friday evening, he would have celebrated it applauding, and Bernard Shaw would have smiled with satisfaction (Zenteno de Leon E., 1943, page 18).

Around this year of 1942, Lucy Richard joined the Cenacle of poetry. At this moment, her poems began to appear in the recitals declaimed by herself. The fifth of these recitals took place on Monday, August 24, 1942, at six o'clock in the evening, in the Cervantes Hall. The salon belonged to the theater of the same name. The great call of the program was the outstanding poet Fide Alessandrini, who took part in her first recital as a soloist.

The program had two parts. In the first one, a splendid and elegant Fide, wondered her audience reciting beautiful verses by Chilean and Uruguayan poets. Among them, she declaimed the poem "Cold" by Washington Espejo; "Artist Pride" by Roberto Sanchez Bolaños; "Three Painful Stages" by Carmen Lys (the only Uruguayan); "The Tear of the Kiss" by Alejandra Victoria; "Sea and Moon" by Maria de la Cruz; "Human Bell Tower" by Samuel Lillo; "Always Rise" by Lucia Richard de Piedrabuena; "Longing" by Javier Vergara Huneeus and "Din-dan-don" by Elena Osuna de Mutis.

Thus, amid a large audience anxious for emotions, Fide recited Lucia's poem "Always Rise" belonging to her 1938 book of poetry entitled *Poems*:

"¡Raise your heart that you are hurt,"
Your spirits rise,
Drown your groan,
Destroy yourself inside, but sing!

Ascend, always ascend,
spur your weary beast;
reach where it extends
in all its breadth, our gaze.

Those fed up with life
perhaps they would envy your brokenness
if they saw the sweetness achieved
many times, after a sad cry.

Separation, uncertainty, death
wait and wait forever
is the metal with which the strong is forged,
blessed is the one who goes after the chimera!
(Richard, 2004, pág. 92).

After five minutes' break, Fide recited several poems by Bolivian authors. Then there was a pause of ten minutes. Next began the second part in which the great reciter put her passionate voice to verses of several authors. Among them, she read "Lullaby" by Patricia Morgan, "Back to Earth" by Maria Cristina Menares, "Cilicio" by Olga Acevedo, and "Creation and Evolution of the World" by Torcuato Luca de Tena. After another five minutes' pause, she recited "The Laughter of the Devil" by the Colombian poet Alvarez Henao, which ended the recital.

The newspapers *La Nación, El Imparcial, Últimas Noticias, El Mercurio, El Diario Ilustrado, El Mercurio de Valparaíso, La Opinión* and the magazine *Variedades* made a wide and complimentary echo of the event. For example, *El Diario Ilustrado* published the following:

> "... Fide Alessandrini knew how to revive each of these romantic poems in the first part of the program. That was the case of her magnificent presentation of Mrs. Paula Jaraquemada, portrayed in a poem by Daniel de la Vega. She depicted her as aristocratic and sober, a passionate and great patriot lady. Only with the performance of this poem, she would gain the status of a grand reciter."

In turn, the newspaper *El Imparcial* published:

> "Fide Alessandrini has a strong dramatic character and a richly expressive temperament. Her faculties fit very well in the "Laughter of the Devil" by Alvarez Henao. She looked ductile in the representation of "The Birth Song" by Patricia Morgan, ranging from passionate to tenderness. Her performance of "The Enchantment of the Cueca" by Carlos Cassasus was festive, near to paroxysm. The piece earned her prolonged applause." (Zenteno de Leon E.,1942).

The excellent performance of Fide Alessandrini also occupied the cover of the Bulletin of the Cenacle of Poetry of 1942. Along with an evocative image of her, its promoters praised the splendid reciter:

> "With resounding success, this reciter has made her debut in the Cervantes Hall. The audience that filled this concert hall denied the saying: 'No one is a prophet in his land.' Fide appeared alone before a demanding public, accustomed to distinguish and appreciate art. Her triumph, so, has a double meaning.
>
> She is a young, beautiful, and intelligent artist. She has crafted her vibrant temperament perfecting her technique after years of patient study. Her

warm voice has rich tones that can produce all the emotional notes. She knows how to sing songs of cradle and roars of a beast, and in her throat sings a lark and rings bells. As a creature made of bravura and sensitivity, she shows the treasure of her artistic uniqueness.

Her introduction at the Cervantes Theater has been her consecration as a Chilean artist. Due to her conditions, Fide is destined for a brilliant career in the difficult art of recitation. She studied at the Conservatory of Declamation, standing out for her enthusiasm and perseverance. For its members, her performance at the Sala Cervantes is a source of pride. There she received flowers and revealed herself as a great reciter. The critics have not spared any praise." (Zenteno de Leon E., 1942, page 2).

Another remarkable poetic recital, the sixth of our series, took place in the same Cervantes Hall, on September 30, 1943. Vera Zouroff and her group of students carried out the show. For the occasion, they recorded an album with the Columbia Records. The program had the appeal of offering *the Shubert's Serenade* by Gutierrez Najera. The great baritone singer, Mr. Francisco Fuentes Pumarino, participated in its interpretation, accompanied on the piano by his wife, Mrs. Elena Cienfuegos de Fuentes Pumarino.

The program had three parts. In the first one, the poets of the Conservatory of Declamation recited pieces by various authors. Among them, Amanda Amunategui, Washington Espejo, Caupolican Montaldo, Arturo Lamarca Bello, Beatriz Egea, Jose Asuncion Silva, Amado Nervo and the same Samuel Lillo who declaimed his poetry "The Hunt of the Puma." In the second part, the reciters declaimed *the Shubert's Serenade*. In the third part, the authors read their poems. That is the case of Lucia Richard, who by then had finished her studies in the Conservatory.

The Spanish Emilio Carrere recited "Prayer Like a Bohemian." The Chilean Cristina Menares read "Little Elegy." The Bolivian Ricardo Jaimes Freyre, "The Two Shores"; The Chilean Lucia Richard put her warm voice to "Invocation"; The Chilean Pedro Antonio Gonzalez also recited "Tripentalicas"; The Argentine C. Obligado recited the translated poem of "The Crow" by Edgar Allan Poe; The Panamanian Enrique Geenzier, recited "Psalm to Life"; The Mexican Amado Nervo shone with his poem "The Key"; The Spanish Eduardo Marquino put his dramatic accent to "Romance of War." The performance ended with the declamation of the poetry "Primitive Soul" by the Peruvian Chocano, read by Mrs. Vera Zouroff.

Regarding Lucia Richard, we cannot resist the temptation to hear once again the author of "Invocation," a poem that belongs to her poetry *Sursum Corda*, as if we were in that same hall in 1943:

"Sweet harmony that from the world sprouts,
song of the bird that the forest hides,
the noise of thunder that in the summit roars,
Give me your voices!

I sing to the gods that my homes keep,
I burn in their altars perfumed incense,
raises its aroma like a white cloud,
raises light.

I sing to the beings that make my life happy,
I sing the beauty that the earth hides,
birds and breezes that the wind cross,
lights and flowers.

Sorrowful bard of sad souls,
I am unveiling the veil of the future,
I cover miseries with pink silk,
copy of the sky.

Of life I make a sweet poem:
I rhyme the happiness with mortal sadness,
and even the hours with their progress give me
rhythm and cadence.

Divine Muse that my song inspires,
Sweet harmony that from the world sprouts,
song of the bird that the jungle hears,
Give me your notes!" (Richard, 2004, p. 53).

The recital was a complete success. Reporters from all over the Americas specially sent to attend the event commented on it. They described in their newspapers an evening that made a great impact on them. Their news appeared in *La Prensa,* of New York; *Il Corrieri d'Italia,* of New York; *El Diario Nacional,* of Bogotá, of Colombia; *The Hollywood Time*; *El Telégrafo,* of Guayaquil; *El Diario de la Marina,* of Havana; *El Diario Colombia,* of Barranquilla; *El Comercio,* of Lima; *Mundo al Día,* of Bogotá; *Cine Mundial,* of New York and *El Heraldo de México,* of Hollywood. For example, *El Diario Nacional of Bogotá* published the following:

"Vera Zouroff appeared as an accomplished artist who knew how to interpret the soul of our poets."

La Prensa of New York, said;

"The Schubert's Serenade by the great Mexican poet, Gutierrez Najera was brilliantly performed by Mrs. Vera Zouroff. She is a famous Chilean reciter, whose continental fame in the art of recitation is indisputable."

The Diario Mundo al Dia, of Bogota, wrote the following:

"Vera Zouroff is a sincere admirer of our poets, who has proven to be a leading authority in this art. She has dedicated profound studies to it until reaching perfection, as we could verify on the night of July 20th ..."

El Cine Mundial, from New York, divulged the following lines:

"Vera Zouroff is an exclusive artist of the Columbia Phonograph Company. She has specialized in recitals with musical accompaniment. This time we heard her accompanied by the master Nilo Menendez and the magic violin of Xavier Cugat."

It also seems that the program had an extension. Colombian chronicler Carlos Melguizo picked it up, in *New York's Hispania Magazine*:

The Spider by Julio Florez, performed by Vera Zouroff

"Julio Florez has been the most popular poet in The Americas. That is because he almost always sought inspiration from human pain. Julio Florez knew more than anyone else that in this life, there are many tears. And so he moaned the sadness of each one, in stanzas that have all the grief of sobs. Seldom, very seldom, the author rebelled against the whims of fate. But when he did, he vibrated the accents of a roaring sea or a devastating cyclone. Among his productions of angry protest stands 'The Spider.'

Many times we heard the piece from the immortal poet. We felt the impression of an immense bell ringing within the dark spirit. When the singer died, we thought we would never again experience that sensation. It was a mixture of longing and protest and a combination of cries and howls.

But from the trembling hands of Vera Zouroff, from the unkempt hair, from the depth of her eyes, from the modulations of her voice, from her very soul and her own heart, we have seen again the monster with 'hairy legs and black head' that tormented the dreams of glory of the Colombian bard. Vera Zouroff did not know the unforgettable author of The Spider. But she could interpret his work with amazing mastery. So much so that when we heard her recite it, we felt the impression of an immense bell ringing again within the somber spirit." (Zenteno of Leon E., 1943).

Therefore, Lucia Richard was present and joined all these endearing events. This fact gives a proper perspective of the activities in which she was involved. The sources even collect another recital, the seventh of our series, unfortunately without mention of the date, and that probably took place the following year of 1944.

In this recital of the Cenacle of Poetry, Vera Zouroff introduced many innovations. Through them, the great patron of art evolved significantly in the dissemination of her message. If the authors of the first recitals recited their poems without being present, in the seventh one, they recited by themselves many of their creations. Moreover, the poems were accompanied by music, and everything was recorded on a disc. The program for this recital was much more advanced than the previous ones, as it incorporated several performing arts or plays.

The program had three parts. In the first one, they performed *The Leader of Almaid* (scenes of the life of Peter the Cruel). In the second and third parts, they recited many poems from Chilean, Spanish, Venezuelan, and Uruguayan authors. On that occasion, Silvia Rochefort stood out reciting one of Lucia's emotional sonnets (Zenteno de León E., ca 1944).

The bulletins of the Cenacle of Poetry of the Conservatory of Declamation offer a lot of information about these groups. For example, Bulletin No. 5 of 1944 first points out that the publication was based in Santiago, at 15 Phillip Street. It also had a board of directors composed of 11 people and 72 sympathizers, who contributed economically to its proper development.

They were part of its board Vera Zouroff, Lucia Richard de Piedrabuena, Berta Ernst, Juan de Rochefort, Francisco Barra, Marta Goycolea de Boizard, Edelmira Muñoz, Oscar Jara Azocar, Washington Espejo, Jorge Gustavo Silva, and Carlos Yañez Bravo. Among the sympathizers were the poets Patricia Morgan, Caupolican Montaldo, the academic, poet and writer, Samuel Lillo, Sara Prats Gutierrez, Rene Arabena Williams, the famous historian and genealogist Juan Luis Espejo, the poet Amanda de Amunategui, the professor of the University of Chile Gabriel Amunategui Solar from an illustrious family of educators, the poet Maria Cristina Menares, the mythical writer and feminist Ines Echeverria de Larrain, the first female deputy Maria de la Cruz, the famous Peruvian poet Carlos Alberto Fonseca and a long etcetera.

On the front page, we can see a magnificent photo of Edelmira Muñoz. She was a Chilean reciter that had been introduced on October 5 of that year at the Ladies' Club Theater. In the following pages, the publication pays her splendid homage. For us, it is significant since she was Lucia Richard's companion:

"The reciter introduced herself before the public and the critics at the Ladies' Club Theatre. She gave her audience the rare impression of an artist and especially in a debutant of owning a perfect technique. From her throat flowed a golden voice that looked like the song of a thousand canaries. But Above her natural conditions, she shared her grace, her sympathy, and fragility. Edelmira Muñoz showed in her first recital a true commitment to such a difficult art.

Edelmira Muñoz is a woman of bright intelligence and fervent love to study. She attends University, undertaking studies of philosophy, psychology, literature, and languages. All this learning opens to her young mind wide windows. Through them, she receives the light of culture, illuminating her steps to a broad upward fate. Edelmira is not eager for applause. A cheap glory does not seduce her. She aspires to the triumph of art for the meaning of art itself. That perfection - so tricky to achieve - is what elevates the artist to the summit over material ends. She conquers this emotion through poetic interpretation, bounding technique with the aesthetic sense." (Zenteno de Leon E., 1944, page 1).

The publication also lists various conferences and recitals that took place that year, which is a good example of the scope of their many activities:

"The beautiful Alhambra Palace, the old and stately residence of that magnate who was Mr. Claudio Vicuña and now owned by the National Society of Fine Arts, hosts this year's activities of the Cenacle of Poetry.

Exciting lectures and lively poetry recitals have taken place every two weeks under this kindly roof open to all manifestations of the spirit. Even on the harshest winter nights, the crowd has been numerous and attentive to hear the speaker's word or the music of the verse. The following conferences have been held:

"Argentine Aspects in the Poetry," by Mrs. Vera Zouroff. "Poets of Colombia," by the Colombian Consul General in Valparaiso, Mr. Juan Peñaloza Rueda. "Lovers of the Sea," by Mrs. Lucia Richard de Piedrabuena. "Aspects of Venezuela" by Hon. Mr. Jose Abel Montilla, ambassador of Venezuela. "Poetic Recital Dedicated to the Work of the Peruvian Poet Carlos Alberto Fonseca." "Homeland and Poetry," by the poet and priest, chaplain of the Military School, Bernardino Abarzua. "Poetic Recital in Homage to Spain on the Day of the Race."

"Culture of the Americas" by former Ambassador of Chile to Guatemala, Mr. Gaspar Mora Miranda. It was a profound study of the spiritual differences of our continent, due to racial differences. Finally, "Juana de Ibarbourou Intimate," by the poet Mr. Oscar Jara Azocar. It was a recitation of twenty poems by the Uruguayan poet, given by the reciters of the Cenacle and the Conservatory of Declamation. With this apotheosis last evening, the cycle was closed, leaving for the next year, "Visions of Italy," by the poet Caupolican Montaldo" (Zenteno de Leon E. (1944), page 2).

The bulletin not only praised the most famous, but also the young people who were getting into the world of recitation. That was the case of Leonor Groebe, who saw one of her poems published. The Conservatory of Declamation was an organized institution. The students wore a uniform with a shield, denoting the organization achieved by the group. That same year Vera Zouroff receives a distinction from Uruguay that we can well extend to the whole Cenacle, of which Lucia Richard was Secretary:

"Our General Director has just received a Diploma that grants her the title of Honorary Member of the Institution Group of America." The Diploma reads as follows:

"This entity confers to the Director of the Cenacle of Poetry, Mrs. Vera Zouroff, the title of Honorary Member. She obtains this award for her intellectual values and her effective action in favor of the spiritual unity and peace of the Americas. Given in Montevideo on July 18, 1944. Edgardo Ubaldo Genta, President. Paz Q., Secretary."

This distinction was accompanied by a letter:

Montevideo, July 18, 1944.
Mrs. Director of the Cenacle of Poetry. Chile.
Mrs. Vera Zouroff, eminent writer and noble friend:

It is a great honor and pleasure for me to put this diploma in your hands. We have awarded it to the institution of which you are the most representative figure. It is a testimony of gratitude to the Cenacle of Poetry, for its contribution to the sacred work of unity and culture of the Americas, in the field of beauty. I am very happy to represent the feeling of the "Group of America" in Uruguay. I salute the esteemed and sublime choir of verse interpreters, who support you in such a significant enterprise of art and poetry. The president of the Group of America in Uruguay, Colonel Edgardo Ubaldo Genta." (Zenteno de Leon E., 1944, page 6).

The bulletin also builds portraits of various Cenacle poets. It portrays the Spanish poet Father Manuel Villaseca as someone who invokes the divine. The Peruvian Carlos Alberto Fonseca is described as active and feverish and gifted with great inventiveness. Chilean Raquel Jara Azocar appeared with a "Romance to Gabriela Mistral" and "The Little White House." Another entry reports that the Cuban Government had appointed Chilean poet Maria Cristina Menares to the diplomatic post of cultural ambassador of its Embassy in Chile.

Fide Alessandrini was a highly prestigious reciter at the Ladies' Club Theatre and the Universities of Concepcion and Santa Maria. Eusebia Cosme triumphed in New York, being hired by the Columbia Broadcasting System. Guillermo Gana Edwards is represented as a true fanatic of all manifestations of art. Pablo Neruda is praised for his *Twenty Love Poems*. Patricia Morgan was an eternal traveler, that year very applauded in Argentina. Virgilia Contardo had conquered her audience with recitations at the Cervantes Hall.

Miguel Luis Rocuant had recently been received at the Royal Spanish Academy. The Uruguayan Edgardo Ubaldo Genta had just been honored at the American book exhibition. The Sarmiento Library in Cordoba organized this fair. There he received the first prize, Diploma of Honor and Gold Medal, for his epics, *Platania and the Amazon*. Augusto Iglesias became a member of the Academy of History of Caracas. Young Ernesto Urra entered the Conservatory of Declamation, as did Gabriela Torrealba Cereceda.

The Cenacle also carried out great work as disseminators of culture with its radio broadcasts through *Radio del Pacifico*. An example of this was the *Famous Poems* program that took place at 15.30. Mrs. Lucia Richard de Piedrabuena ran another radio show broadcasted on the same station called *Evocation of the Gone Poets*. This is how the publication expressed it:

"As we noticed a growing interest in our radio auditions, we dedicate a show to the evocation of some Chilean poet who has passed away. This part of the program was in charge of Mrs. Lucia Richard de Piedrabuena, who, with true emotion, brought those romantic silhouettes to the microphone. They gave us one day the best of their souls with their poems and then they left sadly, poorly some, exhaling their last breath in a hospital bed. They lived a life tortured by thorns of that crown, which from Christ's temples descends to those who one day also crucified their souls on the cross of human incomprehension." (Zenteno of Leon E. (1944, p.8).

Also, the Cenacle had another broadcast on the same station called *A Poet Speaks*. It was a program that gave the sensation of reproducing the voice of a living poet, letting him speak through his verses. On the other hand, it is more than likely that Lucia Richard commemorated July 28, 1944, the four years of the Cenacle's existence. The ceremony took place in the Hall of Honor of the University of Chile. On this occasion, there was a conference on the work done, mentioning the supporters.

The members attended a Mass given by Father Manuel Villaseca in memory of the deceased. After that, the reciters Fide Alessandrini, Virginia Contardo, Josefina Silvan, Edelmira Muñoz, Nelida Rigoletti, Alma Montiel, Pedro Reszka and Ernesto Urra offered excellent recitations being all very applauded (Zenteno de Leon E., 1944, page 9). Finally, the bulletin announced the many books they had received that year, which numbered seventeen, coming from countries such as Uruguay, Mexico, Chile, Peru, and Ecuador (Zenteno de Leon E., 1944, p. 14).

Vera offered the most enlightening account of the activities of these groups with a book published in 1947 entitled *The Cenacle of Poetry to its Poets: 19 Poets of the Cenacle of Poetry* (Zenteno de Leon E., 1947). In its pages, we find insightful biographies of all those disinterested artists, engaged in the art of dignifying the word. There, Lucia shared experiences with Bernardino Abarzua, a priest, poet, lawyer, and military man. He was an orator of extraordinary eloquence. His sermons raised applause under the vaults of the temple. He later collected many of them in his book *From the Earth to the Race*.

In 1947, he had published a work called *Poems of the Rosary*. He was a Chaplain of the Chilean Armed Forces, serving in the Military School. Many young cadets adored him, with whom he had created a spiritual family. Another of her companions was Amanda de Amunategui, a writer and poet with a profound philosophical sense. She personified the exquisite lady and the tireless reader. She had nourished her intelligence with serious scientific, literary, and esoteric studies. Already by then, the author had published a huge number of books of prose and poetry: *Giant Threshold*, *Clover Boat*, *Mirrors of Ecstasy*, *Glass Viewpoint*. Amanda also gave lectures, wrote articles in the press, and created institutions designed to cultivate the spirit and strengthen the mind.

Clara Maria Brieba was a woman of great sentimental fiber, poet, author of Thistle Blue, a book praised by critics. Maria de la Cruz showed sensitivity to all art beauties. She published poetry books as *Transparencies of a Soul*, *Dawn of Gold*, and also promoted a magazine called *Light and Shadow*. Washington Espejo had kind-hearted and liked to evoke the simplest things in life. He brought to the presses the following books of poetry: *The Long Way*, *Lost Song*, *Canto to the Castilian Romance*, *Nothing New*, *Poems of Man*, and *Sonnets*. In his day, his poems covered the American continent and also reached Spain. Many academies and intellectual institutions in Chile awarded him.

Carlos Alberto Fonseca was the highest representative of Peruvian poetry. He created and maintained the magazine *American Word*. Through this publication, he launched a spiritual message of union among the Hispanic republics, establishing a current of thought exchange. Several of his poems gave him recognition. Gabriela Huneeus came from a refined family of intellectuals and artists. Like her elders, she had an intense inner life, devoted to all the manifestations of art. She published *Voices of Time*.

Oscar Jara Azocar knew how to express the beauty of the landscape of Viña del Mar, dedicating many stanzas to children. The Ministry of Education commissioned him to travel abroad to improve children's theater. In the fulfillment of this mission, he met the highest intellectuals of the countries he visited. Reserved, ascetic, and almost unsociable, he confined himself in his study buried in books. He was the author of *Songs of Youth*, *Glass of Blood*, *The Garden of Prints*, *The Theater and School Poetry*, *Viña del Mar*, *Children's Book*, etc.

Raquel Jara Azocar, Oscar's sister, was a woman with no sense of vanity. She published *Poetry to Declaim* and *Celestial Fables*. Carlos E. Keymer was a mystical and sensual poet, who gave voluptuous form to thought and spiritualized the erotic. Samuel A. Lillo was a lawyer, professor of youth, and former rector of the University of Chile. A poet of great imagination, his loud and vibrant stanzas were like Wagnerian orchestrations. They had the strong tone of Chocano, the lyricism of Dario, and the pure tenderness of Nervo, the three poets who were the pride of Latin America. He received the highest distinctions. Among them, the Royal Spanish Academy awarded him a Prize for *Canto Filial*, the best song that sang to Spain in the Spanish language. Lillo represented at that time the most significant figure in the poetic and literary panorama of Chile.

Maria Cristina Menares was a vibrant poet of rich inventiveness. She had published *Distant Pumas*, *The Star in the Water*, and *Eternal Root*. Later on, The P.E.N. Club of Chile released many of her poems. Patricia Morgan worked as a businesswoman, alternating the bustle of the stock market with poetry writing. She published *Fata Morgana*, *Restlessness of Silence*, and *Light Travel*. The critics made a favorable review of these books, being some of them translated to other languages and recited abroad. Ecuadorian Eduardo Olmedo Lopez, although classified as a modern poet, wrote verses which preserve the classical molds. He was erudite, reserved, and sentimental. Many cultural institutions brought his poems to light.

Miguel Luis Rocuant, son of Valparaiso, journalist, and diplomat, became the editor of the magazine *Artes y Letras* and secretary of important literary institutions. Goldsmith of the form, each one of his books, was a perfect work of art. Among them, *Mists*, *Poems*, *Ashes of Horizons*, *Impressions of the Military Life*, *The Lyrics and the Epics*, *Earths and Cards*, *The Sacred Whitenesses*, *Twilight of the Cathedrals* (Novel), *In the Boat of Ulysses* (Greek Impressions), *Dead Eyes* (novel) and *Landscapes of Gospel*.

He was a member of the Chilean Academy of Language, correspondent of the Spanish one and others abroad. He received many decorations, among which stands Officer of the Legion of Honor. Jorge Gustavo Silva was a poet of a delicate sensibility, a profound scholar, a well-cultured man, and jurisconsult.

Gema de Tharsis was born in Chile and educated in Spain. She devoted to classical readings. Her first book was *The Letter that Carlota did not Write to Werther*. This essay went to be a literary jewel impregnated with tenderness and femininity. Her second book was poetry and held the title *Orbit of Dreams*, publishing later the novel *Guanabara*. Finally, Father Manuel Villaseca was ordained as a priest in Spain, dedicating himself fervently to literature and painting (Zenteno de Leon E., 1947)[6].

In 1947, Vera Zouroff sent a signed copy of her work to the Institute of Hispanic Culture. Today, this institution preserves for immortality the committed work of all the members of the Cenacle. Not even in her wildest dreams could Vera have imagined that Lucia Richard's grandson (the one who directs these lines) would find her book. In it, we can contemplate the photographs of each one of her companions. The images show them meditating, looking with a strong posture towards eternity. Each profile is accompanied by a grateful biography and some of their poems.

We can say that the review included in the book about Lucia Richard is one of the most beautiful. It is not surprising for the same reason, the mutual admiration that there must have been between both artists. As a result of this relationship, Lucia became the Secretary of the said Cenacle (Zenteno de Leon E., 1942). Vera Zouroff was a woman of great talent and intellectual foresight who professed great friendship for Lucia Richard. We cannot assume otherwise after reading the generous commentary she wrote about her in her work, *The Cenacle of Poetry to Her Poets*:

---

[6] About this book appeared a brief review in 1948 in Books Abroad, vol. 22, edited by Roy Temple House, Ernst Erich Noth, University of Oklahoma. There a critic named under the acronym of W.K.J. wrote: *19 Poets of the Cenacle of Poetry*. Santiago, Chile. Nascimento. 1947. 85 pages. *"Under de sponsorship of Vera Zouroff, 19 Chileans have published three pages apiece of their writings, preceded by one page introducing them and their work and containing a pasted-in picture of each writer. Some of them, like Samuel Lillo and Rocuant, are already well known. Others have not yet made a reputation, but the present volume gives them a wider reading public."*
Original and even exotic was the profile of the little-known Carlos E. Keymer. According to Nomez Nain, in his *Critical Anthology of Chilean Poetry*, Volume I, 1996, Keymer was a lawyer. But his profession did not prevent him from developing a hidden passion to poetry, versing sonnets of subtle, intimate tone. He was fluent in several languages and was attracted to Hindu rites and mythologies. He meditated on Buddha and Eastern religions. *The Book of the Dead* and funeral customs of Egypt fascinated him. Their motives left a mark on his work. He wrote innovative modernist sonnets that evoked exotic and distant cultures. From this mysterious archaic world, he extracted intertextual elements imbued of certain kabbalistic scriptural notions. He published *Feelings* (1898), *Phoenix* (1922), *Emblems of Light* (1945) and his complete work, *Lyric amphora* (1949) (Nómez, 1996-2000).

"I have said on another occasion that in Lucy Richard there is something transparent, like those images where the light is turned on.

Transparent!

She has exquisite femininity and the distinction of a great lady. These traits show the intense personality of a strong woman, as described in the Gospel. Yet, this temperament fades into the pale and sweet softness of her somewhat pearly face. These are the crystals in which reflect the many changes of light of the internal flame. Her poetic taste oscillates at the call of the outbursts of her artistic restlessness. To fulfill this need, she is always studying, going on a perpetual pilgrimage along the paths of art. Born in an aristocratic home, educated according to her lineage, she shaped her literary tastes in the ancient European culture. There, she acquired the impeccable classical correctness of her elegant style. She also developed a serene eclecticism to look at the things of life from the height of her thoughts.

Travels and readings have enriched her mind, which reflects in her writings. She has published several poems and prose. She has given many lectures and talks on the radio and has an essay on the way. Her verses and stanzas are richly carved gems. In them, we can see the spirit of the Christian woman, the tender mother, the lady, and the artist of boundless inspiration." (Zenteno de León E., 1947)."

For years Vera sent a report of all her activities and publications to the Institute of Hispanic Culture. In 1945 Vera published *The Art of Declamation, Teaching, and Practice of this Art*. Its cover reads *"For the Institute of Hispanic Culture in Madrid, with love for the race."* In the prologue to this work, Vera tells us that in 1938 the University of Chile called on her to create there a recitation chair. Later she called it the Conservatory of Declamation. It became a great success. Her classes were attended by celebrities. Among them were lawyers, professors, professionals of all kinds, and even priests.

She also tells us how badly Chileans spoke Spanish at that time, which she describes as an Indo-Spanish jargon. According to Samuel Lillo's testimony, Lucia Richard went to this Conservatory or Center of Declamation to learn to recite. Consequently, she must have read Vera's book, which was fundamental to her initiation into the art of declamation.

In this book, she taught how to breathe, (aspiration, breathing through the nose, expansion of the lungs) and according to Vera:

> "During breathing exercises, the student should occupy his mind only with pure thoughts of kindness and love. He should accept only ideas of health, happiness, goodness, and beauty. Never, for any reason, should he allow during this activity, depressing ideas of diseases, hatreds, grudges, or envy." (Zenteno de León E., 1945, page 23).

The book also shows how to dominate the voice, diction, Spanish spelling, the importance of consonants, the care of punctuation, intonation, the end of sentences, emotional appearance, gesture... (Eyes, eyebrows, mouth). Vera gave transcendental importance to the expression of the hands: *"The hands speak and express everything: joy, pain, evil, goodness, anger, terror, anguish, humility, love, hate..."* (Zenteno de León E, 1945, page 92).

She also explains how to move your fingers, wrists, elbows, and shoulders. Vera also talks about the precision and measurement of the gesture. It was essential to achieve harmony between gestures and words. Figure and interpretation were also crucial. They included such exciting aspects as adapting to the spirit of the poem.

In the last chapter, there is a section entitled "General Culture," which explains very well the nature of a true artist:

> "The poet is different. He is an intermediary between God and other men. He lives on another plane, where vulgarities do not reach. Poets are misunderstood beings."

Taking up the words of Emilio Carrere, she defines poets as:

> "Those who go through life dazzled with their eyes blinded by the miraculous ideal."

So, according to Vera to understand a poet you have to:

"Place yourself on the same emotional plane as him and enter the sanctuary of his intimacy with your bare feet and your forehead free of prejudice." (Zenteno de León E., 1945, page 174).

As for classicism, Vera was convinced of the need to adjust the poetic exercise to the rules established by the masters of the classical school:

"People can say what they want about modernism and its versatile freedoms. It will resonate with those who are unable to follow the rules of classicism. But the coming time will eclipse all those manifestations and movements that now predominate. Today, humanity is going through a mediocre period, reflected in jazz, cubist painting, and bizarre verse. The masterpiece that rests on classicism will endure with the majesty of the Egyptian pyramids. This perfection has the consistency of what is solid, firm, serene, and immortal."

To which she adds:

"The well-recited classical verse is the most beautiful wonder that the art of speech can offer the ear. It is a piece of spoken music. Any disturbance in the tones, the slightest alteration in the rhythm, immediately breaks the harmony of that music. It introduces perturbations in the cadence of the verse as well as in the sonority of the poem. Even the person who recites gets out of control and can easily forget and distort the words." (Zenteno de León E., 1945, pp. 177-178).

Therefore, Vera Zouroff and many of her generation are entirely against the trend they call "Modernism." They consider it a messy movement whose followers write whatever they want, in rows, without measure, calling the product of all this, "verses." Vera will refer to them all as pseudo-poets.

Another aspect that concerns the author of *The Art of Declamation* is the artist's spiritual ethics. Here, she puts the virtue of humility in the foreground:

"...The more greatness there is in an artist, the more humble he must be. When an artist makes art out of vanity, it means he is a poor artist. The artist ceases to be him and becomes the poem. Vanity and art are at odds, and he who is a slave to his narcissism cannot preach generosity."

Then she continues talking about sincerity:

"The artist must be profoundly honest in expressing his art. He must not fail to be true to himself because of the ephemeral applause of a vulgar audience. He must not prostitute what is noble, pure, and authentic to please certain mediocre audiences."

Later she reinforces her arguments defining moral honesty:

"That is what makes the artist not deceive himself. He must recognize the superiority of other artists of the same genre, without this causing him envy or bitterness. A feeling of fellowship, almost of spiritual kinship, should unite those who cultivate the same art."

Regarding the applause, she concludes:

"There are several types of applause: spontaneous, polite, conventional, claque, and enthusiast. It is the latter, the one that translates the feeling of hundreds of beating hearts. The intelligent, sincere, and honest artist knows when the applause corresponds to what he has given. He feels when that ovation is true, spontaneous, or simply of compliance." (Zenteno de León E., 1945, pp. 171-191).

These are some of the ideas that Vera professed religiously regarding the art of declamation. For us, they are important because Lucia attended her courses at the Declamation Center. Then she progressed in the Cenacle of which she was its secretary. Lucia absorbed all these principles by integrating them into her personality. They were aspects of life in which she believed fervently, as her verses express it very well. In short, all these ideas define Lucia Richard.

CHAPTER III

THE INFLUENCE OF RENOWNED ACADEMICIANS

Miguel Rocuant: The Eternal Traveler

uch could we say about all these delicate souls mentioned by Vera Zouroff in her beautiful book *The Cenacle of Poetry to its Poets: 19 Poets of the Cenacle of Poetry*. These words could help us to narrate with greater glory the true human dimension of their personalities and lifework. Not wanting to distort the meaning of this writing, I will stop only at four essential figures: Miguel Luis Rocuant, Jorge Gustavo Silva, Samuel A. Lillo, and Enrique Nercasseau y Moran. They were real Colossus of the letters of that time, representing the barometer that measures the authentic intellectual stature of Lucia Richard.

Miguel Luis Rocuant Sir was born in the port city of Valparaiso on May 11, 1877. He studied humanities at the National Institute. In 1898, the future writer joined the National Guard in the knight's weapon. From Valparaiso, he moved to Santiago, beginning his literary career. In his youth, he directed the *Arts and Letters magazine*. Later on, in 1903, he collaborated with the magazine *Pen and Pencil*. His sympathy and talent opened the doors to poetic creation, journalism, civil service, and diplomacy.

He entered the public administration thanks to a writing contest organized by the president of the republic Pedro Montt. In 1910, he was appointed Secretary of the Fine Arts Council that presided over Gonzalo Bulnes. In 1914, he was elected Section Head of the National Library of Chile. All his collaborators recognized his work capacity, natural modesty, and perseverance. In 1918, he reran the *Arts and Letters magazine*.

Thanks to his refinement at dealing with people and his great courtesy, he began a brilliant diplomatic career. That same year of 1918, the Government of Chile to Brazil entrusted him with the approach of both nations. He was appointed Secretary of the Legation and Chargé d'affaires of Rio de Janeiro and Undersecretary of Foreign Relations. In 1921 he was sent to Europe representing Chile's interests. In 1922 he returned to Brazil being named delegate of Chile to the Economic Expansion Congress of Rio de Janeiro.

In 1923 he held the post of the counselor at the Rio Embassy and in charge of businesses as well as Chile's delegate to the Social Welfare Congress held in the capital of Brazil. In Brazil, he led a very intense diplomatic and intellectual life. Everywhere he worked well, sang hymns, gave lectures, and enlarged his public persona. In the metropolis of Rio de Janeiro, he gained people's sympathy with his book *San Sebastian del Rio de Janeiro*. Brazilian newspapers said in 1921 that this publication, along with his *Announcing Rhythms*, would do more than decades of diplomatic formulas and protocol documents.

He published his *Biographical Sketches*. In 1924, the Brazilian Academy of Letters appointed him as a corresponding foreign member. He also joined the Society of Brazilian Literature and the Association of Brazilian Academies of Letters. In addition, he was president of the Chilean-Cuban Institute of Culture. In 1925, Aurelio Martinez Mutis described him as: *"tall, princely in his manners, elegant in dress, abundant in conversation ..."* Grown in popularity and already mature of soul, he reaches in 1926 the Under Secretariat of Foreign Relations.

In Rio, he experienced the claws of envy, as well as the nostalgia for his poetic intimacy. There he was interviewed on October 14th of that year, being his words collected in his work *Unipersonal Annotations*. The journalist there notes: *"He is always the same: affable, sincere and modest, despite his high position."* The interviewer then talked to him about his mission in Brazil and on the many flattering comments he had received, concluding that:

- It is justice that comes.

- "I do not have a biography, he said."

  - But I have the data to write it, like your intervention in the press, in poetry, in Brazil, and this Under Secretariat.

- "Nothing is worth that. Instead of being in this position, I would prefer to work alone, confined in my home. I have two unpublished works. I do not bother publishing them. Glory does not appeal to me, and I do not want to be caught in its nets. Here I am in an atmosphere of suspicions, mistrust, and uncertainties. One sentence can have disastrous consequences. We have to live in silence. This idea is terrible for those of us who have lived in the vast spaces of thought."

  - Are you tired of living at this point?

- "Completely and my greatest desire is to use my time again in what serves me to live my life. I need to release my fantasy and my tastes."

At last, someone heard about his discomfort, and in February 1927, he was sent to Mexico to occupy the position of minister plenipotentiary. In March 1928, he went as a minister on a mission of friendship to Bolivia, to finish the treaty of 1904. He handed over to the Bolivian government the section of the Arica to La Paz railway, which ran in Bolivian territory. Yet, climate and heights were detrimental to his health. Finally, he exchanged his plenipotentiary post with Cuban Minister Manuel Bianchi.

In 1928, he was part of the Embassy, which sent him as minister plenipotentiary to the shift of the presidential command in Argentina. On that occasion, he attended the ascension to power of the Hon. Mr. Hipolito Irigoyen. At the end of that year, on November 28, the president of the Committee on Relations of the Chamber of Deputies, Mr. Tito V. Lisoni, gave him a farewell dinner. The event took place at the Union Club before his departure as minister to Cuba, Santo Domingo, Panama, and Venezuela.

On June 10, 1930, he retired from the diplomatic service, moving with his wife Lucy Chatelet to Paris to continue his many literary activities. He made a trip to Greece that inspired a beautiful book. Returned to Chile in 1943, the Chilean Academy of Language chose Mr. Rocuant as corresponding to the Spanish Academy. Because of this election, he became its perpetual secretary and treasurer. He represented the Government and the University of Chile in several international congresses. The writer was also a Chilean delegate at the Institute of Intellectual Cooperation of Paris, presided over by Eduardo Herriot.

He belonged to the Society of Writers of Chile. He was president of the Pen Club of Chile, a member of the Ateneo of Santiago, and the Union Club. The poet received many decorations from foreign governments such as Official of the Legion of Honor (France), Grand Officer Juan Manuel de Cespedes (Cuba), Condor of the Andes (Bolivia).

He wrote notable works: *Impressions of Military Life (1899)*; *Mists,* poetry *(1900)*; *Poems (1905)*; *Ashes of Horizons,* poetry *(1920)*; *The Sacred Whiteness (1921)*; *The Lyric and the Epic (1921)*; *San Sebastian del Rio de Janeiro (1921)*; *Lands and Pictures (1921)*; *In the Boat of Ulysses (1933)*; *The Twilight of Cathedrals,* novel *(1934)*; *With the Eyes of the Dead,* novel; *Landscapes of the Gospel.* There are also his posthumous books: *The Bergson Wall; Aesthetics of Language and his Memories.*

In lines written for his first book of verses, published in 1898, Marcial Cabrera Guerra said:

> "There is, in the essence of this book, a mystical cult of pagan beauty. The poet feels a voluptuous adoration for lines and forms, exhaled through a religious sensualism. This combination gives an original and strange character to his poetry. In each step, he drives his ideas to a sensual emotion, idealized in the chastity of a virginal reverie (Rocuant, 1902)."

Alejandro Sux, in his book *The Intellectual Youth of Hispanic America*, tells us about a journey to Montevideo. There, he talked to some young Uruguayan intellectuals about Chilean literature and his most outstanding authors. In the talking, they mentioned Mr. Miguel Luis Rocuant as one of those who formed the vanguard of the brave phalanx of poets, who in the New World made the Castilian letters shine. Later, after a pleasant interview with the writer, he thought of including him in his *Hispanic American Album of Art*. That's why he turned to the study of his work. He was convinced that the fame he had in Chile and abroad was well deserved, as a poet of a fruitful and brilliant inspiration (1911).

Manuel Ugarte, in his book *New Literary Trends*, describes Rocuant as *"one of the best writers of Chile."* Some said of him to be an admirable landscaper who, with his pen, achieved what no painter with his colors. That's because he not only described but embraced with his unique perspectives all who knew how to read his brilliant rhymes (1908).

Minchero Vilasaro, in his *Universal Dictionary of Writers*, synthesized the figure of Rocuant as a poet, critic, and essayist. In his view, he was an imaginative and idealist writer, enamored with beauty. His work was sensual, serene, elegant, and rich (1957). Mr. Miguel Luis Rocuant died in Valparaíso on February 2, 1948 (Donoso & Wilson, E., 1910).

Think the reader that when Mr. Rocuant enters the 1940s in the Cenacle of Poetry, he is at the pinnacle of his career. Therefore, this Cenacle was not a leisure center, nor an amateur club. It was an institution that brought together into its ranks the first national talents. As a poetic academy nourished by academics, it performed a selfless and responsible work committed to its art. Besides, despite the great opportunities of leadership promotion males usually have, Lucia Richard, thrived among them in full parity of talent.

The Cenacle of Poetry was perfectly comparable to the Madrid Academy of Good Taste. It was a poetic academy created in 1749, led by the Countess of Lemos and Marquess of Sarria. In its halls gathered the most celebrated figures of the eighteenth-century Spanish intellectuality. It is believed this academy emerged, imitating the Parisian gatherings that revolved around the Rambouillet palace. Curiously, like the Cenacle of Santiago, these were poetic sessions directed by a woman.

Jorge Gustavo Silva: The Lawyer Who Embraced a True Passion for Poetry

nother figure impossible to ignore is that of Jorge Gustavo Silva. He was a lawyer, teacher, journalist, writer, and poet. This companion of Lucia descended from an illustrious family of literati. Both he and his brothers Hugo and Victor Domingo formed a trilogy. They prevailed in poetry, in dramatic performances, in sociological theses, in books, in law, and even opinion platforms.

Jorge Gustavo Silva, born in 1881, was the eldest of the three brothers. He studied humanities at the Lyceums of La Serena and Valparaiso and Law in the Lyceum of Valparaiso and the State University. He graduated with a degree in Law before 1921, becoming a lawyer in 1929. Beyond these activities, the author worked in journalism from an early age, and for the Administration. Mr. Silva was a clerk of the Navy Directorate, translator, and secretary of the Navy Attorney-General. Then he became a professor at the Naval School in the subjects of Spanish, Civic Instruction, and International Maritime Law. Later, in 1925, he led the international section, library, and publications of the General Directorate of Labor.

At the same time, he worked in the press, as head of the "Foreign Information Section" and as news commentator of the *El Mercurio* at Valparaiso, and editor and director of *Sucesos*. The future poet was also editor of the *Revista de Marina* and director and editor of *La Mañana de Santiago*. Furthermore, he was the founder and editor of *La Nación*, and collaborator of *El Sur de Concepción*. The writer also published several booklets, short stories, novels, poems, and books.

His journalistic themes were sociological, political, and legal. We can see this in most of his productions: "Is There a Social Question in Chile?", "Political Liberalism," "Belligerents, and Neutrals in Maritime Warfare," "Espionage," "Economic Independence," "Guide of the Prosecutor," "The Municipality and the National Economy," "Journalism and Journalists," "Civic Duties of the Chileans," etc. He also wrote novels and short stories, such as *Doctor Leroy* and *The Sailor*, and a collection of poetry that surprised the public in 1925.

In the literary contest of 1923, he was awarded by his thrilling story, *The Sailor*. He dedicated it to the distinguished officer, frigate captain Arturo E. Whiteside, who offered his life aboard "El Pinto" at the beginning of the century. The Direction of the Navy published it in a pamphlet the following year, preceded by a prologue signed by the ship's captain Olegario Reyes del Rio. Referring to the author, he said: *"He was one of the firmest and solid values of our intellectual world, as a man of the press, as a man of letters and as a man of study."*

To these encyclopedic achievements, he added a new book published in 1929 entitled *The Workers of Journalism in Chile*, and several lectures on law. He also practiced the section of legal-popular consultations held in *La Nación* and took his examination of extraordinary professor of Social Economics and Labor Legislation in August 1930 before a university committee. Omer Emeth, a French priest, considered the most cultured and accurate literary critic of our country included him in his work *The Literary Life of Chile*.

Beyond the rationality of law or formality of pedagogy, this man embraced a true passion for poetry and culture. He lived with delight the intellectual activities of Valparaiso and took part in its Floral Games. In the first, celebrated on the occasion of the anniversary of the country on September 22, 1910, he emphasized with his poems: "The kiss First" and "Train in the Night." In the third of these contests celebrated in the Victoria Theater on May 21, 1913, Jorge Gustavo acted as Maintainer (Figueroa V., 1930, page 827).

Later he caused a sensation with his poem "The Voice of the plane," full of lyrical beauties and grandiose metaphors. This poem impressed Gabriela Mistral. On July 20, 1947, from Llolleo, Chile, Jorge Gustavo wrote to Mrs. Mistral to discuss literary issues. Thanks to this letter, we know that Jorge had sent this poem to her in 1923. In an earlier letter whose contents are collected in the present one dated, 1947, Gabriela expressed:

"Your poetry is the first that thrill my spirit: it is full of movement, vigor, and beauty." (Silva, 1947).

It is interesting to note that many companions of Lucia in the Cenacle maintained correspondence with Gabriela Mistral. To conclude this brief biographical review let's recall the words of Vera Zouroff:

"Jorge Gustavo Silva is a profound scholar and a very cultured man. As jurisconsult, the Civil Code has not enclosure him in its arid pages. The daily struggle with life has failed in annulling the poet as it has done it with many forgotten authors. But above all, Silva is a poet, and the routine could not obstruct his wings, which stretch in a swift flight towards the blessed regions of feeling. In this place, he quenches his thirst for pure air to refresh his forehead. In his high and muscular body, there is a child who looks to the sky to fill his pupils with light. And in his heart, there is a lark that sings to eternal dawn." (Zenteno de Leon E., 1947).

Samuel A. Lillo: The Sweet Singer of Arauco

oetaneous of all those excellent souls and great happenings was Samuel Lillo. He was born in Lota in 1870, land of coal and miners, the cradle of martyrdom, and libertarian struggle. After studying humanities in the high school of Lebu and Concepción, he followed studies of Law at the State University and of Teaching at the Pedagogical Institute. He graduated as a lawyer in 1896 and a professor of Spanish in 1904. He preferred his post as a teacher rather than his role as a jurist.

He taught from 1894 onwards and also worked in the University Secretariat since 1891. He remained in this educational establishment, becoming Vice-rector for 37 years (1891-1928). He taught the subjects of Spanish and Literature at the National Institute and the Military School. Later on, Mr. Lillo was in charge of the university's Mining Code Chair, and that of Chilean Literature in the Pedagogical Institute. In his position as a university's rector, he was the soul and the engine of the prestigious institution.

In May 1925, he inaugurated in the university a course of Literature. For the occasion, he gave a speech. In it, Lillo listed the most well-known authors. The author emphasized those who, in various literary genres, had written works of national interest. In June of the same year, he gave a lecture on learning and studying Spanish. To illustrate and strengthen his literary lessons, in 1918, he published his *Chilean Literature*. It turned out to be a controversial work that had its apologists and detractors. However, the Faculty of Humanities approved it. Even more, it was used as a textbook for Secondary Education, having many editions. After remarkable services that lasted for 40 years, he got his retirement in 1928 (Figueroa V., 1930, page 48)[7].

Also, Samuel Lillo was an academic member of the Faculty of Philosophy and Education at the University of Chile. The writer also belonged to the Chilean Language Academy, corresponding to the Spanish one. But above all, he was a generous spirit, a romantic poet, a singer of Arauco, and its people. With his fine brush, he portrayed the natural beauties of his land. In 1927, the Royal Spanish Academy awarded him with the prize of Hispano-American poetry for his *Filial Songs*, in the race's festival contest. This award represented the most significant trophy that an artist of the race could have.

Carlos Rene Correa, in his work *Chilean Poets* dating from 1944, referred to him as: *"the patriarch of the current Chilean poetry."* (Rene Correa, 1944, page 52). Pursuing those ends, he created the Ateneo of Santiago. From there, he guided a whole generation of students, neophytes of letters, and raiders of deep thought. This detached man, already in the serenity of his last years, remembered the Conservatory. In his work *Chilean Literature*, he evoked it with the following words:

"Under the leadership of the distinguished writer, Esmeralda Zenteno de Leon, better known in intellectual circles by her pseudonym Vera Zouroff, operates a Conservatory of Declamation. It maintains in its classrooms a literary center called Cenacle of Poetry, which gives frequent lectures on the highest poetic values of Chile and Latin America. These lectures are artistically animated with recitations of poems by the students of the Conservatory. In 1947, director Vera Zouroff published a select anthology of 19 poets from the center, whose lives and works she depicts with knowledge and good taste." (Lillo, 1952, p. 290).

---

[7] A loving anecdote of this endearing character is that he always wrote his name as Samuel A. Lillo. This way, he prevented people from mocking him by calling him "Samuelillo," that is, little Samuel.

Enrique Nercasseau y Moran: The Philologist and Hispanist Committed to the Purity of Language

iving a turn to our narration, and without claiming chronological accuracy, it is imperative to talk about Hermelo Arabena Williams. He was a corresponding member of the Royal Academy of Sciences, Fine Arts, and Noble Arts of Cordoba in Spain, also an academician of the Chilean Academy of Language. In his *Essays of Literary Exegesis*, he passionately speaks about Ricardo Dávila's literary gatherings. These, according to the author, took place in the street Mac Iver, no 120, fourth floor, on Thursdays at four in the afternoon. They were organized by Ricardo Davila Silva and his wife, the painter Emma Formas de Davila.

Until Ricardo passed away in 1961, there was an intense intellectual life in his house. To his home came regularly, writers, artists, politicians, and diplomats. For example, Miguel Luis Rocuant, author of *In the Boat of Ulysses*, or the Mexican ambassador, Jose de Jesus Nuñez y Dominguez, well remembered in intellectual circles. The presbyter Alejandro Vicuña Pérez also joined the meetings. He had an independent spirit and mastered the art of writing biographies.

Likewise, appeared the Sociologist Valentin Brandau; the Uruguayan novelist Carlos Reyles, author of *The Land*; the Peruvian essayist Francisco Garcia Calderon; the novelist Paul Bourget, also the author of *Essais de Psychologie Contemporaine*; the Countess poet Mathieu de Noailles, unique in singing love; poets like Victor Domingo Silva who was splendid in the talk; politicians like Hector Rodriguez de la Sotta and Enrique Cruchaga; the Texas philanthropist Jack Danciger, an admirer of O'Higgins and his American work, and many others.

The host of those pleasant evenings, Mr. Ricardo Davila, was classic to the core. He liked to reflect deeply on all kinds of subjects, and cultivate metaphysics, sociology, and essay. He became a great lover of poetry, feeling much admiration for Leopardi, whom he knew in his vernacular language. Ricardo was also a great apostle of liberal ideas. The intellectual saw in them the exalting key of personality, as well as the motor of all progress.

In these warm encounters of beauty lovers, immerse in talks and philosophical exchanges, Mr. Ricardo liked to play at the piano, the adagio of *Beethoven's Patétique Sonata* or *Anton Rubinstein's Romance*. There, among puns and amphibologies, between sighs and declamations, the guests remained confused in a cloud of subtle thoughts. Then the host offered them delicious appetizers and invited them to have vermouth. Also in this group were poet Gabriela Huneeus, painter Dora Puelma, Misia Enriqueta Figueroa Larrain, Olimpia Fernandez Concha de Rocuant, and Marta Nieto de Brandau. Mingled with them was also Lucia Richard de Piedrabuena, who enjoyed the privilege of being the favorite disciple of Mr. Enrique Nercasseau y Moran in the Pedagogical Institute (Arabena Williams, 1986).

Note that this assertion is of enormous importance. Mr. Enrique Nercasseau y Moran (1854-1925), was a Chilean philologist and Hispanist. He was the first one who requested before the Board of Education to create a higher course of Spanish Literature in the Faculty of Humanities of the University of Chile. This course would embrace the general study of rhetoric and aesthetics. He was one of the founders of the old Atheneum, the promoter of a Hispanic-American Center, Hispanophile, and the one who fought for the rapprochement between Chile and Spain. Furthermore, he founded the Pedagogical Institute, together with Domingo Amunategui Solar and a group of eminent German professors.

Nercasseau was a purist of the language, extremely scrupulous with the grammar, with a thought close to Menendez Pelayo's. It could not be otherwise in Elizabethan Spain. He liked Bello. He explored Cervantes' work in-depth, followed Nuñez de Arce, and was also a member of the Chilean Academy of Language, corresponding to the Spanish one.

He was, therefore, a demanding man, very rigorous with adjectivization, obsessed with style, spelling, and all aspects of language. He turned to be a staunch enemy of the literary illness of "modernism" that he considered real flu. So, this statement made by another scholar, Mr. Arabena, that Lucia Richard was the favorite student of Mr. Nercasseau, is of enormous importance since such a figure would not easily grant such status to any of his pupils.

Note that Lucia Richard had to study some kind of humanities degree at the Pedagogical Institute, where she met the distinguished professor. Consequently, she had to have in her hands works such as the *Elementary Treatise of Castilian Grammar*, according to the doctrines of Mr. Andrés Bello or another one recommended by the learned professor. He also had access to the rich library of the center, which housed no less than eighteen selected editions of *Don Quixote* (Arabena Williams, 1950).

Other sources inform us that Mr. Enrique Nercasseau y Moran was born in Santiago, Chile, on December 9, 1855, the son of Enrique and Maria Mercedes. He received his first instruction in the Sacred Hearts. Then he entered the University of Chile, where he graduated in 1872 in Philosophy and Letters.

His main activity was teaching, with which he earned considerable credit throughout his life. He was a university examiner of grammar and Latin since 1881. He taught Spanish at the convents of San Francisco and La Merced, at the Bradford School, at Adrián Araya's and Filomena Rojas de Rebolledo's.

In 1889, he was appointed as a Spanish teacher at the Pedagogical Institute. Ten years later he held the same post at the Technical Institute of Commerce. Other interesting aspects of the Chilean scholar are that in 1905 he was a professor at the University of Chile, as well as a general professor of Spanish Literature. He dedicated himself to the no less exciting subject of professor of Mythology at the School of Fine Arts.

He stood out in all these prolific activities, being chosen for the Royal Spanish Academy, the Association of Writers and Artists of Madrid, as well as the Chilean Academy of Language. He wrote notable works: *Notions of Castilian Orthography*; *Metric Treaty*; *Archaic Castilian Anthology* and *History of Spanish Literature*, which he translated from French (Parker, 1967).

So, Lucia Richard was in contact with these academics. That was the case of Miguel Luis Rocuant, a diplomat and poet, member of the Chilean Academy of Language, correspondent of the Spanish Royal Academy, with whom she shared finesse and beauty in the Cenacle of Poetry. He also exchanged experiences with Ricardo Dávila, who embodied the major humanist. He was a professor of Greek and Latin literature at the Pedagogical Institute of the University of Chile and also an academic. Another figure was Samuel Lillo, academic and companion of Lucia in the Cenacle. All these groups of influence moved around the Pedagogical Institute and the Athenaeum. They promoted the glorious poet Nuñez de Arce in the early 1940s when purity and excellence in declamation were sought.

Therefore, this is an earlier generation than the so-called "modern poets," with whom they did not get along very well. For this reason, it is not surprising that Lucia Richard leaned towards clarity, simplicity, and neatness of language. She was like her elders, a convinced Hispanist. The writer belonged to the Chilean Institute of Hispanic Culture, and in her thinking, there are many reflections on Hispanic issues scattered throughout her work. But if we want to be more specific, we have to refer to the words of Lucia Richard herself, who in an article entitled "Understanding Hispanic America" wrote:

> "From Spain, we inherited the admirable respect for human dignity, the cult of freedom, the vital sense that descends into the bowels of the people and nourishes their culture. From Spain, we received a language that has given and continues to give generous fruit to its poets and writers. Spain made us the depositories of its religion of love that once made Europe great. Now it has the value of a panacea again, in the face of the many ideologies that seek terror and violence." (Richard, 2004, pp. 459).

In Lucia Richard's work, we can trace many Hispanic interests: the well-constructed lecture given by the author in 1945 on the occasion of the commemoration of the 300th anniversary of Quevedo's death; the biographical essay entitled *Doña Marina Ortiz de Gaete*, wife of the conquistador Pedro de Valdivia before 1947[8]; the article entitled "Women of Don Quixote" written in the *Revista de la Sociedad de Escritores de Chile* in 1946[9].

---

[8] The author wrote this biographical essay on the occasion of the commemoration of the Fourth Anniversary of Santiago (1941), "... the reason for which there was among us a true movement towards the Spanish culture, which has not diminished after leaving that glorious ephemeris." (Richard, 2004, pág. 268).

[9] She wrote this newly found article, which does not appear in the *Complete Works,* in 1946, in the *Revista de la Sociedad de Escritores de Chile.*

Another article entitled "Prado Museum: Summary of the History of Spain" written around 1950; the article entitled "Dream of Toledo," appeared in *El Mercurio* on 24 April 1955; "A Visit to El Escorial" also appeared in *El Mercurio* on 16 October 1955; "Once Upon a Time There Was a Young Ercilla," written in *El Mercurio* on 19 February 1956; a poem from his poetry *Blue Smoke* entitled "A Vision in Toledo" written before 1962; the work *Bells for the Dead* before 1962 and the work *At the Edge of Dawn* before 1969[10].

Despite all these achievements by Mrs. Richard, there is one thing that intrigues me. Several authors have expressed in various literary works the idea that many women of Lucia Richard's generation were limited by the models of the time. Moreover, they were believed to be self-taught, dilettantes, amateurs, which had led them to carry the stigma of being minor figures.

In my view, these ideas are pure subjectivity. We must bear in mind that the most applauded aesthetes support the notion that art does not progress, nor it improves, but simply evolves, mutates, changes. Therefore, we cannot speak of a better or worse period. For example, if we read the preface of *The Picture of Dorian Gray* by Oscar Wilde, we can realize how the author in a whole page exhibits maxims that define art, and then concludes: *"all art is quite useless."* (Wilde, 1996).

On the other hand, Hugo Montes, a member of the Chilean Academy of Language, in the prologue to Lucia Richard's *Complete Works* (2004), explains this phenomenon. He refers to the fact that at that time, few women went to university, and most girls in private schools did not take valid exams. The first women's book clubs did not appear until 1915. According to him, they also had many difficulties in publishing and the burden of domestic duties. He also emphasizes that Gabriela Mistral and Marta Brunet remained single and did not attend systematic secondary studies, nor even university... to finally state: *How much lost intellectuality, how many artistic possibilities cut off from the beginning!* (Richard, 2004, pp. 7 and 8).

---

[10] The last two plays deal with important aspects of the colonial past, at a time when Chile was still Spain.

It is also revealing that Mrs. Richard grew up on the shoulders of giants, under the tutelage of such scholars as Nercasseau, Rocuant, Davila, Samuel Lillo. If her poetry was limited, so was that of all these titans. Note that Miguel Rocuant did not study higher education, which did not prevent him from being considered one of the best writers in Chile.

Lucia was not only a tireless reader but also an avid traveler. At the age of thirty-three, she made a magnificent journey through Italy. It was a kind of *"Grand Tour"* at the beginning of the 20th century. It became an inexhaustible source of inspiration and wisdom, which would mark her deeply in her later life. Therefore, despite the limitations that the time imposed on the intellectual expansion of women, the poet had an excellent education.

The word "passion" is not "exciting" just because someone stamps it on a piece of paper. In the difference between "writing" and "feeling what we write" lies talent, and Mrs. Richard certainly has it... As for whether she's a minor figure, Bach's work was buried for 200 years. Vivaldi's was ignored and forgotten for 300. John Keats, an English romantic poet, died at the age of 25 and left to posterity a meager but universally recognized literary work. So what is the definition of a minor figure? Does this have anything to do with the extent of the work?

Fernando Diez Aljaro, a member of the Chilean Society of History and Geography, wrote an article in the newspaper *El Heraldo*. Its subject was the priest Bernardino Abarzua Troncoso, Lucia's companion in the Cenacle. In it, he inserted a quote from the professor and academic of Language, Hugo Montes, who in an essay titled *The World is Well Done* expressed:

> "The authentic poet possesses wisdom not based on intellectual or experimental knowledge, but in a direct and intuitive view of reality." "His task is to show that reality from an irreplaceable angle." (Díez Aljaro, 1997).

In a radio audition dedicated to Maria Luisa Bombal, a great among Chilean authors, Lucia Richard answered herself what in her opinion was poetry:

"What is poetry? Is it the order of words in lines? Is it even the music we call rhythm or rhyme that limits thought? No, it's not that. Poetry is appreciation. It is the capture of the quiet voices of things; the transfiguration of details, the valorization of the minimal and daily beauties, the sublimation of the small and delicate of life; it is a sixth sense that binds us to the universe by giving us back the power of primitive man. It is language, but more than language; it is rhythm, but not only rhythm sensitive to the ears. It is wisdom in the broadest sense of the word, but exciting wisdom." (Richard, 2004, p 578).

But even more incisive is another judgment of Lucia Richard, who in an article dedicated to her colleague Ines Echevarria de Larrain, noted:

"Today, to be an acclaimed writer, it is not enough to know Spanish grammar or metrics. You have to master literary history and even philosophy, sociology, and biology. In a word, you have to learn about the whole man." (Richard, 2004, page 453).

Isn't this beautiful judgment anti-academic *per se*? In some part of her work, Lucia praised Descartes, implying a rationalist view of the world, a denial of all inheritance consecrated by tradition, an enduring doubt before all that exists. *Sapere Aude*! Exclaimed Kant, which means, dare to know! Have the courage to use your reason! Some reflections of Lucia Richard reveal a perpetual dubitation that has become in her a philosophy of life:

"I have in me the sin of not being able to give myself completely to anything. Because everything attracts me with passionate vertigo, the prize reserved for those loyal to their ideals will not be mine." And then he continues: "And here I am empty-handed, having tasted all the fruits, having none roots in me. I go suffering by all the ways of the world and the thought, surprised by everything, absorbed by all. Everything makes me vibrate. I am a paradox made flesh, a living contradiction. I am always indecisive, and my path never has the straightness of the straight trails because I always remain pensive at a crucial point. And because I love all paths, both the one that leads to the fresh meadow and the one that goes to the stormy summit, that is why I stand hieratic, like a sphinx, never daring to move forward." (Richard, 2004, pp. 33-34).

Bravo!

As for Lucia Richard's poetic style, it has a marked lyricism, although, in all poetic techniques, there could be lyricism. According to Hugo Montes, member of the Chilean Academy of Language, several poets of the time contribute to shaping her poetry: Pezoa Veliz, Carlos Prendez Saldias, Pedro Prado, Neruda's beginnings, Gabriela Mistral of *Desolation*, the finesse but not the strength of Ruben Dario (Richard, 2004, p.11). And that may be the case.

However, at least Gabriela Mistral had a poetic style that was grim, mournful, and sad to the point of despair. In contrast, Lucia generally cultivated an optimistic, luminous and joyful poetry. There is also the case of Ruben Dario, who became the main representative of "Modernism" in the Spanish language, leaving many traces of it in his work *Blue*. In general terms, Lucia disdained such a style since, in matters of literature; she was educated in the neoclassical tradition. But aside from issues of poetic technique, this tendency did not prevent her from capturing the great beauty that lies beneath Ruben Dario's work.

We should also consider that at that time, there was a strong influence of a philosophical movement called "naturalism." This movement was joined, for example, by Ines Echeverria Bello de Larrain (*Iris*) and Mariana Cox Stuven (*Shade*). They were immediate precedents of Lucia and also of her contemporaries Marta Brunet and Maite Allamand. What we can deduce from her work is that the natural environment in which Lucia lives invades her thoughts. This natural world would be her first model, captured by her prodigious innate instinct.

It is possible the mystical and pantheistic idealism of her friend Ines Echevarria de Larrain influenced her. She found in nature a poetic charm close to the great Belgian poet Mauricio Maeterlinck. In fact, Lucia Richard dedicated one of her radio shows to this author, for whom she showed great admiration. Lucia had read *Life of Flowers*, and *Life of Bees* works in which she found sources of inspiration. She also praised other works by the Belgian author as *Bluebird*, *Intelligence of Flowers*, and *Pelleas, and Melisande*. The theme of the latter inspired Debussy, a style that placed him among the symbolist poets.

Besides, Lucia left clear signs in her work *Travel Memories*, of feeling great admiration for Saint Francis of Assisi, one of the greatest naturalists of history. On March 25, 1934, she was in Assisi, a small town in Italy, where she could see first-hand the full human dimension of the saint. There she experienced the stature of the man surrounded by exuberant nature. The environment showed the warmest of its smiles along with a beautiful spring already looming.

The Poverello, as people called him, was a humble man, of an austere and simple life, who loved stillness and peace. He lived as an ascetic monk, detached from all the offerings of life, feeling reverence for animals. He considered the sun and the moon his brothers, preached and blessed birds, tamed the wolves, and lived in mystical communion with creation and its creatures.

He also had words for Tagore, whom she portrayed as one of India's greatest poets. Described as a "guru of love," Tagore was an outstanding Bengali sage and reformer. He modernized the arts and letters of his country, showing an enormous naturalistic impregnation in his work. He conceived love as a feeling of truth and a manifestation of the joy present at the origin of creation.

In an article published in *El Mercurio* on Sunday, June 7, 1964, Lucia alludes to Tagore as a mystic and poet. The author was a pantheist of a fertile imagination, a product of the grateful nature of his land. In her view, he was a tender and delicate man. He knew how to sing love either to the child or the little things of daily life. Violence, distorted images, and tormented childhoods never appear in his writings. His defining notes are the simplicity of life, the clarity of his spiritual vision, and the purity of his heart. Harmony with the universe and awareness of the infinite personality of all creation is also manifested in his work. (Richard, 1964).

All these supposed influences–real or imaginary–do not invalidate a marked personal imprint in her writings, a *sui generis* way of understanding poetry.

According to her sons, Lucia was a tireless reader, who also knew how to speak and read English and French. Especially the latter, she spoke it like a native and read it without difficulty. French, the ancient language of culture, of beautiful sounds, had permeated her sensitive soul. No wonder that years later, she got captivated by Lucien Petri's painting, *Poésie des Eaux Dormantes*. Shortly afterward, she based herself on her canvas to write a gracious poem in her book *Blue Smoke*.

Regarding being carried away by emotions, feelings, and lyricism, Lucia expresses it with great clarity in her *Reflections* where she evidences this gap between "what is said" and "how it is said":

"I could not deepen the thought because the grace of the fascinating verb seduced me. This struggle between my philosophical clairvoyance and the treacherous attraction of the word has eroded my energies. My thought rose like a gigantic and threatening wave and died among the whitish foam. It was the trembling truth transformed into an imposing beauty. And so I fought uselessly against the tempting verb. I would have liked to be an anchorite looking up to the sky and smiling at the grace of a flower... I loved the truth too much to dilute myself in fantasy; I loved beauty and fantasy too much to immerse myself in the truth." (Richard, 2004, 33).

CHAPTER IV

THE ENIGMA: SHORT STORIES

An Original Storyteller

ince her first publication in 1925, *Sursum Corda*, to the second, *Poetry*, in 1938, thirteen years passed. In those years, Lucia had eight children. Despite the enormous family burden she had (although she had the help of the maids), after having her last child in 1937, she resumed her literary work at the age of 38, which is commendable. Having children is a beautiful miracle, but who will metabolize my dreams? With such an obstacle, even the most prolific of poets would not have had enough time to cultivate the lyre of Apollo. But the artist's vocation could move mountains.

By those years, Lucia Richard begins to be better known. Her name resounds in Brazil, in Argentina and even in Ecuador. We have proof of this in the work of the Ecuadorian Alejandro Andrade Coello, *Perifonemas*, published in 1939. In the chapter titled "Sketch of the Chilean Letters," read and broadcast in the solemn delivery of the Chilean flag to the Bolivarian Society of Ecuador, he alluded *"to the healthy and not affected verses of Lucia Richard."*

He mentioned her among the most famous of the intellectual pleiad of that time. And so he alluded to the poets Aida Moreno Lagos and Olga Acevedo; the novelist Marta Brunet; the writer Elvira Santa Cruz; the essayist Blanco

Subercaseaux de Valdés; To the catechetical work of Teresa Ossandon Guzmán; the travel impressions and interviews of Letizia Repetto Baeza de Bel-Beltran; the fervor of Rebeca de Fuenzalida; the fine objections and precision of Iris' ideas (Ines Echevarria de Larrain), among others ... (Andrade Coello, 1939, page 319).

From Belo Horizonte, Brazil, Jesu de Miranda, wrote to her on August 25, 1942. He was a poet and writer, author of *Close Woman*, and *Anthology of the Poets of Minas Gerais*. In the letter, he expressed the high impact "her beautiful poem Pray," had caused him. The Brazilian poet had heard about this composition in No. 427 of the *Margarita Magazine*. So overwhelmed he was that asked for her approval to publish it also in *the Jornal das Moscas*, a magazine in which he collaborated (Richard, 2004, 361).

The artist increasingly opens to society. She often attends all kinds of concerts, operas, and plays in the Municipal Theater, even rehearsals! She directed radio auditions too. Therefore, she began to take a keen interest in the national culture. Also, there is evidence that her voice resonated throughout the continent.

According to an article published in the newspaper *La Opinion* on December 25, 1946, Lucia Richard attended a round table entitled "A Question for Six Writers." In this meeting, she shared impressions with the playwrights Lucia Condal, Oreste Plath, Pepita Turina, Oscar Jara Azocar, Jacobo Danke, all forerunners of Chilean letters. In turn, the moderator praised Lucia Richard, saying: *"Public speakers on this continent have spread her verses, which have also given her poetic respectability"* (Anonymous, 1946).

These years of 1946-1947 were very intense in the artist's life. In early 1947, our biographee published a collection of ten short stories under the title of *The Enigma* (Richard, 1947). Many critics commented on the work and not only in Santiago but also in Buenos Aires and even Montevideo. The contradiction and the diversity of opinions about them seem to show the great bewilderment of the critics. They really didn't know how to make a stand in the face of these stories.

A commentator from *La Hora*, on September 2 of that year, writes with a certain interpretive lightness:

"Ten pleasant stories, written with great fluency of language, read with
pleasure, but without causing the slightest spiritual concern... and maybe in
that condition lies their success."

Vera Zouroff, in *La Opinión*, September 9 of that year, refers to the author's
elegant style and light reading of her stories. She also highlights the issues to
which her stories lead, which are somewhat disturbing, resembling Pirandello's endings. Misael Correa Pastene, from the *Diario Ilustrado*, on September
14, offered us a more optimistic view, emphasizing that they were:

"Pieces of life Lucia Richard has sketched with love, emotional simplicity,
a full sense of reality, and human sympathy."

A commentator in the newspaper *El Imparcial* on September 21 alludes not
only to the lyrical beauty of her writings but also to the tragic tone of the stories that remind him of Charles Dickens himself (Richard, 2004, pp. 365-367).

It is interesting to note that Lucia Richard herself attended a literary meeting at the Teahouse on September 21. On a broadcast evening and in front of
the journalists of the newspaper *El Imparcial*, she recited some of her stories.
It is necessary to bring up that these stories were already made known on
December 25, 1946, in the newspaper *La Opinión* in a program called "A Question to Six Writers," previously mentioned. There, said the commentator:

"Numerous stories have seen the light of day in major Latin American
magazines. *Athena magazine*, a publication of the University of Concepción,
has published a large part of this writer's production." (Anonymous, 1946).

Therefore, since 1945, the public knew these stories thanks to the extensive disclosure they had in *Atenea Magazine* [11][12].

---

[11] *Atenea*, Universidad de Concepción, Volume 80, no. 239, page 113, 1945, published
"The Rescue," a tale belonging to *The Enigma*. The stories were also announced in

Besides to the above, we have the testimony of Emilio Gonzalez Lopez, a member of Hunter College, who gave his opinion:

"These exciting stories of Lucia Richard have a common thread that binds them together. They are all small events that suddenly reveal themselves as a shot at close range. In the development of the story, there is always something that ruins the protagonist's illusions. The writer looks for a trivial detail, which produces consequences for the person who suffers it. The title of the first story, "The Enigma" (which is the story of a poor widower who searches the desk where his wife kept her personal belongings, discovering that she was unfaithful), could serve as the title of her other stories. In each of them, Lucia Richard finds many mysteries of the enigma of life." (Gónzalez López, 1950).

Also, Marta Elba Miranda, author of many reviews and books of literature, became interested in the tales *The Enigma*:

The Enigma, short stories by Lucia Richard, Tegualda Publisher. "With a set of ten stories, united under the name of *The Enigma*, Lucia Richard has launched her first prose work. In these stories, facts or scenes, she paints the simple and anonymous life of beings who live, act and suffer, lost in the main events of everyday life. The author handles the dialogue well, which gives interest and movement to the development of the arguments. She does not extend herself in vain analysis or annoying disquisitions, nor does she detail her characters. It is enough for her to point out a gesture to underline an aspect to show the intention and the psychological strength of the subject.

"When Bernard marries, you will give him the bronze cot," says the letter the mother gives to the priest. She gives it to him so that he understands

---

other magazines such as *Antarctica*, *Revista SECH*, *Revista Hispánica Moderna* (Richard, 1945).

[12] Also the work was commented on in *Britanica Book of the Year*. Franklin Henry Hooper, Walter Yust. *Encyclopaedia Britanica*. 1948. Page 62. There, a critic wrote the following: Two collections of short stories, *The Enigma* by Lucia Richard, and *Old Melodies*, by Victoria Orjikh, further proved that Chilean fiction needed a quick change before it reached exhaustion. Consequently, the Chilean fiction needed a quick change before reaching exhaustion, and that change had been achieved with these two works (Hooper & Yust, 1948).

why she is resisting the marriage of his son to the woman he loves. This sentence summarizes the intensity of the conflict that the protagonist has. She is caught between the duty of fulfilling the will of the husband, who orders her to give their son the bronze cot on his wedding day, and the pain of getting rid of her precious wedding gift.

This story, perhaps the best of the volume, shows the creative capacity of Lucia Richard. She is a subtle observer of those small tragedies that afflict humble souls. Peter, the boy who earns his living at the cemetery gate by offering "water for flowers" in exchange for some coins, is another example. These inconsequential characters who suffer and struggle amid simple conflicts, also resolve them.

How about we make the cake he likes so much? Says Cristine, the spinster, at the end of a bitter dispute with her widowed sister, mother of a small boy about to return from school. The love for the child is the bondage, the yoke - as the author calls it- that makes them live together. This bond makes them endure their dissimilar temperaments, which sometimes lead to fights full of hurtful words, bitter reproaches, as in this case where the spinster invites the mother to prepare the child "the cake he loves so much." Lucia Richard joins the many Chilean families of storytellers with a serious and valuable credential. Her storybook is fine." (Elba Miranda, 1946).

Lucia published her stories by Tegualda Publishing House, under the title *The Enigma* (Richard, 1947). Years later, his son Guillermo republished them in *The Complete Works* (Richard, 2004), and one of them, "The Rescue," came into sight in *Atenea Magazine* (Richard, 1945). Although some reviews appeared in some literary magazines of the time, all of them deserve a broader commentary, like the one I propose in these lines.

A story is, by definition, a narrative or short novel, which is also similar to poetry. It is a precisely drawn miniature that expresses a particular emotion, a condensed one, which Lucia knew how to recreate well. I would like to emphasize my astonishment at some stories that denote the author's interest in love as the central theme. She also exposes, in some passages, the suffering, and feelings of ordinary people. In the same way, the author shows her ability to find a balance between content and form. She makes an original attempt at dialogues and lexicography, without forgetting semantics or meanings.

Although enthusiasm always predominates in her writings, it is surprising to see how in these stories, she does not renounce pathos, and her endings are not invariably happy. In each of them, a conflict arises, but the solution as life itself is not always perfect. Serve this commentary as a breviary, like a bird's eye view of her stories. It allows us in a few lines to capture what the author's true intention was and the feeling she had in each of them.

THE ENIGMA

"The Enigma" deals with the terror and impotence that Javier feels in the face of his wife's recent death. With nostalgia, he remembers the best moments, the moving images, the perfumes, and the spring flowers. Almost without noticing it, an embarrassing sexual desire arises in him, before the memory of his sensual and lively wife. But now, by the cruelty of fate, she lies expressionless in bed.

Soon Javier becomes obsessed with the idea of reaching his wife's heart. He tries to understand that well-kept female secret as he observes the small belongings that remain in her bedroom. One day he comes across a literary passage, possibly a fragment of a love letter sent by a stranger to his wife. Upon discovering it, Javier feels cosmic despair, realizing that his whole life could have been a lie. He might not have known his wife. She could have been unfaithful to him and, worse, not love him.

To the impossibility of changing the past or communicating with his deceased wife to solve this enigma, there remains only the memory of the banality of his existence, the lost days of his life in absurd chimeras, in paths of withered glory. Perhaps Javier was looking for the secret of the author, who, between literary lines, could also long for an understood love, a full and happy life.

ANKYLOSIS

Mr. Octavio Mendiburu has to give a speech when entering the Academy of Letters. But as the title anticipates: "he suffers a decrease or impossibility of movement," in this case, of speech. The character is faced with the disjunctive of literature treated as a fossilized object in comparison with life itself, which throbs like the breath.

Then he attends a boring speech, full of old topics, peers who listen without passion and words trampled under the weight of routine. When Mr. Octavio is going to deliver his formal speech, he is among his papers with youthful writing, an unfinished novel which embodies an early love, his only love ...

Soon after, he remembers the betrayal of his life, how he gave up that love for social constraints, for money, for lack of social status ... Now that he has everything, all becomes absurd, and he wants to return to that golden youth, but now everything has changed ... In his mind, he recreates time and again this withered love, but only the harsh reality remains to him: the embalmed environments, the dissected looks, going through life unnoticed with empty hands "without having lost or gained anything."

Lucia Richard denotes in this story her great love for literature and the Hispanic world, showing a great culture, fineness, and erudition in the language. She goes back to the topic of love, and in the small format of the story, we witness the hint of a plot.

THE RECOVERY

For financial reasons, Anselmo's mother has to sell the family home. The young man witnesses the sudden move of all the objects from his old house and remembers them full of life when they lived there. He then becomes intensely nostalgic and begins to recreate his childhood as he passes through the various rooms. He recalls the dazzling lamps where the mosquitoes used to die, the running and jumping with his brothers and sisters, the couch in the living room that they imagined as a boat, the terrifying basement full of adventures, and the secret doors. He keeps inspecting the house and finds the attic full of dangers and mysteries, his parents' room, a symbol of worship and respect, that other room where his grandparents died, etc. Also comes to his mind those characteristic smells that identified the different places in the house and especially the flowery and paradisiacal garden.

Young Anselm leaves the house with sadness and swears to himself that one day he will get it back. He studies; strives to be somebody, graduates, gathers enough money, and one day returns to the house with the intention of buying it. Then a rude caretaker reluctantly shows him the uninhabited house. Anselmo struggles to restore the illusion of other times, the lost childhood, thus nullifying the cursed passage of time.

However, he is perplexed, confused. The whole area, the streets, had changed. The proportions of the house were not the same. The carefree caretaker, without understanding anything, shows him one by one the different rooms of the house. The living room seemed to Anselmo smaller than he remembered. The walls were cracked and unwashed. The strong smells had disappeared, and the garden was a desert.

So Anselmo understands that it was already impossible to recover all the memories of his childhood when his parents and siblings lived there. At that time, the house was filled with laughter and excitement, and each object brought to life a joyful dimension of thought. With nostalgia and disappointment, he has to face the harsh present and the death of past fantasies. Now they vanish like the images of the landscape, which blur when you look out the window of a moving train, the train of life itself.

The author herself chose this story to be published in *Atenea Magazine*. She shows us an optimistic and sincere prose, simple in its structure, vibrant in its content. In the end, the only significant thing is childhood and the best moments. The first years were the best stage of life, of all lives ...

MORNING LIGHT

Anselmo Leclerc is a man who has lost all hope in life. The woman he loved has left him, and now her memory seems disgusting to him. In his desperation, he goes out on a dark and cold winter's night for a walk in the city. He walks through streets, squares, and canteens with a hidden and sinister purpose. Feeling alone, he makes his way through the crowd, immersed in a cosmic terror that consumes him.

He arrives at a river and sees the images of his life pass by. He continues to torment himself with the sufferings of his bitter existence and prepares to throw himself into the waters. The desperate man thinks of the terrible consequences of his act. His body will end up trapped in the mud and eaten by the animals. Then someone would find him, and his acquaintances would celebrate the farce of his funeral. Suddenly, some guards appear guessing his intention. Anselmo leaves and continues walking anguished through the winding and dark streets of the big city.

The light of dawn arrives, and in a final act of lucidity, he walks towards the home of childhood. He climbs to the top of the wall and remembers his mother and siblings and the best moments of his life. Then he goes to a church and feels his mother's presence. A powerful light enters through the stained glass windows illuminating the cross in the center of the altar. Anselmo believes he has a vision and recovers his faith. The light has saved him from the clutches of death and freed him from apathy, obfuscation, and uneasiness. The tender memory of childhood and the mother figure was like a shield against all the vilenesses of this world.

THE BRONZE BED

In this story, Lucia introduces the dialogue and descends to the feelings of the common people, using their slang and idiomatic turns. Bernardo is a young worker who has had an extramarital relationship with Juana, with whom he has had a child. Bernardo is happy and makes all kinds of plans to marry Juana and live together as a family after the baptism.

However, Zoila, the mother, who is ill, stubbornly refuses to consent to the marriage, alluding to the fact that her son is a minor. All pleas to persuade the older woman were in vain. "When I die, I will be glad if you bury me in a pine box, and then you can enjoy all the goods of the house," she says.

In desperation, Bernardo turns to a priest to try to convince his mother. At the tenacious insistence of the pious man, the mother gives in. Then the shiny bronze bed emerges in the conversation, and the mother gives the priest a letter to read. In the letter, Segundo, a sailor, before embarking and suffering a terrible shipwreck, tells Zoila that if he dies, when the time comes for the marriage of his son Bernardo, she will give him the "bed of bronze." The story suggests that the bed of bronze brought back to the mother's memory her best years of youth, her love for her husband, and her moments of joy with him.

The older woman refused to give her consent. Not because she didn't want the best for her son, but because in all conscience, she would have to give him "the bed of bronze." The precious bed meant much more to her than a place to rest. It embodied the full meaning of her life, the evocation of the loving memory of the best years with her husband. It was the typical jealousy of the mother-in-law towards her daughter-in-law, at the idea that she, as in a kind of inverted Oedipus complex, could live in all its intensity what fate deprived her of.

WATER FOR FLOWERS

This story has the taste of the mischievous *Lazarillo de Tormes* (anonymous) or the unfortunate boy *Oliver Twist* by Dickens. Lucia focuses on the feelings of common people, introducing dialogue. To deepen this effect, she makes the characters speak in the language of their social condition.

The main character, "Little Peter," works at the cemetery, along with many other children. There he earns a few pesos, tidying up the graves and offering water for the flowers to his customers. His uncle was Lazaro, the gravedigger who, like his father, had learned the profession. His mother was a washer-woman, and his sister coughed and coughed, being permanently ill.

Lucia takes care of the misery of the poor; mothers abandoned to their fate, who earn their living by the humblest of tasks. The daughter would have liked to be a young lady, but the disease consumes her. One day, some children make fun of "Little Peter," calling him "the son of a gravedigger." A woman asks him why he doesn't go to school and learn a trade.

"Little Peter" realizes the vicious circle in which he finds himself. In his house needs the coins he brings every day to survive. The boy tries to save. He dreams of learning a trade, of reading, and of being someone in life. The years pass, and "Little Peter" continue offering his "water for the flowers," becoming older without realizing it.

One day, the same lady who had been coming for years to honor her beloved arrived at the cemetery. Then a troop of penniless children approached her offering their services, and the lady gave some coins to the smallest ones. The woman does not recognize "Little Peter," and he realizes that he has grown up, and his misery has not changed. It is the misfortune of the poor, who, like their elders, were illiterate and servile. Like them, they wasted the best years of their youth in unhappy jobs, which day after day buried them in the life and successively in that of their descendants.

LABYRINTH

In this story, Lucia looks into the disillusionment of love, entering all the nooks and crannies of the female heart. In an intense drama, Irene finds herself trapped in a psychological labyrinth from which she does not know how to get out. She explores all the possibilities, even thinking about suicide. Then, she remembers that her mother depends on her and how much it took her to pay for her house.

It all started a few years ago. Irene, one day met Gerardo, who arrived in the capital with nothing but a suitcase full of illusions. They studied and explored the mystery of love together. She became a woman with him. She devoted her entire life to caring for him, idolizing him, and trusted his manly judgment before making any decisions.

They worked together, too. They saved money, shared confidences. Irene modeled him, helped him through all those awkward moments until he became what he is now. Gerardo improved economically and intending to move up socially, one day he left Irene to marry Elisa, who was much younger, only twenty years old.

Irene is desperate and doesn't know what she could do to get his attention. How to remind him of that great love they shared? What if she talks to Elisa and tells her everything? But Gerardo would hate her forever. No, no way. That wasn't workable. So, she talks to her boss, Sandoval, who owes her a favor and tells him everything. Sandoval receives her with flattery. But in the face of the young woman's emotional weakness, far from solving her problem, he offers himself as a new suitor. Elisa flees frightened, sorrowful, and hopeless.

She couldn't stand anymore see Elisa's portrait continuously on Gerardo's desk. After packing up her things, she decides without hesitation to leave her work, and with him, the love of her life. The most important memories of her existence were gone. Then, she begins a new path, a dark path of desolation in which she has lost everything.

Female erotic affliction, as some say, is love. And unlike the man who often seems insensitive to this dependence on women, the woman without the man she has chosen often loses hope and withers.

This story has a parallel with "Morning Light." In both, it refers to the despair of a person on the verge of suicide. Yet, if in "Morning Light," the author only expresses the feeling, the outlines of the anguish; in "Labyrinth," she describes not only that feeling but also the reasons for the misfortune. It is curious how, in that story, the protagonist reaches an ending if not happy at least hopeful. Now in "Labyrinth," the ending is pathetic and concludes destroying the protagonist and her story.

THE PILGRIMAGE

Although there is no plot as such in this story, it is interesting because of the customs and the portrait of a contemporary scene in turn-of-the-century Chile: the sentimental vicissitudes of three women who live together in an atmosphere of prejudice and limitations.

It is about a family that, when the gentleman of the house lived, was wealthy and well-supplied. But after his death, the family impoverished, and with it, opportunities and social relationships fled. After the father's absence, Mrs. Gertrudis, his wife, ruled the house exercising her will in an authoritarian way. Her two daughters lived with her. Carmelita, who was forty years old, was always ill and threatened with an imminent attack. Her other daughter, Mercedes, was only thirty years old and was the youngest in the family.

With them live Aurelia, the maid, witness of the endless disputes of the three women. She carries out her daily tasks while becoming the latent conscience of their discord. The mother is a prudish and austere woman who fulfills her religious duties. She imposes on her daughters the model of honest living that has been left for her.

Carmelita, the eldest, would have wanted to get married and once had a boyfriend, Antonio. But the mother opposed the wedding because he was a gambler, and the absent father detested gamblers. The main character is Mercedes, the youngest daughter, who, in her nascent youth, tries to open up to the world. Despite her mother's authority, she struggles to find a groom, a future, a channel for her voice and sensuality.

But all her attempts always succumb to the angry gaze of the mother who represses her or the scathing words of the older sister who envies and attacks her by suffocating her with her offenses. The mother criticizes Mercedes' cousin Marta for her freedoms and her boyfriends. Mercedes, trying to impose her will, argues that at least she had a boyfriend and that she did not know what that was.

In that puritanical environment, everything revolved around the pilgrimage. It was the only opportunity to be seen, to open to the world, and be in touch with people. Mercedes insists to her mother to get in contact with Rebecca since she had a car in which they could go to the sanctuary. But Gertrudis, with her always severe frown, refuses outright. That's because she knew that some male, either Ruben or Luis, Rebecca's brothers, would drive it and did not trust the intentions of those upstarts.

Then Mercedes, in one last try, makes a pink silk dress and prepares to go to the big event. She comes out with a timidly suggestive neckline and a skirt a little shorter than modesty would accept. But Carmelita, already old, bitter, and suffering from illness, which she sometimes exaggerates to increase her sister's guilt, takes advantage of the occasion to humiliate her. Along with her, the mother gives her terrible reprimands and orders to change her clothes.

Finally, the three women and the maid leave for the pilgrimage. During the walk which the mother leads with energy, the young people's car passes by Mercedes' side, to which Mrs. Gertrudis looks grimly. Mercedes instead blushes while gifting to the young a shy smile, to which they respond with a friendly greeting. And so the life of these women passed with the spirit of their century. It was a century of conventions, constrictions, and fear of what people might say. It was a time of religious obligations to be fulfilled and of repression of any impudence.

Drowned in her youth, Mercedes was still trapped in that ambiance of prejudice, confined in this society of stale and shameful morality. This community put decency and virtue first, without allowing her to free herself from the subjection of her elders, without letting her be a woman. In that social environment, she could not develop her personality or open herself to the world.

Lucia, who also suffered some of these hardships, skillfully relates a great picture of a scene that must have been very common at that time, describing women's problems for their personal and social development. Her dialogues are well achieved, and she pays more attention to the details of the narrative, deepening the images she describes.

THE YOKE

In "The Yoke," Lucia narrates the dispute between two sisters, Carmen and Cristina, who one day question why they still live together. The conversation takes place within the daily scene, performing routine tasks such as losing weight, reading the newspaper, or having breakfast. Carmen, through the exercise, tries to rejuvenate and be fresher. Cristina harasses her with sarcasm. Suddenly the sparks fly, reproaches begin towards one another, and old grudges appear.

Cristina alludes to the fact that she was always successful in love, while Carmen had been too selfish to love anyone. Oh, love, love, what would you know about that! Replicates Carmen. Then the emotional drama explodes. Cristina reproaches her sister for being the prettiest, the one with blue eyes and golden curls, whose parents lavished all their praise on her. On the contrary, Cristina was the one who remained in the shade. The dresses did not fit her well, and she languished like a caricature of her sister.

Cristina goes back on the offensive, saying that when she flirted with some guys, Carmen always got in the way, ruining all her love projects. The love of her life had been Hernan, but Carmen had also stolen him from her, marrying him. Then came the breakup of their marriage, and Cristina witnessed in silence all the selfishness of her sister.

According to Cristina, before Hernan's death, he had asked her to take care of the son she had with Carmen. Carmen furiously replies that why Hernan would entrust her with such a thing! Was there something between the two brothers-in-law?

Time has passed, and now everything has changed. Carmen, who based her life on her beauty, reached the age of decadence. She was old and defeated. Cristina, on the other hand, built her life on constructive things. She traveled, had her pleasures, and made a future.

Each of them put in the balance what they had to overcome the other. Then Carmen says: Yes, but I have a son! For a moment, everything falls apart. Cristina sinks psychologically. But, as women they are, they soon embrace each other, feelings of tenderness arise, they forgive each other and cry. As women, they put aside their differences and collaborate because they have the same "yoke." The so-called "yoke" was the child they both loved and had to take care of. After all, the child was their blood and belonged to the man they both loved.

THE FOREST

In this story, Lucia delves into the supposed materialism of women as opposed to the idealism of men. She also shows a great love for the forest and the natural environment, which she describes with great skill. Without abusing, she also resorts to the balanced use of dialogue, which helps her to emphasize certain passages of the drama. There is no doubt that here the story has become a real drama, or has a confrontational development.

Antonio, who lives in an agricultural environment, has married Teresa, who is younger and more contrived than he is. He fears losing her and tries to be less rude, please her and adapt to his new marital status. Then she approaches him mellow, with soft words, telling him why she doesn't plant, to which Antonio replies that he has no money. With cuddles and hugs, begging, and with feminine sensuality, she proposes that he sell the forest and, with its yield, pay his debts and plant again.

Antonio refuses outright. This forest meant everything to him. Besides, he had bought this property precisely because of that wonderful forest. So Teresa, little by little, wraps him up in her web. Furthermore, she claims that the forest provides a shadow over the house that depresses her and increases the cold in the winter. If he cut down the forest, he would have more room to plant, etc. Antonio responds with a dazed look telling he would not cut down the forest in any way. Because if otherwise, he would never see the old tree again, and all that place meant to him.

Then, Antonio leaves the house to clear his mind and prepares to cross the forest once more. How wonderful it was that thick and lush wood, that living and talking gallery of nature! Antonio recreates in his romantic mind each of the tonalities, the perfumes of the different varieties of trees, the smells of iodine, and salt coming from the earth. He climbs the hill and, from there, contemplates a spectacular landscape. He views the sea, the glow of the fire, and gold shining on the horizon, while the evening sun illuminates the sandy soil like gems.

The landscape is mutating. The mists and darkness are arriving, and Antonio is about to return home. At last, he enters his house with a strange feeling that something important came before him. A notice of foreclosure has arrived. After the initial pleas, Teresa now speaks harsh and hurtful words to him. Antonio fears to lose Teresa. Finally, he gives in to the felling of the forest.

The horrible day arrives as if it were the day of an execution. Antonio locks himself in his room while Teresa enthusiastically runs the operations. Operators, machines, and carts come. Antonio hears obsessively the sound of a "rig-rag" all day. The sound of a "rig-rag" inserts into his mind like an endless nightmare. Finally, the deafening silence comes.

Antonio feels a strong pressure in his chest but attempts to leave his room and contemplate the new scenario. Then he witnesses a terrifying sight of stumps, a frozen Martian landscape, like those left by an erupting volcano. Later, he contemplates the rude leftovers of the workers: tins were thrown away, branches crushed on the ground, ashes from makeshift fires, and residues of all kinds...

He makes a new effort to meet with Teresa but falls to the ground senselessly. Teresa, in her pragmatism as a woman, had achieved her purpose, thus annihilating the idealism of the noble Antonio. Antonio's idealism kept him alive and hopeful, something Teresa did not understand. Antonio, wanting to save Teresa and not lose her, renounced his ideals and lost his own life.

As a final reflection, it is revealing to see how Lucia, gifted with remarkable psychological sharpness, in this passage, criticizes her own sex. She makes us understand that women, because of their condition as mothers and women, can be tender, generous, and altruistic. But for that same reason, they can also show us other facets that are not always so kind (Richard, 2004).

CHAPTER V

MUSICAL TEMPERAMENT

Some of Her Musical Aesthetic Ideas. Collaboration with the Musicologist Rene Amengual

nother exciting facet of Lucia Richard is her great love for music. Her fondness for beautiful melodies goes back to her early years of childhood. In one of her radio auditions, she dedicated a program to Claudio Arrau, an internationally renowned Chilean pianist. So Lucia tells when she was six or seven years old Claudio went to her house. It was by then a Claudio very different from the mature pianist he became.

The student went to the house of Mr. Enrique Richard Fontecilla, who at that time was a State Councilor to the Government of Pedro Montt, in the hope of obtaining a scholarship with which to travel to Europe. Claudio played with such skill that he surprised Lucia, who listened to him for hours. Lucia herself wrote:

"How impressed I was then! His princely figure, dressed in white, with his curly blond hair, his air of importance and the prestige of his genius. At first, we the children felt a little intimidated."

Then she added:

> "He played unconcern, looking at the paintings in the living room, which seemed to draw more his attention than the music he played. And they were difficult things for his small hands and his years', works that require four years of piano studies, like *Mozart's Fantasy No 1*." (Richard, 2004, 554).

Note the reader that there was a piano in Lucia's house when she could not yet play it. This fact suggests that one of her parents or siblings played the piano. Thus, Lucia, from a very young age, grew up surrounded by notes, feelings, and emotions that she later translated into words in poetry. There is a popular family anecdote, which says that Lucia was exceptionally talented. Very soon, her father recognized it, distinguishing her from the other siblings, calling her "my secretary."

Lucia tells in her writing *The Kangaroo's Path*, how having reached adolescence, being one day in her father's country house in Ñuñoa, she had a mystical experience with music. Let's listen to her words:

> "On a day that I wandered lazily like so many others, I suddenly felt the harmonious sound of a violin emerge from the other side of the wall. Those pure and lonely notes amid the peace of that garden shook me. Someone was playing Bach from the other side of the fence. He played it not from the unbreathable atmosphere of a hall but the smiling abandonment of a corner in the middle of nature. It was played with love, and I shuddered to hear it. The joy I got from that noble and pure music, I have never felt again neither in the most refined concerts nor in the most cultured halls.
>
> Anyone who has not heard Bach's music played in the deep silence of nature does not know what the voice of God is. Neither does he know how the forests sing, nor how the wonderful transmutation works that make the perfumes, the colors, the flowers, and birds become sounds, notes, and harmonies. All nature was a concert because the flowers sang with their scents, the butterflies with their colors, the foliage with its rhythmic swaying, and the invisible white statues with their placid smile." (Richard, 2004, p. 29).

Although out of modesty Lucia once said that in her adolescence, the mysteries of composition were alien to her or that she did not play like a virtuoso, her sons insist that she played the piano beautifully. There is evidence that she performed with skill pieces by Chopin, Mozart, Bach, Beethoven, Schubert, among others. This great passion for music led her to establish contacts with professional musicologists, such as Rene Amengual Astaburuaga (1911-1954). He was a pianist and composer, professor at the National Conservatory. Besides, the musician had an impressionist style and was very influenced in his career by Domingo Santa Cruz.

Rene entered the Conservatory in 1923, being educated by the masters Alberto Skipin, and Rosita Renard (in piano) and Pedro Humberto Allende (in composition). He was an assistant professor of the opera course (1935), of piano (1937), and professor of analysis of musical composition (1940). This last year, the Liceo Experimental Manuel de Salas appointed him as a music teacher. Among his productions is a song entitled *I Like You When You Shut Up* with text by Pablo Neruda.

Rene Amengual was later in 1940 co-founder of the Modern School of Music, and director of the National Conservatory of Music in 1946. He composed the anthem of the University of Chile. The composer was also the co-author of classics of the Chilean pianist teaching as *My Friend the Piano*, *Selection of Classics*, and *My Friend the Harpsichord* (Besoaín Armijo, 1997).

With Rene Amengual, Lucia had a very close collaboration creating scores for Christmas. They were cataloged between 1932 and 1938, in which the pianist provided the music and Lucia the texts. In particular, these were: *Christmas Eve*, music with one voice; *Easter on the Boulevard*, for four-voice choir and piano; *On the Way to Bethlehem*, for two voices; *Rockets, Firecrackers*, for a single voice[13].

---

[13] *Christmas Eve*, score kept in the National Library of Chile, BNCH, photocopy of the *Journal of Musical Education* year 1, number 6, September 1946, page 6. *Easter in the Alameda*, score BNCH. *On the Way to Bethlehem*, for two equal voices, score BNCH, printed in AME, R. 1, page 8. Rockets, *Firecrackers*, score BNCH, Santiago Institute of Music Extension of the University of Chile. Despite the cataloging of the BNCH, everything leads one to think that this collaboration with Rene Amengual took place in 1946, the year in which Lucia had a great intellectual and social flourishing.

It is important to note that some of these songs appeared in school texts. So for example in *Rockets, Firecrackers* we can read:

"You see rockets, firecrackers, and lights,
Easter has come here and to Bethlehem,
little kids are awake
The mass of the rooster we came to see,
there you see the birth of that cute one,
the Mother and Child and the good St. Joseph."

There is also great tenderness *On the Way to Bethlehem*:

"Dancing, singing, on the way to Bethlehem,
there will be the Child, Mary, and Joseph,
singing we'll get to see the tender
Shepherds, the mule, and the ox,
a sprig of basil, jasmine, and carnation,
wheat spikes and honey buns."

Therefore, the artist felt a great inclination towards music; she was concerned about the music scene, strengthened ties with the Conservatory, and cultivated the friendship of the outstanding figure of Rene Amengual. In her radio program broadcast in 1950 entitled *Centenary of the National Conservatory of Music*, Lucia commemorated the anniversary of the noble institution. In the program, she set aside all the criticism from the skeptics, highlighting the more positive and commendable side of a task that had already achieved generational achievements.

To do so, she went to Compañia Street, the headquarters of the Conservatory. There, she interviewed Rene Amengual about the orientation of his activities, and the projects he had for the future. Rene - who in Lucía's words was one of Chile's most outstanding composers - explained the main lines of the Conservatory's forthcoming projects. Among them were the training of performers, composers, teachers, and amateurs.

Lucia tells us with passion about these plans that would contribute to raising the status of Chilean culture. The Symphony Orchestra would integrate as soloists the graduates who had stood out for their exceptional conditions. The teachers would meet the needs of public and private education, thus improving the level of musical education. Well-oriented fans would contribute to maintaining the concert programs. The composition would play a key role in the objectives of the century-old institution. To this end, the Conservatory would increase composition classes, instituting special awards for the best students. Moreover, the educational establishment was to give a great boost to new talent so that people could listen to them. These activities would be promoted in close collaboration with the Institute of Musical Extension, which was a branch of the Conservatory.

Lucia Richard had a close friend named Lucia Correa, who gave her regular piano lessons. This woman seems to have been linked to the Conservatory and the Municipal Theatre. In fact, there is evidence that she conducted benefit concerts for them and was the leader of a choir. In the fifties, Lucia accompanied her friend to Europe, being the secretary of the choir she directed, touring several cities.

Although some doses of isolation are always necessary to develop an artist's creativity, there is clear evidence that Lucia was not only a writer confined to her studio imagining the world through her poetry and writings. She was fully integrated into the so-called intellectual generation of the 1940s (especially in the late 1940s and early 1950s). And so, she took part in its main endeavors and initiatives, following the evolution of Chilean culture and its main representatives.

We could emphasize Lucia's periodic follow-up of the artistic panorama of the country. She did so both in music, for instance, the *Trap Chorus Concert* or the performing arts, as recorded in her radio program titled *Theatrical Season*. In the latter, she analyzed the play *Montserrat*, the comedy *Alvarez Quintero*, told us about Bernard Shaw's *Pygmalion*, and the ballet *The Beggar Prince*. She also announced to us concerts, works by Mozart or gave us a preview of the visit to the Municipal Theatre of Marisa Regules. This artist was a young Argentinean concert performer acclaimed in London, New York, and Buenos Aires.

In another part of her work, she talked about Erik Satie's *Musical Humourism* (Richard, 2004, page 597). This composer's music arrived in Chile with the full version of his play *Sports et Divertissement,* performed by Claudio Arrau at the Municipal Theatre. Likewise, in her radio program *Window* by Wally Ossa (Richard, 2004, page 593), she described *Man's Life Expressionist Paintings.* Lucia also had the opportunity to see this piece at the Municipal Theatre.

This great liking Lucia had for music and theater, she reproduced at her home, writing small pieces for her grandchildren or other plays of higher significance. Every year when Christmas arrived, it was a perfect occasion, in which Lucia created a small private theater performance. Her daughter Carmen remembers it this way:

> "Since then, we celebrate Christmas. Mom organized everything: from writing the comedy to choosing the characters, the costumes, and the setting. She accompanied us on the piano playing a Chopin prelude, as we sang Glory to God in the heights and peace to men of goodwill.
>
> She assigned to each child-brother or cousin-a role, representing the Virgin, Saint Joseph, the Child Jesus, the Angels, the Magi, and the Shepherds. In fact, she managed to celebrate Christmas Eve as a family, as it should be, and her grandchildren gave little importance to gifts." (Piedrabuena Richard, 1995).

We see other evidence of her great musical passion in her radio program *Art Guide*. For years, Lucia followed the most renowned composers, both national and foreign. For instance, she showed interest in the lifework of Claudio Arrau, Rosita Renard, *Chopin's Centenary* on October 17, 1949, Haendel, *Beethoven and Goethe*, the *Small Chronicle of Magdalena Bach*, Edward Grieg, Richard Wagner, Erik Satie, Arcangelo Corelli, and Frederick Smetana. She also focused on other musical themes such as rhythm, the writings of famous musicians, or the origin of Waltz.

Throughout her life, Lucia Richard sought purity in all artistic manifestations and longed for a state of intellectual grace. She tried to find the philosophical stone of art, its most intimate secrets. Such a vision she summarized in a harmonic-geometric union of the world, in mystical communion with a perfect universe. Much of this we can trace in her musical conceptions, with some notable exceptions.

In her radio program dedicated to Richard Wagner, Lucia dared to deepen into a complex and contradictory personality, which she defines as Dionysian. She began her speech by dazzling us with all the revolutionary elements of Wagner. So, she tackled his vanguardism, his ability to transform German music, his fusion of the classical-romantic symphonic tradition with modernist elements, or his capacity to unite absolute music with musical drama.

New aesthetic horizons appeared in Wagnerian opera, bringing together various performing arts, theatre, music, and speech. It is flowing music, without recitatives, which gradually rises in search of something superlative. Its melodies suggest colors, gradual states of the soul. These sounds translate through the evolutions of the states of mind, everything that is immense and ambitious in the spiritual and natural man. It is music defined as ardent and despotic, which emerges from the deepest darkness. It is torn from an exciting and fatal dream, which runs like the dizzying images of opium.

Musicologists have also compared it to a supreme cry of the soul close to paroxysm. Baudelaire said about this music that it had the power to express the totality of nature and the fusion of the arts. Many critics claim that this music–as unique as it is revolutionary–had its precedent in the "Decadentism," according to which the musical language could represent meanings and images, like other arts. They also conceived it as the reflection of the totality and unity of the world.

Many blamed Wagner's first wife, Minna, for loving the man but not understanding the artist. In Lucia Richard, there is an inverse relationship: she revered the artist but distanced herself from the man. In Wagner's music, there is a fusion of philosophy, sociology, and politics. That's the danger according to the angle from which people look at him.

Thus, Lucia points out that in her time, this innovation of musical drama had its violent detractors. This opposition came on the part of the supporters of pure music (among them Tchaikovsky and even Stravinsky). Soon the public deified Wagner to the point of exaggeration, erecting him a temple, being worshiped by many of his followers. Then critics attacked him, seeing in his art and myths the symbol of threatening German authoritarianism.

Part of this reticence, Lucia already expressed in an article that appeared in *La Hora*, which referring to Neruda, she wrote the following:

> "Neruda's influence on our lyrics has been somewhat overwhelming, comparable only to Wagner's influence in the late 19th century." (Richard, 2004, 495).

Therefore, Lucia claims that after several movements in the 19th century, such as impressionism, the Russian novel, or musical romanticism, Wagner disrupted them all. He wanted to reform everything, introducing a new impulse into art and society. And in this situation, Lucia points out the confusing ideas that underlie in Wagner.

A man of the past and the future says, Lucia Richard. A man from the past because to create his musical drama, he inspired both by German myths and legends as in the knights of the Middle Ages. A mixture of values, in which he equally worshiped Catholicism, as in *Parsifal*, or praised dogmatic Protestantism as in *The Singing Masters*, or immersed himself in a remote pagan and barbaric past. He was also a man of the future since, through unknown concepts and procedures, he had the impetus to change and reform everything.

Therefore, according to Lucia, if we forget the playwright and his truculent mythological subject matters—and this is remarkable since in her view it is something to get rid of—remained the great musician, the great instrumentalist, and orchestrator, who had achieved a synthesis of all the arts. Were not cinema, ballet, and theater themselves a fusion of all the arts? (Richard, 2004, page 596).

Although Lucia was not explicit enough in her lines dedicated to Wagner, her writings, however, show contempt for a man with whom she could not feel aligned for many reasons. He was a bohemian, a reveler, a womanizer, somewhat impolite and rude in his manners. The author was a charlatan who could not stand interruptions, being refractory to the French language he did not want to learn. In his early youth, he also admired the Russian anarchist Mikhail Bakunin (1814-1876). This appreciation led him during his later life to devote himself to biased essays. The playwright even revealed in one of his writings the idea of the collapse of social order and end of private property.

There is also his anti-Semitism, which has, as a counterpart, the controversial German nationalism. Faced with the light emanating from Lucia's thinking, contrasts the darkness projected by Wagnerian thought. Clarity floods the work of Lucia, and the shadiness that of Wagner. Critics have denounced in Wagner his unacceptable ideas and opinions fed from his youth by a pile of non-systematic readings. At the core of his mindset, it was the influence exerted in his work by Arthur Schopenhauer (1788-1860), the philosopher of pessimism. From him, the German musician imported much of the dramatic meaning of his work.

If life sprouts with force in Lucia's poetry, Wagner's message is a howl of pain and tortured souls. These spirits wander, lost in the darkness of their intemperance. Then we must talk about the approach of Nietzsche to Wagner, the one who said, "God is dead!" An idea Lucia could not accept. Despite all Lucia omitted, praised, or attacked, for many, Wagner's mythological immersion is the most sublime of his operatic production, where we can perceive effluvia of the Greek tragedy.

The character of Siegfried evokes the struggle between good and evil, the symbol of life and purity. He is the hero who stands victorious in his fight against the dragon. *The Ring of the Nibelung* was the most significant play of Wagner's production, to which he dedicated twenty-five years of his life. In it, he deals in all its depth the subject of the essential freedom of man, importing many ideas from the Nordic imagery. It is breathtaking to contemplate the fabulous worlds built by Wagner, from which characters like the god Wotan emerge or the transcendence of certain scenes like the twilight of the gods. These are representations of an overwhelming intensity that have not yet been surpassed.

Wagner's immediate predecessor was Ludwig van Beethoven, Bonn's genius and one of the greatest innovators of musical theory. Beethoven, in his youth, picked up the threads of the Setencist tradition. That is, the so-called Viennese classicism embodied in the figures of Haydn and Mozart. But at the end of his compositional evolution, he liberated the formal structure of the symphony, chamber music, and even sonata. He created a revolutionary new musical language for the time that produced masterful scores. Yet, these productions were sometimes, at the limit of the orchestra's capacities of execu-execution.

Beethoven despised Italian opera and all its festive air. Many times, he expressed great esteem for the austere person of Cherubini and his neoclassical operas. Under the auspices of the Napoleonic era, the tragic and solemn gesture, the gravity of the Greek tragedy, became fashionable again. In his encounter with Rossini, he mocked the Italian from a position of superiority. He censured him for sticking only to the comic genre, withdrawing from the tragic and dramatic.

He also disapproved of the fact that Mozart had written operas in Italian, even recognizing their high quality. He saw in this the cynicism with which the *Ancien régime* had mocked the ideals of the French Revolution. This contradiction clashed with his convictions nourished by the rigor and morality of Immanuel Kant's philosophy. Besides, Lucia Richard devoted only a few sentences to Mozart, who perhaps she perceived as too mechanical. Yet, the genius of Beethoven absorbed her, being for her was much more sentimental, emotional, and transcendent ...

Therefore, Beethoven felt much closer to a national theater, with plays performed in German. Together with this nationalism, he gave a new air to concerts, especially those of piano and orchestra. He transformed the relationship between the different instruments and their performers. In the end, this improvement enhanced the orchestra, which had never been so powerful, or so ductile.

Beethoven sought new stylistic paths. He was a great precursor of the renewal of the musical language, taking its possibilities of expression to the limit. He developed an original and innovative style that powerfully influenced musicians such as Schubert, Schumann, Liszt, Berlioz, and Wagner. Despite some reluctance towards Wagner, Lucia considered Beethoven as one of the greatest geniuses in art history. In her essay entitled *The Art*, which belongs to her work *Sursum Corda*, she pointed out:

"If human intelligence had produced only the three sublime geniuses, Dante, Beethoven, and Michelangelo, we would still lack time to study the history of art." (Richard, 2004, p. 73).

When someone values an artist to that extent, it means that the admirer appreciates the artist's work and possibly also feels an attachment to the essence of the person admired. Beethoven was a libertarian, a transgressor, a bourgeois of Dutch origin. Hence, he added the preposition "van" to his surname. In his youth, the musician became soaked with all encyclopaedist ideas spread by the French Revolution. They were progressive ideas that he reproduced intensely in his music.

These ideas emerged from the so-called *Sturm und Drang*, a movement based on a wide range of themes. They were not only aesthetic but involved a radical transformation of the philosophical, political, and social order. Among its immediate theoretical background, we can recognize the philosophical thought of Leibniz and Spinoza, the criticisms of Rousseau and English empiricism.

Through their actions, the Sturmers sought to overcome the limits of conformity, tradition, and the norm. The body of this group was an emerging bourgeoisie, aspiring to emancipation. It advocated a break with the past and a constant struggle against all forms of oppression. Moreover, the philosopher Immanuel Kant fascinated Beethoven. Many ideas converged in the musician: the rationalist tradition (Leibniz and Wolff), the scientific knowledge of the world, and the natural sciences (as in Newton's theory), the English empiricism (Hume), or the ideas of Rousseau.

Other important aspects of this set of doctrines were anti-metaphysics and the rational theory of knowledge, as well as Kant's moral theory projected as pantheism. Beethoven had an unshakable faith in the absolute and a concept of divinity. But he reached these positions through a conception similar to deism. This belief was a great natural construction, in which God was perceived as the great architect of the universe.

For the first time, Beethoven fights for the dignity of the artist, his freedom, and emancipation from the nobility. Also, following the slogans of the

German Enlightenment (*Aufklarung*) on the role of the artist, he will act as an intermediary between the transcendent and humanity, promoting the spiritual elevation of man. The artist, as a prophet or guide, will discover his inner self through progress and freedom. In that world, the true aristocracy was that of thought.

Beethoven was a pre-romantic, halfway between the Enlightenment and its powerful reason that explained everything and Romanticism as a movement of feeling, nostalgia, and devotion to nature. From another perspective, he also swung between the interests and ideals of the bourgeoisie and those of the aristocracy. This was a complex era that came from enlightened despotism. It was a zone of shadows, in which significant social advances occurred, but, the aristocrats continued to keep many of their old privileges.

No doubt that the Bonn's musician was drenched with encyclopaedist ideas and aspirations. He conceived Napoleon as the greatest hero of these claims. To the sound of the Marseillaise and carrying the tricolor flag, the troops of "the Corso" propagated those ideals of the French Revolution of freedom, equality, and fraternity. However, this first admiration vanished when Napoleon self-proclaimed Emperor. The fact shocked Beethoven to the point of withdrawing his dedication to Napoleon from the title-page of his *Third Symphony, "The Heroic."*

Many have seen here the ideological contradictions of Beethoven. Even if he condemned Napoleon, he considered acceptable emperors like the Austrian or the Russian, and sovereigns as Louis XVIII, the Bourbon who had just sat on the throne of France. Therefore, if encyclopaedist ideas were an essential first reference to understand the musician, he did not hesitate to flirt with the highest exponents of Viennese society, to cultivate snobbery, and to adhere to the postulates of the Restoration.

Countless critics have interpreted that break of the title-page of the *Symphony No. 3,* not only as disenchantment with Napoleon but also as his willingness to align himself with the moderate and nationalist environment of the Habsburgs. So much so that Beethoven composed some pieces to commemorate the crucial and victorious moments of Europe's struggle against Napoleon. These include the Cantata *The Victory of Wellington* or *The Battle of*

Vitoria, or *Der Glorreiche Augenblick* (the glorious moment) to welcome the participants of the Congress of Vienna, which would redesign a new Europe after the fall of Napoleon.

Although the composer strove to renew the language of music, incorporating many progressive ideas, his progressiveness was spiritual, but at no time did he support a policy of reform or renewal. In other words, in Beethoven, we can glimpse an intellectual progressiveness, but not a social or political one.

This same eclectic attitude occurs in Lucia Richard. Lucia was a woman who embraced beauty, cultivated truth, and was progressive in thinking. But she never broke the mold of her upbringing, nor did she want to irritate the bourgeois society to which she belonged with too many bold thoughts. Although there are strong indications, that she harbored them in the depths of her heart. This progressivism has been called "aesthetic progressivism."

Between ideas and words, there is an abyss, and between them and facts a universe. It is difficult, not only for Lucia but for any true intellectual, to find the perfect formula of intellectual sincerity. Intellectuality and progressiveness are related, without being able to cultivate one and dispense with the other. It is difficult to reconcile ideas, words, actions, attitudes, roles, education, religious beliefs, pantheism, prejudices, moral Manichaeism, double standards, and to find the perfect equation of intellectual sincerity. Here, Beethoven, the musician for whom Lucia felt so much admiration, acts as a tuning fork, as a gauge, of the intense ideological struggle she faced in secret.

The *3rd, 5th, 7th, 9th* were Beethoven's best symphonies, the innovative ones, those that represented a transition to modernity. At that time, both Friedrich Schiller and Johann Wolfgang von Goethe occupied the vortex of German culture. Beethoven was keenly interested in Schiller's work, especially in his historical and political dramas. Because of this, the musician incorporated the *Ode to Joy* into his *Ninth Symphony*. He also showed interest in *Goethe's Egmont*.

In her radio program entitled *"Beethoven and Goethe,"* Lucia referred to the meetings of these two great men in the bohemian city of Teplitz in July 1812. She called them "the two greatest geniuses in Germany and perhaps the world" (Richard, 2004, p.590). It is interesting to see how she combines this passion for these two titans with the German *Aufklarung*. Lucia considers this to be a period of great intellectual flowering, comparable to Pericles' Greece (and its democratic advent), or the Italian Renaissance (with its return to neo-classical paganism).

Therefore, by making a synthesis between what Lucia said and what history has established, we can recreate how those encounters were. At first, there was a mutual admiration between the two men. Thanks to the intervention of an intermediary, the German writer Bettina Von Brentano, the meeting was possible. Yet, the magic and curiosity that both harbored towards each other's genius quickly dissipated.

The cold, fierce, and violent character of the musician frightened Goethe. Beethoven's manners broke the social ideal forged by the poet. He even said he had never seen an artist so concentrated, energetic, and profound. But this praise was also accompanied by many reservations about his volcanic character. Beethoven reproached Goethe for spending so much time at the Weimar court. In his opinion, he took more pleasure in its elegant atmosphere than would be permissible for a poet.

What was at stake here was the collision of two visions of life: one bourgeois and the other aristocratic. Beethoven was a titan, imbued with rationalist ideas, engaged in translating into his music his message of the progress of humanity. After the clash, the musician perceives that Goethe is bribing himself to the aristocratic and conservative environments of Weimar. He was stifling the progressive ideals nurtured by the generation of the late 18th century. Thus the writer was betraying that "poet mission" the German youth had attributed to him in previous years. He forgot everything for the glitter of the tinsel.

Despite these objections, Beethoven set Goethe's *Egmont* drama to music and planned for a long time to compose for the *Faust*. However, that aspiration could not be crystallized. The advisors who surrounded the poet in Weimar felt none sympathy for Beethoven, especially after they had met him in Teplitz. Besides, Goethe not only condemned Beethoven's rude manners but had even come to fear the disorders of the genius.

As for Egmont's drama, Lucia expressly referred to it, outlining the plot. She uttered passionate words but did not take a clear position on the subject. Thus, Lucia said the following in her radio program dedicated to Beethoven and Goethe:

> "The passionate republican and libertarian who was the musician from Bonn found a great subject in Goethe's drama that exalted the hero of the Thirty Years' War. His tragic end, full of beauty, was the culmination of a life devoted to freedom. As history recalls, Count Lamoral of Egmont, having served Charles V and the Duke of Alba, led the rebellion in the Netherlands. Finally, the Duke arrested him and sentenced him to death. The execution was carried out, despite numerous pleas to Philip II. This heroic end did not lack an emotional note. Jeanne Lavil, Count Egmont's mistress, fell dead from shock after witnessing the torture and death." (Richard, 2004, p.591).

In her radio show *Art's Chronic*, Lucia dedicated three programs to the Dutch people: *Contemporary Holland, the Netherlands*, and *Belgium*. In the program entitled *Contemporary Holland*, she strongly condemned the German occupation, pointing out the enormous damage that the usurpation of her well-earned freedom had caused. Moreover, she underscored the heroism and rebuilding capacity of the Dutch, who could overcome adversity. As Lucia said:

> "The hard-working spirit of the Dutch, their constancy, and the political tranquility they enjoy will make them find the means to defeat the enemies of today, as they knew how to defeat the traditional enemies of yesterday ..." (Richard, ca 1950).

Those "traditional enemies of yesterday" to which Lucia refers were no other than the Spanish. The United Provinces were one of the world's greatest commercial and maritime emporiums. There lived an advanced and prosperous people who experienced freedom for the first time, long before revolutionary France. In that oasis of wisdom, the most far-sighted minds in Europe took refuge. They came for reasons of conscience, fleeing from intolerance and persecution on religious grounds. Spain's most enterprising Jewish families also came there. They were expelled by the intransigent policy of a hermetic and barbaric Spain.

Philip II was nothing but an obtuse and fanatical monarch. Despite the recommendations of his closest advisors, such as his secretary Ruy Gomes, he sent his most narcissistic, ruthless and arrogant general, the Duke of Alba, to the Netherlands to impose the religion of Spain by force. He arrived in Brussels on August 22, 1567, establishing the so-called Court of Blood. He led thousands of people to the gallows for reasons of conscience. Among them, he executed Count Egmont, committing indescribable atrocities to the Dutch people. This struggle lasted for generations, and to pay for it, Spain spent all the gold so harshly extracted from the mines of Latin America.

In her radio programs dedicated to the Netherlands and Belgium, Lucia made a perfect compendium of the most sublime qualities of their main cities, telling us about the great artistic wealth they had. With great skill, she depicted their cathedrals, paintings, altarpieces, and the pantheistic dream of their poets ... She praised Leuven among other cities, which she called "the expression of science and knowledge," perhaps the most beautiful definition of all the towns she described (Richard, ca 1950).

We must not forget that in Louvain, many intellectuals practiced Erasmism. There, the influence of the Hispano-Flemish Erasmists on the ideological foundations of the Spanish Monarchy was evident. In contrast to the hermetic and religious humanism of Nebrija, in Louvain, scholars generated a universal and pagan humanism, setting their sights on Renaissance Italy. This group revived the taste for Greco-Latin traditions. Besides, they questioned the widespread medieval scholasticism in which Spain had plunged.

As for the intellectuals, Lucia refers: "... to the gigantic figure of Maeterlinck", a pantheist poet for whom she felt great admiration, dedicating him an exclusive radio program; to the music of Cesar Franck; to the young and pearly bodies of Rubens; and to the magnificent painting by Van Dyck, as an outstanding representative of the Baroque."

Before, Lucia had highlighted the heroic character of the Dutch people in the face of an unjust invasion. But now she was much more eclectic in describing the occupation of ancient Flanders by the troops of the Duke of Alba. She perceived some glory in that feat, putting her emphasis on the chivalry of the lofty *hommo hispanicus*. Furthermore, the author pointed out the religious fervor that encouraged them. Thus she refers to:

> "... Everything revolved around the domination of Philip II, the Duke of Alba, and the bloody struggles for freedom. To achieve this, the Thirds of Flanders went brave and proud to the battlefield but returned biting the dust of defeat."

Adding:

> "The ground was stained with blood, and the cities were burning. But on top of the bells, as eternal symbols of faith in God and spirit, the chimes still rang harmoniously." (Richard, Belgium, ca. 1950).

Closing this exhibition on what Lucia thought of Beethoven, she was original in her luminous interpretation of the artist's personality. It is paradoxical how the volcanic, virile, and intense genius of Beethoven did not intimidate Lucia's delicate sensitivity. She does not stop before the melancholic and overwhelming beauty of the *Moonlight Sonata*, nor in the drama of the *5th symphony* that evokes - according to Beethoven himself - destiny knocking at the door.

Neither is she frightened by Beethovenian impetus, nor by his irritable temperament, nor by the deafness that made him an asocial being and led him to the progressive isolation of his surroundings. Neither does she pay attention to the misery of his last days, his taciturn personality, his misanthropy, or his deep sorrow and torment.

The visionary Lucia skips all this and only sees the greatness of the musician who knew how to express joy. She implicitly refers to the *Ninth Symphony*. This work is the culmination of a whole life of spiritual and musical search, a piece that achieves the most sublime aspiration of man. After a race of anguish and misfortune, humanity marches triumphantly in its desire to master its destiny, singing its glorious hymn of joy. *The Ninth* is a universal language of love, which liberates the tensions of life. It is a clear message of peace and brotherhood in the world.

This is how Lucia describes it:

> "In this overwhelming task of entering the sanctuary of the great, the first one that comes to mind is Beethoven. He was a genius among geniuses—the one who knew how to sing joy with its triumphant notes. No artist felt or expressed the inner joy as he did. The musician lived a tormented existence and yet knew how to keep those pains to himself." (Richard, 2004, page 593).

In Lucia's work and her artistic conceptions, there is a propensity to look for joy. We can also trace melancholy. We see this as a nostalgic evocation of feeling, a memory of a lost past, an affliction in the face of a mutant world, such as the changes of season. Never does this melancholy turn into anguish, pain, drama, or pathos.

In her radio audition entitled *Theatrical Season*, Lucia feels uncomfortable in front of this chaotic world, full of atrocities. That is the case with the play *Montserrat*. She explains that the theme of the performance is dramatic, with touches of existentialism and resistance. Its action takes place during the Venezuelan War of Independence.

With great eloquence, she describes the content of this drama. It is the imaginative influx of a sensitive author who rejects what she exposes:

> "... We can conclude that hatred, reprisal, caveman instincts are not the unfortunate inheritance of this epoch. These conflicts between good and evil are as eternal as the world." "... The author spreads existentialist ideas as if it's licit to let the innocent die and other perplexing issues." "Man abandoned to his instincts, excited by danger, shows more cruelty than the beasts themselves. Emmanuel Robles, in his main character, has embodied the man given over to his passions." (Richard, Theatrical Season, ca 1950).

However, when she describes the *Cheerful Mood* play, her prose is enlightened. Her ideas convey a placid, almost pastoral, idyllic, and joyful worldview. She is not interested in politics, philosophy, or bloody drama. Death, darkness, calamity, or violence does not entice her. Lucia eliminates from her ideology, everything that implies abjection, baseness, or lack of humanity. Let us listen to her words:

> "With what pleasure I went to see the play *Cheerful Mood* that nice comedy by Alvarez Quintero set at the other end of the scale of feelings. There the theme is the joy of living, peace of the soul, youth alien to intellectual or social concerns."

> "*Cheerful Mood* is like an *intermezzo*, a break between performances overloaded with complications. The modern theater is a theater of anguish. Infected with the current unrest, it could not be otherwise. How much I enjoy when resting a little of philosophies and realities and wander in the merely poetic and sentimental." (Richard, Theatrical Season, ca 1950).

Lucia's critics have defined her as a classicist, as also demonstrated by many of her aesthetic judgments. But I have always suspected that there is also a romantic side to the author. This is so because one of the main pillars of Romanticism is the love for nature, as well as the cult of feeling, the nostalgic evocation of ancient civilizations, ruins, etc.

But we are entering a contradiction. Romanticism seeks to describe the ineffable, but it does so by highlighting the supremacy of the creative genius in search of his universe, which is above neoclassical reason. Now, creativity, originality, the emphasis of feeling prevails over the classical rules consecrated by tradition.

There are elements of Romanticism that fit well with Lucia Richard's thinking, but other aspects are dissonant to her spirit. Romanticism is full of natural scenes, deserts, ancient and mysterious ruins. All this leads to a relationship between nature and human feelings. Some critics have claimed that Romanticism is a precedent for Naturalism, which suits well with Lucia's ideology. It is also a world that exalts passions and a burning spirit of adventure. We can trace this temperament in the transhumant and restless spirit of Byron or Chateaubriand.

We know that Lucia strongly defended the classical rules. This fact clashes with one of the main premises of Romanticism: the break with classicism. The ideas of this movement reject absolute faith in reason and are based on the objectivity of art that defends neoclassical poetics. However, Lucia also passionately defended in many parts of her work the need to create her own lanlanguage, far from imitation.

Romantic aesthetics sublimated the power of genius, in its particular way of interpreting art as action and movement, free from all external precepts. Romanticism even took care of the myths of antiquity, but this recovery did not emerge as a desire for mimicry. It sought to revive the old clichés so that it could unfold on them its own conflicts and passions.

The exaltation of the heart, the lit language, the love for nature, the worship of the original genius (with nuances and limits) are aspects that we can glimpse in Lucia's thinking. What is not so clear is to see Lucia aligned with all that is torn, disturbing, and stormy in Romanticism. Let us speak, for example, of its marked nationalist spirit, its struggle for civil rights, its revolutionary heritage, its libertarian aspirations, its disordered passions, its sensual and libertine incitement, its impiety, its proclivity to transmigrate towards the tragic, seeking out extreme situations...

Chopin, the last of the Romantics, was Lucia's favorite musician. Clues and testimonies suggest that Lucia regularly played his waltzes, nocturnes, and some of his preludes. Chopin's music springs from the most profound feeling. It is a kind of music full of sensitivity, originality, and poetry. For this reason, women and artists love it. His playing, silent, diffuse, elegant and delicate, creates an atmosphere that leads the listener to lose himself in a kind of sentimental trance, driving him to a vital question.

Lucia Richard dedicated two radio auditions to Chopin. One of them was held on the occasion of his centenary, on October 17, 1949, and the other focused on the analysis of his twenty-five preludes. These programs show that our presenter made a great effort to study the artist, offering a splendid overview. About this figure, she expressed passionate words, as passionate as the Polish musician himself.

Chopin was born in 1810 and, from an early age, revealed himself as a true child prodigy. Refined and with impeccable manners, he frequented the salons and palaces of the Warsaw nobility from a very young age. In 1826 he entered the city's Music Conservatory and studied composition with Jozef Elsner for three years. The young man left the old professor so astonished that at the end of the academic years, he wrote about him: "that he was a singularly gifted student"; "he had remarkable aptitudes"; "he was a musical genius."

Elsner was very attached to the German classical tradition embodied mainly by Haydn, Mozart, and Beethoven. Paradoxically, he sees in the young man a promising future despite abandoning the usual paths. That's because the professor considers his talent truly unusual. In 1828 Chopin traveled to Berlin, where he attended many opera performances. Later he went to Vienna, where he met countless musicians, being acclaimed by the most distinguished figures in the society of his time.

The magazine *Allgemeine Musikalische Zeitung* praises the artist by portraying him in the following words:

> "The exquisite delicacy of his touch, his incredible mastery of technique and the perfection with which he passes from one note to another reveal a deep sensitivity. The sharpness of his interpretation and his compositions bear the stamp of genius. They show the virtuoso gifted by nature which, without the endorsement of fame, appears on the horizon like a shining meteor." (Nachrichten, 1829).

In 1831 the Polish revolution broke out, and Chopin emigrated to Paris. He suffered economic hardships and went through other good times. In time, the pianist dazzled everyone with the virtuosity and melancholic depth of his music. He liked Italian singing and established ties of friendship with Vincenzo Bellini, whom he greatly admired. He was a musician in vogue in the Parisian salons, being the greatest exponent of Italian opera.

At the City of Light, Chopin made contact with artists and intellectuals. He met the poet Heinrich Heine, and the pianist and pedagogue Friedrich Kalkbrenner. He also coincided with the music critic François-Joseph Fétis. Despite his reputation as a fearsome and irreducible adversary of avant-garde music, the writer filled the young Pole with compliments. In the *Revue Musicale*, Fétis alludes to the fact that Frederick, abandoned to his own impressions and without following any model, had carried out a complete renovation of piano literature. In the Frenchman's vision, his playing was elegant, soft, graceful, brilliant, and clear.

Schumann had already published a generous article about him on German soil. In it, he inserted the famous phrase: *"You have to take off your hats, gentlemen: here is a genius."* He later mentioned that with Chopin: *"the soul of music has passed through the world."* Liszt also supported him and was one of the first to understand the young man's innovative music. He met a Polish exile, Prince Antoni Radziwill, who opened the doors of the most elegant salons in Paris to him. The Parisian high society invited him to continuous receptions and evenings, rubbing shoulders with princes, aristocrats, and wealthy bourgeoisie.

The ladies adored him, and he gave many piano lessons to the daughters of the nobility. Chopin led an expensive lifestyle, went to eat at the best restaurants, and had many expenses. His biographers refer to his supreme elegance, his noble gestures, his refinement in dressing, the luxury of his lifestyle, as well as polite manners. Many bowed before him as if he were a true prince. He met Hector Berlioz, Mendelssohn, and a multitude of artists. The musician traveled all over Europe, achieving success and adhesion wherever he went.

Three loves tortured his existence. The first was the Platonic one of Konstancja Gladkowska, which dissipated in the complexities of exile. The second was Maria Wodzinska's passionate love, frustrated by the young woman's cowardice. Furthermore, her parents refused a marriage of different social status, with a sickly young man. The third one was George Sand's absorbent, which ended up in a shipwreck due to the disparity of temperaments. Nor did it help that the French intellectual exercised a masculinizing dominance over the delicate Frederick.

Lucia alludes to the fact that Chopin does not represent the triumph of force or cunning. However, he has the virtue of making us dream, leaving us suspended in time. His melancholy notes, sometimes sickly, or snatching, are always very personal and beautiful. They have the power to awaken the poet who sleeps in the heart of every human being. She traces three axes in the life of the genius: misunderstood love, a broken homeland, and inexorable illness.

All of them are loaded with sentimental epithets, as if he yearned for the best of his friends, unjustly beaten by a cruel fate (Richard, 2004, p 569).

Chopin was a deeply sentimental man who loved women, and many of them in the shadow sighed for him. Lucia denounces the behavior of Maria Wodzinska, Chopin's true love, who acted cowardly, moving away from his life. She gave in to the pressure of her relatives and the ever-intransigent social conventions. It is ironic to think that if we mention her name today, it is only thanks to the large entity of the man who did not love. Frederick had to face the harsh reality that in his time, the nobility of spirit could never reach the level of the aristocracy of blood.

Lucia is also upset by George Sand's attitude towards the musician." The two of them spoke at the same time —she says—, but they didn't listen to each other." In her opinion, misunderstanding reigned in the couple. The writer was unable to penetrate the intellectual sanctuary of the Pole. George Sand appears under her pen as a banal, artificial, exhibitionist woman, who lived only for social recognition and external appearance. She did not understand Chopin's heart. At the moment of truth, the novelist could not bear sacrifices or renunciations. She did not hesitate to abandon him when he could not continue with her social demands of enjoyment in an elegant, snobbish, and superficial world.

There are many similarities between Lucia and Frederic. His music moved the author, penetrating the most intimate sanctuary of her personality and feelings. *"Chopin is still alive... he continues manifesting himself among us, those of us who love spirit more than matter, the dream more than reality,"* says Lucia (Richard, 2004, p.569). Chopin is a person who belongs to the upper bourgeoisie, full of grace and nobility, refinement in his manners, and moral integrity.

He has a nature that fits perfectly into the sumptuous story of her poetry "The Chariot," full of smooth and aristocratic beauty. *"With pomp and circumstance the ducal carriage crosses the cobbled streets, and among silks and feathers the duchess, with indolence in its interior, rests."* (Richard, 1938, p.65). The musician is an apolitical figure who, in 1830, fled not only from the Polish revolution but also from the Parisian one in 1848. He was a poet of music and never got interested in politics or social philosophies, as George Sand did in her novels.

Chopin was terrified of the uncontrolled masses, and the irrational and bloody struggles, and he did not hesitate to walk away from them. He sought a quiet refuge where he could create, like that cottage in Nohant, where he composed his most beautiful scores. They were oases in a desert of incomprehension or monoliths in the desert, in Lucia's words. These places remind her of that secluded path like the one she described in her work, *The Kangaroo's Path*. They also suggest her garden at Conchali's farm, where the author meditated and wrote her most precious verses.

Lucia doesn't like superfluous social gatherings or empty talks full of trivia. Like Chopin, she has the disease of infinity seeking. To achieve this, the writer devotes her most chosen moments, in the intimacy of her personal world. There, out of the worldly noise, she gives free rein to her imagination. In the same way, Chopin did not like to exhibit himself in public. He felt uncomfortable in his soloist role. He once confessed to Liszt that the crowds overwhelmed him. In addition, the pianist felt suffocated by the noise of their compulsive breathing. Their curious glances paralyzed him, feeling silenced by so many strange faces.

Frederic liked to play the piano surrounded by a small group of chosen friends, in a dark room, in the late afternoon. At that moment, the vital hustle and bustle reduced to a minimum. It is a time when the suspended and evanescent notes of his *Nocturnes* flowed ethereally from the noble instrument. His pulse was fine and light, like the imperceptible line that separates life from death. His small audience remained trapped in his magical world. The artist's music hypnotized them, beginning to dream.

On other occasions, a halo of kindness permeated his music, as in his *Berceuses*. Here we find another parallel with Lucia, who wrote several poems full of tenderness dedicated to her newborn children and grandchildren. Chopin liked to cover his slender hands with elegant white gloves. Many have drawn a metaphor for life from this fact. The gloves would act as an aseptic screen with which the musician protected himself from a world addicted to materialism, selfishness, and iniquities.

Frederick had a pale, sad face, dark eyes conveying gentleness and goodness, a fine and sweet smile never becoming bitter. The young man had a melancholy as seductive as reclusive. His muted voice heralded great inner grief, and his delicate body gave off a distinguished air. His constitution was fragile and morbid and reflected tuberculosis that consumed him. He had feelings of death. Premature disappearance obsessed him. The musician feared not being able to return in time to his beloved Poland, to see his parents and siblings again. These torments grew worse as the disease beset him.

He was a wounded child, and Lucia, in her radio program dedicated to Liszt, thanked the Hungarian musician: *"... for the care and affection he gave to Chopin"* (Richard, Chronicles of Art: Franz Liszt, ca 1950). To relieve his lung condition, his doctors recommend him going to a warmer climate. To this end, in 1838, Frederick, George Sand, and her son, Maurice, left for the island of Majorca. They lived first in the village of Son Vent and then in the old Carthusian church of Valldemossa.

At first, the weather was mild, everyone wore summer clothes, and at night they listened to songs and guitar music. But in a few days, the weather got worse and became wet and windy. Then Frederic had a persistent cough again, which aroused a superstitious fear among the islanders. The French writer overjoyed with this eccentric adventure. But Chopin, housed in a monastic cell, felt like being in a grave where he literally was dying of cold and terror.

It was in this environment of baneful omens where Chopin composed his most intimate scores: his preludes. All create a unique atmosphere, sketch an image of a feeling, and suddenly they dissipate like the flight of a bird when posing. Their importance is uneven: some are suggestive, others terrible, but none lack character. These preludes represent the most enigmatic and ambitious expression of Chopin's creativity, who made few concessions to fashion and the aesthetic canons of the time.

It is well known that Chopin fled from classical music models. He especially avoided those enshrined in the Germanic tradition, based on symmetry and regularity. Chopin's music, whether on its virtuoso or its slow side, flows freely, full of fantasy and originality. His works condense a great richness in modulation but drag a certain disorder in the union of the phrases. Yet, this gives more of a feeling of listening to improvisation than a written composition.

Germanic ears, used to a symphonic tradition based on complex structures, found it challenging to assimilate Chopin's music. This music was too light and lacked the depth of post-Beethovenian symphonism. The preludes reveal a very intense and expressive musical style, not only in the choice and development of the harmonies but also in the balance between harmony and melody. This liberation from tradition also happens in the use of piano tones, which now appear with unusual colors and perspectives.

Lucia dedicated an extensive radio program to them, importing numerous music reviews from specialists, and interspersing her judgments. What is being discussed now is the struggle between traditionalists or supporters of "absolute music" and progressives or authors of "music of the future." In her first program entitled *The Centenary of Chopin*, Lucia enters this debate, with an innovative approach. In the end, despite her rigid aesthetic conceptions, she made a notable exception with Chopin. He was a musician for whom she felt true worship. The writer summarized her ideas with the following words:

"Amidst the cathedral of Bach's music, Beethoven's impetus, Wagner's storm, and Liszt's jubilant bells, his work filtered through the windows like a graceful and delicate ray." (Richard, 2004, p 569).

She then reaffirms these ideas, showing again the great support she has for Chopin:

"His music is immortal and survives the whims of fashion or the dictates of new techniques. Because it is a music that comes directly from the heart and penetrates the heart." (Richard, 2004, p. 569).

"Techniques" could be the problem or the solution, depending on how we address this dilemma. From Lucia's program on *Chopin's preludes*, we can deduce that the musician's creativity and originality came from the classics:

"When Chopin was composing his *Preludes*, his relationship with George Sand could have dragged him into a decadent romanticism. Yet, it is at this time that his imagination matures, and he relies most heavily on Bach and the classics." (Richard, ca 1950).

Therefore, there were elements of the romanticism that matched her personality, but others were alien to her spirit. So Lucia says that the danger of being in touch with George Sand—a woman of fantasy, and predator of avant-garde artists—might have dragged Chopin into a "decadent Romanticism." In my view, Lucia considers Romanticism to be decadent because it exacerbates the creative self, beyond the desirable objectivity of art and its untouchable classical rules.

Lucia offers her support to a "more serene imagination" compared to one that is out of control or irrational. Here again, we see the immobility in Lucia, or, more precisely, her traditionalism, being a partisan of pure music. We can check this in the following paragraph of the same radio program:

"The music of Bach and the sketches of his *Preludes* were the only things he took with him on his famous trip to the island of Majorca. Chopin never stopped advising his students to study the great master, as he considered him the substructure of all his piano fantasies." (Richard, ca 1950).

In Lucia's opinion, we should look for Chopin's success in the pre-existing framework of musical classicism and not necessarily in the uniqueness of his inventive genius. Let us not forget that a significant part of his piano production evokes and extracts elements of the folklore of his homeland as in his mazurkas and polonaises. There is an anecdote that when the musician was in Paris, the music teacher Kalkbrenner insisted on giving him piano lessons.

Chopin hesitated on this point and even consulted his relatives and teacher Elsner, who advised him not to take such lessons, urging him not to get entangled in the intrigues of Kalkbrenner. Mikolaj Chopin wrote:

> "You've never cared much for technique. Your spirit works much more
> than your fingers. Others may spend whole days playing the keyboard. But
> rarely have you spent more than an hour playing other musicians' composi-
> tions."

Chopin agreed to take such classes only out of courtesy. Moreover, this relationship opened the doors of the most prestigious musical circles in Paris to
him. Returning to Lucia, she seeks peace, serenity, happiness, placidity of spirit, and rejects anxiety, pain, disorder, or chaos. From this explicit formula, her
aesthetic conceptions emerge. And they have their charm, but they also harbor the limitation of what they lack.

Tragic, fateful, and mournful feelings also have their dynamism, sometimes
of brilliant execution, which can be exploited in works of literature or any artistic manifestation. Lucia, however, seems to want to get rid of the bicephalic
nature of human feelings, divided between good and evil, the Apollonian and
the Dionysian. Instead, she advocates a man full of happiness and devoid of
vileness, misery, sadness, and cacophony. In her program dedicated to Richard
Strauss, she portrays Chopin again with the following words:

> "Chopin also enjoyed the company of his favorite friends, who were art-
> ists, writers, painters, and poets. But he was too big and complete to use
> resources outside of music." (Richard, 2004, 606).

Lucia again indicates that Chopin was a music purist, who did not use other
resources (such as the performing arts) to create music that flowed from the
heart and went to the heart. Summarizing her most representative thoughts
about the *Preludes*, we can classify her judgments as condemnatory and apol-
ogetic. Together they embody the paradigm of her aesthetic conceptions in
musical art. Thus, for example, regarding *Prelude Prelude nº 2*, Lucia wrote:

> "The *Second Prelude* has something strange and disconcerting that antici-
> pates a musical avant-garde. Although Chopin never wrote ugly music, this
> violent and irritating piece is hopeless, grotesque, and even discordant. It is
> an asymmetrical melody. Its lazy march suggests the deepest depression.

Consequently, these are thoughts lodged in the souls of suicides. The tone is vague and shows all the morbid and conflicting characteristics of Chopin."

"These notes show hatred of life, a kind of hypnosis and sentimental atrophy. These are the characteristics of the one who expects nothing and only faces the great mystery of death with its dilemma of annihilation or survival." (Richard, ca. 1950).

Concerning *Prelude nº 22* we read:

"Written in a minor tone, it destroys the nerves with its bold dissonances. The recklessness of this *Prelude*, its audacious harmonies, its dramatically cut phrases makes it a worthy companion to the *number 18*." (Richard, ca 1950).

From this, we can deduce Lucia's rejection of avant-garde music and her preference for order and balance in musical creation, with clear support for the traditional method of composition. Along with the above, an appeal to beauty in art is implicit in her words. It is an element inherent to it and without which it cannot exist. We can confirm this in the coming approving judgment:

"But we arrived happily at the *Third Prelude*. We left that tunnel of shadows and abandoned ourselves in a happy, smiling world. Its lightness does not resemble that of the *First Prelude*. Here the lightness of the soul floats like clouds in a clear sky. The left hand has a murmuring role, similar to fine rain. It is a study that is better adapted to a salon but without falling into artificialities. This is a joyful and graceful piece that reflects Chopin's sensitive nature." (Richard, ca 1950).

It is in this peaceful and smiling world that Lucia, lying in her fabled hammock, meditates on her eternal dream of beauty, happiness, and poetry. Lucia is minimalist. She does not think about great universal ideas or complex philosophical concepts. Her retina dwells on the greatness of the small things in life. In another paragraph of the same program, Lucia defines Chopin and his art, which is a living reflection of his personality:

"Chopin was reluctant to love things that were too big: Michelangelo, Shakespeare, or Beethoven. His temperament sang the beauty of the small, finding poetry in the insignificant things. The nuance, the reflection, the perfect, and revealing detail attracted the pianist. He was a melancholic who liked memory. He had a somber personality that took pleasure in torturing himself with his nostalgia. Art was for him a carefully filtered wine, a liquor from which the fragrance of memories came out.

All music has a magical effect on us from the moment it speaks with the language of our past. Chopin constantly lived in exile, and only heard the oldest voices in his memory. That was his only poetry. His music flourished amid the cathedral of music. Like the majestic compositions of Bach and Beethoven, the choirs of Cesar Franck, or the impressive staging of Wagner and Liszt, his pieces appeared like the wonderful and impalpable glassware of Venice, endowed with delicious sonorities. It is the essential chalice of refined art, illuminated in a romantic sunset by a green ray of imprecise and divine pallor." (Richard, ca 1950).

These are beautiful and sincere thoughts that come naturally from Lucia's heart. They could hypnotize anyone. In her program called *The Origin of the Waltz*, Lucia recalled Chopin again, stating that he was the musician who most dignified and embellished the Waltz. She also had evocative words for Chopin about his work entitled *Waltz of Farewell* in which she said:

"It embodied the greatest love of his life. In those painfully repeated notes, he poured out his nostalgia, his pain, and his misfortune." (Richard, 2004, page 603).

Lucia's interest in entering into these passionate feelings, together with the auditioning of her music, makes one intuit that in the intellectual field, Chopin was perhaps the greatest love of her life ...

Throughout this writing, we see the struggle underlying Lucia Richard's thinking. This conflict arises, on the one hand, from her need to adapt to her education and to the ideas that prevail in her environment. On the other hand, the necessity she has to fulfill her insatiable thirst for knowledge and to discover many enigmas. In her radio program dedicated to Arcangelo Corelli,

Lucia flees from dogmatic ideas or absolute truths. She is expansive, revealing herself as a true intellectual.

If before we saw Lucia moderating her writings with rigid aesthetic conceptions, now she appears as a true "polymath." This term emanates from Renaissance humanism and evokes a universal man (Homo Universalis) who strives for a global understanding of knowledge. He is limitless in his capacity for development and tireless in his feverish interest in embracing new truths and areas of expertise.

She begins her presentation by alluding to the fact that the Renaissance was a time that had great creations in philosophy and culture. These productions not only copied classical antiquity. They built a vigorous humanism in opposition to or as a complement to theology.

Here are two interesting elements. First, the author recognizes that there was a transformation of pre-existing knowledge. Therefore, she praises the work of the creative genius in the face of the axiomatic truth inherited by the ancients. Secondly, she openly expresses that from this transformation, a "vigorous humanism" emerged in "opposition" or as a "complement" to theology. Thus, from these words, it seems that the revealed message, although supported by the authority and credit of tradition, is not exempt from explanation and interpretation.

She then reformulated her message, which, as we know, was a radio program, pointing out that of all the arts, it was music that changed the most. Monteverdi, Frescobaldi, Boccherini, Vivaldi, and Corelli - says Lucia - were the Italian masters who paved the way for Bach, Handel, Haydn, and Mozart. Later they reached the pinnacle of musical composition. Among them, she alludes to Corelli as the "prince of music," who had the honor of being buried next to the tomb of Rafael Sanzio.

In subtle but transparent words, Lucia adds that when the culture was broad, and the clergy did not conceive of different specialties, Corelli lived "observing the perpetual miracle of life." Note that Lucia is speaking to her audience from *Radio Chilena*, a broadcast channel attached to the Church that belonged to the Archbishopric of Santiago. The intellectual discloses these ideas with great dissimulation, under the abstract concept of "different specialties," which hides a thought or at least a technique in opposition to the dictates of the ecclesiastical hierarchy.

She reaffirms these ideas in the following passage:

> "Corelli enters the musical scene when religious art falls into a prolonged lethargy, and lyrical and instrumental art show their childlike face through the windows of time."

With the innocence of a child's angelic face, Lucia slowly imposes her thought. She talks about art, but between the lines, she shows us that lyrical art (poetry, humanism, man, and his concerns) emerges in the face of a decaying religiosity.

The next paragraph is even more enlightening, and as an upward wave explodes in its content:

> "He was like every creator a revolutionary of the gained knowledge. When his innovations surprise and even more, scandalize the official talents of the time, he only declares he does not know how to appease those critics, who have no other knowledge outside the basics of composition and modulation."

Lucia here reveals herself to be open-minded, talking about revolution, innovation, and criticism. The "official talents" are none other than those that depend on the ecclesiastical authority. They are the ones who observe the artistic model imposed from the highest levels of the prelature. Therefore, they are surprised and even more, scandalized by humanistic innovations, which announce an art as new as it is pagan. So Corelli does not know how to "appease," that is, "adjust" to the dictates and pressures of these critics, who lack sufficient instruction to understand them. Here again, we see the Church's reluctance to advance culture and science, all of which Lucia expresses with great subtlety.

Then she adds more:

"But the true genius does not shrink from the comments of those who want to keep the tradition. They are afraid of any change. Corelli went ahead and composed his remarkable *Concerti Grossi, Sonata de Camara, and Sonata da Chiesa*. Vivaldi and Bach studied these works carefully. In some of the latter's compositions, we can perceive the Corellian spirit that invaded Europe and changed the course of music."

"... We must worship precursors because no genius suddenly creates a system or a style. Later composers inspire their works from earlier ones. Bach took elements from the Italian masters. Others do from Bach and so on. It is as if the sacred torch of genius were passed on to humanity from hand to hand."

"Human judgment is unpredictable when it comes to standards of beauty. They change from century to century and from generation to generation. Those artists acclaimed in one era don't have as many followers in the next." (Richard, 2004, pp. 598-600).

All these thoughts of Lucia are important. If before she suggested being rigid in her aesthetic conceptions, now she tells us that the canons of beauty are in perpetual change, seeing this as a normal process in the cyclical flow of history. Therefore, she offers us a tolerant view of the transformations of art, a progressive vision in the face of the sacrosanct classical rules. She even disavows all those who defend immobility and oppose any form of avant-garde, in this case, music.

What is peculiar is the perfect balance she achieves between humanism and religion. The author is able to impose her thoughts without disturbing anyone. Under the aura of expressions such as "miracle of life," "child's face," "fervent devotion," "sacred torch," Lucia defines the contours of a humanist triumph, clothed under an air of Catholic spirituality. It seems that the Augustinian attempt to reconcile faith and reason permeates Lucia's work.

Lucia also cared about contemporary times and their innovative music. She had read Charles Baudelaire and at least knew his famous *Flowers of Evil*. This work could not arouse her admiration because of its burden of immorality and Satanism, although she quoted some of its passages in her radio auditions. Likewise, she was attracted to Debussy, possibly due to the naturalistic impregnation of his work. Debussy's music emerged as an original expression that opposed the traditionalists, the undiscerning avant-garde, the academic and official hierarchies, and the Wagnerians. The latter focused on defending the supposed truth of the music.

Although Lucia always opposed dissonances, she made an exception for Debussy, despite being one of the greatest representatives of musical impressionism. The French writer Émile Zola supported the new movement, becoming a passionate advocate of Impressionist art. On one of her radio programs, Lucia broadcast a piece by Debussy entitled *The Submerged Cathedral*. In this and other works, the composer created a musical expression out of silence. It was a silence full of suspension of the soul, of rapture, of transport to multiple spiritual states. This quietness did not leave the Chilean poet indifferent, who adored that unclassifiable serenity.

Charles Baudelaire is considered today the father of modern lyricism and the starting point of movements such as Parnasianism, the Decadence movement, Modernism, and Symbolism. His works *Flowers of Evil*, *The Little Poems in Prose* and *The Artificial Paradises*, were so innovative that they became banned in his time, due to their obscurity and immorality. Symbolism was a literary reaction against naturalism and realism. It fostered the exaltation of spirituality, imagination, and dreams.

Some variations of Symbolism, such as Hermeticism, allowed for free versification and a disregard for clarity and objectivity in art. The fatal side of Symbolism is that its followers identified with the terrifying works of Edgar Allan Poe. Other great precursors of Symbolism were Paul Verlaine and Arthur Rimbaud. Both were involved in a fiery love affair, beginning the movement with their ravings.

The most influential was Rimbaud, only seventeen years old, nicknamed "Le enfant terrible." He was a gifted writer who strove to seek the alchemy of the verb, trying to become a seer through the disorder of the senses. His work "Drunken Boat" is perhaps the most representative of wild creativity. Paul Verlaine, in his work *The Damned Poets*, showed the true essence of the movement. Both carried out a wave of excesses, which led them to a tragic, asocial, and self-destructive life. Linked to the previous ones was the poet Mallarme, also a significant exponent of the Symbolist movement.

Since the 1950s, there is evidence to believe that Lucia was changing in her aesthetic conceptions. Her moderate defense of Pablo Neruda or Gabriela Mistral or her hesitations in her approach to Wagner induces this idea. Her interest in Orientalism, in distant and unknown cultures, also suggests this. Lucia was seeking new forms of intellectual expression beyond Western canons and possibly conventional spirituality.

In the last stage of her life, she radicalized her message, questioning herself about the nature of truth. We may find an example of this in her unpublished essay *The Disturbing Question*. Despite Lucia's turns, she built an enormous eulogy around the figure of the Belgian writer Mauricio Maeterlinck which in some respects turns to be perturbing.

Culture is so complicated that it is difficult to seek a univocal system of values in a person and even more so in an intellectual. Lucia always opposed - with nuances - the lack of objectivity in art, drama, experiments in the theatre, darkness, and pathos in human feelings. Now, however, in her program dedicated to Maeterlinck, she praises the Belgian writer, dubbed "the poet of death," who was not only a poet but also a playwright and a scientist.

Lucia explains that the writer went into the mysteries of the beyond as well as the details of everyday life. His *Life of Flowers* and his *Life of Bees* —says Lucia— introduce us to the admirable universe of the minimal beings. His messages from the beyond and his constant concern for death elevate us to unknown planes. Furthermore, Lucia tells us that the poet joined the symbolists. As a playwright, he had his ideas, becoming one of the fathers of modern theatre. She also points out the breath of mystery underlying in his works close to Ibsen's. (Richard, 2004, p 600).

It is puzzling to realize how much Lucia admired an avant-garde author as Maeterlinck, which leads us to think of the complexity of human thought. Lucia liked the Naturalism in the work of the Belgian poet. Despite its symbolist influence, she expressed her most beautiful feelings when referring to pieces such as *The Bluebird* or *Pélleas and Melisande* (on which Debussy based to compose his homonymous opera).

Debussy's friend was Erik Satie, a French composer and pianist (1866-1925). Satie was an eccentric musician who opposed the musical romanticism and impressionism that the music of Debussy and Ravel represented at that time. Despite this, he cultivated dissonance and gave very rare titles to some of his works (*Three Pieces in the Shape of Pear*). The musician also cooperated with the Cubist movement. For example, he created the ballet Parade, for the Russian businessman Diaghilev, leader of the Russian ballets, in collaboration with Jean Cocteau and Pablo Picasso.

Around 1950, Claudio Arrau brought to Chile a play by Erik Satie entitled *Sports et Divertissements* that was to be performed at the Municipal Theater. As many times before, Lucia went to the theater to enjoy the experience and gather material for her later work as a music critic. The evening had a bitter-sweet flavor for Lucia as she then expressed on her radio show *Erik Satie's Musical Humor.*

As a commentator, she begins by saying that the audience listened to these satirical pieces with little pleasure. All this had made them meditate on the value of humor applied to art. Another debate arose about the old dispute between the supporters of pure music (music for its intrinsic value), and those who use descriptions in music. Lucia acknowledges this modernist author had original ideas, but he opposed Debussy's musical impressionism and pure music.

Bored with so many interruptions, the artist tried to understand this music. Finally, she concluded that the author's concern to apply titles or intentions in his compositions hindered their appreciation. Note that Chopin always opposed this idea while Schumann practiced it to explain his works better. Therefore, Lucia thought that description in music had its limitations and diminished the greatest thing that music had: "its power to awaken vague sensations, alien to the intellect." In her view, humor applied to music was a failure.

Once again, Lucia opposes avant-garde music: disorderly, disconcerting, and modernist. From the sublime to the ridiculous, there is only one step, she says. For her, musical humor is incomprehensible without ballets or fragments of comic operas. They are plays that combine word, sound, color, and movement; music that nobody played in isolation. She goes on to say that after so many masterful performances and unforgettable evenings in the Municipal

Theatre, came this mediocre work. With cubist confusion, it talked to us about golf, tennis, fishing, hunting, or the tasteless coral.

Lucia finds a greater affinity in understandable, serene, transcendent and balsamic music and so she expresses it:

"The privilege of the world of sounds and harmonies is the freedom in which they leave our sensations. They only dare to insinuate them through diffused images... In the song or the chorale, the suggested word leaves the soul in suspense. It awakens a world of feelings that was waiting for someone to open the liberating door."

Finally, she summarizes her thought with the following words:

"Fortunately, that entire false atmosphere was soon dispelled by the wonderful composition of Ravel *Water Games*. The piece came to refresh the room and cleanse it of the impurities of the so-called "musical humor." Other musicians had cultivated humor, but this was an innocent joy and not a deformation of the intellect." (Richard, 2004, pp. 597-598).

Lucia was inaccurate here. Ravel was an avant-garde musician, who emerged from the atmosphere of outmoded musical impressionism. In this movement, Debussy's evanescent dissonances reigned. But Ravel always denied being influenced by them, even though he appreciated them. Ravel knew how to maintain a balance between tradition and progress, incorporating into his music the latest conquests of musical language.

The inaccuracy is that Ravel claimed to be especially influenced by Erik Satie and, like him, practiced descriptivism in music. For example, *Water Games* is a piece inspired by the sounds of the changing movements of water, waterfalls, and streams. This pairing with Satie's style was the main reason that led the Municipal Theater to perform both works in one program. At the same time, it offered a more refreshing and more eclectic version of a similar way of conceiving music, at least as far as descriptivism is concerned.

Therefore, Ravel practiced the evocation of images through sound. He did this either by imitating the sounds of nature or scenes from natural life, depicting scenes from exotic ports in the East, using Spanish folklore, or translating poetic texts into music. Among them, he translated one of his favorite poets, Mallarme, for whom he had great admiration. In other words, Ravel joined the Decadence movement, believing in the ability of music to reflect reality as accurately as poetry and painting. We may find examples of this in works such as *Scheherazade*, *Moths*, *Sad Birds*, *A Boat on the Ocean*, *The Child of Sorcery*, *Natural Histories*, and many others.

All this leads to thinking that it is not so much the avant-garde music, the dissonance, nor even descriptivism in music that bothers the author. What irritates her is the surrealism in music. That is to say, they are works that have no sense and that are no more than an overlapping amalgam of musical stanzas without a truly human meaning. The artist's soul vibrates with works full of emotions capable of reaching the heart. They have that "liberating force" able to take feelings out of their state of confinement.

Lucia talks about "cleaning up impurities from music," "fleeing from a false environment," or "a search for the genuine." She finds all this in pure music or any melody of a healthy spirit. At other times, the writer conveys the idea of the "power that music has to awaken imprecise feelings beyond the intellect." She even tells us that "works are love and not good reasons." So, in her view, emotions and feelings cannot be evoked through rational machination. These siblings of sensations arise spontaneously from the entire being by the power of suggestion.

All this leads to the conclusion that, although she once made some adverse comments about pictorial impressionism, she did not have the same opinion about musical impressionism. Consequently, musicians like Debussy, Ravel, or Chopin, despite their dissonances and transgressions, were of her liking by the simple allure of their music. Therefore, it is not so much a rigorous criterion towards the evolutions of music that limits the aesthetic conceptions of the author but conceiving beauty as a guiding and inescapable principle of art.

I am sure regarding the experimentalist Ravel, Lucia would have been ecstatic at hearing relaxing works like *Boat on the Ocean*. It is a piece full of relaxation, rich in silky colors blending in a natural setting, where emotions flow freely in an infinite space. But she would have despaired at the obsessive rhythm of *Bolero*. This work reaches the highest point of musical technique but may not convey the sweetness of images that conquer the spirit of our author. Lucia always opposed to brain constructions, to hypertrophy of the senses or any creation that did not come from the heart.

Lucia included in her radio programs a musical thought according to her sensibility. After portraying Richard Strauss, she looks at other nationalist composers, who worked hard to revive the popular folklore of their lands, such as Gluck, Smetana, and Grieg. Gluck heard the voice of nature in the green hills of Bohemia. Ancient legends and customs inspired Smetana, as did the beauty of nature, the imposing mounds, the rivers and forests of his homeland. But especially Grieg would be, in her opinion, the most relevant personality of all these naturalistic composers.

Edvard Grieg was the first national musician of Norway, who evoked the sensitivities of the Nordic world. He created a spontaneous and fresh language, whose originality fostered the most modern styles. Lucia, in her program dedicated to Grieg, avoids the historical data of the musician. Rather she emphasizes the natural and sentimental elements of his life. The author says nothing about his meeting with Liszt or his time studying at the Leipzig Conservatory. It is as if she had grown tired of circumlocutions and ran freely through the meadows to meet her spirit.

At the beginning of his career, the musician became Germanized, letting foreign figures influence him. But he soon returned to his homeland and felt the powerful force of the land, in search of his identity. Lucia conveys to us the idea that German music, too rational, loaded with structures and logical divisions, could not replace the one that emanates from the most authentic dictates of the heart. In the depths of those fjords, in those blue coves, you could not create by relying solely on reason. There one dreams, one sees visions...

After meeting Ibsen, he asks him to put his *Peer Gynt* play to music, a task that took him two years of his life. Lucia points out that in this gigantic work stand out for their beauty: "Dawn," "The Death of Ase," "On the Threshold of the King of the Mountain," and the "Song of Solveig." Later, she broadcast many of these passages on her radio program. It is interesting, however, the way she approaches the plot of the *Peer Gynt* drama, not in her own words, but the ones of Jose Enrique Rodo. He was an Uruguayan writer, professor of literature at the University of Montevideo. The scholar became famous for his work *Liberalism and Jacobinism*, his essays in defense of Latin America, and his criticism of American culture.

Peer Gynt is a young and naughty villager who longs to be rich and powerful but also has artistic affinities. The whole plot is a struggle of identities. This need for self-affirmation will lead the young man to the very Sphinx of Egypt in search of himself. It is, therefore, a drama that links with the romantic tradition of impossible loves, journeys to exotic places, and abandoned ruins, interweaving all this with Nordic legends.

After attending a wedding, Peer meets Solveig with whom he falls madly in love. Given his eccentric personality, Solveig at first rejects him. In the act of desperation, he kidnaps the wedding bride, Ingrid, taking her to the mountains where he abandons her. There, Peer seduces the daughter of the King of the Mountains, and the trolls threaten to eat him if he does not marry her. From the union of the two, a monstrous son is born. Not wanting to be part of this grotesque world, Peer runs away from the fantastic beings that pursue him.

After the death of his mother Ase, Peer travels to Africa, where he becomes a slave and merchandise trader. Led by a prophet, he joins a sheik's entourage. He kidnaps the beautiful Anitra, who finally escapes from his clutches, leaving him abandoned to his fate in the desert. Then Gynt returns with his wealth to his country, but a terrible storm sinks the ship near the coast, and his return delays even more. Twenty years later, he is a tired man who meets a character called the Shadow. This character makes him see that his destiny lies with Solveig, the woman in love who is still waiting for him.

Finally, Peer returns home. In a scene of redemption, Solveig hugs him tenderly while singing a lullaby. In short, the story of Peer Gynt represents the search for the true meaning of life. Where is this true meaning found? Perhaps in possessing more wealth, in love, in exotic travel, in gaining power? Nothing seems to fulfill him, and after a journey that lasts twenty years, he returns home. There he manages to redeem himself from his chimeras in the arms of his beloved Solveig.

Lucia tries to find out the true meaning of life using Rodo's words. On his return home as an older man, Peer maintains a dialogue with a natural God, a Nordic God who surrounds him. On the way from the mountain to the village, the leaves of the trees swirl at his feet. "We are," they say, "the words you should have spoken. Your timid silence condemns us to die in the furrow." The wind would be the song he did not sing. The dew held the tears his eyes did not shed.

The herbs were the thoughts that never inhabited his mind. In short, Lucia, through Rodo's ideas, asks herself where happiness is. At the end of the day, a euphemism meaning the end of life, the Supreme Founder (a kind of god of nature or Gaea), in the name of justice that presides over the integrity of the moral order in the world, in the manner of the ancient Nemesis (the goddess of retributive justice, revenge, and fortune), stops him to ask where the fruits of his soul are.

And that is the true moral of the story, since in Lucia's vision (following Rodo's ideas), a life that does not reach its meaning is not worth living. In the same way, a soul that is not capable of releasing its aroma must burn with others in an immense purifying fire. Moreover, upon its past incarnation must fall the oblivion of the eternity of nothingness. This passage of overwhelming beauty tells us that a soul incapable of expressing itself must be erased from the face of existence, being relegated to the icy wind of oblivion.

The worst thing about this anonymity is that after death, there is no second chance. The problem is to know where that "meaning of life" lays. Lucia, with this passage, goes back to the Renaissance's idea of *Vanitas*. She wants to convey to us that we cannot find this meaning in the increase of wealth, neither in ostentation nor in the maintenance of power. We can only achieve happiness at the moment when the heart releases its corolla and makes it accessible to the rest of humanity. That is true happiness (Richard, 2004, pp. 594-595).

CHAPTER VI

HER CONTRIBUTION TO CHILEAN FEMINISM: MAIN FIGURES AND ACTIVITIES

The Pan American Round Table of Women of Chile. Contacts with Gabriela Mistral

At the end of the 1940s, Lucia Richard took part in many cultural initiatives and became a member of several institutions promoting such enterprises. Lucia Richard was Secretary of the Pen Club, Secretary of the Cenacle of Poetry, member of the Society of Writers of Chile, member of the Board of Directors of the House of America, and delegate of the Pan-American Women's Round Table of Chile. She also had a long time ago, her radio program called *Art Guide*.

Over the years she gave many lectures: the already mentioned "Death of Stefan Zweig" given at the Cenacle of Poetry (May 28, 1942); "300 Years of Commemoration of the Death of Quevedo" (1945); "Sara Hubner," read at the Central House of the University of Chile (1947); "Stained Glass of Brazil," presented at House of America (November 17, 1954); "Guillermo Valencia, Colombian Writer," addressed at the Catholic University of Chile[14].

---

[14] As for "Sea Lovers," the sons of Lucia Richard think it was a conference given its extension, although they cannot assert where and when it took place. Thanks to the *Bulletin of the Cenacle of Poetry*, we may know it was indeed a conference. But it bore

If we analyze the data in the previous paragraphs, we can easily realize that Lucia Richard belonged to an intellectual elite that promoted Chilean feminism. And this is a dense issue since there was working-class feminism, middle-class feminism, and high-class feminism. Lucia pertained to the latter category, and within it, she made great contributions.

The feminist claim in Chile began at the end of the 19th century, with figures like Martina Barros de Orrego, a tireless fighter for women's equality. In 1873, as President of the Ladies' Club, she dared to give talks on the female vote, when few ventured to mention such a thing. As far as the period in which Lucia Richard lived, we can divide this struggle into three periods.

The first one was from 1900 to 1935 when women collected their concerns and pushed for greater participation in society. To this end, the first women's associations, not yet considered as political, emerged. The second phase went from 1935 to 1953, when women organized themselves politically. The women's movement reached its peak. They obtained the right to vote and were involved in numerous social actions. The third period run from 1953 to 1970. Once the right to vote had been achieved, women's participation channeled through the parties that had women's sections (Santa Cruz, Pereira, & Zegers-Valeria Maino, I 1978, pp. 227-229).

The pioneers of this difficult struggle were women from the upper class. At that time, they were the only ones capable of carrying out this urgent transformation of Chilean society. Among them stood out: Ines Echeverria Larrain (nicknamed "Iris"), Delia Matte de Izquierdo, president of the Club de Damas, Sara del Campo, widow of Montt, Josefina Smith de Sanfuentes, Gabriela Mistral, Sara Hubner, Amanda Labarca Huberson, Elvira Santa Cruz Ossa, and Gines de Alcantara. All of them constituted the immediate precedent of Lucia Richard. She got many references from this previous generation and even knew some of them. The exception would be Amanda Labarca, who, having been born in 1886, died in 1974 and lived longer than Lucia.

---

the title of "Sea Lovers" (not in love with the sea) and took place in the Alhambra Palace of Santiago in 1944 (*Bulletin of Cenacle of Poetry*, no 5, 1944, page 2). In addition, she had a radio program called *Evocation of the Gone Poets* (same *Bulletin*, page 8).

These courageous women, not only denounced traditional society with their writings. They also carried out many social action initiatives through charitable organizations. In them, children got special attention. During these years appeared institutions such as the National Board of Children (1901), The Association of Ladies Against Tuberculosis (1901), The Creches (1904), The Women's Charity Society (1906), The Children's Pots (1908), Saint Lucia's Blind Society (1923), The League of Chilean Ladies (1912), The Chilean Red Cross Women's Association (1914), The Women's Club (1915), The Women Center of Studies Center (1919), The Ladies Reading Circle, etc. (Santa Cruz, Pereira, & Zegers-Valeria Maino, I., 1978, p.232).

Especially important for us is the Ladies' Club, founded by Delia Matte de Izquierdo, to which Lucia expressly referred. This club pursued social action, fought for the emancipation of women, and promoted cultural activities. It was one of the first institutions not sponsored by the Church and one of the most advanced organizations of the time. It encountered great opposition from both the Church and men. They did not tolerate women joining a club in the evenings to talk about cultural endeavors or discuss their rights. This institution also aimed to educate women from the upper classes. In 1915, "Iris" said:

> "Then we feared that if the ignorance of our class lasted two more generations, our grandchildren would fall into the common people and vice versa. We could not delay the issue. The symptoms were alarming ... And so some ladies, who were not retrograde, felt the need to meet. Thus they joined the new society that had formed, in spite of the old family traditions." (Santa Cruz, Pereira, & Zegers-Valeria Maino, I., 1978, p.234).

Regarding this statement by "Iris," it is laughable to think that the most influential feminist of the time, presumably also an intellectual, on the one hand, claimed the right to self-affirmation of women, as a prerogative sought to raise their cultural level. On the other hand, she wanted this intellectual supremacy to exclude women from ordinary people or to distinguish themselves from them. Class fusion is impossible in Chile. The permeability between the strata is an insurmountable barrier, which we see clearly here.

That is to say, in this passage, the feminist demands a liberal position to oppress the ignorant later. Then, she considers that this is not retrograde but advanced. In other words, she advocates the emancipation of women, freeing them from men. But once this power is achieved, she tries to subjugate ordinary people to it. This idea is a *"reductio ad absurdum,"* a conceptual contradiction, characteristic of this nascent feminism. But Latin America is like that: a caste society, difficult to understand from a European perspective. Rights yes, but not for everyone, comes to say, "Iris."

Concerning this Club and its Reading Circle, Lucy Richard wrote:

> "The origin of this Club was modest. To this end, four ladies met in July 1915: Mrs. Luisa Linch de Gormaz, Ines Echeverria (Iris), Manuela Herboso de Vicuña and Mrs. Matte. They could not imagine the uproar and scandal that their purpose would produce in the peaceful society of that time. This community lived entirely under the shadow of the parish and the narrow mentality of family prejudices. Soon angry voices, mockery, insults appeared in all the newspapers and circles of the capital.

> They appealed to ridicule, were criticized, and some condemned the idea because women would neglect sock darning. Of course, they also had their defenders. Finally, the Club prevailed with its great program of weekly conferences, art evenings, concerts, numerous and chosen classes, like those of the piano teacher Mr. Bindo Paoli." (Richard, 2004, p. 449).

In 1935 the MEMCH (Movement for the Emancipation of the Women of Chile) was created. This organization brought together all ideological and religious tendencies. It encouraged its members to fight for the social, economic, and legal liberation of women. A highlight was in 1949 when women obtained the right to vote in the parliamentary and presidential elections. The Congress of Santiago in 1937 established the objectives of the movement:

1. The protection of mothers and the defense of childhood.
2. Improve the standard of living of working women.
3. Obtaining women's rights.
4. Raise the cultural level of women and ensure the education of children.

5. The defense of the democratic regime and peace.

This committed organization achieved great strides through its continuous action. For example, it obtained fairer regulations for everything that belonged to the female sphere. During this decade, which coincided with Lucia Richard's great intellectual revival, many women's organizations were created. Among them, we can mention the Women's Rights Committee (1941), the Women's Civil Defense (1941), the Committee for Women's Rights and Defense of the Race (1941), the Women's Civic Action (1942), the Chilean Federation of Women's Institutions (1944) and the Chilean Women's Party (1946). Also, in these years, between October 27 and November 1, 1944, the first National Congress of Women of Chile was held.

The Chilean Women's Party has a special interest for us. Its board of directors included Maria de la Cruz (president), Georgina Durand (vice president), Mimi Brieba de Aldunate (treasurer), and Olga Aguilo (secretary-general). Both Maria de la Cruz and Mimi Brieba de Aldunate had been Lucia's companions in the Cenacle. They belonged, along with others, to a well-consolidated group that gravitated around Vera Zouroff. This party—whose evolution Lucia had to follow very closely—received violent attacks from many sectors.

For example, some groups of Catholics tried to prevent women from joining the movement, arguing that there was a divorced woman on the board. Others questioned the candidacy of Maria de la Cruz, raising a wide controversy and an unanswered question for political agitators. The candidate's rivals defeated her at the polls. However, many judged her defeat to be a moral triumph because of the few means with which she carried out the electoral campaign (Santa Cruz, Pereira, & Zegers-Valeria Maino, 1978, pp. 238-242).

In any case, what matters most to us is to point out that although Lucia Richard took advantage of the achievements of the previous generation, she rather belonged to "the generation of the forties." To this generation belonged women like Marta Vergara (1898), Magdalena Petit Marfan (1900-1968), Marta Brunet (1901-1967), Maria Flora Yañez Bianchi (1898-1982), Marcela Paz (1902-1985), Chela Reyes (1904-1988), etc. (Santa Cruz, Pereira, & Zegers-Valeria Maino, I., 1978, pp. 291-231).

Many of these writers questioned in their writing the role given to women in the patriarchal society. For the first time, they denounced the moral bias of conceiving of women as mere objects. They tried to exonerate women for having a sensual body. Now women could enjoy the eroticism of their bodies without being mortified by the historical burden of their sexuality. Women like Vera Zouroff in her work *Liberation* criticized marriage. They did not consider it a suitable path for their personal, emotional, and erotic fulfillment.

This group conceived of marriage as an instrument of control over women's sexuality and reproductive capacity. Thus, it became an object of abomination. The space reserved for the single woman was opposed to that of the single man. Society relegated this single woman to contempt and compassion, eventually becoming an individual without an identity. She was a family burden and ended up being reduced to solitude. In the face of this, the single man would be the champion who freely enjoyed his sexuality.

The speech is broad. Yet, Lucia Richard did not want to take part in that kind of writings that would have led her to endure attacks. These would have been hard to bear for a married woman. The poet did not want to get involved in those risky ideological disquisitions of the time. She preferred to focus on history, beauty, architecture, psychology, and music. In short, she wanted to embrace all that is transcendent and universal in the human spirit. But that did not prevent the writer from being familiar with the ideas that her colleagues published in their books. She also shared with them many of their social actions.

However, in her work, we see how she subtly cared for her colleagues, although she did not always restrain her thoughts. As for Ines de Echeverria, nicknamed "Iris," she descended from Andres Bello, one of the most aristocratic families of the time, and was a staunch feminist. Some branded her fanatical, selfish, anarchic, and a transgressor of her class values.

She was an independent woman, who vilified with her pen the foundations of a society she considered retrograde. The feminist even courageously attacked the Church itself and all those who opposed the emancipation of women. Because of these issues, the activist became the object of several criticisms and even threats of ex-communication. Nothing mattered to her, but to impose her judgment and will.

To this pioneer woman—whom Lucia once met at the Municipal Theatre—she dedicated a lavish article, putting on her lips the words that the haughty lady wrote in her work *Virgin Land*:

> "The current Chilean race is insensitive, utilitarian, and unsightly. It will not be the ancient nobility of the colony with its moth-eaten coats of arms, nor the nouveau riche, the inhabitants of this paradise." (Richard, 2004, pp. 451-453).

Then, Lucia continues displaying all the nuances of her well-written defense. And so she points out her virtues, her theosophical piety, her pantheism and her capacity as a novelist, lecturer, and polemist. Little by little, she disarmed all the sharp criticisms that some had written about her in her time.

In her article published in *El Mercurio*, entitled "Renovales de Maite Allamand" (1911), a writer of French descent, Lucia sketches a pleasant picture, full of detachment. Her setting is the Chilean countryside and Creole customs. Here, Lucia penetrates all the foliage of the fertile southern nature. She immerses herself in a green mass of spectacular images, at the slow pace of a peasant cart. In that thicket, the author dissolves into the fog. Then, she rescues from Maite's prose all those images of the rural world that fascinate her, and where "suddenly" characters emerge of whom we know nothing.

Maite Allamand's biographers see this, of course. But they also perceive in her narrative a repeated denunciation of a peasant woman abandoned in a patriarchal society in a context of local customs with traces of colonialism. There, women are subjected to multiple types of humiliation. Maids, washerwomen, peasants, humble figures, are victims of marginalization in a hostile environment. All this leads to paternal or marital subjection; sexual harassment by masters and bosses; violence and ill-treatment in marriage; rape and other abuses by a drunk, quarrelsome and jealous husbands, etc. (Rubio, 1994-1999, p 246).

However, none of this caught Lucia Richard's attention. Here she was missing the pepper, the counterpoint, the dynamite. She is a perpetual refuge of beauty, where only harmony and goodness reign. Her pen leaves a trace of grace and lightness, seducing us with its silky hilarity. Renoir once said: "In life, I am only interested in my paintings and my flowers." In life, there is already too much tragedy. Why create more?

Lucia herself confessed the tendency she had to see in the works of others, only poetry. In a radio commentary dedicated to Maria Luisa Bombal, she expressed:

"There is much talk of her creative fantasy or her immersion in the unconscious. But for me, her book *Sea, Sky, and Earth* was above all an exquisite poetry. Perhaps because we see in others only the part that finds resonance in us; perhaps because poetry for me is the measure of the elevation of the spirit, I am tempted to find poetry in everything I admire. The work of Maria Luisa Bombal deeply impressed me with its integral poetic sense." (Richard, 2004, page 578).

Something very similar happens with *Aunt Eulalia*, a novel by Chela Reyes (1904-1988). Chela Reyes was a poet, narrator, novelist, essayist, playwright, lecturer, social worker, and one of the founders of the Pen Club of Chile. Not by chance, Lucia examined her work in an article that appeared in *El Mercurio*. Everything indicates that Lucia and Chela led parallel lives. They agreed in many aspects of their intellectual lives. Besides, both writers met frequently at the Pen Club, to which they both belonged.

This article shows Lucia particularly ingenious and intelligent. She knew that her contemporaries would read it and that her words could affect their relationship. This review proves how Lucia read her peers' books and was imbued with their ideas. One author recently interpreted *Aunt Eulalia* as a work inserted into the set of conceptions that made up Chilean feminism at the time.

For this critic, the novel subverts the patriarchal order. It tells the story of three women reduced to solitude. In her opinion, they saw their lives frustrated by submission to a dominant order. Even more, she finds a break with the hegemonic order through the critical analysis of the patriarchal discourse on women's bodies. Therefore, some limitations weigh on women's erotic desires. It is a story of rebellion or tortuousness in the pressure exerted by the dominant rule. Women are subject to double repression: that of the society and that imposed by themselves when internalizing this censorship, etc (Rubio, 1994-1999, pp. 170-178).

There may be a lot of truth in this discourse, or contemporary feminism could have exaggerated it. Anyway, Lucia Richard does not grasp any of this. For her, in the novel, the literary genres are confused, seeing in its development, a great poem, a great work of art. Lucia does not enter into the plot, the difficulties of the characters, or the dramatic evolution of the project. Nor does she examine any sorrow, pathos, or desolation. The work under her retina is a sublime aesthetic realization, a fabulous scenic world. In it, the reader plunges in another plane of reality lost in the Elysium of the imagination.

Human passions are left aside in Lucia's interpretation, to enhance the ornament, the plastic aspects of the work. Luxury objects, velvety hedonism, and perfectly polished adjectives are omnipresent. The opulence of a language full of musicality envelops us in the constant narrative flow. All this voluptuousness encompasses the quintessence of what she describes as "an exquisite work of art." She still has time to think about the quiet things. Under her contemplation, they have the greatness that surpasses our small lives full of tribulations.

In the quietness of things that remain immutable, she perceives the shelter of eternal wisdom. When she closes the book, she does so with the pain of a newborn baby. It is as if she leaves her magical circle and joins a much less paradisiacal reality (Richard, 2004, pp. 520-521). Yet, it would be nonsense and even a historical mistake to conceive Lucia Richard only as a superficial author. She didn't have only luminous prose. The writer didn't just paint with her words an ugly reality, full of misery.

The university indeed denied women access, and this led her into a dilettante position. But her strong vocation made Lucia read for years on all kinds of subjects. Through her efforts, she acquired a solid intellectual formation. The poet embraced a range of realities, from which her rich personality emerged. She had a deep mind, endowed with an excellent capacity for psychological penetration. She knew how to express with a language of sweetness and beauty, all the greatness and transcendence that the human spirit can achieve.

In 1947, Lucia gave a lecture on Sarah Hübner (1888-1930), at the Central House of the University of Chile. In it, she showed a unique insight into the intellectual and human figure of the Chilean writer. Sarah emerges before her eyes as a complex woman, who had a mysterious and multifaceted personality. It all began with a career of mistakes and truculence in childhood. Little Sarah possessed an impressionable and haughty soul and endured a hostile environment from a very young age. As the only way out of the weariness that consumed her, she virulently projected her feelings onto paper. Mysticism and sensuality, stillness and movement, ethics and aesthetics, kindness and sadism, encouragement and sarcasm, fatherhood and egomania, are in synthesis the polysemy expressed in her writings.

In her interpretation, Sarah was sometimes shy and even tender. But suddenly she became angry, expressing herself in violent language. The author used harsh phrases, full of sarcasm, whose aggressiveness was only the mask of her sadness. Her self-esteem made her feel superior, a pedestal from which she uttered her disturbing phrases. The contrast would be in her sincerity. This frankness contradicted her as a lacerating woman and placed her on a plane of intellectual greatness. The writer dared to say things as they came to her mind, in an era of pretense and hypocrisy, which gave quality and refinement to her work.

Despite her apparent frivolity, Sarah was a woman of great curiosity and broad spirit. This inquisitive personality led her to take an interest in the advances of science, biology, and medicine. She also engaged in the problems of the world, religion, life, and even ventured into philosophical speculation. But after her periods of expansive lucidity, the tormented woman returned. Then, she showed proud, extravagant in her dress, inconsiderate of people, with whom she maintained a certain distance. The writer developed herself in a framework of originality and distinction, hidden beneath her gestures of a great lady. Her intellectual narcissism, her intransigent sincerity, and Byronian mood would have led her to say the following:

> "No philosophy will give me the meaning of life. I know that I must seek it only within me, unfolding myself." (Richard, 2004).

Sarah was a contradictory person but very attracted to beauty. She expressed herself in a beautiful language, nourished by a luminous verb, with a huge influx of grandiloquent epithets. As an epilogue, Lucia Richard draws a cunning parallel between the physical heart, like the weakened organ of an exhausted woman, and the sentimental heart of the same woman who is desperately seeking her audience. In this fight, she ended up dying prematurely of incomprehension, being relegated by others to oblivion.

According to Lucia, the intellectual would have been intensely subjective. Therefore, all her journey through the universe of ideas, psychology, culture, her whole ideology in sum, was born and died in her own heart. When she woke up to the social milieu, family prejudices seized her with their sharp claws. This fact reduced her into one of those women who go through life anonymously. In Richard's interpretation, this had been the turning point at which her physical and intellectual collapse began. Here started the struggle, which broke her health, transforming her into a corrosive and angry being. In her last moments, she didn't cease insulting, while her heart stopped beating (Richard, 2004, págs. 393-405).

Turning our account on the subject of feminism and social action, Lucia Richard from an early age became interested in feminist vindication. In her letter of 31 December 1926, entitled "Letter to the Women of America," addressed to Mr. Gregorio Martinez Sierra and published in Viña del Mar, the young poet said:

> "In Chile, there is no political or theoretical feminism, but rather a factual one. In this case, we understand feminism as a woman who occupies her rightful place in life, improving her skills. This new woman acquires that self-confidence, which makes her someone in her home and society. Gone are

the days when women, hidden by a dimly lit lamp, made a living from tedious embroidery and underpaid sewing.

Work no longer dishonors! Chilean women go to universities and sign up in art schools. They are interested in agriculture, shine in commerce, distinguish themselves as professionals and face life with integrity. They are valuable at home and many times support for their family. However, this healthy and advanced feminism that rages between us urgently needs a defender. We have much way ahead, and we have to fight against everyone and against everything." (Richard, 2004, 457).

That defender was Gregorio Martinez Sierra, whose supreme quality in Lucia's eyes was his marked optimism. Martinez Sierra (1881-1947) was a prolific Spanish writer who stood out as a poet, storyteller, novelist, and playwright. In this last field, he achieved notable scenic triumphs. He founded inspiring literary magazines such as *Vida Moderna*, *Helios*, and *Renacimiento*. Together with Catalina Barcena, the producer directed the Eslava Theatre in Madrid. From there, he made known musicians of the stature of Falla, Turina, Conrado del Campo, and Angel Barrios, among others. He translated the works of Rusiñol, as well as many other foreign works, such as those of Barrie, Maeterlinck, Bernard Shaw, Molnar, Andreiev, Pirandello, Pagnol, and Nocodemi.

Martinez Sierra was a writer of the so-called "spiritualists" for his themes and "stylists" for the care and gallantry of his language. With a delicate soul and fine artistic spirit, everything that came out of his pen was polished and refined. She had a way of seeing life without complications, very similar to Lucia's feeling, unaware of any dramatic intrigue. He was an extremely sentimental man with a sweet and delicate tone. Someone accused him of being maudlin, calling his literature feminine. He usually, combined his emotions with a certain irony, not violent, but warm and healthy.

Gregorio was an exquisite and generous man, gifted at describing scenes and creating dialogues that flowed easily. He was tender and emotional. His poetry tended towards an endearing intimacy and a delicious melancholy. His stories and novels attracted the public with their clean prose and good descriptions, full of warm and luminous scenes. He supported the cause and the feelings of women, together with his wife, Mrs. Maria de la O' Lejarraga, also a passionate feminist.

Her masterpiece was *Lullaby*, a play that explores the maternal instinct of all women and whose action takes place in a convent. Premiered in November 1911 at the Lara Theater in Madrid, the performance was an international success. It was later translated and staged in many countries. In May 1926, Martinez Sierra was on tour with his acclaimed theatre in Chile and Argentina. In these countries, he achieved many triumphs and gained great sympathies.

In Santiago, the Chilean ladies led by the famous feminist Delia Matte de Izquierdo received him enthusiastically. He returned the gesture with courtesy, leaving indescribable signs of his rich personality in the capital. The tour continued through Valparaiso. From Viña del Mar, a young Lucia addressed him in December 1926, her "Letter to the Women of America." In this article, she praised the virtues and understanding that Mr. Sierra had always shown towards the cause of women. Opposed to political struggles, he lived his last sixteen years outside of Spain (Sainz de Robles, 1953)[15].

Apart from this brief experience of youth, her true vocation as a public feminist began two decades later. On June 1, 1946, in her article entitled "Gratitude or Interest," she showed her commitment to the Pen Club's campaigns to help the miserable condition of French writers (Richard, 2004: 455). A year before the intriguing lecture on Sarah Hübner, Lucia was at her best, and her career as a writer and intellectual was on the rise. Lucia was fully involved in many feminist initiatives. They were driven by various representatives of the beautiful sex, along with some inspired men, for the benefit of women, youth, and especially children.

In December 1946, the newspaper *La Opinión* invited a group of six writers to a colloquium. Each of them had to reflect on the topic that interested him

---

[15] This visit to Latin America also appeared in the magazine *Blanco y Negro* of 30 May 1926, p. 95, and in the newspaper *ABC* of Friday 11 February 1927. A good example of the warm welcome Martinez Sierra received in the capital of Santiago can be traced in a book he gave away. Entitled *"Primer Ciclo de Conferencias Presentadas en el Club de Damas I,"* I, year 1925, the book is preserved in the National Library of Spain. On its cover, we can read: "To the distinguished writer and playwright Gregorio Martinez Sierra, very affectionately, Zamorano and Caperan."

most. These were Lucia Condal, Oreste Plath, Pepita Turina, Oscar Jara Azocar, Lucia Richard, and Jacobo Danke. The journalist from the publication interviewed them one by one. Addressing Lucia Richard, she had beautiful words for the children, giving great importance to their education:

"An appropriate book for children is one whose author puts himself in the child's place and takes as his subject the life of the child. All the classic books of children's literature have a child as their main hero: *Heart of Amicis*, *Alice in Wonderland*, *Oliver Twist*, *Three Years of Vacation*, etc. The influence of these first readings is enormous as the first window that opens to the outside world. Before being able to read, the child creates his universe with his little things.

After that age, he crosses the borders of his intimate and vegetable life and takes his first steps in the outside world. The heroes in his books are the first companions of his life. For this reason, we must be cautious in choosing these friends. I think the book they need is the one that describes the lives of famous children. Thus, he places himself from the beginning in the company of select beings who will become his models and teachers.

In our own country, we have the exemplary lives of those who forged our nationality. It would be interesting to make stories of the childhoods of O'Higgins, Perez Rosales, Blanco, Arias, Plaza, Alfredo Lobos, Gabriela Mistral, etc. We could complement these stories with fictitious accounts of the figures of America and the benefactors of humanity. I believe that this book awaits the Chilean child, but not only the Chilean. Because when we talk about childhood, we cannot talk about nationality. In those first years of life, there are no marked racial or social differences. All children are like a vast undiscovered jungle." (Anonymous, 1946).

In another interview published on September 5, 1949, she expressed similar things. There the interviewer alludes to Lucia Richard de Piedrabuena as:

"...a widely known poet and writer. She is a member of the Pen Club of Chile, the Society of Writers of Chile, the Cenacle of Poetry, and the Pan American Women's Round Table of Chile. Among other activities, she directs the radio program *Art Guide*. As a feminist, she doesn't need much introduction because she is an ardent fighter for the cause of women." (Richard, 2004, 447).

In the interview, Lucia Richard responds resolutely to the barrage of questions from the interviewer. The main topic of discussion is the equal intellectual capacity of women with men. She strongly defends the same capacity, and whether society relegates women to the sidelines is merely a cultural issue. Women must struggle to achieve their true potential.

Nor does the writer believe that a broader culture could deprive women of their femininity or divert them from their roles–quite the contrary. The woman is the first educator of the child, and a higher culture would transform that child into a worthy man. Therefore, this woman educator would promote the progress of the country. The most educated and discerning woman, taking advantage of women's right to vote, would be better at creating laws and managing the city.

There is a debate about whether the woman should be a teacher of children. Lucia emphatically resolves that women understand childhood. Therefore, they should be in charge of preschool and primary education. But that do not mean that they cannot devote themselves to other educational tasks, in which women, because of their great instinct, can also be successful. The interviewer also asked her about the creation of the Women's Atheneum, an idea that the feminist strongly supports. Lucia sees in its achievement the revival of the old Ladies' Club, which she considers an urgent need.

Lucia Richard was involved in various feminist activities. Many of these stemmed from initiatives carried out by the Pan American Women's Round Table in Chile. She worked closely with this association. That is why it is interesting to know its beginnings and the reasons that encouraged it. It was an institution that emerged and was established in Santiago. Its most genuine aspiration was to promote fraternity and peace among peoples. But also to be in constant contact with many other Tables of the continent. It was founded in Chile by Mimi Brieba de Aldunate, Georgina Durand, Elena Guiller, Ines Oliveira, Amalia Hamilton West, Maria Delia Prado, Gladys Gomien and Teresa Vasquez.

They forged the following ideals in its charter:

"Our project will be primarily cultural. We conclude that only through culture can man fulfill his duties and responsibilities. And we will begin, according to this principle, to work for ourselves. We want to become spokesmen for a desire for perfection that will enable mankind to live in peace. That is why we founded the Pan American Women's Round Table in Chile.

Its mission will be, first of all, to praise women spiritually. Furthermore, to overcome the circumstances that have so far prevented them from fully collaborating with men in determining political and social improvements. It will also claim their rightful place in history. It will bring the demands of the wife and mother to the great debates. These women will fight in these forums against the deafness of men, to the call for human compassion and pain. They cannot allow men to give in to arrogance or madness, letting the world fall into a hecatomb.

Our purpose is to respond to a local claim. The Pan American Round Table has been constituted in Mexico and Cuba. It will be formed in all the countries of the Americas to carry out coordinated work throughout the continent. Thus, thousands of women bounded by an intense spirit of peace, and inter-American fraternity will contribute with their enthusiasm. But they will also convey the hope of mothers and wives. We will fight to the end against the forces of barbarism and destruction. With our hands united as a symbol of brotherhood, firmness, spiritual understanding, and solidarity, we form the Pan American Women's Round Table of Chile." (Mariategui Oliva, 1953, 174).

The Round Table as a concept came from the Arthurian legend. It refers to a series of knights who sat around a table to discuss and debate their concerns. But this table was exceptional because it lacked headboards. It represented the highest aspiration for equality among those who shared its ideals. The realization of and respect for ideas of social good were at the core of the institution. In short, it pursued moral and political ends that were permanently valid.

Therefore, the Pan American Women's Round Table of Chile intended to continue that legendary yearning for equality, whose tradition of beauty could shape the human mind. Its founders hoped that many good things would germinate in the motherland and Latin America. They hoped that when the Round Table was created in all countries, it would be the torch from which a civic consciousness would emerge, giving humanity an era of peace (Mariategui Oliva, 1953, 174).

Apart from the charter, it is also interesting to learn about the activities of this institution, to which she and many of her colleagues belonged. There is a letter dated September 14, 1949, sent from Santiago by Mimi Brieba de Aldunate to Gabriela Mistral. Mrs. Aldunate was the President of the Round Table and Lucia Richard's companion in the Cenacle. In it, she told the Nobel Laureate that the Round Table had learned of notification No. 433 from the Ministry of Foreign Affairs. In the communication, the latter invited the Round Table to celebrate United Nations Day, October 24, designated as "Peace Day."

After accepting the commision, the Round Table agreed to organize a solemn ceremony at the National Stadium. For the occasion, children's choirs and dancers would participate. *The Hymn of Peace*, a composition by Lucia Correa (a friend of Lucia R.), would also be sung. The organizers would reward the best work presented by the students on the theme "The commitment of the United Nations to world peace." After announcing her plans, Ms. Aldunate asked Ms. Mistral to contribute to these events. She was to send a message of peace to the children of Chile, which would be broadcast by them (Brieba de Aldunate & Guiller, E., 1949).

The following year, The Round Table promoted these contacts again. This time it would be Mrs. Ines Oliveira de Nuñez, national president of the institution. In a letter addressed to the famous Chilean poet Gabriela Mistral, she thanked her for sending several checks to support The Round Table. Mimi Brieba de Aldunate, former national president of the institution, collected the checks. In the letter, Ms. Oliveira gave Gabriela Mistral a complete description of the spirit that animated the multifaceted institution:

"The Round Table was constituted on July 7, 1947. Its postulates were the promotion of world peace, the strengthening of cultural relations among the peoples of the Americas, and the improvement of the social, legal, and cultural status of Chilean women. To make these three wishes come true, a group of women created this institution. Today, they work actively for the cause, hoping for better days for humanity.

The Round Table, in pursuit of its ideals, worked energetically to win the political vote. Today, it is engaged in public education campaigns for women. It has collaborated intensely with the United Nations. The institution has also organized the United Nations Association in Chile and maintains relations with different women's or cultural institutions in Latin America. This brief presentation of our work will give you a general idea of what we are and what we represent.

Echoing your thinking on women's suffrage, regardless of any ideology, the Round Table remains on the sidelines of political and religious doctrines. In fact, in its ranks, there are women from different parties or who profess different religious beliefs. The members of the Board of Directors did not belong to any political group, and the institution did not deal with such issues." (Oliveira de Núñez, 1950).

CHAPTER VII

VERA ZOUROFF: PERSONALITY AND CAREER

Her periodical Women of America. Participation with Lucia Richard in the Foundation of the House of America in Santiago and Other Events

ext to these figures and in the vortex of many activities, stood always Vera Zouroff. She became a lifelong friend of Lucia Richard and a leader who took part in many feminist initiatives and social actions. And it is time to say it. Who was Esmeralda Zenteno de Leon, better known as Vera Zouroff? Well, she was one of the greatest female talents of her time, whose genius flourished beyond the second third of the 20th century.

Vera was a convinced feminist, gifted with an extraordinary capacity for work and organization. The arts, poetry, religion, and the dramatic scene interested her greatly. She wrote many articles, books, and engaged in activism on behalf of women. Among them, the intellectual wrote the novel *Martha* and *Liberation*, in which she describes men very poorly. She also collaborated in the *Book Commentary section* of the newspaper *Las Ultimas Noticias de Santiago*. With this post, she started in the field of journalism.

In 1921 she created the Circle of Women, participated in the Ateneo de San Fernando, traveled to the United States, Mexico, and other northern countries and was a correspondent for Zig-Zag magazine. Her works include *Chile* (1922), *Hollywood* (1932), *Mexico Outside and Inside its Borders* (1932) and *Worker's Home* (1934). She founded *America magazine* in 1934. She wrote the essays *The War* in 1937 and *Appearances at Lourdes* (1939). She also trained actors and actresses for the theater. In that field, Vera exhibited a true vocation and histrionic knowledge, enhanced by her experience in Hollywood. Tired of a society plagued by conflict and class struggle, the essayist wrote *The Other Way* (1944).

She was the patron and promoter of a literary cenacle, from which a school of declamation emerged. As a poet and teacher, she published *The Art of Declaim* (1945), *The Cenacle of Poetry to its Poets* (1947), and *Evocations of Peru* (1949). The writer also wrote another novel entitled *Beatriz Sandoval* (1954), Edgar Allan Poe's study called *The Raven* and other stories and essays gathered in the work *Dust Shot*.

That's what her biographers tell us, but Vera did a lot more. She communicated with cultural institutions all over the continent, founded the House of America in Santiago, and attended countless Americanist conferences. Mrs. Zouroff participated in many events with all kinds of great personalities from culture and politics, organized poetry recitals, and gave lectures. Several institutions honored her for her countless efforts. Besides, she also transmitted her message through radio programs, participated in the activities of the Pen Club, at the Round Table, and made inroads into the cinema. As a playwright, along with Marta Brunet and Maria Luisa Bombal, she carried out innovations on the stage and many other initiatives that we will learn about next.

For many years Lucia Richard was the wake of this cyclone that passed through our cultural scene. The influence of her great personality also mesmerized many other artists of both sexes. Another very evocative testimony, full of clairvoyance and intuitive lyricism, is that of the Peruvian Dr. Ricardo Mariategui Oliva. In 1952, Vera invited him to Chile to attend a series of cultural events and give some talks.

Mr. Mariategui speaks of a woman of great genius, very feminine, with gestures close to arrogance. She had made incursions into all fields of knowledge and life. She not only wrote books but also painted canvases, modeled statues, played dramatic roles, recited verses, and gave birth to children. Vera fought fervently for the awakening of women of her country and devoted her entire energy to uniting women all over the world.

A descendant of an ancient lineage, Zoila Esmeralda Marina Zenteno was born in 1880 in Antofagasta. She was the daughter of its first governor, Mr. Nicanor Zenteno Urizar. In her early years, she attended the Santiago College in the Chilean capital. Since her youth, the writer collaborated in newspapers and magazines, holding the record of having published her first book at the early age of sixteen. For the Peruvian, Vera was a generous and philanthropic woman, frank, brave, and with a determined character. In addition, the activist possessed an excellent sense of organization, brilliant intelligence, and a fine sensibility.

Esmeralda Zenteno de Leon, better known as Vera Zouroff

A great social emotion vibrated in her being, and she possessed a powerful spiritual force. She was a combative journalist, and a convinced feminist, fully aware of her actions and sure of her mission. The activist faced her time with determination. Vera always had a strong conviction and perseverance. She did not hesitate to pursue the political rights of Chilean women from her earliest youth.

The feminist loved the ideal of peace and dreamed of uniting people through better spiritual understanding. She was extremely human, softened many anxieties with her wise advice, and saved many lives on the edge of the precipice. Conscious and selfless, Vera was a creator of life, including her own, and she revived lives created by others. That is why her friends called her "a master of life."

The women's rights advocate also had a facet of a historian. Her work *Evocations of Peru* depicted its cities, historical relics, and the kindness of its inhabitants. She also described charmingly the many people who received her.

The writer loved Peru. In a prominent place in her living-room, among works of artistic merit and on an elegant console, Vera had the six volumes of *Peruvian Traditions* by Ricardo Palma, the illustrious Lima's traditionalist.

The great affection she had for Peru moved Mr. Mariategui. So he asked her about that collection of books. Then, she answered: *"They are my favorite children, precious jewels, like those that adorn the most sumptuous palaces."* The historian closes his presentation by pointing out the high prestige she had, the nobility of her character, the femininity of her feeling, her strong personality, and how determined she was. She represented one of the most exceptional figures in her country.

We also know from the prominent Peruvian that in 1952 Vera was writing her memoirs and was 72 years old at the time. The charismatic woman never published her memoirs, suggesting that she must have died a few years later. But not before 1954 because at least that year there is evidence she became the president of the House of America (Mariategui Oliva, 1953, 63).

In September 1947, the first edition of the newspaper founded by Vera Zouroff *Women of America* appeared. With a bi-monthly circulation, it was distributed throughout the continent and carried the evocative slogan *"United Hands, Strong Hearts."* The ideology of the magazine is a little strange for a current European. We can only understand it by taking into account the historical and geographical context from which it emerged. The newspaper was an emanation of upper-class feminism. The freedom of women and their achievements were present in its columns.

If the publication gave priority to the emancipation of women, this combined with all kinds of Catholic expressions. Here, for example, we do not see any debate about "abortion" or "divorce," archetypal demands of modern feminism, and even of the French one of that time. These are issues that currently generate frontal opposition from the Church. Still, Vera had stated in New York that there were half a million women in Chile who wanted to divorce.

It is refined feminism, considered progressive but allied with the great factual powers of the time. That means minor strata had no place in it. Military men, prelates, ambassadors, diplomats, and intellectuals were all in its ranks.

This movement pursued the representation of women in various political and social institutions. It also fought for their right to vote and their participation in society. Besides, it sought to ensure that they had access to the workplace and higher education on an equal footing with men. But women were not involved in other initiatives labeled as subversive.

Another ideological pillar of the periodical and its promoters was continental union. Of course, they knew that was Bolivar's old aspiration. This union could prevent regional revolutions, dictatorships, political destabilization, and poverty. In the mindset of these groups, they could only achieve this goal through the democratic union of the entire continent. In other words, they believed in centralism over local regionalisms. In doing so, the question arises on whether this position was really liberal.

To this end, a phalanx of artists and intellectuals worked throughout the continent. They were like living cells of an immense constellation of initiatives and projects. We can also define them as bastions of freedom, conceived as profoundly progressive and lovers of democracy. Another priority of the gazette was to disseminate the conquests and achievements of these women. Its promoters wanted to make known their associations and political institutions, not only in Chile but also in other parts of the continent. In addition, the publication praised many of these women who belonged to the Cenacle of Poetry. Among them, it highlighted the figure of Lucia Richard, attached to these groups, and committed to their ideals.

Luckily, Vera Zouroff had regular communication with the Institute of Hispanic Culture. Shortly after she founded the periodical, she sent some issues to Spain. Thanks to this relationship, the Hispanic Library of Madrid maintains this bi-monthly newspaper. It has it from number 5, printed in May-June 1948 to number 26 appeared in November-December 1951. All of them were issued in the printing houses of Phillips Street nº 15 in Santiago. These copies offer a lot of information about the activities of these groups. For the benefit of the reader, I will only extract the most significant.

For example, we can read in number 5, May-June 1948: "Our director receives an honorary distinction for her Americanist work." It was a "Pan-American Diploma of Honor" awarded by the Haitian Honor Guard. Ms.

Zouroff received this tribute for honoring Bolivar on the anniversary of his birth and exalting the heroes of his native country on their most emblematic dates. She also deserved it for promoting civility, culture, and Latin American exchange. Along with the diploma, there was a letter highlighting her hard work in pursuit of culture, her writing skills, her spirit of self-improvement, and her message of brotherhood (Zenteno de León, C. de Guzman, Deccarett Jaar, Jarga Gana de Lazo, & Mayer de Zulen, 1948).

The article "Women in Diplomacy" reported on the appointment of Marta Brunet, by the then Consul of Chile in La Plata and Cultural Attaché at the Embassy of Chile in Buenos Aires, as Secretary of the Embassy of the Republic of Argentina. (Zenteno de León, C. de Guzman, Deccarett Jaar, Jarpa Gana de Lazo, & Mayer de Zulen, 1948). The column "The absurdity of colonialism in Latin America, America for Latin Americans..." gave ample coverage to the IX Pan-American Conference in Bogota. The attendees claimed many issues of sovereignty over Antarctica, the Falklands, and other islands. They also denounced the Colombian revolution, orchestrated, according to the publication, from Moscow. So, in their opinion, there was an urgent need for an agreement against communism. Furthermore, they extolled as the highest values of Western culture: God, country, and family (Jarpa Gana de Lazo, 1948).

The last pages of the issue paid a beautiful tribute to the painter Dora Puelma:

> "She is the most accredited brush in Chile, as well as a fine writer of great psychological penetration. She is tireless in her artistic work and brilliant in her motifs, carrying within her a temple of beauty and talent." (Zenteno de Leon, C. de Guzman, Decarett Jaar, Jarpa G. de Lazo, & Mayer de Zulen, 1948).

In issue number 6, July-August 1948, the promoters of the journal extracted excerpts from the Magna Carta of Catholic Youth. It was published at the Congress of the International Union of Catholic Women's Leagues held in Rome (Zenteno de León, and others, Social Problems, 1948). On the next page, we can read for example the heading "Women in Diplomacy" where this time they praised Juliana Victoria Sanchez de Guevara, who was the cultural addict of the Argentine Embassy in Chile (Zenteno de León, and others, Women in Diplomacy, 1948).

On the penultimate page, a splendid article appeared about Bolivar. It reflects on the legacy that the famous hero left in the conscience of the continent when he expressed his longing for unity in a "confederation of Latin American republics." In his opinion, this was the only way to preserve intact the conquered freedom. However, this dream had vanished:

> "Once the colonial chain broke, the Hispanic republics have maintained their freedom. Some have done poorly, weakening patriotism. This fact has allowed other higher forces to create new chains that have tied our hands. These new difficulties have prevented us from protecting the interests of Latin America."

To then add:

> "The Spanish American nations have lived more than a century asleep, trusting in their freedom. They did not imagine the superb man. That made them exclaim at the turning point of their history: We have plowed the sea!"

For all these reasons, they called on all the women of America to unite their voices in pursuit of this supreme ideal of confederation and brotherhood (Zenteno de León, and others, Bolivar, July 27, 1703, 1948). Lucia Richard, in her article entitled "Understanding Latin America," proved to support this idea. After making some comparisons with the European continent, she emphasizes the following:

> "From Bolívar here, the most eminent statesmen, and politicians who look to the future, have seen in this union the only formula that can strengthen our democracy and save it from the chaos of nationalist individualism."

Then she points out:

"These peoples have realized two strong reasons for seeking this continental unity. One is a common culture uniting them, larger than the regional differences separating them. The other is the imminent danger threatening them all. That menace would make them disappear in a new invasion, in which barbarism and progress would join hands in destruction."

After many paragraphs of great rhetorical eloquence, Lucia states:

"That is why we love freedom, value democracy, abhor racial differences, and try to eradicate social inequalities. We also take pride in elevating the figure of our thinkers, intellectuals, and artists. The time has come for the work of Latin American teachers and political leaders to bear fruit. We understand that this continental solidarity can only be based on the democratic unity of the continent. Then nationalism will fall. In this way, we will see Hispanic America abandon its totalitarian madness and enter the path of sanity. In doing so, it will come close to the dream of Miranda, Bolivar, Marti, O'Higgins and San Martin." (Richard, 2004, pp. 460-468).

In issue number 9, January-February 1949, the newspaper dawns with the following headline: "Chilean Congress grants political rights to women." The column reviews the speech given in the House by the liberal deputy Miguel Luis Amunategui Johnson on December 14. This speech reproduces another by his predecessor, Mr. Miguel Luis Amunategui Aldunate, delivered on February 6, 1877. In the address, there was broad support for encouraging women to pursue higher education and enter the scientific professions. The State had to provide the means for women to earn a living for themselves. The publication reinforced this article with breaking news:

"The political vote. When our newspaper was about to come out, the Chamber of Deputies of our country approved the project on women's political rights. This undertaking was carried out thanks to the determined attitude of the Honourable Member of Parliament Mr. Miguel Luis de Amunategui, to whom we express our profound gratitude." (Amunátegui Johnson, 1949).

All these women were also fervent supporters of Arturo Alessandri. Nicknamed "The Lion," they compared him to Portales. In their opinion, he was a politician with an exceptional personality and a forger of the fate of the Republic. A patriotic man supported by people. He turned out to be a skillful political coordinator and an appeaser of his party. The women of Chile also saw him as a true champion of their feminist demands. He was a senator who had reformed the Constitution and defended their civil rights. Vera Zouroff put it this way:

> "Brilliant, beautiful and intelligent ladies; cultured, modest mothers of the middle class; humble women of the village; unhappy beasts of burden of the convent, all raised the same voice. They all showed the same enthusiasm to proclaim their sympathy for the 'gentleman without fear and blemish.' They found a sensitive man who understood their civic aspirations. They saw in him a man capable of recognizing in Chilean women, women of principle willing to fight for their country." (Zenteno de León E., 1950).

The editorial brought out another interesting headline: "To the Women of the Pan American Round Table in Chile." In beautiful paragraphs, it denounces the horror of women in the face of war and barbarism. Women had to join forces to achieve universal feelings. These emanated from the qualities of their motherhood, with which they would be invincible above all political or religious creeds. They had to defend the integrity of homes against the oblivion to which men had relegated love and understanding.

To achieve these purposes, the women stood up with the red sign of the cross (The Red Cross), joining in the healing of earthly wounds. They did this without asking whether the person they were relieving was Muslim or Jewish, Christian or Buddhist, Russian or English, communist, or reactionary. As members of the Red Cross, they neutralized evil with good, hatred with tenderness, inflexibility, and selfishness with understanding and generosity. In their way of thinking, we could not understand life without human dignity. Therefore, these spirit healers could not admit those regimes that granted privileges to a few while denying others their fundamental rights.

A community that aspired to social peace and justice had to equalize these rights without distinction of sex or caste. That is why they had established the Round Table in Chile: to stimulate cultural exchange between peoples. Even more, these women aspired to extend the Round Table throughout the continent by creating new branches in other countries. As we know, Lucia Richard was totally committed to these ideals (Zenteno de León, and others, 1949).

On the next page of the issue, they published a new article entitled "Continental Political Unity" (Zenteno de León, et al., 1949), in which they revived these ideas with greater nuance. Another headline was "The First Stage of the Women of America," stating that the four pillars of the war monster were imperialism, racism, classism, and partisanship (Mayer de Zulen, 1949).

Other entries awaken our conscience with headings like "Save the Children!" Here, they made an extensive review of the social actions in this field, denouncing the misery and abandonment. These women were devastated after visiting homes in need, which lacked hygienic measures to prevent the spread of disease. But above all, as mothers, they understood the importance of bringing affection, clothes, and toys. They had to instill confidence in this hopeless child. Through these efforts, a new generation of healthy and responsible children would emerge (Garcia and Garcia, 1949).

In the following issues, the magazine made a deep echo of many women who were Lucia's companions in the Cenacle. Thus, in issue 11, May-June 1949, Patricia Morgan was generously portrayed. They also announced new books by Maria Cristina Menares and Marta Brunet.

As for Marta Herrera de Warnken, better known as Patricia Morgan, the magazine strengthened her figure. It portrayed her as a woman who helped her husband in the painful trance of death. After being widowed, she managed to educate her children with dignity and developed a prosperous business. Then it brings out her facet as a poet, her talent for writing plays, and her merit for having created the children's theatre. At the institutional level, the journal highlighted her leadership capacity as director of the Pen Club, the Society of Chilean Theater Authors, president of the Rapa Nui Publishing House, etc (Zenteno de León, and others, 1949).

After she died in 1978, many articles appeared in various newspapers. Today, thanks to them, we can build with great accuracy the remarkable human and intellectual figure that was this enterprising companion of Lucia. For example, we can verify these qualities in the article published in the *Prensa Austral* on July 12, 1978. *El Mercurio of Valparaiso* also portrayed her on the 9th of the same month and year. They described her sensitive side, pointing out that Patricia felt artistic inclinations from an early age, manifesting themselves at first in painting.

The journalist then focused on her poetic gift, as well as her skill as an essayist. She published several portraits of Latin American writers in *Athena magazine*. Later, she became passionate about the theater, after studying drama at the Sorbonne. In fact, she won several awards for her efforts in this field, culminating in the creation of theatre for children. But Patricia Morgan was also a convinced feminist, the leader of an extensive network of organizations.

She was an insurance agent and the owner of two splendid factories. She also held various positions of responsibility: director of the Society of Chilean Writers, leader of the Society of Theatrical Authorities, president of the Union of Latin American Women and the Women's Legion of Chile, vice-president of the Inter-American Commission for the OAS, member of the Pen Club, of the Poetic Fire Group, of the Society of Writers of Valparaiso, advisor to the Society of Theatrical Authors and permanent director of the Children's Theater. The author traveled extensively abroad, giving poetry recitals in several Latin American countries. Thus, she was in contact with the most acclaimed intellectuals of the time (Araneda Bravo, 1978) (Simpson, 1978).

Another interesting woman with a penetrating gaze and overwhelming personal power was Mrs. Mimi Brieba of Aldunate. She became Lucia Richard's partner in many educational forums and at the forefront of a whole legion of women in their feminist demands. In issue 13, September-October 1949, Ms. Brieba addressed all the "Women" (with a capital "W") of the continent. As president of the Pan American Women's Round Table of Chile, she wrote: "Let us contribute to the historical rehabilitation of women."

She began her speech with great wit, sensitizing her audience to the lack of women in history. In her view, in the last half-century, the cultural heritage of nations had produced a variety of artistic, scientific, religious, and social manifestations. Libraries had collected them in hundreds of books. However, the creators of this Babylonian cultural monument had unintentionally or deliberately committed serious omissions. The reason was obvious:

"Since the vast majority of those who forged literature, art, and science were men, they had forgotten to highlight the influence of women in determining historical events and culture. Where is that book that describes women's thought and action through the various cultural cycles? Where is the one that synthesizes the painful epic of women sacrificed in their most noble feelings, for the warrior feats of men in all ages?"

The feminist leader asked herself. These questions had, of course, an answer:

"There are no women's works for women. What is missing is a volume showing their historical truth, actions in the past, and aspirations for the future. Men are the ones who have tried to define the soul of women. Men are also the ones who narrated the drama of their motherhood! They judged their irresponsibility and lack of interest in historical truth! They dogmatized about women's psychic reactions to the imperative of love, the influence of love on their actions, and the impact of this enormous driving force on women's thinking! Will, we ever say our word, confess our truth, define our feelings, specify our role in history, express our deepest yearnings for social justice and peace?"

All these shocking truths struck at the consciences of thousands of women. That is why they raised their voices in the hope of speaking out against the oppressive force that had erased their identity from the cultural face of the earth. It was time to tear down those totemic cults, those phallic monoliths that had drowned out women's voices for centuries! It was time to stand up against that tyranny and undermine the vigorous pillars on which the macho culture was based!

For all that historical injustice, the Round Table of Chilean Women agreed to form an *Encyclopedia of Women*. As representatives of the institution, they would write the book themselves in all the countries of the Americas. The great work was intended to include the biographies of women who had some involvement in history. The idea was to highlight their influence in the gestation of events.

Historical rectification was not their only aim. With this great compilation of personal profiles, they intended to produce an intellectual exchange in all Pan American countries through research work. Research in folklore and all sciences was necessary to magnify the achievements of women so far, barely evoked. They wished to promote inter-American cultural dissemination, thanks to the coordinated work of all the Round Tables of the continent. Women from various countries would carry out this research work, helping to broaden their mutual knowledge. To build this immense tribute of courage and tenderness, the Round Table invited all its women to take part in the project to create the *Encyclopedia* (Brieba de Aldunate, 1949).

The cover of the journal, number 12, July-August 1949, dawned with the following heading: "Cultural work done in Brazil by the Chilean poet Mrs. Gabriela Huneeus de Izquierdo." This article reported on the poet's trip to Brazil. There she contributed to strengthening the intellectual ties of both countries. The Pen Club invited Gabriela (Lucia's partner) to give a talk. On the occasion of their meeting, she had beautiful words for the Chilean writer Maria Luisa Bombal, referring to her work *La Amortajada*.

Gabriela was elegant, cultured, and beautiful: the crucible of the talent of the aristocracy of art and blood. She made a great impression on Brazilian intellectual circles. Their authorities invited her to the most prestigious cultural centers in Rio de Janeiro. They also had the gesture of translating into Portuguese her poems collected in her book *Voices of Time* (Zenteno de León, and others, 1949).

In the following pages of the journal, we can read the exciting profile of Dora Mayer de Zulen, a German woman who lived in Peru. After contemplating her portrait sketched in charcoal, her silhouette invades us with a kindness that transcends. Her generous features radiate serenity, wisdom, and self-sacrifice. But more than that, she was a woman of vast culture, committed to her ideals. The writer developed great intellectual work, focusing on her productions. She worked far from the worldly hustle and bustle under the aura of her peaceful retreat in Callao.

This intelligent woman stood out as a humanitarian and Latin Americanist, pro-Indian, and always a defender of the weak and humble. Ms. Mayer wrote in several languages for newspapers and magazines in Europe and America. She quickly assimilated the feeling of her adopted country, to which she rendered selfless service. The native peoples found in her strongest support. This genuine altruism led her to attend several indigenous and Latin Americanist congresses, held in the main capitals of America and Europe.

She was a polyglot who spoke in Buenos Aires, Santiago de Chile, Panama, London, the United States, and Berlin. She always did so in defense of the oppressed or to remedy human pain. Besides, she was fond of philosophical and sociological studies since she was a child. This inclination earned her the reputation of being an eminent sociologist and internationalist. In the study of international politics and metaphysics, the thinker found the great passions of her life. The National Library of Peru treasures many of her works: *The Peruvian Indigenous, Monograph on Female Intellectuals of Peru, The Feeling of the Peruvian Race, and Synopsis of a New Teaching of History*. Librarians preserved them as an everlasting tribute to her memory (Zenteno de León, et al., 1949).

Among the many stories published in the *Women of America* newspaper, one was crucial. That was when the publication reported in its issue 18, July-August 1950 on the founding of The House of America in Chile. This important event took place on July 8, 1950. Lucia Richard participated in it, becoming a member of its Board of Directors. Since its foundation, The House of America raised the flag of the continental union, holding it up as a sign of Latin Americanism.

This new cultural forum, founded in Santiago de Chile, was intended to be the home of the continent's most acclaimed intellectuals. Its promoters planned to give light to all kinds of cultural events. They wanted to do so by bringing to the media their conferences, recitals, concerts, exhibitions, and any initiative aimed at uniting the republics (Zenteno de León, Mayer de Zulen, Vilchis Baz, & Huertas Oliveira, 1950). On July 8, 1950, the *Women of America newspaper* published on its second page the founding act of The House of America, which read:

The following persons attended the first session of The House of America: Ms. Esmeralda Zenteno de Leon, Mr. Daniel de la Vega, Ms. Marta Goycolea de Jara, Mr. Cleofas Torres de Perry, Mr. David Perry Barnes, Mr. Oscar Jara Azocar, Hector Paul de Viale Rigo (Consul of Venezuela), Mr. Rene Arabena Williams, Ms. Edelmira Muñoz, Ms. Amanda Brieba de Lorca, Mr. Roberto Meza Fuentes and Ms. Sara Prats de Meza, Ms. Hilda Corvera de Guzman, Ms. Blanca Merino, Ms. Lucia Richard de Piedrabuena and Ms. Maruja Brunet.

The session opened at 7:00 p.m., "in the name of God and the good of Latin America." Mrs. Zenteno de Leon explained the work already done and offered the Hotel Crillon as the headquarters of the institution. They would have rooms in the hotel to hold conferences and other similar events and a place to receive correspondence from abroad. The Army physician, Mr. Arturo Tamargo, offered free professional services to the guests of the institution. The poet Mr. Washington Espejo gave away a book to start the future library.

She then outlined the main guidelines for the normal development of the institution, which are summarized below:

We have created several commissions to encourage correspondents outside and inside the country, the exchange of books, and the organization of conferences. We have also coordinated our institution with the diplomatic representations accredited in the country. Our members organized social meetings, established social care for the sick, planned exhibitions and secretarial and treasury services:

Foreign correspondent: Ms. Sara Prats de Meza Fuentes.
Correspondent inside the country: Mr. Rene Arabena Williams. Recording Secretary: Mrs. Hilda C. de Guzman.
Press Secretary: Mr. David Perry Barnes and Daniel de la Vega.
Book exchange: Mr. Oscar Jara Azocar.
Organization of conferences: Mrs. Maria Flora Yañez de Echevarria.
Coordinator with diplomatic representations: Mr. Hector Paul de Viale Rigo.
Organization of art exhibitions: Mrs. Blanca Merino Lizana.

Organization of social events: Mrs. Marta Goycolea de Jara, Mrs. Goycolea de Viale Rigo and Maruja Brunet.
Reception in Los Cerrillos: Amanda Brieba de Lorca.
Social visit, attention to foreign guests: Mrs. Teresa León de Gallardo and Mr. René Arabena Williams.
Treasurer with wide powers: Mrs. Cleofasa Torres de Perry.

<u>Mrs. Lucia Richard de Piedrabuena</u> had the idea of forming file cards. According to her proposal, she was asked to take care of it. Then, Mrs. Esmeralda Zenteno de Leon ended the session by adding: "In the name of God, we found the House of America." (Zenteno de León, Mayer de Zulen, Vilchis Baz, & Huertas Oliveira, 1950).

The newspaper *Women of America*, in its number 21, January-February 1951, published the statutes and objectives of The House of America in Chile again. Highlighting only the most significant ones, The House of America set out to solidly unite all citizens of the continental vanguard. It wanted to reach out to those who were capable of understanding the need to join all the peoples of Latin America on a truly democratic basis. This end excluded any imperialist attempt. It also urged for raising the standard of living of the less privileged classes in each country, and it sought cultural unification.

Furthermore, The House of America promoted the friendship of Latin American communities. It encouraged cultural exchange among Latin American teachers, writers, artists, professionals, and students. It developed an inter-American tourist exchange and created commercial links. Likewise, the new institution fostered the cult of the heroes of each country. Its members wanted to start a Latin American Peace Prize comparable to the Nobel Prize itself. They desired to spread the Americanist ideals in Chile, through radio broadcasts, press, conferences, books, etc.

On the other hand, the statutes of The House of America distinguished among its active members, honorary members, and protectors. The new institution had a General Directorate, which was subdivided into a Central Committee and a Council of Delegates, which set their respective renewal periods, their fields of action, etc. It also announced the creation of a magazine that would register its activities, and that the establishment would be based in Santiago.

This first General Directory had several signatories: Esmeralda Zenteno de Leon, Eugenio Orrego Vicuña, Roberto Meza Fuentes, Amanda Brieba de Lorca, Sara Prats de Meza Fuentes, Blanca Merino Lizana, Marta Goycolea de Jara, Hilda Corvera de Guzman, Hector Paul de Viale-Rigo, Maruja Brunet, Maria Flora Yañez de Echevarria, Oscar Jara Azocar, Berta Loeser Soza, David Perry Barnes, Cleofas Torres de Perry and Lucia Richard de Piedrabuena (Zenteno de León, Mayer de Zulen, Huerta Oliveira, & Silva de Santolalla , 1951).

In 1952, Rafael Larco Herrera in his book, *The Last Letter of Democracy*, reported in a section on the founding of the House of America in Santiago (1952, pp. 161-162). In addition, the publication contained several opinions on the need to hold an Americanist congress. It would openly discuss the necessity to unite the continent under the same political institutions. They judged this modern idea to be profoundly democratic. And if anyone still believes that these projects were utopian, you can see the enthusiasm with which they defended them:

-Asked Mrs. Esmeralda Zenteno de Leon, a prestigious intellectual and Chilean writer, founder of the House of America in Santiago, she answered:

"I am convinced that this congress must be held soon in Peru. The events that precipitate daily are already calling for it. I think the mood and the atmosphere are ripe for the work. Everything we want to do, we must do immediately. Time, as we live today, is the present. For you, the greatest moment of your life has come. Don't wait for time to pass: do it!" (Larco Herrera, 1952, page 198).

Besides the above, The House of America had an annual Bulletin. Vera Zouroff made great efforts to publicize her activities abroad. Thus, the intellectual sent a copy of the 1951 Bulletin to the Institute of Hispanic Culture. Thanks to this gesture, today we can find this periodical in Spain. On its cover, we can see the official page of the institution, together with the striking image of the Hotel Crillon stamped on it. Then a long list of countries where there were other Houses of America appeared. All this was closed with the following motto:

Latin American:

"Love your land above all things on earth."

Therefore, at the end of that year of 1951, the Bulletin offered extensive information on the intense work carried out. In fall, the House of America received a Colombian student delegation. In July, its members declared the Bolivarian month to commemorate the independence of three republics liberated by Bolivar: Venezuela, Colombia, and Peru. On July 24, they recalled the birth of the great liberator.

On the 8th of the same month, The House of America celebrated the first year of its foundation. To honor that date, its members gave thanks to Divine Providence by celebrating a *Te Deum* in the Basilica of Our Lady of Mercy. *Radio Mercurio* transmitted the event to the entire continent. The highlight of this month of events and celebrations was the sending of copihues to Caracas. The aim was to decorate the tomb of Bolivar on the anniversary of his birth. The press of Santiago and Caracas widely reported this initiative.

Each year, for one week, the O'Higgins Committee celebrated O'Higgins' birthday. Its president, General Ramon Cañas Montalva, invited The House of America to these meetings. Its members joined in these tributes with a magnificent evening at the Hotel Crillon. The brilliant speaker, Colonel Edgardo Andrade Marchant, and the lady of Chillaneja, Ms. Maria Brunet, gave exciting lectures. Other commemorative events took place in the town "Isabel Riquelme" of the Emergency Housing Foundation. The wife of His Excellency, the President of the Republic, presided over the event. The organizers also gave conferences in some prisons and other places (Casa de América, 1951, pp. 1-2).

As for the memorial held at The House of America, the newspaper *Women of America* attested to the celebration in its issue 19, page 2, September-October 1950:

Tribute to O'Higgins at the House of America

In the Tudor Lounge of the Crillon Hotel, headquarters of The House of America, distinguished personalities gathered to listen to the lecture of the historian Mr. Eugenio Orrego Vicuña. With this speech, the Americanist entity paid homage to the Liberators of Chile and Peru, General O'Higgins and San Martin. The audience listened to the scholar's words with respectful silence, giving him warm applause. Afterward, the organizers offered a cocktail. The singer Miss Iris Labora, accompanied by the pianist Garcia de Paredes, gave artistic performances. On that occasion, they mentioned the supporters of the institution. They also read an affectionate letter from The House of America in Montevideo. The message ended remembering its Chilean brothers. Attendance was withdrawn after 9 p.m.

Among the attendees were prominent personalities from the official and diplomatic world, the Army and Navy, as well as Americanist institutions. Among them, we can mention the lecturer Mr. Orrego Vicuña, Ms. Vera Zouroff, Ms. Maruja Brunet; Ms. Amanda Brieba de Lorca; Ms. Berta Loeser Soza; Mr. Hector Paul de Viale Rigo, representative of Venezuela; Mr. Oscar Jara Azocar; Mr. Pedro Melendez, counselor of the Embassy of Colombia; General Ramon Cañas Montalva and Ms. Lucia Richard de Piedrabuena. In addition to these distinguished guests, there was a long list that included delegations from the Argentinean Embassy, the President of the Miranda Institute, correspondents from *El Mercurio*, envoys from the Ministry of Education and members of the O'Higgins Committee (Zenteno de León, Mayer de Zulen, De Miranda , & Sosa Mendy, 1950).

These events were added to other activities developed by the Pan American Women's Round Table of Chile. Subsequently, the newspaper *Women of America* published them in full. Thus we can read the following headline: "The Pan American Women's Round Table of Chile will solemnly commemorate the centennial of the death of the Argentinean hero General Jose de San Martin, declaring the St. Martin's Week - August 10-17, 1950."

After the headline, the article continued:

The Pan American Women's Round Table of Chile, with the full attendance of its delegates, agreed in a general assembly, among other important things, to declare the St. Martin's Week from August 10 to 17. This celebration is a tribute to the memory of Jose de San Martin, liberator of three nations, and to whom Chileans owe so much. The Round Table entrusted Lucia Richard de Piedrabuena, its delegate from Argentina, with the organization of the commemorative program and the talk with the cultural attaché of the Argentine embassy, Mrs. Teresa Bo, for better collaboration.

As the anniversary of Peru's Independence Day approaches on the 28th of this month, the Round Table assigned Ms. Esmeralda Zenteno de Leon, its delegate in Peru, to prepare and send a program to commemorate this event.

On the occasion of the commemoration of the independence of the Argentine Republic, a sister country, on 25 May, the representative of the Round Table, Ms. Lucia Richard de Piedrabuena and her colleague Ms. Zenteno de Leon held a radio audition on *Radio Mercurio*, with the collaboration of the reciter Ms. Edelmira Muñoz. The cultural attaché of the Argentinean embassy, Ms. Maria Teresa Bo, addressed a word of thanks to the Chilean delegates:

"This is one of the happiest dates for us, in which thousands of Argentines express their joy and faith in the future. This date moves me deeply, filling me with great emotion and enjoyment. That is why I am addressing you, Chileans, to remember the men who gave us a country and a destiny." (Zenteno de León, Mayer de Zulen, Vilchis Baz, & Huertas Oliveira, 1950, page 1).

In the months following its foundation, the House of America, through its diplomatic coordinator, Mr. Hector Paul de Viale Rigo, contacted the embassies accredited in Santiago. These, in turn, assigned delegates to represent them, as well as an assistant to the Steering Committee. The aim was to promote cultural, intellectual, scientific, and artistic exchange with other American republics.

After the lectures on O'Higgins, the eminent professor, Mr. Moises Poblete Troncoso, spoke on "Human Rights and the United Nations." This topic was of great importance at that time. On Wednesday, November 8, the Honorable Ambassador of Colombia spoke about "Colombian Figures." On the 30th of the same month, there was a singing recital by renowned students of Ms. Emma Ortiz (Zenteno de León, Mayer de Zulen, & Huerta Oliveira, 1950, p. 1).

Almost always, what remains of a person's life is nothing more than the wreckage of a shipwreck. Lucia's life must have been much more exciting and full of enriching events. What remains of a person is what the written evidence says it was. However, at least thanks to these testimonies, we have been able to reconstruct Lucia Richard's human and intellectual profile much better. We can now see her not only as a woman of great literary talent but also as a reference for a whole generation of intellectuals and thinkers.

At the end of 1951, the House of America, at the suggestion of David Perry Barnes, laid the foundations for a Latin American Literary Contest. The idea was to invite university students from all over the continent to take part in it. They would develop topics of interest to them and Latin America. For everything concerning the challenge, Mr. David Perry Barnes, Roberto Meza Fuentes, and Oscar Jara Azocar formed a commission.

The possible subjects were twelve:

1. Economic and Intellectual Cooperation between the two Americas.
2. Ideas on Latin American Unity (Miranda, Bolivar, O'Higgins, San Martin, J.M. Carrera, Morazon, Jose Marti, Artigas, Washington, Franklin, Jefferson, Vicuña Mackenna, M.Egaña, Sarmiento, C. de Madariaga).
3. The current meaning of the Monroe Doctrine.
4. The spiritual and material dimension of Latin America.
5. Coordination of Port Policy.
6. Possibility, convenience, and effects of universal peace.
7. The Good Neighbor Policy and the OAS.
8. Understanding and Interpretation of Walt Whitman, Ruben Dario and J.S. Chocano.
9. Understanding and Interpretation of Mrs. Eugenia Vaz Ferreira, Dalmira Agustini, Alfonsina Storni and Gabriela Mistral.
10. The influence of Women in Latin America from independence to the present day.
11. The historical significance of Mrs. Isabel Riquelme as the mother of the liberator of Chile.
12. "Latin America's canto,"; "Song to the seas of Latin America,"; "Song to the Andes mountain range."

The awarded works would be considered "Valuable Works of Literature." For each theme, the organizers would award a first prize, a second prize, and an honorary mention. The reader should note that all these themes synthesize the ideology of the group. They speak very well of the spirit that animated these people and where they directed their energies. To resolve this important event, The House of America selected a jury. It was composed of the most distinguished intellectuals, educators, and professionals of the time.

Therefore, the members of the Jury were Roberto Meza Fuentes (poet); David Perry Barnes (poet and writer); Oscar Jara Azocar (poet); Maria Flora Yañez de Echevarria (writer); Lucia Richard de Piedrabuena (writer and poet); Agustin Benedicto (historian); Socrates Aguirre (internationalist); Vera Zouroff (writer); Daniel de la Vega (poet and journalist); Gaspar Mora Sotomayor (diplomat, lawyer and internationalist); Fidel Araneda Bravo (Academician, poet and historian); Edgardo Andrade Marchant (writer, poet and historian); Eduardo Gonzalez Ginouves (jurisconsult and internationalist); Augusto Millan Iriarte (Internationalist); Carlos Valdovinos (jurisconsult); Augusto Iglesias (academic, historian and poet); Osvaldo Illanes Benitez (jurisconsult); Enrique Molina (Rector of the University of Concepcion); Juvenal Hernandez (Rector of the University of Chile); Hugo Lazo Baeza (Casa de América, 1951, pp. 3-5).

The *Women of America newspaper* also published all this in great detail (issue 26, November-December 1951). The journal also mentioned Lucia Richard as a member of the jury of this prestigious literary contest. As we have seen, it gained an important political dimension.

In parallel with these activities, the Bulletin reported on other social events that took place throughout 1951. The House of America invited the Honorable Ambassador of Spain and his wife to dinner. They celebrated the Fifth Centennial of the birth of Isabella the Catholic, known as the "Godmother of America." Likewise, they gave a lunch for the poet Roberto Meza Fuentes. A cocktail was also offered to the Consul General of Venezuela, and to Hector Paul de Viale-Rigo and his wife.

Another event was a family cocktail party called "Race Day" or the Discovery of America. On this occasion, the organizers gave a reception to the distinguished representatives of the five Central American republics. There was much to celebrate, as their foreign ministers had just signed an essential document of mutual collaboration. This agreement would be considered as the first step towards continental union. At this event, the Minister of the Supreme Court of Justice, Mr. Osvaldo Illanes Benitez, spoke about the Congress of Panama, "Peace, Freedom, and Justice." The wife of the Ambassador of El Salvador spoke on behalf of her husband, who had lost his voice.

The annual publication also reported on six members of the Steering Committee who had received awards that year:

—   Amanda Brieba de Lorca received an award from the town's mayor for the special services she had carried out at the Red Cross.
—   Eugenio Orrego Vicuña was elected a member of the Royal Academy and invited by the Government of Mexico to attend the Spanish Language Congress.
—   The poet Roberto Meza Fuentes won the Municipal Prize in the Literary Contest of the V Centennial of Isabella the Catholic.
—   The artist of recitation, Miss Edelmira Muñoz, received a grant from the Government of Spain to study in Madrid.
—   The poet Oscar Jara Azocar received an award from Ecuador for winning in a poetic contest, being invited to visit that country.
—   Mr. David Perry Barnes got a prize from the University of Chile, for his intellectual collaboration with its Department of Culture (Casa de América, 1951, pp. 5-6).

Finally, the publication reported on the many personalities invited as speakers at The House of America that year. Lucia Richard did not take part in the 1951 lecture series. But she did on November 17, 1954, when she gave her wonderful lecture "Colorful Brazil." In 1952, The House of America in Santiago invited the Peruvian art critic, Doctor Ricardo Mariategui Oliva. He was the director of the Research Institute of Peruvian and Latin American Art and had published more than twenty books in his field.

From there, he continued his tour of Buenos Aires. In the capital, he attended the First Inter-American Congress of History and Colonial Religious Art. Later, at the Crillon Hotel in Santiago, Vera Zouroff and Maria Flora Yañez gave him a warm welcome. Mrs. Yañez had just been appointed president of that great cultural forum. At the event, the audience highly praised him. Later, the historian left a generous memory of this warm meeting in his book *Vision of Chile*, published the following year in 1953.

He wrote touching and affectionate words about Vera Zouroff, Miguel Rocuant, Maria Flora Yañez, and Dora Puelma. All of them, as we know, were companions of Lucia Richard. For example, he portrayed Maria Flora as an outstanding novelist, with refined qualities as a woman and writer. In his opinion, she was delicate and emotional, with exquisite sensitivity. But this did not prevent her from holding a strong character and powerful will. She was comfortable when talking to people, showing herself to be pleasant and eloquent, truthful, and profound. The writer also had an elegant literary style with a deep philosophical sense. In a word: she was a prestigious intellectual.

Her novels were for Mr. Mariategui, the product of a robust and creative inspiration, with evidence of great interpretive talent. In her own style, she used beautiful expressions, presented in a harmonious balance. From her prose flowed the moral physiognomy and intimate temperament of her characters. This ability reflected a woman of great spiritual strength. Her writings vibrated with great feeling, and a natural emotion shared in all its truth. For all these praises, Mrs. Maria Flora invited him to The House of America. There, she gave the illustrious Peruvian a copy of her work *Ashes*, accompanied by a tender dedication.

The illustrious researcher also portrayed Dora Puelma, describing her as a remarkable Chilean painter. She had an ardent artistic vocation and represented one of the best brushes in Chile. The greatest masters of color: Alberto Valenzuela Llanos, Richon Brunet, and Pablo Burchard taught her. Besides, Dora had exhibited her paintings in Seville (1929), Bogota (1939 and 1946), Ohio, New York and Washington (1941-1943), Valparaiso, Viña del Mar and Santiago (1950 and 1952). For this reason, she received many prizes and the acquisition of her work.

She became a teacher at the School of Fine Arts of Viña, and then at the Catholic University. In both places, she showed signs of being a capable teacher, endowed with a dynamic personality and a tenacious temperament. The painter mastered oil, watercolor and the secrets of light. All this allowed her to create luminous paintings, in which she knew how to combine with excellent talent, original sets of tones and nuances. Dora Puelma also drew skillfully and sketched out forms with dexterity.

Under the pen of the Peruvian, Dora Puelma's work had a lively rhythm that reflected the true expression of moral superiority. All this revealed the intimate temperament of a subtle artist. She was also a devoted pianist and a writer of exquisite sensitivity and great culture. She managed to express herself with literary turns full of vitalism and deep human sense.

Mr. Mariategui tells in his book how a few days before his departure from Santiago, on September 29, 1952, he attended the Pro Arte exhibition "Landscapes of Europe." On that occasion, he was able to contemplate many of the painter's paintings. Among them were the most beautiful corners of Paris, Marseilles, Rome, Naples, Florence, Venice, Barcelona, and Seville. In short, Dora was an exceptional painter: the incarnation of simplicity and harmony, with great skill to capture the beauty, oblivious to extravagant influences.

Every year, The House of America celebrated the birth anniversary of the hero Bernardo O'Higgins and his respected mother, Isabel Riquelme. On the evening of August 20, 1952, the Americanist institution invited Mr. Ricardo Mariategui to attend a lively program as its guest of honor. The literary part was in charge of General Jorge Berguño, who gave a speech about the life of the brave man. The poet Roberto Meza Fuentes read a fragment of his beautiful "Ballad of O'Higgins." Baritone Mr. Fuentes Pumarino and Miss Georgina Vial sang the musical part. They interpreted among other pieces a romance, with lyrics by the poet Meza Fuentes and music by Mrs. Emma Ortiz.

Numerous participants attended the event, particularly U.S. diplomats accredited to Chile. Maria Flora Yañez, as President and Vera Zouroff, received them with the chords of the National Anthem. Maria Flora Yañez addressed her audience with a brilliant speech. Then, both women praised Mr. Ricardo Mariategui, presenting him very honorably to their guests. Later, they invited him to speak, and he was acclaimed with unanimous applause.

Mr. Mariategui highlighted the Peruvian side of the hero. He especially emphasized the financing and final organization of the liberating expedition to Peru. The academic also spoke of his resignation from the supreme command of his country. He took refuge on Peruvian soil, where he had many friends and true brothers. In Lima, he recalled, there was a plaque commemorating the first house he lived in. Later, the Government of Peru donated him the Hacienda de Montalban, as a reward for his efforts in the Independence.

Therefore, Bernardo O'Higgins was, in his opinion, Marshal of the Army of his homeland and symbol of friendship between Peru and Chile. In short, he embodied a bastion of the Americanist ideal of uniting their peoples. After the conference, the attendees congratulated him and applauded effusively. As the anniversary of the death of Saint Rose of Lima approached, The House of America invited him again to give a lecture on the pious woman.

El Mercurio and the *Diario Ilustrado* announced the talk, scheduled for August 28, at 7:00 p.m. For more than an hour, the Peruvian intellectual spoke about the sublime qualities of the saint. He described her exemplary virtue, illustrating his audience with little known facts of her life. A photographic exhibition followed this description. It was composed of valuable canvases and sculptures from the 17th to the 19th century. They were unique items that caught the public's attention. Before the end of the conference, the poet Roberto Meza Fuentes, Chilean Ambassador to Ecuador, talked about the guest. In his speech, he highlighted the merits of the speaker and the warm welcome he had in Santiago.

Along the same lines, the Pan American Women's Round Table of Chile invited Mariategui on Friday, September 26 of the same year. The meeting took place at 7:00 pm, to give a conference entitled: "Women's Happiness in Today's Life." President Maria Delia Prado and Secretary-General Regina de Amestica welcomed him greatly. Vera introduced the wise man, praising the merits of the speaker.

Mr. Mariategui pointed out in his talk that the world today was going through a crucial time in which man was struggling in a muddy sea of moral stupidity. It was an epoch of morbid individualism in which people seemed to be going mad. Our existence was based on the binomial of pleasant life and contempt for moral values, using force as the only right. We were faced with a reality that led us on a continuous march towards perdition, where everything pointed to the collapse of society.

He blamed the contemporary man for living deafened by selfishness and envy. In his eagerness to satisfy his interests, he had destroyed many lives of others, as well as his own. Therefore, the time for reflection had come. It was inevitable to seek happiness, rectify behaviors, and defend ideals. He also reflected on how routine made men automatons. People should know how to face the challenge of governing their own lives. They had to fight against the dangers of pessimism and fatalism. He based the foundations of happiness on the value of education and experience. He also stressed the importance of knowing how to combine the past, present, and future of our lives.

Once the conference was over, the audience cheered enthusiastically for Dr. Mariategui. President Maria Delia Prado gave him a fraternal Chilean-Peruvian message to deliver to the women of Peru. Along with the message, Mrs. Prado also placed in his hands a spike that was the symbol of the Chilean Women's Round Table. With this symbolic act, the scholar's trip to Santiago ended. He took with him good memories that later inspired him to write his book *Feminine Confidences* which was then in preparation (Mariategui Oliva, 1953, pp. 64-76).

The activities of these people were not limited to a select group. Women throughout Latin America knew and encouraged their achievements, including the universal poet Gabriela Mistral. Long before receiving the Nobel Prize in 1945, she had led a nomadic life in various countries. However, the famous Nobel Prize winner never forgot her compatriots. In fact, she maintained an extensive correspondence with them over the years.

We have seen above how Mrs. Brieba de Aldunate, and Mrs. Oliveira de Nuñez, sent letters to the author of the famous *Sonnets of Death*. In them, they informed her of the activities and purposes of the Pan American Women's Round Table of Chile. In fact, Ms. Mistral was an enthusiastic and regular reader of the newspaper *Women of America*. So she knew very well the steps taken by her feminist colleagues in Chile. She even subsidized some subscriptions to the newspaper. Vera Zouroff in a letter to Gabriela Mistral from Santiago, Chile, on October 6, 1949, said:

Thank you also for your generosity in supporting *Women of America*. I will fulfill your wish by sending those subscriptions to women's institutions where the newspaper will find many readers. I'm intimately pleased to know that you approve of the work done by *Women of America*. I put my heart and soul into this work. I am convinced that we can only save Latin America from the coming catastrophe if we unite. God have mercy on us all! (Zouroff, 1949).

Gabriela Mistral's generosity and empathy towards the work of her fellow citizens was evident in the journal. In it, its promoters published the following article:

"Generous gesture of Gabriela Mistral"

The illustrious poet who brought the Nobel Prize to our America, despite the distance from her homeland, keeps in touch with her compatriots. Some time ago, we thanked her in these columns, for her generous sending of money to pay the free subscriptions of those who could not afford them. Now, at the Pan American Women's Round Table in Chile, we have witnessed another human quality of our poet. She has sent a sum of money to stimulate a poor and intelligent girl who shows skill and effort in her studies (Zenteno de León, Mayer de Zulen, Vilchis de Baz, & Huertas Oliveira, 1950, page 2).

In addition, several members of the Cenacle, including Edelmira Muñoz, Nelida Rigoletti, Virginia Contardo, and Fide Alessandrini, wrote to Gabriela Mistral in Mexico City. In the letter, sent from Santiago and dated June 1950, they informed her about the activities of the Cenacle in Chile. All this shows that Gabriela was very aware of the achievements of her colleagues in poetry. The letter said:

Dear Mrs. Mistral:

On the occasion of the tenth anniversary of the founding of the Poetry Cenacle of the Conservatory of Declamation, we students wents join together to pay a tribute of admiration and gratitude to our great teacher, Mrs. Vera Zouroff. As principal and founder of this Cenacle, she has prepared us to receive the poets better and to spread their message.

This tribute will take place on the evening of July 21 in the Honor Hall of the University of Chile. For this celebration, we kindly request a verse or a short poem as an expression of sympathy for Vera Zouroff. Her superior spirit has maintained an interest in poetry. She has achieved this despite the many difficulties involved in humanistic work in today's world.

We hope we can count on your support in this matter. Yours, very truly,

Edelmira Muñoz and the rest of the Cenacle's companions (Muñoz, 1950).

There are also several letters from Gabriela Huneeus, Lucia Richard's partner, addressed to Gabriela Mistral, in which she talks about literature. Let's keep two paragraphs from two letters, one written in 1951 and the other in 1955:

Dear Gabriela:

I am very glad that finally, although late, Chile gives you the deserved prize. It is painful to see how this land of hope and beautiful landscapes also has children who shamelessly ignore justice and the imposing truth. You are one of our highest values. You express yourself with all the depth and richness that the heart of our land possesses and the elevated spiritual stature of its summits (Huneuus, 1951).

In the second letter, Mrs. Huneuus expresses herself as follows:

Dear Gabriela:

A few days ago, I received from Parral a copy of my book *Eternal Prairie* along with your affectionate letter. You can imagine how much your words of encouragement have meant to me! And that's a lot. When we observe the world, the painful smallness of so many beings induces us to take refuge in the inextinguishable light of the soul. From this comes up happy moods almost impossible to express and a wonderful liberation of everything vulgar (Huneuus, 1955).

All this is very interesting because it shows the relationship of a whole generation of intellectuals with the most celebrated literary prodigy of the time:

Gabriela Mistral. There are also letters addressed to Gabriela Mistral from Patricia Morgan, Maria Flora Yañez, Jorge Gustavo Silva, all of them Lucia's companions. In the following letter, written by Vera Zouroff from The House of America a few months before the previous one, we can clearly see this relationship. All this shows that Lucia was fully integrated into those great towers of female thought that were the generation of the fifties.

Santiago, September 8, 1954

Sublime Gabriela:

When you won the Nobel Prize for Literature, it was the continent where your country is located that first received it. Today, as you return to your homeland, the Board of Directors of this Americanist institution, on behalf of our America, welcomes you.

Sign with their names: Esmeralda Zenteno de Leon; Colonel Agustin Benedicto; Santiago Aguirre Amengual; Carlos Valdovinos; Sofia Flores de Aguirre; General Teofilo Gomez Vera; Hilda de Guzman; Ema Ortiz; Luis Consiglieri; <u>Lucia Richard de Piedrabuena</u>, Amanda Brieba de Lorca; Berta Traversari from Ureta; Adela Perez de Larrain, Edelmira Muñoz; Carmen Alonso; Dora Puelma (Zouroff, 1954).

MEMORABLE LECTURES

Stained Glass from Brazil

The House of America. November 17, 1954

Vera Zouroff, director of The House of America, commissioned this exciting lecture from Lucia Richard. She gave it on the occasion of the arrival in Santiago of the Charge d'Affaires of Brazil, Colonel Benedict. At first, Lucia confessed the great difficulty of defining a country as vast as a continent where many races and climates coexisted. Only religion and language seemed to be the common denominator.

Lucia, who had traveled to Brazil and studied its history, began her speech by quoting the words of Americo Vespucci: "If Paradise exists somewhere, it is here." She remembered Ruben Dario, who exclaimed: "Land of sun, poetry and wealth, promised land for the work and energy of men." She also remembered the words of Sarmiento with his beautiful descriptions of Brazil as a vegetal paradise.

If there was one thing that symbolized Brazil, it was its flag: a vegetal background on which rested an enormous flower that for her represented the soul of a nation. Then she pointed out the beauty of Rio, a city of witchcraft, described so many times by pens like Stefan Zweig, Tibor Mendes, and others. The Guanabara Bay surprised the spirit of the traveler with its extra-human landscapes, its islands, coves, hills, trees, and blue mirrors. Then we found its avenues, incredible and extensive beaches, palaces, and gardens. Its colonial vestiges framed in a tropical and picturesque environment announced one of the largest and most revealing countries in Latin America.

Santos, with its natural beauty, was the prelude to what awaited us in Rio. São Paulo was the pride of civilization: modern, avant-garde, the country of the future. Bahia symbolized the charm of the past, its colonial period, the corner of history where traces of the metropolis remained. Unlike Bahia, São Paulo grew with the power of its tropical vegetation.

She also praised how independence had come about, transforming a country into a republic after mere negotiation. That was because Brazil always sought peaceful means to resolve its differences. It did not present examples of absolute and bloody dictatorships. For its most challenging problems, it found friendly and generous solutions. But the most exemplary was that the country abolished slavery and tolerated its racial diversity.

The Brazilian was quiet, a product of his climate, his Lusitanian blood, his soft tongue, or the nature that gave him fertility lessons. The enormous extension of land in an underpopulated country favored that relaxation and cordiality. There was an abundance of space and a profusion of material means.

This tranquility of the Brazilian was no stranger to a certain melancholy. Paulo Prado, one of his poets, said: "In a radiant land lives a sad people." The Portuguese, besides his language and religion, had brought the "*Saudade*." It was a kind of longing, a mysterious feeling. Benjamin Garay defined it as "not only the sadness of a farewell, the joy of memory, the delicacy of emotion, the truth of hope, the nostalgia of a homeland, but also that melancholy of absence. He also felt it as the affection of friendship, strength of a bond, shadow of pain, and even as an imperishable thought."

Among the leading men of Brazil stood out the illustrious man, Jose Bonifacio de Andrada e Silva. He was a complete humanist, a wise man, diplomat, philosopher, and poet. He promoted independence and built the nascent nation. Together with Miranda, Bolivar, San Martin, and many others, they formed the pléyade of the titans of the Latin American epic. They represented the demigods of a new mythology. Another outstanding figure in Brazil was the emperor, Pedro II. He was a man of a calm character who loved science and art. He had a humanitarian spirit, which made him the prototype of the ideal ruler, the leader who abolished slavery.

Brazilian literature became one of the most fertile in the Americas, conditioned by its diverse regions and libraries. Rio's library was one of the largest and well-equipped. Its architecture was vigorous and original, influenced by the brilliant French architect Le Corbusier. In music, Carlos Gomez stood out with his opera *El Guaraní*, an excellent example of how Brazilian composers could shine among the modern ones.

Among the greats ones was also Hector Villalobos. He knew how to look at the folklore of his country, finding in nature his most genuine inspiration. Hector listened attentively to the harmony of the jungle, getting rid of the false melodies of sambas and rumbas. He based himself, instead, on the artistic and the national. Besides, the musician was passionate about choruses, gathering the energy to make hundreds of people sing. A tireless worker, he published two thousand works, some of which were very extensive, such as operas, symphonies, and choirs. He was a great innovator of Brazilian music.

The sun and the natural environment have always influenced Brazilian poetry. It was also affected by the Afro-Brazilian poems of Jorge de Lima, Rau Bopp, or Camargo Guarnieri. As sensual and tropical verbalism, Lucia defined the poetry of Gilka Machado or Ronald de Carvalho. She also spoke of the markedly religious poetry of authors such as Murilo Mendes, Jorge de Lima, Augusto Meyer, or Murillo Araujo.

She also mentioned women poets, qualifying Cecilia Meireles as intimate and sensitive. Adalgisa Nery was pompous and symbolic, and Henriqueta de Lisboa tender and simple. Her *Children's Poems* strongly impressed Gabriela Mistral, who gave her a lecture. She added that Gaston Figueira said Brazil was one of the most favorable countries for poetic creation. It had inexhaustible motives for the poet's inspiration in that lush nature, a mixture of dream and grace.

Finally, she highlighted its painting and sculpture, its economic and industrial development, confessing how difficult it was to leave Rio de Janeiro, its beautiful landscapes, beaches, and bays ... The powerful and luminous Christ the Redeemer was the symbol that opened us his arms in a gesture of invitation and goodbye. He remained with us for a long time, as if defying separaseparation, distance, time, and oblivion (Richard, 2004).

About the Death of Stefan Sweig

Conference given at the Poetry Cenacle, May 28, 1942

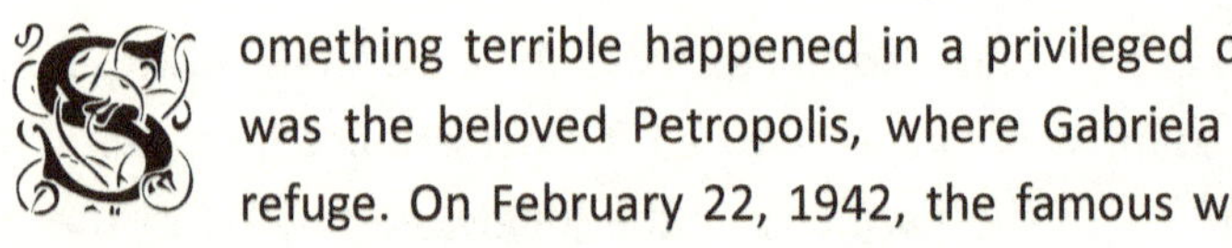 omething terrible happened in a privileged corner of Brazil. It was the beloved Petropolis, where Gabriela Mistral also took refuge. On February 22, 1942, the famous writer Stefan Zweig and his wife were lying dead in their bed. Nobody understood at first the reason for their suicide. Lying down and serene, they remain in their bed holding hands, with the expression of those medieval kings, who in their stone tombs, defy eternity.

Apparently, Stefan has no credentials or coins to give the boatman in his transit into the unknown. Just one last act of love, redemption, and exorcism... given to the world as the authenticity of his memory. His gestures show no repentance, no sign of terror, and no visible illness. The writer declares with this final act that his words are not traces piled up on a piece of paper. He is an intellectual who speaks to humanity with a sincere pen and will demonstrate this to the last.

Lucia does not delve into the historical circumstances of the character. Let's talk about his doctorate in philosophy, his studies of literature, his life in Austria, or journeys around the world. That is the case of his trip to India, China, and many other countries. She ignores the chronology. In the aesthetic feeling that floats, she finds the precious motive. For her, it is the fictional beauty of a dramatic act, worthy of being staged in Shakespeare's theatre. In her ability to transmit sensations is where her genius, full of tenderness and depth, refines:

"His eyes remained serene, intensely pale, in the magnificence of the lavish nature. They shined aristocratically like white candles, amid the polychrome splendor of a Byzantine basilica." (Richard, 2004).

Lucia strives to know the reasons for this abrupt and inexplicable end. It is an enigma that she intuits very well, and yet it can only be revealed by understanding the character and his vital discourse. Stefan had a lonely heart, one of those that torment stateless people. Born into a family of wealthy Jewish bankers in Vienna, he never delved into such an identity, nor did he practice Judaism. His destiny would have been to perpetuate the family business. But after his stay at the University of Vienna, he proved with his exceptional talent that his life was destined for higher purposes.

His youth was restless. He constantly traveled to Vienna, Berlin, Paris, and Brussels. He rubbed shoulders with the intellectual avant-garde of the beginning of the century, including Sigmund Freud, Paul Valery, Auguste Rodin, Rainer Maria Rilke, Romain Rolland, Yeats, Pirandello, Thomas Mann, Richard Strauss ... He traveled for several years until he settles in Salzburg. Suddenly, with the assassination of the Archduke of Austria, a thousand-year-old dynasty collapsed. World War I broke out, and Ştefan, who was a pacifist, fleed to Switzerland.

The ordeal of his exile began. He protested Germany's intervention in the war. The pacifist had to confront the nationalism of the time and its vengeful spirit. In 1930, on a trip to the United States, he met Einstein at Princeton. With the rise of the Nazis in 1933, his books are banned and burned in public places. In 1934 he traveled to Latin America. In 1938 he divorced his wife after infidelity with his secretary. He then took refuge in Paris, London, and then Bath, but he feared that the Nazi's clutches would reach there as well. He left for New York.

There he met a culture very different from his own. He felt oppressed among hundreds of refugees who asked him for money. In 1940, he gave many lectures in various Latin American countries. Throughout these years, the author faced with deep melancholy being away from his homeland and wandering the world. He worked on the biography of Magallanes and on that of Erasmus of Rotterdam. Like him, he was a pacifist who believed in a united Europe.

An eternal war that had not yet reached its climax overwhelmed him. What world will be left after the devastating conflict? Where will be the dream of uniting men of goodwill from all countries, of all races and classes, in a great league of enlightened and educated people? He thought. His idealism *à outrance* led him to an itinerant life that was a continuous flight and desertion. A successful figure, flattered by the public and women, had to leave Vienna like a criminal. He witnessed the First and Second World Wars. He felt like an outlaw.

He then hoped to find a creative exile where he could start over and put down roots. In 1941 he arrived in Brazil with his new wife. The beautiful tropical country represented for him a counter-world, a heavenly place. There you could live in peace without racial divisions or social tensions. It was a multicultural country built on European values. Everything was soft and sweet around them: nature, beings, and events. There they found another dimension of space and another sense of time.

In this beautiful country, the degree of tension in the atmosphere is less; men are kinder, contrasts are less vehement, nature is closer. Time runs smoothly. Energies do not compromise in the extreme. But even better, one lives more peacefully and humanly. In those years, he wrote his novel about chess and read Montaigne with passion. Then he wrote *Brazil, Country of the Future*, an exalted and optimistic book. If there was a country of the future, there was a future for the world. Like Goethe, who fell in love at the age of seventy, Zweig experienced a joyful rebirth. This change led him to conquer a vast area of freedom in these virgin lands and promising jungles.

But then the horizon turned dark. Thunders foreshadowed storms that disrupted the vegetal tranquility of the tropics. People were giving lectures. The formidable war machine rose, and hostility grew. The government restricted freedoms, and there were expectant silences. War again! Here too? He wondered. In the weeks before the tragic outcome, two German ships had sunk in Brazilian waters. He, as a German speaker, felt pointed. The writer thought that the terror of Nazism was spreading all over the world.

He sensed an inordinate fear for the future. Signs of a disillusioned man appeared on his face. He believed that Europe no longer existed and refused to cry as if it had died. He wrote to a friend saying: "Without having lost a father, I am mourning, for Europe and humanity." Unable to accept the shipwreck of his European dream, he carried the burden of having been expelled from the city that had shaped his identity. He was also humiliated by how Nazism had appropriated the German language.

Lucia believed that the tragedy of Zweig was much more than personal and represented the embodiment of universal evil. We could repair the devastating material destruction, but the spiritual damage would be perpetual and disastrous. The burning debris could be reborn as the Phoenix from its ashes. However, the illusion of people, the joy of living, the lost intellect, would be difficult to recover. The young brains of future scholars immolated by war, the schools demolished, the madness imposed on the minds of thousands of children; all this would be very difficult to erase from the consciousness of humanity.

The destruction also brought with it hunger and a generation of malnourished people. The apocalyptic wind dispersed the artists and silenced the wise. Now they were forced to evoke the catastrophe. All the human pain was concentrated in a heartrending groan. That entire ordeal erased the smiles, turning them into gestures of despair. The massive dose of evil had poisoned souls and seized hearts. We would never repair or forget this enormous damage.

Stefan Zweig understood all this and felt it in his skin. His fine sensibility presaged it. As always, he ran away, even from himself. The writer could not face the wicked destiny shadowing the world. He lacked the courage to denounce Hitler out loud. Stefan would never speak ill of Germany. He believed an intellectual should not interfere in politics, and instead, his concerns should focus on his books.

He could not bear to see his language, his beloved German, become the language of the executioners. The author had news of a ban on translating his works into English or French. He understood he could never return to a place no longer existed. In his homeland, his compatriots despised him because of his ethnicity, and in the New World, people questioned him for his nationality. He was a citizen of nowhere. He no longer had the strength to start over or the arguments to reinvent himself...

In his last letters, he complained that he would never again have a home, a country, a publisher... He's trapped in a small town in Brazil thousands of miles away from his life, his books, friends, and conversations. He lacked the intellectual environment and people of his cultural level with whom to share impressions. The novelist no longer went to the theater or concerts. He saw no one, and even the infinite jungle oppressed him. The loneliness that once was reassuring now distressed him.

He tried to keep working but confessed he had half his strength. How could I convince without being convinced? How could I enlighten hearts with my writings, if I can no longer be moved? He thought. He feared that without the right books, a good library, a quiet spirit, he would not finish his work on Balzac. Even the carnival he attended in the days before his departure did not deter him from his final decision.

Then, in his last moments of life, he wrote a short note that began with the title of *Declaraçao* and continued with some lines in German. In it, he said goodbye to this world "in his own will and lucid mind" and thanked Brazil for its hospitality. He left this world at the very moment when Europe, his homeland, was destroying itself as a product of the Second World War. Finally, she preferred to end his life at the right time on his feet. He made that decision as a man whose cultural work had always been his purest happiness and freedom.

We can think if, consciously or unconsciously, he didn't dramatize his own life. We will never know if, with this tragic ending worthy of a Greek tragedy, he might have wanted to gain legendary fame. This fact could have allowed him to increase the interest in his works, or on the contrary, it could have ruined his literary greatness. But one can never deny the authenticity of his ideals, the openness of his thought or his commitment to humanity.

For Lucia, the one who forgives the error instead of the evil should have taken them in. Romantics are all those who want to clothe the miseries of this world with illusion. They satisfy with kind words, the eternal thirst for beauty and truth that afflicts human hearts. This universal care is proof of their high spiritual origin and their lasting destiny.

Sara Hübner

Central House of the University of Chile, 1947

arah Hübner (1888-1930), was the daughter of the writer Carlos Luis Hübner and Teresa Bezanilla. She belonged to the movement called avant-garde spiritualism and aristocratic feminism. These movements were close to literary modernism (with a French influence and anti-positivism) but with clear differentiating shades. Critics recognized her as part of an intellectual vanguard of the early 20th century. These precursors tried to raise awareness of feminist thought and fight for women's rights.

Other authors also participated in this movement, such as Ines Echeverria Bello (Iris), Maria Mercedes Vial, Teresa Wilms Montt, Maria Luisa Fernandez de Garcia Huidobro, Mariana Cox Mendez, and Morla Lynch. Sarah was a journalist and writer. She cultivated lyrical poetry, social and literary criticism, and reporting. She wrote for several newspapers and magazines, including *Zig-Zag, Eventos, Artes y Letras,* and *Últimas Noticias*. Many critics, like Alone, agreed that her works were scattered. Mrs. Hübner published them in several publications, making it difficult to define her personality.

But to understand a woman's personality, her physical presentation also helps. Sarah had a somewhat peculiar physiognomy. Her narrow skeleton and small size gave her the proportions of a 13 or 14-year-old boy rather than a woman. She was very pale. She had bright golden hair and supernatural green eyes because of their brightness, color, dimensions, and expressive strength. When she walked down the street, people stopped to look at her, speechless. Her face evoked that of a Russian princess or the Black Lady from a spy novel (Vergara, 1962, págs. 23-27).

Lucia explains how the essential feature of her figure was the paradoxical complexity of her person. She also highlights her proteiform quality: "constantly changing forms and ideas." All this personal contradiction dispersed her work in various newspapers and magazines. Besides, It did not constitute a thematic unit or a literary genre. To prepare her lecture, Lucia studied the author's work in-depth, but not everything. That's because Sarah, as a true artist, was always dissatisfied with what she wrote, destroying much of her literary production.

From childhood, she had a mysterious and privileged brain, as intense as it was convulsed. Since her birth, confusion had marked her life. Clashes of races and nationalities, of different temperaments, had produced constant misunderstandings between her parents. Luis Eduardo Hübner, her father, was a distinguished writer of vast culture. Yet, he was weird. Her mother, of exceptional beauty, married very young. But her marriage went through many difficulties and the intransigence of the family.

During her childhood, the delicate and impressionable girl had to endure all kinds of travel, economic uncertainties, and truculence. She was brought up in a hostile foreign environment. Her family settled in Lima, where her father held a diplomatic post. All the notables of the country came to her house. But there, people hated Chileans because the war was very recent in everyone's memory. During her school years, she showed signs of shyness and extravagance, exposing herself in front of her teachers. Lucia thought that a talent like hers, with a markedly haughty and aristocratic stamp, could not follow the routine of official teaching, calculated for average intelligence. At that time, she was more interested in life than in books.

She once confessed to Fernando Santivan, her unhappy childhood. She had been precocious in suffering, and now she longed for those days he had not lived. Her father was a handsome intellectual who liked to go to clubs and socialize. His children knew nothing about his life. He arrived late at night, got up at noon, and left again. Because of a disagreement between the spouses, her father had promised never to talk to anyone in his house. He passed in front of his children like a shadow: serious, and completely silent. Like a stranger, he created a heavy and unforgiving atmosphere around him.

His children loved him, but that stern, cutting muteness terrified them. He showed joyful with his friends, but with his children, he was instead like a living statue, cold and distant. In this Victorian environment, her mother, sweet and gentle, spent the day crying. Without wanting to, she projected onto her children the anguish that oppressed her. In this scenario, Sarah lived in a state of shock. She always expected a supernatural and terrible event, suffering constant nightmares. One night she woke up next to her parents' bed, crying because she thought she had heard fighting voices in her sleep.

Her parents forced her to marry when she was only fifteen, to a good-looking boy from a wealthy family. They went to live with her mother-in-law, who led a monastic life. She was an austere person, surrounded by priests and saints. In her home, you had to whisper, as in churches. The young couple had to keep their eyelids down. The mother would have considered excessive laughter sacrilegious. They had to hide like criminals to kiss each other. She had left the house in the hope of breathing new air. But instead, she had found this gloomy atmosphere (Santivan, ca. 1920, pág. 7).

With these precedents, it is easy to guess her angry and contradictory character. Her figure was light, and a legend surrounded her name. Her personality gave off melancholy, sadness, and a volcanic desire to conquer infinity. She showed exacerbated feelings, and sometimes even aggressiveness. But for Lucia, it was no more than the mask with which she hid her great shyness, her passion, and the burning desire to fill an unsatisfied yearning. She also stood out for her histrionics, theatricality, and spectacular manners. All this was a product of her arrogance and overestimation of herself. In her *Intimate Diary*, she wrote: "To Gabriela Mistral almost with humility." (Sudermann, 1918).

Sarah had a dual and bipolar spirit. She was as human as paradoxical and could be as mystical as sensual. The writer enjoyed stillness and movement and ethics or aesthetics. But she could also be gentle or sadistic, refined or sarcastic, maternal or egocentric. Her writings speak of a tremendous internal contradiction. That is the case of her *Intimate Diary*, which she signed under the pseudonym of Magda Sudermann. She had a fire that consumed her, and incomprehension of life and the world, but above all, a misunderstanding of herself.

Suddenly, these dilemmas, this lack of trust, turned into narcissism. From there, they moved to an intense desire for greatness that was almost megalomania. Then the author turned to tenderness and from there to loneliness, sobbing, despair, and helplessness. Along with this, she showed high sensitivity to beauty, a promiscuous libido, and great sexual intensity. Her aristocratic sense made her say things like "those of my race were the deepest dreamers, and some of their dreams still linger in me."

Her style displayed powerful and exciting images. And although she declared that no one could understand her, this did not prevent her from being fraternal and generous and wanting to do good. She indeed repudiated banality and selfishness. As a consequence, her elusive soul sought to distance herself from people. The intellectual liked to read the literature of heroines. She said that this contributed to her balance and reduced her constant anxiety. She also enjoyed ridicule and sarcasm.

Lucia also focused on the writer's curiosity about beings and ideas. This questioning led her to become interested in the advances of science, medicine, and biology. But she also devoted herself to philosophy and was concerned with the problems of the world, religion, and life. Her faith often came up in her works. Sarah believed that there was a disproportion between the advances of civilization and the progress of spiritual forces. People had to have these values to behave properly. Humanity, the so-called Christians, did not have the slightest awareness of what the spirit of Christ was.

Despite her apparent frivolity, she showed a bold ability to enter into philosophical speculation. She had even dared to study and comment on Spengler's most outstanding work: *The Decline of the West*, publishing her study in *La Nación in Buenos Aires*. Lucia also referred to her pride, the consequence of which was sincerity. This feeling went beyond frankness and became intransigent.

In a time of pretense and hypocrisy, that sincerity brought her many disappointments. But it also gave quality to her work and allowed her to expand her powerful personality. In her *Reflections*, she said: *"Worthy women are always sincere."* And elsewhere, she wrote: *"No philosophy can give me the meaning of life. I know that I must seek it, right within me, by developing myself."* (Richard, 2004, pág. 398).

Because she believed herself to be superior to others, she felt to have the right to show herself as she was. Sometimes, this sincerity turned into impertinence, if not frankness and intemperate aggressiveness. So in 1919, she dared to write derogatory things against the Araucanians in the press (Hübner, 1919) .

On other occasions, she openly criticized the Chileans, calling them players who were wasting their lives on cards. They always worried about the lives of others, magnifying the slightest news. She also spoke of their "spiritual laziness" and their "narrow-mindedness." Sometimes Sarah wore pants, talked about love, referred to the loneliness of the Creole woman. However, just because she was one, she did not hesitate to use a harsh tone.

Joaquin Edwards Bello explained that she had died with a reputation of being "weird." This word in Chile was synonymous with an exceptional being, one who crossed the line or skipped conventions. For him, Santiago was a city that expelled misfits, those who could not accept everything. In his view:

> "Nothing was as atrocious as the inability of well-endowed people to discharge excess energy in an adverse environment. This unused energy poisons the organism." (Calderón, 1991, pág. 14).

Speaking of clothes, according to Lucia, she loved to surround herself with a frame of originality and distinction. She liked to show her superior class, with refined gestures. Fernando Santivan, a writer and a decade later winner of the National Literature Prize, also gave news about her pride and clothes. He told how Sara's generosity towards people of her affection knew no bounds, referring mainly to her husband, son, or brothers. She had an extremely strong character, which did not prevent her from having an attractive personality. Today we would talk about a *femme fatale*, of whom Fernando was her victim.

Fernando made the big mistake of pouring some allusions of plagiarism on Jorge Hübner. The suspicion was centered on the work of Vicente Garcia Huidobro, questioning the quality of Jorge as a poet. Sara, his sister, soon after finding out, did not hesitate to present herself in his office as a tigress. For the confrontation she hoped to provoke, she wore a severe black velvet suit, very tight to the body, and a large tail in the style of the time, and a wide-brimmed hat of the same fabric, in the style of the Marquise of Montespan. On her chest gleamed an authentic cross of diamonds, hanging from a ribbon of fine pearls.

So, she walked into his office. After Fernando's first courtesy greeting, she extended her gloved fingertips, piercing him with a dramatic, haughty look, leaving him intimidated by her imposing emerald green eyes. After a few moments, her face seemed more serene. But, without further ado and without "losing the righteousness of her body," she threw a shower of harsh words and many hurtful phrases. With this, Sara showed extreme anger for the treatment received by her brother Jorge and the group of poets of his age.

For minutes that seemed like hours, Sarah relentlessly continued her merciless attack screaming *"thugs," "scoundrels," "cowards..."* without allowing Fernando to explain himself. The scene was gaining more and more energy and intensity, arriving at a drama that the best of the actresses would envy. Fernando, who was already getting sullen, taking advantage of a gap in her terrible attack, said: *"Madam, I cannot allow..." "If you continue to insult me, as I cannot answer you as a man, I will have to withdraw and leave you alone..."*

But Sarah, far from stopping, interpreted Fernando's words as a new threat to her brother or her husband. At that moment, her face reached apocalyptic tones, and her words became more and more hurtful. Fernando, seeing that his efforts to calm her down were futile, tried to flee his office. He knew that several employees and one of his bosses were listening around his office door. So he feared that the whole episode would degenerate into a big public scandal. But the proud lady cut him off, preventing him from exiting, leaving him trapped. Then, she poured out a new torrent of frightful grievances.

Feeling Fernando cornered, and already close to exasperation, with a pronounced tragic attitude shouted: *Get out ... Get out ... or I do not know what I could do!* Such was the tone and expression of his gesture that Sarah finally shut up, looking at him with lost eyes, leaving the room in silence. After that,

Fernando was highly shocked, fearing the husband's anger and even the possibility of facing a duel ... Then two friends of his knocked on the door of his office, thinking that Fernando would be in a state of madness. They had just met Sarah Hübner on the street. She had explained to them that they should go and calm Fernando down because he was about to leave armed to kill her brother Jorge. After which the three friends looked at each other puzzled and did not stop laughing (Santiván, ca. 1930).

That was Sarah. What a woman. Lucia confessed that her interest in her figure was not based on admiration. For her, she stood out as an intellectual reference. That's why Lucia wanted to make a serene judgment of her works. Fernando Santivan tells how much she impressed him the first time he met her. But that admiration was not exempt from a lot of criticism. This meeting took place in her home with her brothers. Sarah burst into the conversation abruptly, imposing herself on her brothers. Her talk flowed like a waterfall. The words that came out of her mouth were lapidary phrases loaded with clear and convincing reasons.

There she was among her brothers. It was impressive to see her thin scarlet red lips embedded in a snowy face. Her large seawater eyes rested gently under the fan of her golden lashes. A magnificent blond hair accompanied these rare traits. For him, Sarah still carried in her blood the vehemence of a schoolgirl's gestures and the androgynous beauty of the medieval pages.

Her silhouette looked vaguely like Teresa Wilms and Berta Singerman. Later, she became friends with them, with whom she shared certain affinities. Fernando argued that mixing Saxon metals and Spanish gold in Creole crucibles produced strange results. He did not hesitate to compare her to "la Quintrala," a sinful female product of antagonistic races. In his opinion, this mixture had produced monstrous flowers in the society of colonial Santiago. All these women, like Sarah Bernhardt or Mariana Cox Mendez, had in common complexity, moral chaos, and inner torment. They were also characterized by an unbridled desire to live, analytical subtlety, mental clarity, bitterness, and disenchantment of the past.

Fernando came to doubt Sarah's sensitivity. He believed that the tenderness of these beings was more of a mental game, responding to well-defined interests. Later, the writer expressed his esteem for her. He did not want to tarnish her merits. But he didn't believe in her charity for the poor and helpless. In his opinion, feminine gentleness was not the cause of her empathy for other people's feelings. Neither was her willingness to avoid their family's pain. To him, Sarah was an analytical woman, acting with the coldness of a surgeon. In such circumstances, it was difficult to feel the pain of others as one's own.

He thought Sarah behaved cruelly as beautiful, flattered women do. Positive-minded beings were like that. Fernando said Sarah flirted with her suitors, played with them, forced situations, and then used sarcasm. She liked to get her friends together to make fun of those unhappy lovers. But just as she was cruel to these poor guys, she was harsh to herself. This paradoxical woman became unable to love or could not enjoy love.

Sometimes some talented men interested her. She approached them, entangling them with her deadly threads. But when she had them at her mercy, Sarah lost interest in them because of the smallest detail of their privacy. On one occasion, she became enthusiastic about a well-known poet, perhaps the most delicate of our poets. The writer thought she was in love. But one day Sarah noticed that his teeth were dirty and she couldn't get any closer to him (Santivan, ca. 1920, pág. 7).

Lucia also described the intellectual's aesthetic concern for herself and her work. This desire to seek harmony and beauty was omnipresent in her work. Yet, it altered the effects of love itself or made her follow her own philosophy. These sets of ideas were like a dogma or a canon under which she embraced all her actions. Her ideology was active and belligerent and shaped her sensibility into a holistic plan.

The author sought the exquisite, and through her feelings, she channeled that supreme attraction for beauty. She had an aesthetic mysticism, conceived love in a refined way, and longed for a superlative truth that inhabited the Elysium of higher realities. Her body, gestures, and clothes were poetry. Her personality shaped the air by creating artistic dimensions of her thought. She firmly proclaimed her uniqueness, which allowed her to be at the same time song and star, crystal and perfume, verse, and poetry.

But the shadows of a fateful destiny loomed over her existence. On one occasion, she confided to Fernando Montivan her intimate secrets: *What is the meaning of my life?* She said more than once. *"Believe me, if it weren't for my husband and my son, who need me and whom I would leave as orphans, I would rather die."* (Santivan, ca. 1920, pág. 7). Her observations turned out to be premonitory. All her contradictions, extravagances, and mortifications came together in one fatal result.

A son lit up her life. He was smart and beautiful, but his mother bore a terrible stigma. One day he died in an accident in the middle of his youth. The tragic event devastated his mother, and she detached herself from earthly things. In her fits of madness, she plunged in a perennial melancholy, destroying almost all her literary production. She also turned away from many people and disappointed virtually everyone. In Fernando's opinion, Sara was a nihilist. Such was the emptiness of her soul that she would have done anything foolish to accumulate intense sensations. She had a deep need to fill the immense dissatisfaction of not having enjoyed a great love (Santivan, ca. 1920, pág. 8).

Her heart could no longer bear the weight of all that pain. In addition to the devastating misfortune, she had to carry the weight of misunderstanding. The writer could not find anyone to share her life and ideas with. She shut herself away with her most intimate and genuine feelings. But she tried to give something of herself, and when her voice did not resonate, she suffered the torture of spiritual suffocation.

Her death was the culmination of disenchantment and detachment from matter to conquer the spirit. She could no longer bear the burden of a fragile body. Her soul was anxious about infinity and longed for a hurried flight. On the last page of her diary, written a few days before her death and already feeling the tremor of the unknown, Sarah wrote:

"In front of me, I am. I have never loved a soul as I love my own, and yet I, a great magnet for all sorrows, stood timidly on the threshold because I was too lonely to enter into myself. My head bows silently, and on my forehead, I leave my white and bloodless kiss." (Richard, 2004, pág. 405).

For Lucia in that kind of spiritual narcissism, we find perhaps the key of many anomalies, anxieties and worries which made Sarah Hübner the woman best endowed by nature and most tormented by life.

Quevedo

Conference in commemoration of the 300th anniversary
of the death of Quevedo. September 8, 1945.

Francisco de Quevedo was born in Madrid on September 14, 1580, into a family of hidalgos. He was one of the most outstanding authors of Spanish literature. Mainly known for his poetic work, he also wrote narrative and theatre, as well as several opuscules on philosophy, politics, morals, asceticism, humanities, and history.

He was born lame, with both feet deformed and severe myopia. These defects made him spend a lonely and sad childhood, putting up with other children's jokes. He was orphaned at the age of six, and at eleven, his brother Peter died. All these factors influenced his misanthropy and fostered his love of learning and study. His parents held high positions in the palace, so that during his childhood he grew up at court, surrounded by nobles and potentates.

Francisco was of superior intelligence and much inventiveness. As a child, he spoke fluent Greek, Latin, Hebrew, Arabic, Italian, and French. Later, the young studied at the Imperial College of the Society of Jesus and the University of Alcalá. He lived halfway between the Renaissance and the Baroque. It was a time when the man claimed his position in the universe and recovered classical culture. These advances contrasted with a time of disappointment in which man was an orphan in the cosmos. He was a curious humanist.

Before the age of fifteen, he graduated as a doctor of theology, although he was not ordained. The future writer mastered civil and canon law, as well as mathematics, astronomy, medicine, and natural philosophy. During his student years, he corresponded with the famous Belgian humanist Justo Lipsio. The scholar was also interested in philological and philosophical subjects. While he was in Valladolid, his endless enmity with Gongora, "the Cordovan swan," arose. Hence the duality between "conceptism" and "gongorism," the former defended by Quevedo and the latter by Gongora.

The Duke of Osuna appointed him as a counselor with whom he traveled to Italy in 1613. In this position, he trusted him with delicate diplomatic commissions in Naples, holding several public offices in which he excelled in leadership and organization. During these years, the intellectual traveled between Spain, Naples, and Sicily. He had meetings with the Pope and the King. He fled Venice accused of conspiracy, where violent persecution of the Spaniards had unleashed. Disguised as a beggar, he escaped by confusing the guards with his perfect Italian accent.

Quevedo was a contradictory man: as revolutionary as conservative, as moralist as immoral. For his friend Jose Gonzalez Salas, he embodied the most elegant poet of his time. But to his enemies, he was *"a teacher of errors, doctor of shame, professor of vice, and devil among men."* His love poetry shows him as the greatest singer of love, while his satirical poetry shows him as a misogynist. He climbed up the ladder of court, helped by powerful people. But, later, he did not hesitate to attack the corruption of his former mentors. Spain worried him, and he defended it as a patriot. He was a quarrelsome man who drew his sword for any reason.

It was a complex world: a transition from the Renaissance to the Baroque, the struggle of two concepts of life, two antagonistic ages, two definitions of man, a clash between humanism and mysticism. All this came together in Quevedo like a barrel of gunpowder thrown at the world. He had a fixation on unmasking things, condemning hypocrisy, and showing the corruption of vices. He liked mockery and satire. In his youth, his parody, and shameless pamphlets ran through the streets. Later he tried to deny them, but in the end, he could not stop them from spreading.

Conceptism was born from that world of opposites. Literature was an art of educated minorities. It was an elitist craft that despised the vulgar. Although Quevedo could be rude with his sayings and word games, he denounced gongorismo for being a style loaded with formulas and empty at heart. For this reason, he believed poetry should flee from the vileness of words and had to nourish by voices away from the common people.

In several writings, the poet sarcastically criticized the affected lexicon. But then, he complicated his love poetry with cultisms and hyperbatons, thus approaching his archenemy more than once. The hostility between the two literary rivals was terrible. In *La Perinola*, cruel miscellany satire, he launched horrific attacks on Gongora. Quevedo called him *"an unworthy priest, a homosexual, a dirty and obscure writer, a big nose, a card player, and indecent."* Gongora answered him with the same violence, presenting him as *"a lame, drunk, deformed, and poor Hellenistic."*

Quevedo also excelled in poetry, whether refined, cultured, amorous, or satirical. He relied on colloquialisms and vulgarisms that reproduced a prosaic reality. The author was also interested in moral poetry, which used elements of the Christian religious discourse. In his writings, we can see as well the influence of neo-stoic currents of moral philosophy. His love poetry bifurcated between those poems in which the poet hyperbolically praised the beauty of the beloved, following the Petrarch tradition, and those in which he despised female figures.

In both cases, he applied the code related to literary style. So it can't be called misogyny, but language congruent with the literary genre he used. Some themes obsessed him like *carpe diem*, the brevity of life, the inexorable passage of time, human vanity, or the body as a grave. For Damaso Alonso, he was *"the greatest love poet in Spanish literature."*

He emphasized sentiment in his poetry, which anticipated the romantic tears and made a model for modern writers. Hope, love, and beauty overcame the relentless passage of time. In *Constant Love Beyond Death*, he valued love as an eternal feeling. Referring to the soul in love and other parts of the body, he wrote:

> They will leave his body, not his care;
> They will be ash, but they will make sense;
> Dust they will be, but dust in love

Lucia Richard's great originality in her lecture on Quevedo was to say that the Spanish author had read *La Araucana*. He knew the Chilean people perfectly. Under his pen, Chileans were cautious and did not trust appearances. They received the embassies with their army and were very brave. The Chilean people fought for their land and freedom and did not submit to slavery. They were patriotic people proud of their nationality (Richard, 2004).

Quevedo returned to Italy with the Duke of Osuna and organized the Treasury of the Viceroyalty of Naples. There he entered the Academy of the Idle, meeting daily with a cohort of aristocrats and literati to discuss literature and poetry. The writer met the neo-Latin poet Giulio Cesare Stella and other intellectuals. He translated the Greek poet Anacreon into Italian. Spying missions were also part of his duties, receiving in 1618 the habit of Santiago.

He went from triumphalism to Baroque's disappointment, from believing in the greatness of Spain to witness its decline. With great mordacity in *Dreams* and other writings, he made fun of everything: customs, protocols, vices, all kinds of trades, women beggars, cuckolds, marginality, and the underworld. To do this, he did not hesitate to use the jargon of crime and all kinds of colloquialisms, proverbs, and famous sayings. He portrayed the figure of the rogue, a mixture of the cynic and stoic, anarchist, and anti-hero of the upper classes, who fought for the truth. Each mockery was in pursuit of a moralizing ideal.

In *El Buscón*, he recounted the vital vicissitudes of the rogue Don Pablos of Segovia from his childhood to his planned flight to the Indies. From his humble origins, the character goes through a series of adventures, always catastrophic for him. He seeks social climbing and economic stability. He is the false nobleman, whose claim to nobility is always unmasked. In his eagerness, he enters the court, but all his attempts always end in humiliation, hunger, and hardship. After his efforts, he becomes a comedian, living in sin with someone, dreaming of going to the Indies. But its materialization seems unlikely.

In his metaphysical poetry, he is interested in the moral sense, the reflection on life, and the anguish of man in the face of death. In doing so, the author advanced concepts of modern existentialism. Quevedo became passionate about Seneca and introduced many of his motifs into his works. For example, he dealt with the misery and brevity of life, the inevitability of death and the need to prepare for it, the defense of virtue and eternal values, transcendence, the rejection of material goods, and the deception of appearances.

In his historical and political prose, he spoke of defending the homeland and reclaiming the values outraged by the enemy. He praised the Hispanic culture in all its fields: its history, language, and literature, contrasting it with the foreign one. At the beginning of Olivares' government, he supported its regeneration and economic policy. Censorship called his work *Politics of God Government of Christ and Tyranny of Satan* subversive. To them, the piece was against the government.

His work reflects on the characteristics that the sovereign should have. It also describes the values with which he should govern and the limitations of power. The monarch represented God on earth, and as such, was to serve the people and the common good. The text does not allow for injustice and arbitrariness. With these ideas, he opposed Machiavelli and his reason of state.

The fall of the Duke of Osuna also dragged Quevedo down, as one of his trusted men. For this reason, in 1620, he was banished to the Tower of Juan Abad. There he spent months writing some of his best poems, relying on Stoic doctrine, completing his *Dreams*, and other political works. Later, the enthronement of Philip IV brought new winds of hope, and the new government released Quevedo from prison. Reborn for a moment, he accompanied the monarch on his travels through Andalusia and became his Secretary in 1632.

Quevedo lived one of his most creative stages, along with a messy private life. He smoked a lot, frequented taverns and brothels, lived with someone called Ledesma. One day his enemies at court found a diatribe under the king's napkin, criticizing the policies of the Count-Duke of Olivares. In all crudeness, they arrested him in the middle of the night and confiscated his books. Barely dressed, he was confined in a dark and damp dungeon in the convent of San Marcos de Leon until the favorite fell in 1643.

That year he came out of his confinement, but by then, he was very ill. So he left the court and retired to the Tower of Juan Abad. There he arrived, *"hurting his speech and weighing the shadow,"* as he put it. Shortly afterward, he left in search of better weather and some medication for Villanueva de los Infantes. In that place, he died after receiving the last rites.

Finally, as Lucia wrote, his legacy is immense, being one of the most outstanding members of the Golden Age. He was one of those lucid beings who built the magnificent cathedral of our language. In his writings, lovers of bold metaphors have found an inexhaustible arsenal of modernist images and motifs. Those who wanted to document an era have seen in Quevedo a rich source of details of all kinds. Those who seek laughter have found in his epigrams all the ingenuity and grace of Castile. All of them have been pleased with his quips and serene reflections, thus surviving the fashion of the times (Richard, 2004).

In Commemoration of the Colombian Writer Guillermo Valencia

Conference given by Lucia Richard at the
Catholic University of Chile

In this great conference, Lucia confessed her shyness to her audience, for daring to occupy the same rostrum where eminent professors and renowned artists had preceded her. However, she added that she felt legitimized by the professorship her father held for many years at the university. This task was the most precious duty of her life. Somehow, it continued in the figure of her son, who was studying at the university at that time.

As for Guillermo Valencia, once again, we are witnesses to Lucia's preference for these aristocratic characters. He came from a wealthy conservative family of Spanish descent, one of the most dazzling coats of arms in Popayan, Colombia. As on other occasions, she was not interested in the details of his political career. For example, his performance as Secretary of Finance in Cauca, his election as a deputy at the age of 23, his diplomatic posts in France, Switzerland, and Germany, his diplomatic missions in Brazil, Chile and Peru, or his position as governor and senator of the Republic since 1908. Nor was she impressed by his presidential candidacy for the Republic.

Lucia is only interested in the man: his personality in all its breadth, his human quality as a poet, his interiority, and his feelings. Lucia does not inform, but narrates, recounts, vivifies his figure. She achieves it using adjectives and comparisons that arise from her imagination and interests. The writer recreates and understands his different states of mind. And she does so with style so personal that she drags us into a hypnotic dream, a trance or a bath of sensuality.

Guillermo Valencia, in Lucia's words, was a pale, aristocratic figure with refined manners and elegant oratory. On his face was the look of a frightened child who had lost his mother when he was ten years old. He had an insatiable curiosity about things and carried with him a rich heritage, which made him seem, predestined to rise above and lead men.

Graduated in Philosophy and Literature, he was a man gifted with a great capacity for public speaking. This fact enabled him to speak fluently in Parliament, where he served for 27 years. There he met Baldomero Sanin Cano, with whom he established a close friendship, later joining the Bohemians of the Symbolic Grotto. He began his wanderings in Parnassianism, later focusing on French symbolism. In 1898, Guillermo met Ruben Dario in Paris. From then on, he adhered to his rich personal imagery, defending literary modernism.

In Lucia's opinion, he was a man surrounded by contradictions. He could be conservative in politics, and yet he inclined towards modernism in poetry. Withdrawn and lonely, he sometimes retreated into the darkroom of his unhappy childhood. But this anguish did not prevent him from engaging in intense activity. He was equally interested in the transcendent personalities of the old world, and the warmth of his beloved Popayan. In 1899 he published his exceptional book of poems, *Rites*, which made him famous as a poet.

The anchorite opened up to the world with intense and renewing light. The old romantic patterns collapsed under the allure of a work in which reflected young people eager for transformation. More ethereal than ever, the poet pursued the spell of the East and exotic motifs. He longed for the conquest of other planes of reality, in which he evaded from his time, space, and his own being. And he did so as one who sketches a tender and sensual drawing, exquisitely refined. He used an expressive beauty in words, which he caressed in perfect symmetry.

Other poets like Gabriela Mistral, carved their poems in rough rock. But Valencia needed marble to chisel his lapidary and incorruptible phrases, his eternal and perfect truths. He loved color and music and often inspired by paintings. In them, he sought the sublime beauty, the hidden message, the soft and discreet tones, the white, grey, and blue. In these pictures, the light dissolved, and all the stridency of this world faded away.

Just as we cannot avoid delighting in female physiognomy, we can't resist the author's literary world. He patiently wove it, embellishing it with his most beautiful words. There was his secret garden, where he seemed to harbor the fear of awakening the untouched, the little giant of consciousness, the deafening silence, and the mute voice. He feared to violate the dream of the lustful satyr who sought to corrupt the virginal harmony. The poet also worried that the dream would not arrive in time to cover the nakedness of the pagan reality.

Like the statues that don't see, he does not pay close attention to current events in his country. He makes his way through the ages of man, skipping the centuries, reaching the peaks of Olympus, the marbles of Athens, and even the sphinxes of Egypt. In his work *Catay*, he showed his deep attraction for Greece, Rome, Marco Polo, and legendary China. His style tends towards perpetual evasion, and a static view of the world based on themes imported from history or books. His gaze is set on distant places and times that disconnect him from reality. For the avant-garde, Valencia embodied one of the greatest Latin American poets of modernism.

Lucia finds in his oratory pieces and speeches the ferment of his patriotic and traditionalist ideas. This love for his homeland also fostered his cult of heroes, his knowledge of history, and Creole feel. However, the poet is not interested in patriotic legends, popular heroes, romance, folklore, or peasant motives. His world is that of Apollo and Aphrodite, and sometimes that of the crucified man from Jerusalem.

He also stood out for his formidable translations of foreign authors such as Goethe, Victor Hugo, Baudelaire, Mallarme, Oscar Wilde, D'Annunzio, Verlaine, Maeterlinck, Flaubert, Stefan George ... But his greatness lay mainly in his status as a poet. For his critics, the author was musical and plastic, very correct in language and architectural in his way of composing. Yet, he expressed himself with a bit of coldness. He lacked that essential intimate warmth, that spiritual strength of other authors. But the grandeur and beauty of the structure filled this insufficiency.

After his last electoral defeats, he became disenchanted with politics and took refuge in his family home in Belalcazar. There he collected ivories, medals and dedicated himself to writing and translation. He surrounded himself with many precious things, works of art, books and documents, hunting expeditions and pheasants, friends, and servants. Time passed, and loneliness consumed him. In the autumn of life, illusions fell like leaves. He turned melancholic after cultivating his inner self too much.

In the last moments, unreal things filled his mind, and in his hands, he held a crucifix. The day finally came when, as always, he set out in search of the unknown regions. He left our world wrapped in the mystery of his divine words to find his double immortality. And at his door stood a drowsy hound, guarding his eternal sleep... (Richard, 2004).

Sea Lovers

Santiago, Alhambra Palace, 1944

 he sea is a bluish reflection of space, an infinite field for expansion, a place to dilate thoughts, a living fable where the spirit runs unimpeded in search for its freedom. There, our being enriches, under the weight of old legends and unfathomable mysteries. With it identify the predators of dreams, those who abandon themselves in its imprecise impressions, and those who explore its presumptions of presences. The sea represents pure frankness: it always transmits what it feels; beats at the same time as its waves.

Lucia tells us about the attraction of the obsessive vertigo of its constant swinging. On its shores, stay the lovers of the sea. They are beings of a unique and imposing race, endowed with special psychological conditions. They come to it to understand that unlimited world, which connects them to superlative realities, beyond the real. There the absent and lonely remain; those who pose their abstract gaze in its unreachable distances.

In the contemplation of its golden horizon, we come into contact with the indecipherable mystery of our own conscience. And so it awakens the primitive man who lives in us. Those lost in thought, and those focused on their interior, arrive there silently. The hypnotic power of the sea seduces them. It is a phenomenon that Augustus D'Halmar compares to the subjugating power of fire.

Salty smells, floating laughter, light and warm breezes, sweeten our hours and allow us to make a serene judgment on what the sea is. And if the popular imagination has constructed a contemptuous and fearful view of what the bandit is, it has praised the pirate and covered him with a legendary aura of heroic fantasy. If other professions fall into boredom, the sailor is a restless being who feeds on winds and suns from all latitudes. Thanks to these voyages, he enjoys the dealing and experience of all peoples and races.

Sea lovers, with their restless spirit and erratic life, are not bored or affected by routine. For Lucia, the sailor faces the challenge of the sea with steadfast courage, while the woman often looks at it with fear. The women wait for their men on the shores in uncertainty. Love never fades. They take on the departure with pain and then are moved by the unexpected return. In between, the sailor crosses the seas, trying to master the untamed waters that have never subdued man. Nothing magnifies and purifies more than the journey by sea. Our soul changes and expands; it mutates under the benevolent cadence of inexhaustible sensations.

But the sea can also be a metaphor for anguish. Its overwhelming forces and terrible violence awaken our Dionysian feelings. Its changing currents express contradiction and evoke fatal thoughts. Heart's burdens sometimes resemble a fragile paper boat, crossing a terrible storm in the middle of the night.

Then, we shock before thunder and lightning. Flashes of light overwhelm us with their terrifying message. Darkness swallows everything, but our boat still feels an impulse to live, to surmount the hurricane winds of uncertainty. It strives to overcome the crashing waves, and enjoy the enigmatic gleam of a silver moon over the sea...

Lucia saw in this impenetrable sea a sibylline truth whose resonances reached mythology. Ulysses and his odyssey was the legendary hero with an unwavering faith in his mission. He crossed the Greek islands to conquer his destiny in the Trojan War. Poseidon was the god of the sea. Called Neptune in Roman mythology, he became a powerful entity on Olympus, a protector of the Hellenic cities. The vanished Atlantis described by Homer remained an eternal mystery. The beautiful nymphs and the enchanting mermaids seduced the brave men with their female torso and their fishtail. They splashed in the waters, attracting the sailors with their irresistible melodious voice. They tried to make them crash into the rocks or direct them towards fatal destinations.

The sea for Lucia had something absorbing for its admirers. When one of them felt its claim, he no longer belonged entirely to himself. That was the case with those magnificent Venetian Doges who married the sea by throwing in the symbolic ring of the first voyage. The passion of this man for the sea became a vocation. His desire was a constant obsession; his aptitude, something that displaced all other activities. For the sailor, land was neither a goal nor the end of his aspirations. Instead, it turned to be the starting point for a new journey, new embarkation, and greater communication with the sea.

This excitement for the sea would be the case of the skilled Genoese captain Juan Bautista Pastene, who took part in the early stages of the conquest of Chile. It amazed Lucia the moral temper, courage, stubborn resolution of these first navigators. Other conquerors, eager for gold and riches, went in search of mines and "encomiendas." But Pastene, generously and perhaps driven by the legend of Columbus, departed intrepid with small ships to discover the unknown coasts of Chile, exploring its seas until the Southern end.

After him came Juan Ladrillero, the Spanish navigator who continued to explore the Strait of Magellan in both directions, after the death of its discoverer. Juan Fernandez discovered new sea routes and left his name in the middle of the Pacific, on islands famous for their beauty and legend. Centuries later, they were the starting point of a novel as important as *Robinson Crusoe*. Chile, because of its long coast, lives turned towards the ocean. Its waters benefit from the temperature and the intense blue of the tropical seas and the foggy cold of the southern land. It is a marine homeland, which has lived its history and linked its destiny to the sea.

Later, visionary men, artists, writers, and poets spoke of their love for the sea. Painters tried to capture on canvas the transience of the moment, the eternal immobility of the waves, and the changing colors of the waters. With just a little paste, they reproduced the clarity of the waters, their different tones, and the vivacity of their diverse range of colors. Among them, the marine painter Alvaro Casanova Zenteno made his art the seal of a true vocation.

He was the most genuine interpreter of the sea. For years he studied Chilean naval history and became familiar with shipbuilding. Casanova applied this knowledge to the difficult task of portraying the sea. It turned for him an arduous task because the sea was a changing and dynamic element, with different intensities of lights and shadows, and different transparencies. He did not paint an academic sea, which spoke of school technicalities, but a lived, caressed and sensed one.

Casanova was a student of the English marine painter Thomas Somerscales. He learned much from him, especially from his insatiable curiosity and his patient and expectant observation. What he painted came not from a closed workshop, nor from the shore of a distant beach, but from the sea itself. In his youth, he built a floating studio, and in the company of six crew members, he traveled the seas in search of motifs for his paintings. This tenacity shows courage in pursuit of an ideal.

In literature, many love the sea for its own meaning. They carry it in their blood like the mystic carries his god. One of its most exalted representatives was Augusto D'Halmar. He was a man with Nordic roots who claimed to descend from a saga of seafaring ancestors. He enjoyed the long coast of Chile. The sea fascinated him to the point of saying that many nights he had to hold on to the railing in order not to give in to the attraction of jumping into its waters. Only the members of an exceptional race could give up everything for the sea: their homeland, home, and ambitions.

They were hard-working men who understood greatness differently. They could not comprehend the eagerness of these city dwellers to destroy themselves. Until the end of their days, all they cared about was the annulment of others. There was a sublime gesture in their genuine appeal to the mystery of the ocean. In the sea lies an eternal truth that enters the personality and becomes the companion of great solitude. The writer conceived of a sea without a country. It was for him a universal reference, where he found a refuge for all his affections and illusions.

The writer Francisco Coloane, winner of the National Literature Prize, described the seas and winds of Chile intensely. He was born in the southern city of Quemchi, Chiloé, on July 19, 1910, the son of a whaling ship captain and a small farm owner. In his youth, he worked as an employee of the Chilean Navy and later as a member of the oil expeditions that took place in Magallanes. He grew up facing the ocean since his childhood. For Coloane, the sea represented a genetic and fundamental experience. In these latitudes, it manifested itself in all its pathetic grandeur.

There, at Cape Horn, in those wild and rugged landscapes, he wrote his most realistic and vigorous pages. In *The Last Prince of the Baquedano*, we can feel in our face the splash of the great waves, and the strong wind of the southern region. Its sea is dramatic. There's something tragic and desperate about it. In that place, the man struggles continuously with his environment. He is a hard-working man who experiences the loneliness of the sea. In order to survive, he faces a still untamed and unexplored nature, in one of the wildest and most inhospitable places in Chile.

The Pacific Ocean is winding and brittle, full of channels and rocky expanses that make navigation difficult. Ice floes float silently through these inlets. It's a place where civilization has not reached, nor the decline of the West. Man is in direct contact with a genuine and courageous nature, not yet plundered by unscrupulous caciques. It is a nature that speaks to him in a clear language and looks at his face with its ancestral eyes. The first navigators crossed the Strait of Magellan to meet its two seas. This feat allowed these two watery immensities to come together in a cyclopean embrace.

This land is of abysmal beauty, where the wind screams, hoots, and expels wild puffs of air and water. The ocean manifests its fury and unleashes its stentorian forces. When it rains, it is as if another sea were falling on you. The marine fauna is exuberant. Birds are majestic. Being in Tierra del Fuego is like being at the end of the world. It's the last frontier. Beyond it is Antarctica, the icy territory, the world uninhabitable without the help of external means.

The Chilean sea is an impetuous sea, where fish and seafood multiply. The waves rise like eyelids, as Pablo Neruda, another passionate of the sea, said. Collecting shells and snails fascinated the poet. Many times he put them in his ears to listen to the sea. That distant rumor whispers secrets to us and connects us with mirages from other worlds. He also collected figureheads, objects of pure art and symbolism, from which seductive women emerged. They looked into the distance without looking, imposing themselves on the horizon with their expressive esoteric faces.

He also collected miniatures of boats confined in bottles, spyglasses, compasses, books, and treatises on malacology, that part of zoology that studies mollusks. His enthusiasm for the sea led him to sail around many parts of the planet. His conception of the sea was transcendental: love, distance, and time. He expressed it this way in his *Desperate Song*:

> You swallowed everything, like distance,
> like the sea, like time.
> Everything about you was a shipwreck.

For Garcia Lorca, Neruda was closer to death than to philosophy; closer to pain than to intelligence; closer to blood than to ink... There was something about him that was anthropomorphic. He worshipped the sea, trying to interpret its sidereal questions. And he did it with the magic of one who knew its legends. That was the case of the Caleuche, the ghost ship, the son of Chiloé's imagery, which advanced in the thicket with its fantastic silhouette.

The Chilean sea is home to incredible creatures like the albatross or the pelican. One glides weightlessly showing off its slender figure, and the other is extravagant with its enormous beak. It's a sea full of gulls and sea lions that are not afraid of man. It's also a sea of pirates in the stories of Vargas Huneeus. A sea of civilization and tourism emerges in Jara Azocar's writings about Viña del Mar. For Jorge Hubner, the waves swell like a golden dome and then crumble in a fatal cataclysm.

Lucia was also concerned about women's feelings about the sea. It seems as if the sea were too imposing for them. They admired it, but they did so from afar. Maria Monvel wanted to be a sailor's bride and, through his lips, taste all the continents. Chela Reyes saw the sea as a symbol of life. Domus Aurea contemplated the sea from the heights, in a house hanging from the hills. Gabriela Mistral preferred the land to the sea. Her voice of a peasant woman was linked to the earth. However, in "Bow Man's Song," she also referred to the sea:

> The man sitting on the bow
> The man with the face of anxiety
> How ardently he sails north;
> His eyes are enlarged with eagerness!

The sea is also feminine. It creates beauty and welcomes us with tenderness. It attracts us with its sinuous silhouettes and understands and listens to us. It rocks us in its eternal swaying and relieves our sorrows. When it is all over, it receives our ashes and transforms them into a new dawn (Richard, 2004).

Luis Felipe Contardo, a Priest Poet

Born in Molina in 1880, Contardo received his education at the seminary of Concepción. Then, he continued his studies at the Pedagogical Institute of Santiago, where he graduated as a Bachelor of Arts in 1898. He studied Theology in Rome. In 1901, he took his degree in Theology. In 1902, Luis Felipe graduated in Theology from the Gregorian University in Rome. He received holy orders in 1903.

He toured the United States, Europe, and the East. On his return, he worked as a teacher at the Seminary of Conception. There, Mr. Contardo directed the newspapers *El Pais* and *La Union* and was Secretary to the Bishop. In 1917 he was appointed parish priest of Chillán. The Supreme Government of Chile sent him to Tacna at the time of the plebiscite where he could gain followers for the Chilean cause. In Bolivia, he gave notable conferences on culture and art.

His most important works were *Flower of the Mount*, 1903; *Palm and Home*, 1908; and *Songs of the Way*, 1918. He knew how to harmonize the elegance of the classical form and the dazzling brilliance of modernism. His poetry in the Parnassian style assimilated much from Ruben Dario, Verlaine, Mallarme, and Baudelaire. From his travels to the Holy Land, he drew much inspiration for his verses. Through all these activities, he developed his vocation as a poet, diplomat, journalist, sacred speaker, and patriot.

Felipe Contardo was above all a mystical poet, compared to San Juan de la Cruz or Fray Luis de Leon. For Lucia, he was a classic, far from the cosmic and transcendental poets. He was a simple poet, abandoned by anthologies, but a true poet. His work, *Songs of the Way*, became his most accomplished creation, for which people remembered him. With its sale, he intended to rebuild his church.

The poet was humble and generous. There was never any ambition or exaggerated feeling in his poetry. His world was that of the people, the rustic buildings, the home, and, above all, nature. With his verses, he evangelized. But he did not forget the beauties of the universe or the stars, omnipresent in his poetry. The stillness and silence attracted him deeply. In his stanzas, he sought eternity: a mixture of spiritual longing and human transience.

His verses evoke the beauty of the world, the sweetness of life, the search for the ideal, and meditation. Rural life, the countryside, and shepherds, the fragrance of flowers, and idyllic simplicity attracted him. Many of his poems reveal the great love he felt for his mother and the memory of home. The tenderness, delicacy, and innocent games of children abound in his writings. Also, in his pieces is the sense of flight, the weightlessness of the birds, and the slow-motion images.

At other times, passaging time disturbed him. So he recreated the medieval abbey or the feudal castle. But he didn't intend to exalt a heroic act or praise courage. The charm of the better times, of mysticism, memory, and asceticism, attracted him. In *The Desert*, he wrote about passaging generations and centuries, seeing in the pyramids a perennial altar. Remains of stone, dreams of centuries in which the pharaohs slept, bones of villages, all were magnificent monuments built to satisfy the vanity of the flesh. Then he felt the weight of eternity, the millennial breath of death, and the great fatigue of humanity.

In Lucia's opinion, his "Ancestral Voice" poem portrayed the author. He praised the century in which he lived, describing it as a robust period of enterprise, audacity, and noise. However, he kept within himself something primitive, naive, and rude, some strength and candor. He thought he must have once been a monk, childish and elusive. A monk absorbed in his work. Like the Poverello, he was smiling and thoughtful, or he was participating in a noble crusade, or he was a dark friar like the one who accompanied Columbus.

In many of his poems, he depicted some Italian places, praising Francis of Assisi. The writer identified with the Saint for his love of nature, animals, and plants. As a genuine ascetic, he emulated his poverty and his austere and dreamy mood. He went in the footsteps of Francis, picking up the peace of the forgotten valleys, listening to the wild music of life.

His poetry is full of generosity, human sympathy, communicative benevolence, and frankness. Soft rhymes, without superfluous words or dislocations, abound in his stanzas. One can perceive his sober diction and pure inspiration. In his poems, there are no metaphors or complex constructions. He looked for authentic and genuine in life. He fled from falsehood. The Alexandrian verses were his favorite.

Sometimes in his poetry, we may see melancholy, obfuscation in the face of pettiness and bewilderment at the impurities of the world. But hope always returns. It is like the search for something unattainable that tears between dream and reality. Despite everything he was optimistic. The illusion overcomes the disenchantment. An essential aspect of his numen is the stillness and loneliness. The serenity of the countryside, the modest roofs, the frugal life, and the rustic walls shaped his worldview.

Often this dialogue with himself emerged in the imperturbable calmness of nature. He loved the last light of the evening and the last rays. Then the joy of living in peace arose. Sometimes his writings conveyed the emotion of reading. In his hands, he held a book in which he found an echo to his sorrows while he concentrated in a contemplative gaze.

Under Lucia's lenses, the author was a great physiognomist, a psychologist, and an artist. He interested in current events, trying to capture the fleeting moment that escapes from our hands. But he also felt a preference for the ancient times, the biblical passages, and dialogue with God, aspiring to understand his immense kindness. In God, he found peace and truth. He rested in his lap, like a wounded bird, to calm his anguish, finding in his heart a sweet nest... (Richard, 2004).

Felipe Contardo's poetry has many parallels with that of Lucia Richard. His world was archaic. He sang of serenity and inner peace. She had a pure and kind soul, like that of St. Francis of Assisi. His voice resounded with prayer and radiance. The honesty and tenderness of his emotion influenced many and contributed to the poetic rebirth of the century. In Lucia's view, he was a beneficial rain that sweetly inspired her poetic creation.

CHAPTER IX

AN ACCOMPLISHED COLUMNIST

Her Aesthetic Opinions on Painting, Literature and Poetry, Especially Regarding Pablo Neruda and Gabriela Mistral

he following years of 1955 and 1956 were very prolific in the career of Lucia Richard, publishing numerous articles mainly in the newspaper *El Mercurio*, where she enthusiastically showed her knowledge of history, art, architecture, etc[16].

Her articles could be classified into four groups: the first one would be those collected in her book *Travel Memories* of 1934. It is a miscellany chroni-

---

[16] Regarding Lucia Richard's articles, only thorough research could give us the exact number of these. Although in the *Complete Works* many columns have been collected, some are missing, as well as some dates. For example, they are missing: "To Gabriela Mistral," 1922; "The Women of Don Quixote" (*Revista de la Sociedad de Escritores de Chile*, in 1946, vol.II, No. 6/7, pp. 36-38); "Who is Gonzalez Vera?" (*La Hora*, 19-VI-1950); "The Book of Hours" (1-1-1957 as verified by El Mercurio Documentation Center). As for dates, the *Complete Works* collected "Claudel's Words" without a date reference and according to the Documentation Center, the poet wrote this article on March 13, 1955; "The Day Has Always 24 Hours." (According to the D.C. she wrote it on 11-13-1955 and not on 05-11-1955); "A Notre Dame Prayer" without a date in the *Complete Works* appeared in the D.C. of *El Mercurio* on July 29, 1956. Besides, *Hoy magazine*, vol. 12, nº1, 593-605, p. 28, of 1943, mentions the poetry *Disorder* corresponding to the unpublished poetry collection *Blue Smoke*, which was recited in a poetic recital in Santiago.

cle, full of interesting curiosities. It conveys all the excitement of a traveler astonished before some wonders of art and culture she contemplated for the first time. She shares with the reader the climax of mysticism and rapture, of a Chilean group that went on a pilgrimage mainly through Italy (Richard, 1934).

The second group would be those articles that could be classified as having a social scope. In it, the author deals with subjects of general interest (for example, "Rebellious Youth" or "The Day Always Has Twenty-Four Hours"). The third group would include those articles in which the author comments on her colleagues' books (for example, "Renovates by Maite Allamand" or "About Aunt Eulalia"). The fourth group would be those pieces of cultural or artistic interest ("Life, Passion, and Death of the Portrait," "Dream of Toledo," etc.).

Taking only a sample and referring to her social articles, we could talk about the entry entitled "The Day Always Has Twenty-Four Hours." The exciting thing about this article and others in its series is that Lucia improvises, writing almost in a state of flow the sensations she perceives from the world around her. It is a world full of constrictions, in which man lives alienated by an accumulation of conditionings that prevent the global projection of his personality. She quotes Paul Sartre, and we can perceive the influence of existentialism.

Man's first enemy would be "time." This evil results from the complexity and increase of communications, the internationalization of human manifestations, and global legislation. The need to produce more, and to do it faster to compete in an increasingly demanding market, has transformed the modern man into a neurotic being. This man is caught up in a race against time, overwhelmed by pressing needs and tormented by a bacchanal of invading noises.

This cult of the god Cronus, usurper of everything beautiful, and harmonious in life, had suppressed artisan work. Instead, it advocated a vision of synthesis, an economy of space and time, which led to mediocrity in production. Lucia criticized the banal writer who was not sincere in his art but prostituted himself in the service of the puerile mentality of the vulgar. He sought easy applause, and excessive propaganda would cooperate in this confusion of values.

There were many people tired of the noise and movement. For example, the painter was producing accelerated works. The journalist standardized states of opinion with the speed of a great juggler or a conjurer of the word. Politicians combined the interests of a heterogeneous plurality of people. The patriarch of the house saw his family's burden increase and his income decrease. Although Lucia did not mention it expressly, we can think Picasso would be the archetypal figure of this dehumanized urban world, full of disorder and cacophony. This mess was what Lucia referred to as "orchestral painting." Here the artist poured his unconscious images, abstractions, and delusions into the work.

As for music, she criticized the dissonance and agglomeration of musical sensations. Intermingled, they were a faithful reflection of the disordered world of modern society. Possibly, Lucia was referring to modernist musicians such as Stravinsky, Schoenberg, or styles such as Jazz and other related musical manifestations. She also opposed dark and confusing poetry, full of distorted images that produced exhaustion to those who read them, probably thinking of Neruda. She made the same statement regarding literature. In her opinion, writers crammed their writings with events and characters. Exposed in cross-sections, they intended to show a multiplicity of life, defined as orchestral literature (Richard, 2004, page 490).

Lucia had a classic spirit, which made her enjoy peace, tranquility, and backwater. In this state of the soul, the author found the greatness of things and the perfection of art. Even more, it meant for her the mystical union with the universe and the mastery and purity of eternal realizations. Adopting this position, she rebelled head-on against that hell that Sartre called "immobility." That would be the most irritating position in our nature. Lucia abhorred novelty and experimentation. She idolized tradition, academic structures, and the norms enshrined by the wise men of antiquity.

However complicated the culture, Lucia in her way of thinking - consistent and legitimate without a doubt - approached from very different ideological positions what the National Socialists called "degenerate art" (*Entartete Kunst*). This view also had its variant in music (*Entartete Musik*). Based on totally spurious asepsis, they eliminated from German ideology, everything they considered impure and abstract art. And so they condemned writers like Thomas Mann or Marcel Proust, creators of literary masterpieces. They also rejected painters such as Francis Bacon, Wassily Kandinsky, or Marc Chagall, the highest current exponents of modern painting.

The premises are radically different. Lucia rejected brain constructs, the product of artifice, and cold reason. Yet, she believed in the spontaneous freshness of feelings that arise from the depths of being. The poet moved away from the insane, and everything she considered was not beautiful, but an amalgamation of anything. What was not genuine beauty or a naked heart, she did not consider being art.

The National Socialists believed that art was degenerate for philosophical-political reasons. They praised a superior man, Aryan youth, Greek vigor, and power. They, therefore, attacked what they considered being Jewish, Slavic, Marxist, and other art. Lucia started from a premise of goodness and the National Socialists from an assumption of evil.

But most aesthetes and art scholars agree that beauty is not found in objects, but in the subject who experiences it. Beauty is eminently subjective. But art is not only beauty. An unpleasant scene like *The Shooting of the Second of May* by Goya is art because it manages to move, excite, whip up the lethargy of our imagination. All the great geniuses of painting were people who, starting from academic education, broke with the established rules and followed their own instinct. We can see this rupture in Turner, Goya, Velazquez, Delacroix, Picasso, Dali, Monet, etc. And this can be extended to all manifestations of art.

A good intellectual contradicts himself many times in his life. He will also make errors of judgment. We can see this in the distance that Lucia Richard keeps from the two greatest literary geniuses of her time: Pablo Neruda and Gabriela Mistral. Lucia's different social origin with them may be the source of this misunderstanding. The fact that Neruda joined the Communist Party may also have been the main reason for her rejection of the poet.

But apart from this speculation, Lucia condemned the obscurity of their poetic styles, something that was unforgivable in her opinion. But, to abhor two Nobel Prize winners in Literature (Gabriela Mistral in 1945 and Pablo Neruda in 1971) and to do so publicly seems to be imprudent. All this shows that many people supported her ideas.

In her article "Neruda and the Chilean Poets," she clearly expressed her way of thinking:

"I belong to a generation that has fallen victim to Neruda's dazzle. Neruda's influence on our lyrics has been somewhat oppressive. It's only comparable to the impact of Wagner at the end of the 19th century. Gabriela Mistral has few followers. Her pathetic voice as a biblical prophet represents a unique case in our literature. Apart from Garcia Lorca's ephemeral fashion, foreign poets have left no trace in us. The poets copied Pablo Neruda in his forms and procedures without - with some exceptions - matching his depth." (Richard, 1950).

A few years later, Lucia Richard paid tribute to Gabriela Mistral and Pablo Neruda in her radio program *Art Guide*. After what we've read, it's hard to believe that she didn't maintain reservations when making those programs or if she surrendered to the mainstream instead. Be that as it may, she reflected again on their literary personalities, extracting from these characters the best and most valuable of her pen.

For example, in her homage to Gabriela Mistral, Lucia picked up the melancholy humor of a poet who lived abroad and looked back on her homeland and childhood with nostalgia. In her exploration, she made an imaginary journey into the writer's mind, from her self-imposed exile to the modest home of her childhood. No matter how many high-profile personalities she might have associated with, how much she had read, or the scholarly conversations she had had. All her generous literature originated in that house with its narrow and vulgar walls, in that small town, in that popular and provincial world.

It is in that rural world, where Gabriela Mistral grew up surrounded by a boundless nature. Lucia confessed that she was moved when she thought of that peaceful and challenging childhood. That small town of vast horizons was the origin of the deep emotions that shaped the tones of her poetry. In that place, the great matron held in her bosom all the anguish of the universe. It was there "where the poet dignified with her voice the discourse of The Americas and confirmed the grace of the Spanish language itself." (Richard, 2004, page 576). Therefore, the essential elements of her feeling were God, death, childhood, and the earth.

Gabriela Mistral (1887-1957)

According to Lucia, this dialogue with God and death in her poetry would have fostered her immense love for children. The images in her stanzas were a direct reflection of her observations of nature and had a taste of the biblical and evangelical parable. Her poetry was that of the sad Indian, the old Castilian fed by the popular saying, or the early Christian who still retained the miracle of love.

This elegiac, harsh, and apocalyptic poetry could not be more opposed to Lucia Richard's feelings. They only coincided in their love for nature and children but from very different angles. In contrast to the off-key, sordid, popular, mournful poetry, although rich in images of Gabriela Mistral, Lucia's poetry rose like a luminous beacon, with rhythmic accents, and refined rhetoric. In front of the high priestess who trumpeted despair as a harbinger of death, the aristocrat of the vibrant word was opposed. Unlike Gabriela, Lucia's most sublime desire was to capture the beauty of the world or the mystery hidden in the smallest things.

But Lucia had her own opinion. Let's hear her words of praise for the winner of the Nobel Prize for Literature:

> "For that reason and for all the authenticity that Gabriela transmits of herself, her poetry is a living being and not a rhetorical and cerebral toy, hypertrophy of images, and atrophy of sensitivity. She is palpitating, vivid, spontaneous, unstoppable, boiling, and bitter at times, crystalline and simple at other moments, and always great and sincere." (Richard, 2004, page 576).

Everything suggests that trying to increase the listeners of her radio program and following the mainstream, Lucia Richard saw the convenience of dedicating a program to Gabriela Mistral. It is possible that Lucia had to decide between her way of thinking about poetry or ingratiating herself with a com-patriot Nobel Prize winner and leader of many feminists. If one adds the num-number of epithets that reveal adverse connotations to her figure throughout the broadcast, one might think that Lucia had reservations about the style of the famous poet.

As she expressed so well in her *Three Sonnets of Death* or *Desolation*, it was a style of high dramatic intensity. In these works, she dealt with the theme of mercy towards the suicide victim, loneliness, intimate pain, the sorrows of love, poverty, dry, and stony ground. This style was totally contrary to Lucia's. But as on many other occasions, the radio announcer left aside her personal feelings. She saw greatness in a tribute that benefited all Chilean culture[17].

Regarding Pablo Neruda, we saw above how she described him as an *"oppressive poet, Prometheus of modern times, iconoclast and destroyer of metrics to place the products of his fantasy..."* However, over the years, she exhibited a very different view of the famous poet on her radio show *Sweet Country of Pablo Neruda*. Now the author is much more serene and eclectic, much more flexible to new trends. Lucia began her speech, giving little importance to the political inclinations of the man or his participation in class struggles. The historical circumstances were passing, but the glorious poetry would remain.

If at first Neruda's darkness scandalized her, she questions now the sacrosanct classical rules, and intones the *"mea culpa."* The lack of understanding of his poetry was due to *"our incompetence and not to the apparent irrationality of what he said."* (Richard, 2004, page 577). Then she mentioned the apocalyptic prophecies, the *Dwellings of Saint Teresa*, Gongora, and Quevedo. All were as ingrained in our literature as they were obscure. She even mentioned

---

[17] We can find an example of this in her recently discovered article entitled "Who is Gonzalez Vera," published in *La Hora* in 1950. In that article, Lucia did not allude to the fact that the character was a radical leftist. Instead, she focused on praising the most representative of the work of the recently elected National Literature Prize. Although, she also launched a bit of irony by referring to the author's "Volterian smile," which also means "cynical and mocking impiety".

Garcia Lorca, who said that *"poetry requires a long initiation..."* (Richard, 2004, page 577).

Leaving behind the fear of the dark, a field that Lucia preferred not to enter, she now felt admiration for Neruda's use of the myth. It was not the Greco-Roman mythology that the immortal Chilean introduced in his work. It was a new mythology, an invented one, taken from the great American nature, the epic of the conqueror, the tragedy of the natives, the ruins of the disappeared civilizations. *"Even though we have to respect the nobility and ancestry of certain things, it's about time someone innovated!"* She said (Richard, 2004, page 577).

Lucia Richard now demystified or questioned certain expressive resources repeatedly used by classical poetry. Such was the case with the lark, the nightingale, and the dove. *"Are not the rest of God's creatures entitled?"* (Richard, 2004, page 577). He also extended this claim to the world of plants. Lucia implicitly referred to the recurrent use of the laurel, symbol of epic poetry, or ivy, a frequent motif in lyric poetry. With Neruda, a whole Latin American Noah's ark would raise its song, among them the queltehue, the loica, and the condor. Among the plants, lemon balms, boldos, and copihues would appear.

In another part of her work, Lucia had criticized the man locked up in a rapidly growing city. She had also opposed cities that developed in disorder, full of conflicts, profuse in spiritual and acoustic pollution. The machines and the race against time turned man into an automaton that went through life, like a domesticated animal. This city dweller was not interested in beautiful and vital things. In her work *Blue Smoke*, she even said, referring to this man: *"Rip out those eyes that don't see!"* Now, however, she seemed to have a different opinion.

Therefore, Lucia considered an innovation in Neruda his exploitation of the conquests of science, modern inventions, mechanization, gunpowder, bullets, railways, warehouses ... All this seemed to her worthy of being used in poetry, although she confessed that it was difficult for them to get used to these innovations. She also thought that our language was full of idiomatic twists. The language was developing as something living and changing, so it was time for someone to carry out this transformation. If her professor Nercasseau had been here listening to this it would have been a shock to him! She also high-lighted the patriotic aspect of Neruda, praising the figure of Jose Miguel Carrera. He was an aristocratic figure par excellence. All this, along with her verses dedicated to St. Martin and Bolivar, would form pages of great beauty (Richard, 2004, page 577).

Whether by popular acclaim or by her own conviction, Lucia reconsidered her previous opinion and tried to understand Neruda, which was an admirable advance. As we saw before, Lucia sympathized with figures like Jose Miguel Carrera, San Martin, Bolivar, and O'Higgins. They were national heroes who had helped bring Latin America together. She conceived these events as pro-foundly democratic.

Lucia's admiration for this beautiful "Ode to Jose Miguel Carrera" could lie in the patriotic aspect of the character. That makes sense since he was a figure who helped the independence of Chile. But perhaps it was the aristocratic side of the general that pleased her. This empathy was parallel to the one she felt for Bolivar and his dream of uniting the continent under a constellation of democratic republics. Carrera had a complex personality. He was a Mason whom Neruda called in his poem "the prince of the people." Yet, he assumed full powers to avoid political chaos. Neruda's support for this figure suggests the altruistic goals that guided him. Lucia's praise of this poem would mean that she aligned herself with this set of liberal ideas.

However, considering this issue from another angle, in Neruda, there is an important popular sublimation. Let's say an ideological bias that deserves analysis, and that Lucia preferred to ignore. But Lucia also made some clarifi-cations regarding Neruda. For example, she stated: *"Besides certain allusions to class struggles, it is very humane for him not to want to get rid of."* (Richard, 2004, page 578). In this "besides" lies much of the Nerudian conflict Lucia had.

Although she tried to reconcile herself with Neruda's writings and acknowledged some of his merits, in the end, Lucia Richard distanced herself from the modernist poet. His style did not fit her artistic conceptions. We do not know if that is good or bad, but in any case, it is a respectable position. As in the struggle between "culteranists" and "conceptists" in the Spanish Baroque, the poet closed ranks with the literary faction opposed to that of Neruda.

It was a rather conservative faction concerning grammar and its rules. Its members did not line up themselves with a surrealist way of making poetry. We may go even further, trying to understand why she condemned class struggles. The author felt uncomfortable with the politicization of poetry. Its ideal of purity and beauty she could not see as blackened, much less handled as a mere instrument of mass propaganda.

Lucia advocated the asepsis of lyric art. In assuming this position, she maintained an ideological point of view, opposing the detractors of that option. In Lucia, we can trace refined prose, which fixes its gaze on the beauties of this world. This is a place where happiness and harmony reign. In her poetry, the Creole literary movement and costumbrismo are absent (with occasional exceptions such as in "Fishermen's Life," "Peasant Sketches," "The Huaso," or some stories of *The Enigma*)

We could establish a comparison between Rosalia de Castro, a Galician poet from the last century, and Lucia Richard. Rosalia (1837-1885) was a writer who had social poetry and an existential one. In her social writings, although she came from a noble family, she concerned about the pain of the Galician people. She focused on the marginalized, the problem of emigration, poverty, the suffering of the peasant, the evil of others, and the relegated woman. All this helped to elevate her to the status of a myth after her death. Today, she embodies the soul of the Galician people. The famous poet also had existential poetry, which comprises a set of regrets and sorrows.

Lucia, on the other hand, except for some passages of slight melancholy, strove to pursue her desires and a state of happiness. Like the Galician feminist, she cared for the needs of women and children. However, in general, the Chilean poet was not interested in ordinary people but in the heart as a reflection of a global feeling. She did not identify with the rural people, but she did not judge them with the stately pride of Emilia Pardo Bazan. She simply omitted them.

Her poetry is intimate, and through it, she generously related her inner and personal world. But Lucia did not intend to conquer the feelings of other people, beyond her close acquaintances. Instead, she developed a role as a columnist, in which the poet described the most outstanding artists of her time. Lucia had a sense of others, through which she conquered spiritual excellence. Yet, it is unlikely that she would find this kind of perfection in the feelings of ordinary Chileans. It is a rather bourgeois version of literature.

When we speak of bourgeois literature, we should not understand this term as pejorative. Nor does it mean that this literature has no quality. It is enough to analyze Balzac's work and especially his *Comédie Humaine*, to realize how exquisite this literature is. In Lucia's case, she spread her thought with a degree of delicacy, craftsmanship, and purity, comparable to that of the glassmakers. Behind her elegant art, we can glimpse a comfortable life without hardships, but not one that is given away or easy on a spiritual level.

Her prose is elegant in using adjectives, but not hedonistic. She was never interested in enjoying the comfort of bourgeois life. Rather, she refused to accumulate material goods, and opposed snobbery. The poet found her rightful place in the sublime and generous simplicity of nature. Therefore, we can only speak here in part about bourgeois literature.

Her writings tend towards order, moral integrity, and the absence of lower passions or unbridled ideas. They also reflect a value system based on religious education. But, this mystical aura of her work is not alien to other poets of her generation either. In any case, it is a literature that has the lack or the virtue - it depends on whom - of not being reconciled with popular sensibility or with a standardized feeling of life.

In Neruda, we see a conscience cracked by a universal drama, the perennial struggle of an oppressed people, a memory of the impoverished, an evocation of human pain, a ship loaded with dreams that nevertheless sinks. It is a vision perhaps more infamous, but also more realistic of man's destiny and his circumstances. As such, it permeated the masses, representing the medicine that came to heal Chile's great wounds.

Pablo Neruda was one of the greatest literary personalities that universal history engendered. His invasion of realms is certainly orchestral. His cosmogonies are so vast that any attempt to delimitate them seem irrational. He is a living metamorphosis, mythopoetic giant, boiling sap of the earth, a hidden heartbeat in the thicket, transvestite of the form, space-time violator, meta-phorical orgasm, an embryo that sleeps eternally in amniotic waters, a reciter of unconsciousness, and the pain of a thousand births. He is also a prehistoric, pre-literary, pre-human man; an anthropomorphic creature, the one who aus-cultate of all that exists; ambassador of distant stars, interpreter of eternities, seeker of light and darkness, a synaesthetic orgy of the concept and mysteri-ous spawn of nature. All that and much more is Pablo Neruda. Any attempt to define man diminishes his human stature and ours.

Pablo Neruda (1904-1973) in an evocative street graffiti

Another article that confirms what Lucia Richard thought about the rules of poetry was "The Conferences of Alberto Hidalgo." Lucia had gone to the Mu-nicipal Theatre to listen to the poet's lectures. There, the Peruvian exhorted before an expectant audience a new theory: Literary Modernism. According to him, we should remove all musicality from the verse, stripping it of rhythm and rhyme. These were true obstacles to inspiration. We had to reduce the poem to its purest expression: the metaphor.

Lucia recognizes that rhyme lends beauty to form, but it often becomes an obstacle to inspiration. However, she argues that rhythm is innate to man and imposes some discipline on the verse. Rhythm embodies the triumph of order over disorder. This cadence saves effort and gives effectiveness to movement. Therefore, the poet believes that pure poetry, without bonds or frames, would become a wild horse, like a torrent without channels. It would be anything but art, since art, in her opinion, conveys the polished beauty of forms. That "difficult ease of making art" was its greatest charm and what made it last.

Reading the following paragraph, we can perfectly understand why Lucia Richard had so much difficulty in aligning herself with modernist (or more precisely post-modernist) poets, among whom we can include Pablo Neruda and Gabriela Mistral:

> "To deprive poetry of some of its musical elements is to reduce it to an exciting brain game, to a coquetry of the spirit. In doing so, we take away all the emotion; all the cordial warmth that the poem transmits to the reader and makes him vibrate. It turns the verse into a game of wits or a myriad of inventions that flatter the vanity of the writer but do not reach the heart of the listener." (Richard, 2004, page 534).

An example of her social or general interest articles is "Rebel Youth." Here, she masterfully mediates between two groups in permanent conflict: the young and the old. It is only through her ability to observe that Lucia understands the virtues and defects of both sides. Far from putting one group above the other, she conducts an ingenious literary debate between the antagonists, finding solutions so that both would have a better future. Analyzing her judgments, we can also observe the attributes of her personality.

What is really at stake is change versus tradition, progress in the face of stagnation, innovation against conformism, creativity versus *dolce far niente.* This dispute is ancient and already had significant implications in the Age of Enlightenment. On the one hand, there were the encyclopedists, in favor of overthrowing a tradition infected with superstition. On the other hand, the scholastics were opposed to any scientific advance that did not comply with the Holy Scriptures. In time, this struggle ended in the secularization of society, producing a profound transformation of its ideological foundations, now inspired by the new cult of reason.

However, in Lucia's interpretation, this power struggle does not seem to lead to an ideological confrontation. It would rather be a clash of attitudes, an emancipation of the will, and a search for self-affirmation. We can also read it as a liberation of young people from the domination exercised by their alter egos.

The young man, swinging on the plates of the Goddess of Justice, had the vice of letting himself be carried away by the indigestion of the data provided by books, being blinded by the brilliance of technique. He had an enormous appetite for erudition but forgot to think for himself and create a philosophy of life. In his eagerness to reach high horizons, he became a great emulator, looking for models and heroes to reflect upon. Meanwhile, he imitated the fashion trends of costumes and customs, which, according to Lucia, created "a standard and repellent type."

This last statement allows us to delve into new facets of Lucia. If in other poems, she had spoken with disdain of the uneducated masses and their inability to see the greatness of the smallest things, now her sting penetrated the banal, ignorant, and materialistic people. They lived only to adorn themselves and could not go deeper into the true meaning of things. Fashion would be at the center of this reproach, whose proselytes would be frivolous men and women, the bourgeois snob, the young.

Ignorance is an evil that has no social origin. This repulsion to the homogenization of society brings as a counterpart an exaltation of the uniqueness of human beings. This rejection seems to praise the genius and artist. With the power of his creative mind, he can free the human spirit from the limitations that oppress it. It doesn't matter if these obstacles come from his origin, social environment, gender, country, century, continent, creed, ideology...

This myopia and lack of introspection make the young man look for support in the masses, in the guild, to hide the distrust in himself. Intuitive and visceral, he has difficulty controlling his impulses. In that tragic ardor, he ends up losing time, health, and possibilities. The older man, on the other hand, is pragmatic, analytical, skeptical, and distrustful, which makes him live in a routine prison. In his extreme selfishness, he tyrannizes the young man by silencing his voice, "filing the claws of his greatness." He sacrifices the beauty of his passion for a space of security, which often becomes tedious hypocrisy.

She praised the generous attitude of the young people, ready to be persuaded by the eloquence of their elders. They induced them to do great deeds, and in their audacity, they despised a danger that they ignored. Finally, she assessed the pros and cons of both groups, providing solutions for a perfect coexistence. Thus, Lucia affirmed that *"to change is to be human, to stagstagnate is to make a caricature of God."*

This last thought reveals that Lucia Richard was not a regressive, puritan woman anchored in class prejudice. To some extent, she was a dissident or at least a critic of her social group, always willing to learn and evolve. She showed an inexhaustible curiosity, ready to solve new enigmas at every step. This struggle between vice and virtue, past and future, ends in the latter's victory. Lucia seems to support this progress. But because of her shyness, fear of being censored, or out of conviction, she did not always fight enough for this change. Nor did she expand her rich personality in all its nuances (Richard, 1955).

Lucia Richard deeply admired the Italian Renaissance, a period of history that fascinated her. After some fourteen centuries since the death of the Redeemer, in which man had lived immersed in obscurantism and mortification, condemned under the weight of original sin, the gaze turned to classical antiquity. This new era was a pagan rebirth, a resurgence of mythology, a liberation from ecclesiastical authority, discredited by notorious papal scandals. The man now occupied the center of the universe and not God. Lucia was enthusiastic about this optimism, shown in many works of art and manifestations of the spirit.

The Renaissance was a powerful movement. It meant openness to the intransigence and dominance of thought exercised by the Church. Besides, it was a time of schisms. Scholars and priests questioned the orthodoxy of Catholic dogma and the unity of the Church. Erasmus opposed these questions in his writings, as did Luther, irritated by papal excesses. Angry about the extortion of money through indulgences, he advocated a return to early Christianity.

It is also a time when doctrines such as Epicureanism -living life with pleasure-, or Neoplatonism -love for women- are being reborn. Intellectuals extolled love and read Petrarch and other Greco-Roman authors. Gutenberg invented the printing press, and there were significant advances in medicine, anatomy, music, architecture, and the way people controlled time. During this huge crisis in Christianity, art flourished as never before.

In her article "On the Fourth Centenary of Michelangelo," Lucia showed her rapture at the beauty and restlessness of the Renaissance. She focused on Michelangelo's David, a work that transported her. The poet felt a certain paroxysm before the soul, the passion, and the suffering of the inert marble. Under the hand of the genius, it came to life, throbbing within its material shell. To this David, she dedicated some words that, even out of context, bring us closer to what Lucia thought about progress and youth. All these ideas allow us to go a little deeper into the author's mind:

> "The willful gesture, the clenched fist, and the calm brow are the imposing features of David. Always ready to throw his stone, he represents the faithful effigy of our youth and that of the world. They are ready to challenge the Goliaths who, since the beginning of time, have stood up against the progress of Humanity." (Richard, 1964).

Another interesting article to understand Lucia Richard's spirit is "Life, Passion, and Death of the Portrait." In it, the author discusses the different stages in the evolution of the portrait. Her journey begins in the Renaissance, which produced the most accurate representation of the genre. Then, it gradually deteriorated by introducing technical elements in Baroque, Romanticism, Impressionism, dying totally with abstract art.

Therefore, what is really at stake here is whether the artist's subjective participation in the creation of his work can overlap or coexist with the faithful representation of the model, or if this interference can destroy the personality of the person portrayed. Let us not forget that the neo-classics - who were the ones Lucia seemed to follow - believed in the objectivity of art. For a long time in the history of art, artists questioned whether they should represent the portrayed person with his or her defects and miseries or if they could idealize the character.

We can ask ourselves if it is we who contemplate the portrayed person or if it is he who looks at us. To what extent do we influence, with our particular way of looking, the transformation of the recreated model? Could I interpret and therefore alter Lucia's authentic personality? Or is it she who, through this interaction, beyond time and space, is modifying mine?

Lucia began her presentation by pointing out that during the Renaissance, the portrait had reached its peak. This portrait was an individual expression that tried to capture the fleeting nature of an instant or gesture - the rictus - by recreating the image of a proud man. He is a renewed man, who has discovered himself and freed himself from the moralizing stigmas of the past. It's about capturing the emotion of the face with its worries, concerns, malice, and passions. What matters now is the character's mood or psychological disposition. The wonderful portraits of Giotto, Leonardo, Titian, and Raphael emerge. *The Giaconda* would be the most resonant work of art in all Christianity.

Painters such as Dürer, Holbein, Velazquez, El Greco, and Ribera exported the Renaissance portrait to Flanders, Germany, and Spain. In doing so, they gave rise to those willing, sensual, or mystical faces of their time. It is the most serious and profound attempt to reveal the human soul, to make it tangible and visible through its gestures and expressions. Lucia makes us see that beauty was not always the priority. Alongside the beautiful ladies, there were also the old, the dwarves, the beggars, and the deformed. This modality was defined as counter-portrait and characterized by the absence of idealization.

For Lucia, this time synthesized the apotheosis of the portrait. Painters brought the human figure to the canvas. They painted a confident man who felt at the center of the universe, and the genre reached its highest splendor. This man was no longer satisfied with the afterlife and wanted to seek his immortality here on earth. This period enhanced the vision of the man for himself, with no additives or superfluous attributes. The church, the court, or the high nobility could commission the portrait, in which the individualized man was the undisputed protagonist.

The artist's sensitivity was important in bringing out the character's interiority. But this sensitivity will not distort the temperament of the person portrayed. Painters will follow this principle with some exceptions. For example, we find the case of Arcimboldo, with his superimpositions of fruits and vegetables, or the anamorphic portraits produced through advances in optics.

Little by little, this uniqueness of the person portrayed faded in time. In the Baroque period, refinement prevailed. The need to highlight the social position of the patron was also of major significance. The look or the gesture was no longer of particular interest. Chiaroscuro took over the whole canvas. Some people stood out for the sumptuousness of their clothes and the artifice. In doing so, they showed ostentation and theatricality. Now the portrait enjoyed progressive democratization. It became no longer the exclusive prerogative of the privileged classes but covered the entire social spectrum.

With romanticism, the landscape was added as a complement to man. The hero and the impersonal nude emerged. With Impressionism, it would not be the gesture, or the personality, the most important elements of the canvas, but the plays of light and color. The portraitist painted portraits more than ever, including self-portraits. There was an academic liberation that sometimes approached caricature.

According to Lucia, this process of degeneration and loss of human uniqueness continued with the arrival of the masses. The man became confused in his amorphism, and the group appeared in the murals, as in the Middle Ages. The crowd with its impressive anonymity always predominated. The world went beyond the private world of man, where he used to confine his personality (Richard, 1956).

With the arrival of the 20th century, a stylistic revolution took place. This change led to the collapse of academic standards and rigid principles of realism. A strong charge of renewal was imposed. Its proponents advocated a vision of reality with new plastic forms and values. It was a century of exhibitions, travels, and publications that involved a rich exchange of ideas.

It was also the century of psychoanalysis, in which the portrait became a tool to reveal the darkest areas of the human soul. The artist's inner visions reigned over his work. The relationships between shapes, colors, lines, and planes mattered more than the actual figure or his feelings. For many, these distortions and freedoms of the artist were not capricious. They turned out to be the vehicles to achieve a more faithful representation of the person portrayed.

Lucia Richard was totally opposed to all this disfigurement, which for her summed up the "death of the portrait." In her mind, this transfiguration encompassed abstract art. And although she did not mention it, it also included Fauvism, Cubism, Expressionism, Futurism, Abstraction, Surrealism, and even Pop Art. The stereotype was now a pluralistic man, competing with his environment, prevailing trends, and the passage of time. The portrait would enter the twilight. Abstract representations looked at the subconscious and deciphered the artist's dreams. He gave us a transcription of his restlessness, instead of transferring the sublimated image from the model to the canvas.

Therefore, with these thoughts, Lucia defined herself again as a classical person who believed in the purity of form, simplicity, and nobility of academic standards. These ideas brought out their best representation in the Renaissance portrait. For Lucia, everything was superfluous except man himself and his deepest feelings. She abhorred anything that did not come from man's genuine emotions. In those emotions was the true, rich, and immeasurable personality. There the true identity, the immortal entity, of the ontological being was expanded. And it needed no adornments or artifices to adulterate its true nature.

The greatest horror for the poet was the arrival of the masses, speed, and machines. In these elements, she finds parallels with the atomic age and all its destructive power. Once again, she denounces the "reification of man," the loss of his spirituality and uniqueness. This man was confused in the ignorant mass, diluted in the unifying power of the anonymous as opposed to the originality of the authentic. Abstract art would represent the apex of a series of degenerative processes that cooperated in this loss of identity.

Once again, we are witnessing the struggle between progress and regression, what we can preserve, or must change. In this cyclical environment of history, every person interprets the most transcendent part of his reality. It should be noted that the Renaissance was also an innovation with respect to an earlier era. Under this perspective, every thought, trend, or idea is anachronistic. Every movement, epoch, style, is valid and old-fashioned at the same time. The word is self-explanatory: Renaissance means rebirth.

We find an echo of these ideas on her radio program *Painting News*. In it, she commented on an exhibition of thirty-two works by artists from the Americas that was being held at the Museum of Fine Arts in Santiago. By way of introduction, she denounced the lack of originality of the Chilean painting environment. For years it had revolved around neo-impressionism, expressionism, and surrealism. These were styles that Lucia did not appreciate, especially the last two. She then developed these ideas further in the following paragraph:

"Painting goes through a theatrical period. Artists represent many exacerbated images to produce sensations to scandalize the bourgeois. But the bourgeois is very intelligent and has entered art through snobbery, and is not afraid of anything. Surrealism can paint furniture on trees, as Salvador Dali did. Even more, it can depict faceless orthopedic mannequins, which hug each other. Such is the case with Giorgio de Chirico's painting entitled *Hector and Andromache*. But the bourgeois, far from being afraid, declares that he understands them." (Richard, 2004, page 602).

Here we find two interesting elements. First, the intense repugnance Lucia felt for surrealism. It was a pictorial movement that subverted all the ideals that had hitherto formed the canon of beauty. It also became an agent who invaded the purity of the rational soul. Secondly, we see her pejorative judgment of the bourgeois, especially the snobs. They were cooperators in all this transgression of values, and the breakdown of beauty.

Later, in the same program, she praised the neoclassical painting *Return at Night* by the Venezuelan Hector Poleo. It was a work that was fully in tune with her artistic sensibility. Besides, the painting was far from realism. The artist painted it in the Italian way, with solid human drawings, normal figures, and a well-structured composition. In her opinion, this work breathed a well-done neo-Renaissance intellectualism, full of poetic suggestion and plasticity.

She was much less eloquent with Mexicans Diego Rivera and Clemente Orozco. Although she valued Rivera's painting *Girl in a Checkered Dress* as an exponent of a race, she became ironic with Orozco. She thanked him for not using the macabre theme in his work, *Cemetery*. These Mexican muralists did not attract her for many reasons.

The main one was the necrophilia that showed the Mexican art of this time. It embodied an explicit evocation of the bloodthirsty Aztec worldview. Ritual sacrifices, bones, skulls, and other apocalyptic visions were everywhere. No less shocking for Lucia was the muralism, which represented the group, with its consequent loss of human individuality. In this art, she saw a prodigious confusion of elements, which transformed the aesthetic equidistance or the ideal of beauty, into an unrestrained movement. It also brought an ideological message to the painting and a permanent defense of the indigenous.

From the Brazilian Candido Portinari, Lucia commented on the painting *Returning from the Fair*. More than a painting, she said it was a poster, pointing out the following:

"Those who return from the fair are nightmarish beings, disheveled heads, and ghostly figures." (Richard, 2004, page 603).

Lucia did not like ravings, violence, confusion, irrationality. Once again, we can confirm this in her praise of the work of the American Karl Zerc, entitled *The Harlequin*, which she defined as follows:

"This painting offers pure plastics without theatrical influences, imaginative reflections, or outdated literature. It simply shows shapes and colors, something so simple and yet so difficult to paint." (Richard, 2004, page 603).

Finally, she thought that her compatriot Israel Roa represented them with dignity with his canvas *The Painter's Birthday*. It stood out for the beauty of its tonalities, the modulation of the color chords, and the spontaneity of the execution (Richard, 2004, page 603). Once again, we see how Lucia finds her space in placidity, symmetry, proportion, and aesthetic unity. This choice implies some values, which transmit serenity, beauty, rapture, transport of the soul, and meditation. In any case, this position is legitimate and perfectly understandable.

But that doesn't mean that new artistic trends weren't important. The evocation of discoveries in psychology, new philosophies, and prevailing trends prove it. Moreover, the recovery of the indigenous, alienated, or worse, disappeared identity for years, was crucial. Clemente Orozco became interested in universal values. He was eager to recreate a man who would control his freedom and destiny. And he did so beyond the conditioning factors of history, religion, or technology.

In her study entitled "Art," which belongs to her 1924 poetry collection *Sursum Corda*, Lucia defined art. She established a set of principles, wondering if art could have rules. She said:

"Above all, the goal of art in the reproduction of beauty cannot be mundane. To reproduce life is not the main aim of art, but to reproduce it with beauty. Every work of art must have that divine radiance called inspiration. We must show the reality of life with its virtues and defects, as the lights and shadows come together in a picture, giving us a sense of reality. A certain spiritual elevation must go along with physical or moral nakedness. It is impossible for me to conceive a bad-natured artist, a creator without feelings or rude of spirit."

"When I talk about works of art, I always think of sincerity. If people forget them in their personal relationships, much more happens in artistic creation. Anyone who appreciates something must seek its perfection in his inner self. What do schools, teachers, and models matter in the face of the natural inclination, vocation, instinct, which deep down advises, persuade, and imposes?" (Richard, 1925, pp. 81-87).

The eloquence of these arguments surprises and convinces, because of the simplicity of the exposition and the equity of what was expressed. For Lucia, art was beauty, sincerity, good feelings, spiritual elevation, and a glimpse of the divine. Moreover, in this passage, it is intuition as opposed to any academic dogmatism. The grotesque, mannerist, excessively ornate, deformed, hyperbolic, did not fit with what Lucia conceived as art. The author pursued absolute purity, mystical communion with nature, universal harmony, a Pythagorean world order. In her opinion, only an honest artist could reach this state.

The following paragraphs of the same article classify the most significant defects of the artist: vanity, the pursuit of easy applause, and flattering triumph. All this caused him to germinate an attitude of mimicry towards temtemporal styles, producing academic verses and anemic literature. Art without frankness, without intellectual honesty, could only become a mannered vulgarity or a servile imitation (Richard, 1925, pp. 81-87).

In the fifties, on her radio show *Talking about Art. Chronicles of Art*, she explained what she thought art was:

"Art is the only thing in these times of mechanization, and specializations can prevent the disintegration of the human being. It is the only thing that when we face ourselves, it reveals our true essence..." (Richard, 2004, page 555).

Lucia published an article in *El Mercurio* on March 18, 1956, entitled "Reflections on Art." In it, she not only manifested her interest in psychology but also reflected again on the meaning of art. Here we witness new aspects of her character, such as "indignation" and "irritability." These contradictory traits of her peaceful personality very rarely emerged. We can only explain their appearance as a visceral reaction to some of the statements of the psychoanalyst Dr. Edmund Bergler.

The specialist had declared in London in one of his books that literature was the symptom of neurosis and that there were no normal artists or writers. Reading this statement, Lucia felt like a fumigated insect. And so she expressed her anger against the poison of those who wrote trivialities. If this were so, Lucia thought, all the creators of beauty, the interpreters of humanity, the bastions of social consciousness, would be abnormal and hysterical beings. According to this statement, all writers, poets, artists, painters, musicians, sculptors... those who guided spiritual progress and dignified the human species were maniacs.

Lucia went on to point out that the London psychiatrist seemed to confuse normality with mediocrity. Any attempt at self-improvement, and search for an ideal, whether religious, philosophical, or scientific, implied in the Dr.'s vision a psychological tare. He conceived it as an evasion of people who took refuge in the art to escape from their ghosts and petty concerns (Richard, 1956).

We can't say that this is totally untrue. For example, it is a well-known fact that non-communicative, social, and individualistic people are prone to mental hyperactivity. Beethoven, deaf most of his life, was a great misanthrope. However, Schubert was an extrovert, given to social gatherings in his home. These have gone down in history as "schubertiades," and no one denies the musician his status as a great artist.

Some believe that behind Bosch's immense creativity, there was a schizophrenic disease. Michelangelo was unruly, irritable, violent with his collaborators, and self-destructive with his work and also a genius. He lost his mother when he was six, which makes you think a lot. Plato said there could be no genius without mania, associating certain doses of madness with talent.

Saturn is the planet of melancholy. Since ancient times, scholars believed that under this planet, there were poets, philosophers, hermits, older men, loners, sad, melancholic, and fools. However, they also held that those under its influence possessed extraordinary powers. The Saturnines - hence the etymological origin of the word - had superior intelligence and a subtle memory. These qualities gave them access to transcendence. There was some vehemence in creative inspirations and deep ecstasies.

Saturn is a changing, ambiguous star, fed by light and darkness. It's also a planet of extremes, which favors visionary experiences. Taking these elements into account, we can say that Van Gogh had high psychic imbalances. But both Mozart and Picasso were strongly supported by their respective parents. One was a chapel teacher, the other a drawing teacher. Yet, we cannot see any childhood trauma in these artists or any other disabilities. The subject is controversial, debatable, and quite dense.

In her radio show, *Psychoanalysis in Art*, Lucia meditated much more serenely on these issues. This radio broadcast was the result of a visit that Lucia made to the Salon Caveau of the French Bookstore. There she heard a talk by Dr. Gallinato precisely on "Psychoanalysis in Art." So, she based her presentation on this lecture. Lucia began her program by emphasizing that the speaker reported on an exciting work by Dr. Andre Anne on Shakespeare and complexes.

According to him, the theatre of the great Englishman advanced what scientists and philosophers study in modern psychology. The Oedipus complex or mother worship would possess Hamlet, causing him to behave in an unstable manner. In Othello, we can recognize the person with epilepsy. King Lear announced early dementia. All this would confirm that the English playwright was a keen observer of reality. He enriched this quality with his poetic instinct, which allowed him to stage his amazing productions.

Freud had died in 1939. Everything related to psychoanalysis was then in vogue, and his theory penetrated wide branches of knowledge. Among them, art found new ways of interpretation. Freud had studied Leonardo da Vinci. The famous artist was a natural son separated from his father until the age of seven. This fact made him focus on his mother all the emotional power of his soul. It would be this emotional break-up that drove the genius of the multi-faceted man. The attachment to the mother became the impetus that produced the wonderful image of the Mona Lisa. Finally, Dr. Gallinato emphasized the importance of early childhood education. In his opinion, the first four years of a child's life decide his entire future life (Richard, 2004, page 208).

In this radio program, Lucia exposed these ideas without questioning their veracity, giving only hints of her opposition to art being a product of complexes. However, in her article "Reflections on Art," she was much more categorical regarding this controversy. In her way of thinking,

> "Humanity is indebted to the artist or writer, who, by creating works of art, creates a universal language. It is a new Esperanto that unites peoples and individuals, even if separated by religion, ideas, or social conditions."

This is a beautiful message of brotherhood that we must keep in our minds to face what is to come. According to Lucia:

> "When it comes to art, the feeling is the common denominator. We all experience general rejoicing in the contemplation of beauty. Art softens the mood and makes human coexistence possible. Symmetry or rhythm helps

order and harmony. A clear expression of thought makes history and philosophy understandable."

"The beauty instinct cooperates with nature in its work of natural selection. It presides over the deep mystery of sex. Without it, the human species would have fallen into degeneration. The strength and vigor of the race would never be at odds with the beauty instinct. A general principle states that when love is free, it attracts beauty. Moreover, beauty and health unite in their path to perfecting human species." (Richard, 1956).

In this last paragraph, Lucia spread a risky thought. It has been the reason for the historical division between geneticists and biologists, on the one hand, and moralists and guarantors of social equality, on the other. In natural selection, the strongest survive thanks to greater adaptability to the environment. This versatility provides an advantage that individuals pass on to their offspring. Lucia created a parallel between the "beauty instinct," sex, natural selection, the vigor of the breed, and its perfection. And so she concludes that the immanence between these elements is such that if they did not exist, the human species would have fallen into rapid degeneration.

This reasoning is a dangerous thought that has compromised eminent biologists. It has done so by speaking of superiority, predetermination, and pre-eminence, even if they based on scientific criteria. Lucia perhaps only wanted to talk about aesthetic issues, but the text is open to confusion. It is true that in Darwinian terms, this idea of the link between the vigor of the race and beauty makes some sense. But we must consider whether it is desirable to extrapolate it to human society or whether, on the contrary, it is a controversial idea. It is an argument that does not help the brotherhood of peoples, as so many feminists advocate. The beautiful or the handsome survive, and the ugly or the unsightly degenerate. This message seems to be the one Lucia wanted to convey. Whether it is true or not, it implies a rigid vision of the concept of beauty and a certain social iniquity.

But maybe we're misinterpreting her words. Lucia would not have referred to the vigor of one race over another, but to the strength within each race. If so, "the beauty instinct" would act as a competitive factor that would function as a selector that provides vigor within each specific race. But by introducing the term "human species" as an integrative element of all races, the issue is subject to debate. It would have been preferable if Lucia had not entered such a muddy terrain.

Therefore, Lucia bases the success of art on the beauty of its lines, its noble ideals, and everything inherent to it. In conclusion, she finds a parallel between art and the vigor of the breed. Art survives because it is beautiful. So, beauty is art, and art is only beauty. To explain this complex question, we must define what art and beauty are. Is the gloomy atmosphere of ordinary people painted by Van Gogh art or beauty? Is the disheveled madman or the blind guitarist painted by Picasso, works of art or beauty? Are the raggedy children painted by Ribera also art? Are they beautiful? Can we only worship beauty and perfection? Can we eliminate degeneration?

What is degeneration? Does it make any sense to sublimate the beautiful and condemn the ugly? As in the case of Beauty and the Beast, can't the good feelings of the monster prevail over his repugnance? Should we segregate the old by his decrepitude and worship the young by his grace and charm? Should we exult in human nature all the positive, beautiful, and luminous adjectives in the dictionary? Should we marginalize from it the terms with negative, dark or unpleasant connotations? We have already seen how, in the 20th century, there was a reaction against the traditional concept of beauty. Moreover, many scholars have defined modern art as unsightly.

Can beauty be equated with virtue? Should we value beauty only by aesthetic parameters? Are we satisfied with proportionate and symmetrical images or harmonic sounds? Is beauty a mathematical structure, comparable to the golden number, found in many works of art and productions of nature? For Aquinas, beauty is a splendor of goodness and what pleases the eye. Should we judge everything by its appearance, or should we delve into its spiritual meaning? Would Lucia be right in relating the "instinct of beauty" to the vigor of the race? Would Beethoven be right when he said that if order and beauty shine in the constitution of the world, there is God? Let the sharp reader answer these questions.

It must be acknowledged that in Lucia's work, there are some slips or uninspired passages. This lapse is not the only one; there were others. All writers have them. In *Defenses of Man*, she spoke again of "natural selection," exposing a particular way of conceiving the Malthusian disproportion between individuals and resources, now applied to man:

> "...in war, natural selection does not eliminate the weakest and most incapable. That's because the youngest in each country are the ones who go to the battlefields. We must consider that the highest mortality and weakening has occurred among white men. They were a select minority of humanity, which means that the best of the best have perished. This paradox produced by war, instead of having eliminated the excess population, has weakened the active forces, which are the nerve of all production" (Richard, ca 1960).

The most significant thing in this paragraph is that Lucia said that the best died in the war, claiming that they belonged to the white race. Instead of understanding each other, they had fought each other, without eliminating the excess population, that is, the worst. Therefore, this had weakened the ruling class that controlled the means of production. This thinking is conservative and contradicts many democratic ideas present in her work.

In 1933, upon her arrival in Rome and other cities in northern Italy, she let herself be carried away by the emotion of the moment. She lost historical perspective, making some statements that diminished her intellectual authority. Mussolini's regime impressed the author, who set out his political program. Lucia never praised such a regime, but she did describe the political atmosphere of the moment. Her eagerness was informative, and she spoke of order, organization, discipline, being stunned by the political effervescence that surrounded her. On March 19, 1934, she wrote the following in her book *Travel Memories*:

> "... in our country, people fight, slander, plagiarize and caricature fascism, but they don't ignore it." (Richard, Travel Memories, 1934).

Many newspapers published these allusions, which show that Lucia was not afraid of being censored. On the other side of the ocean was her audience, supporting some of these pronouncements. The reader's acceptance of these ideas reveals the "ethos" of conservative Chilean society.

These ideas are difficult for a modern European to assimilate. But we cannot look at Lucia with contemporary eyes. The artist was a woman of the time, a country, a continent, and her social group. If the author had been born in France, she would have been a first-rate talent. But her personality developed in a conservative, prejudiced, and excessively patriarchal environment. A great rigidity in customs, education, and family traditions were the norm. Lucia overcame her education, progressing and conquering. But she could not free herself from everything.

Her father, Enrique Richard Fontecilla, was a prestigious jurist, an eminence in the Congress, leader of the Conservative Party, and a member of the Council of State. He collaborated in the foundation of the Pontifical Catholic University, where he held a chair of Civil Law. Besides, he belonged to a multitude of religious institutions. The notorious statesman was a self-made man endowed with precious virtues: disciplined, orderly, a fervent believer, and an impeccable moral rectitude. Mr. Richard was also compassionate to the needy and a great man. Therefore, we can object that he had a profile that rivaled that of a complete intellectual. We might think so if we did not know that he was also a "powerful philosopher."

When he died on May 13, 1912, there was a great commotion among his contemporaries. They took his body to the cathedral, where his colleagues gave solemn speeches and praised his figure: a myth was born. Lucia was only eleven years old. After his disappearance, his family venerated him beyond measure. Even after his death, his family had great respect for him. He was an exemplary man, immaculate in his habits, truly unique. Throughout her adolescence, the ghost of her father haunted her like a huge colossus. This giant hero settled on her conscience, directing her actions. Moreover, everybody remembered him over the years.

Therefore, Lucia lived her first youth affected by the intense greatness of a notorious man. It is an evocative situation for a girl who was still forming her personality and ideas. His early disappearance left a deep impression on his daughter, who immediately picked up the legacy of all the ethical-moral values of the absent father. This legacy of Christian inspiration permeated her work, but it did not prevent Lucia from striving to explore other frontiers of thought.

Enrique Richard Fontecilla
(1865-1912).
Distinguished parliamentarian

She once spoke of Sarah Hübner, as a person destroyed by the social restrictions of her environment and her family. But this is out of place in the case of Lucia, who always moderated her horizons and expectations.

Enrique Richard Fontecilla was not only an exemplary statesman, and a believer, but also a man of the world. He had a perfect command of the French language. According to his biographers, to the figure of the public man, we must add his private side. It is in that sphere that he revealed himself as an accomplished artist and scholar, a musician and painter of the word. He received an ancient classical education at the Seminary of Valparaiso. Its library contained the prayers of Cicero, the odes of Horace, the stories of Caesar, and the tragedies of Shakespeare. Richard became a profound connoisseur of Latin literature and a devourer of English magazines (Gonzalez Cerda & Casanova, 1913, page 125).

Other chronicles describe Henry Richard as a very bright and happy man. He loved to meet in the evenings with his friends to talk and read literature, including Dickens. He also showed signs of being a man of refined tastes, treasuring many paintings in his living room. Among them, we must include one by Carlo Brancaccio that reflected the Bay of Naples (Fernandez Richard, ca 2000, page 7). For Lucia, her father was an immense monument of reverence, respect, and a model of virtue. But it was also a stimulus from which she inherited a transcendent intelligence. In the long run, this allowed her to reflect with an open mind on the great mysteries of life.

Trying to clarify the polarities of the intellect, we find an echo of these ideas in the Spanish Enlightenment. In this period, there were two groups in permanent conflict. On the one hand, the so-called "innovators," doctors and scientists, fought for the opening up of society, breaking with the inherited tradition. They wanted to carry out an empirical renewal, stripping the university of fables and superstitions. On the other hand, the "scholastics" believed in the truth underlying the Holy Scriptures. Creationism was the backbone of all knowledge.

Faced with these two groups arose what has been called the "Christian Enlightenment," which came to be a middle way between the earlier two. It was, therefore, a group that wanted progress, that aspired to transform things, but not at the cost of knocking down the earlier tradition. By situating Lucia in our 20th century, I place her on that middle path. This is how Carolina Andonie Dracos, a journalist from *El Mercurio,* portrayed her on 30 December 2004: *"The writer who transgressed the canons without breaking them."* (2004).

Lucia opposed almost all "isms": surrealism, cubism, existentialism, modernism, resistentialism. She even despised psychoanalysis, at least in its way of conceiving artistic creation. André Breton had defined surrealism as *"the expression of thought in the absence of any control exercised by reason."* Henri Bergson had declared that *"sleep is the complete mental life because, during sleep, there is no tension."* Lucia opposed these ideas and believed in the need to control the artistic process and subject it to certain rules.

With this way of thinking, she approached Vicente Huidobro, who reduced the surrealists to the status of improvisers. He believed that poetic creation required vigilance, full awareness, a lucid, and supreme effort. *"You have reduced poetry to the banality of a spiritualist trick,"* he once said (Huidobro, year XI, 1956). However, from another perspective, Huidobro broke the usual forms of the metric. The poet adopted free verse without rhyme or rhythm. He also created a new literary movement called "creationism." He encouraged the development of phrases without punctuation, poems composed of single words, experiments with typography, and other innovative effects (Silva Castro, 1961, page 89).

Our artist wasn't exactly a romantic. She did not exalt love in her writings as Jane Austen, or Gustavo Adolfo Becquer did. Not even in the form of disdain or loss as Gabriela Mistral did. In her writings, we can find maternal love, filial love, but rarely the love of a couple. She was a pure and chaste woman. Her style is not anacreontic. Her literary effects place the values of a Vestal over those of a Bacchante. Nothing lewd, or profane, stains her work. She was shy, reserved, and preferred to be a spectator rather than a performer.

Lucia lived absent in eternal contemplation, but she did not lock herself in her ivory tower. She rarely practiced irony or satire. She did not slander, parody, or lose her temper. One could say that moral sense, seriousness, order, blushing, glide over her writings. On the contrary, her eagerness to throw herself into literature gave her the confidence she needed in life. We can also find in her prose much tenderness, sweetness, hope, high sensitivity to all manifestations of art, and a great love for nature.

This general appreciation does not prevent from notable exceptions which, like gentle caresses, also reveal to us the nuances of an epicurean nature. So in "Roses," we can read:

"Smiling mouths of beautiful women, / inextinguishable fire that does not extinguish the air, / beam of hearts of burning desires, / are the reddish roses." (Richard, 1925, 49).

In "Forgive me, Lord," we come across the following verses:

"Forgive me, Lord, if I love the earth / and place my love in things, / you planted my way with flowers, / with fragrant flowers." (Richard, 1925, 79).

In "Moon Night" she surprised us with the following stanzas:

"Who in his youth did not have some / wonderful and enchanted night / under a soft silver moon? / Who did not love under the moon?

Maybe it was that summer night ... / I do not remember it well; the atmosphere / was warm, the burning heart was silent / and in his hands, I posed my hand." (Richard, 1938, page 14).

This tendency not to allude to love refers mainly to poetry. However, in other genres, such as narrative or theatre, Lucia mentioned love extensively. Thus, in her stories, *The Enigma*, she addressed the subject of love several times. This is the case of the homonym, "The Enigma." In the poem, the narrator deals with a husband's suspicion of his recently deceased wife's infidelity. In "Ankylosis," she shows us the lack of authenticity of a man who was very successful in literature and culture. Yet, he had given up his first love for social conventions.

In "Light of Dawn," she explored the feelings of a man abandoned by the woman he loved. This breakup leads him to want a suicide that does not end up being consummated. In "The Bronze Bed," she deepened the jealousy of a mother-in-law for her daughter-in-law. The young woman had deprived her of a unique bed that reminded her of the best moments spent with her husband. In "Labyrinth," she recounted in an intense drama, the affections of a disheartened woman who could not rebuild her life after the man she loved left her.

In "The Pilgrimage," she discussed the obstacles women faced in their social and personal fulfillment in the puritanical Chilean society of the early twentieth century. In "The Yoke," she spoke of two sisters competing for the love of the same man, bringing out their mutual jealousy in their willingness to love. In "The Forest," the author became interested in the idealism of men as opposed to the supposed materialism of women. And so she denounces the wife of this exciting drama for abusing her sensuality to achieve her purposes.

She also made engaging contributions to love in the field of theatre. For example, in *Bells for the Dead*, the author explored the rivalry between two women, Marina Ortiz de Gaete and Ines de Suarez. In the plot, they compete for the love of the conquistador Pedro de Valdivia. The frustrated love of the legitimate wife is opposed to the passionate love of the illicit woman, with original nuances and reasoning. We can also find echoes of this dispute in her essay, *Marina Ortiz de Gaete*.

In her play *Flight*, she dealt with the dilemmas of a mature woman who, after being widowed, fell in love with her administrator. At the end of the drama, the woman gives up her love when she discovers that her youngest daughter had also fallen in love with the same man. Finally, in *On the Edge of Dawn*, she goes into the subject of love as a universal concept. On this occasion, she included stanzas by the famous author of *La Araucana*, Alonso de Ercilla y Zuñiga.

Beyond love, she sometimes liked to recreate history, and then her thinking expands. She seeks the transcendence of great ideals, eternal glory, and the impulse of the epic. Imbued with an aura of solemnity and nobility, she projects visionary scenes of the future:

> "As in Wagnerian choirs, of fantastic grandeur, / with their crushing pace, with their untamed fierceness, / the mobs advance in the universal life. / They are the modern barbarians, the invasion of the ages, / who shake the foundations of old societies, / that fall from their broken pedestals to their wild passing"(Richard, 1938, 82).

Other times she develops an eschatological, afterlife sense. It is not necessarily dark, not even of Christian inspiration. This is the case with her poetry "Oh Terrifying Night," which belongs to her poetry collection *Blue Smoke*. For me, it is the most sublime and overwhelming poetry of all her lyrical production. In it, a tiny and fragile Lucia, imbued with esoteric presentiments, presides over the temple of glorious pantheism, beyond the summit of time. There she comes face to face with the unfathomable mystery of a vast universe:

> Who will remain impassive before you? / Oh great priestess of mystery! / Do you steal our shadows, / or do you turn our bodies in shadows?
>
> How much orphanhood I feel, what abandonment, / how much untranslatable suffering, / as if all human misery / came to take refuge here in my chest.
>
> The nocturnal birds fly grave / launching their moaning doomsayers, / the returning souls cross swiftly / and the ghosts leave their tombs.
>
> Are we a living among the living?
>
> Perhaps we are just a dead cocoon drifting / in the waving current of time! (Richard, 2004, page 252).

She kept a thought close to the poet Paul Claudel. He was the main representative of French Catholicism in modern literature, whom she praised in some of her articles. The curious thing about Claudel is that, due to a strange paradox in his thinking, he tried to make a synthesis between symbolism and realism. Despite his deep religious concern, he knew how to reconcile orthodoxy with modernism.

On the other side of the spectrum, leaving aside love, epic, or scatological, we find the liberal nuances in the author's thinking. In her article "Understanding Latin America," published on March 5, 1957, mentioned above, she wrote:

"That is why we love freedom, understand democracy, hate social differences, try to erase human inequalities, and take pride in elevating the figure of our thinkers, intellectuals, and artists." (Richard, 2004, page 58).

Lucia made great efforts to achieve equality between women and men, following all the feminist concerns of the time. She also advocated reducing social differences. In her recently discovered article "Book of Hours" she referred to Christmas as,

"A parenthesis of joy and happiness, where there are no age or class differences, where we can all feel like children, full of generosity and hopefulness." (Richard, 1957).

For Lucia, this would be a time when people would spontaneously unleash their feelings. They did so without being indoctrinated with complex philosophical systems they did not understand. Or as she put it:

"... the same groups of peasants gathered in the church at that blessed Midnight Mass, are reminders of the fervent joy of the people when they were not concerned with thinking about systems, but with expanding their feelings." (Richard, 1957).

Lucia married lawyer Guillermo Piedrabuena Bories. Mr. Piedrabuena, among other exciting activities, began his political career in the Conservative Party until October 1925. But then he suddenly switched to left-wing positions. This year he left the Conservative Party to support the candidacy of Jose Santos Salas. He was a politician raised by popular and marginal sectors of the Conservative Party and the Radical Party. This party united liberals, radicals, and democrats against the traditional candidacy of Emiliano Figuera.

Some believed that he was a Mason (although in the family, not everyone agrees). Some have demonized this word. But actually, it encompasses the most significant achievements of science, philosophy, and democracy. Many Masons were aristocrats, practiced religious tolerance, and read Spinoza. But they also invoked the "great architect of the universe," according to the model of order and harmony proclaimed by Descartes and later codified by Newton.

In the 1940s, Mr. Piedrabuena gave speeches against the aristocracy, used anticlerical language, and was agnostic. Paradoxically, at the end of his life, he embraced the views of the right and befriended some generals. In any case, although there were differences between the spouses - the main one being that Lucia was a true believer - there must have been some ideological complicity between Lucia and Guillermo. Otherwise, the marriage would have been unviable.

The most logical thing is to think that Guillermo pursued the opening up of society through politics and his wife through the arts. In the intimacy of the home, they discussed their achievements and exchanged impressions. Somehow there was a symbiosis, and the opinions of one spouse affected the other. That's living.

PASSION FOR THE THEATER

Bells for the Dead

he play begins with an introduction, in which Lucia presents all the characters, who founded the city of Santiago del Nuevo Extremo. It's a one-act play. One of the characters is Rodrigo Gonzalez de Marmolejo, a Spanish Dominican religious. At that time, he was the first bishop of Chile, a very kind and generous person. Another is Ines de Suarez, born in 1507. She arrived like the previous one with the conqueror Pedro de Valdivia and was his lover. After his death, she married the noble Captain Rodrigo de Quiroga in 1548 and died in 1580. The Quiroga Suarez couple were the wealthiest landowners of their time.

Another is Marina Ortiz de Gaete, born in 1510, and wife of Pedro de Valdivia. She arrived in Chile in early 1555, after her husband's death. She lived in Santiago until she died in 1592. Her sister, Catalina, accompanied her on her journey, along with her children, the Suarez de Figueroa, who died in the Arauco wars. The whole plot focuses on the supposed meeting between Ines de Suarez and Marina Ortiz de Gaete, in which Catalina supports her sister. The cleric Gonzalez Marmolejo, while condescending to Marina, points rather to Ines' virtues.

The play is brief and simple, set in colonial Chile, in the late winter of 1560. The author shows the scene in one shot: a room illuminated by natural light.

In the setting, we can see an image of the Virgen del Socorro, with a lit candle. On the dais, there is an armchair and other furniture, cushions, and a rustic rug. There's also a desk and a big brazier. Also, we may see a portrait of the conqueror Valdivia, which would be the latent background of the plot. The curtains cover the windows without glass. The walls are roughly plastered.

The play reflects the canon through which Spanish comedy takes place: the royal world, the court, and its intrigues, the nobles, the Church, the young gentlemen, and their love problems. The main features of the 16th-century man are omnipresent: class consciousness, honor, virtue, integrity, and heroism. There is a real spirit. The characters speak the language of their time, lineage, and social rank.

The characters are real, whose authentic lives come from history. There is no invention in the characterizations. The only speculative thing is the encounter between Ines and Marina, which we don't know if it ever happened. This encounter triggers an explosion of feelings, although the plot is weak. We never see a true confrontation to call it drama. It's more like a conversation or an interlude. Even more, there's hardly a break-up or anything abrupt. The unity of place and time takes place. Only the memories of the characters transport them to other scenarios and moments.

As for the scenery, the decoration is scarce, frugal, and rustic, typical of a classical and colonial dramaturgy. It is a sober show, without music or folklore. The stage space is small, without luxuries or ornaments. There is a fixed set, which does not move or change. Only a few characters appear. They do not make gestures, nor do they share their expressions except for a few exceptions. The lighting technology is limited. There are no songs, no dances, and no stagehands.

The costumes are presumably worn by the colonial upper class. We can see this in the case of Ines de Suarez. However, there is nothing mythological or unrealistic. Nor do we find any metaphorical or symbolic complexity. Moreover, perspective and movement are very rare. The little intrigue would make it impossible to qualify the play as cloak-and-dagger or vaudeville. The greatest strength of the performance is the text rather than the acting. Nevertheless, the psychology of the main characters shines in the scene. The struggle of the personalities and a hypnotic state of consciousness drag us into a sentimental trance.

The scene begins with a dialogue between Marina and Rodrigo Gonzalez de Marmolejo. At first, they talk about trivial matters, such as the events of the nascent colony. Then, the subject of Garcia Hurtado de Mendoza appears in the conversation. He was a young man in his twenties recently appointed governor of Chile. Later, they continue to talk about his abuses. The discomfort caused by the distribution of the farms among his soldiers was enormous. He ignored everything that happened before his arrival.

Then there is mention of the cities destroyed by the Indians, later rebuilt by Garcia, to which he gave his name in a moment of vanity. Those were hard times when the savages seriously threatened the colony. There was a lack of food and basic tools. Regarding Marina, Lucia portrayed her as a melancholic woman, a little removed from reality. She carried in her chest the pain of her husband's death. Cruelly annihilated by the Indians, she did not know where his remains were to honor him.

Sometimes Marina and her sister Catalina try to degrade Ines with insinuations to her decency or dignity. In such cases, the bachelor Gonzalez ardently comes to her defense. He tells them of Ines' many virtues. She was a brave and daring woman who dug a well in the desert, without which everyone would have died.

It was also she who denounced and frustrated the revolt of Pedro Sanchez de Hoz. Marina, in turn, openly refers to the fact that Ines slept with her husband. The clergyman excuses her because he could not judge her. The conquistador remained alone for many years and far from his wife. Gonzalez de Marmolejo continues to tell of the exceptional courage that Ines showed in the assault on Santiago. On that occasion, Valdivia was not there, and the Indians had surrounded and set fire to the city.

The population was saved only because of her courage. The two sisters recognize that in that circumstance, a normal, honest woman, like those confined to their home, would have fled in terror by screaming or fainting. They are surprised by the audacity of Ines, who did not hesitate to cut off the heads of the hostages with her own hands. What courage, what cold blood, and what cruelty! They say.

Then it darkens, and the thought enters another dimension. Ines de Suarez arrives accompanied by an entourage of slaves. She displays her rank by wearing a luxurious dress. She crosses the threshold with much pomp and circumstance. At the other end, in the gallery, Marina and Gonzalez de Marmolejo are waiting for her. It contrasts Marina's simplicity, mourning, and dignity with Ines' luxury and imposing attitude.

There's tension in the air. Marina shows herself to be the legal, chaste, and demure woman. Moreover, she embodies the traditional woman who presents her honor and virtue. Therefore, she feels entitled to look over her adversary's shoulder. Ines would be the adulterous and libertine woman, who lived extramarital with Marina's husband. While Marina had been too cowardly to go with the great man in his campaigns of conquest, Ines had shared his experiences. She had understood him, entered into his visions, and promoted his manhood and heroism.

After the first few courtesy exchanges, an exciting discussion ensues. In the conversation, Garcia's excesses emerge and how he had deprived Marina of her farms, leaving her destitute. The solution was to make a complaint to the monarch, but Spain was far away, and communications were very slow.

Other complaints add to these. Marina regrets that this waiting has ruined her life. Remorse makes her cry. If she had been at her husband's side, maybe his fate would have been different; she could have saved him from his fateful end! Gonzalez Marmolejo disagrees. After all, that was his job, which he would not give up so easily. Lately, the conqueror was sick, moody, and sad. He had to face a brave enemy named Lautaro, who had an army that outnumbered him. No one could defeat him.

Everyone leaves, and only Marina and Ines de Suarez stay looking at each other. Ines emphasizes that they have to talk to dispel the misunderstandings of the past. Marina is vulnerable. She tells her rival about her loneliness and how she lost her youth in a useless wait. It wasn't easy. She confesses her anguish in those twenty lost years waiting for her man.

Far from being angry with each other, conciliation reigns. Ines states that life has enormous contradictions that do not allow them to achieve what they love so much. Marina lets her antagonist know the anguish she has suffered. A considerable wait and in the end, when she went to see her husband, she learned of his death. Ines sympathizes with Marina.

Marina claims she can't stand anyone coming between her and her husband. In her opinion, the brave woman has been guilty of their separation. She had deprived her of their love and happiness. Ines tells Marina that Valdivia loved her. Many times he worried about her. Marina believes her man forgot her. Moreover, she wonders if her husband loved Ines. Ines guesses it could be so, even though she thinks we don't leave the one we love.

Ines was the woman who had accompanied the conqueror in his campaigns, poverty, and danger. She had given up everything for him, sacrificing her youth and safety. Marina recognized her cowardice. She was a woman educated for home and children, not for wielding a sword. However, Ines said that when the time came for triumph and rest, Valdivia forgot her. Despite all her sacrifices, he walked away from her.

Marina believes there were reasons of state or conscience. But Ines argues that Marina felt better knowing that her husband was waiting for her. She, instead, in the end, received indifference and contempt. Viceroy La Gasca forced him to separate from Ines if he wanted to keep the governorship. And he did not hesitate to do so. His desire for glory and high ambitions prevailed.

Ines holds that her affection never made the conqueror forget his family, his tradition, his home, his distant homeland, and Marina herself. The two women had suffered a lot: one for not consummating her love, the other for not being able to maintain it. According to Ines, at least Marina could cry for him; shed tears for him without hiding them.

Ines had rebuilt her life by marrying again. But, Marina was a lonely woman, immersed in her memories, her mourning, and eternal sadness. In this curious encounter, they make concessions to each other until the end. Ines complains once again that she will always have forgetfulness and death engraved on her heart. Marina, on the other hand, concludes that the regret Valdivia expressed in his last moments was for some memory he could not forget. Surely, that discomfort was caused by the abandonment of the woman with whom he was really throbbing, to comply with the social canons (Richard, 2004).

The Flight

It is a play set in today's contemporary world, aimed at the petite bourgeoisie. It is a performance for the masses, designed for the middle class. The idea is to make money without significant stage complexities, neither lofty nor elitist. It uses everyday language and addresses domestic problems. The developers of this type of drama try to finish with the spectator audience to turn it into a participating audience. The piece does not direct a political or ideological message, nor does it seek to convey any ritual, sacred, or cultural content.

In the play, there is no parallel or characteristic of avant-garde performance or any symbolism. Lucia seeks the collective unconscious through the current events of modern life. Nothing announces elements of absurd representations. She does not use the slowness of the characters as a tool to awaken the subconscious of the audience. The author uses dynamic actors, who come and go, adopting different body postures and expressions. In this way, they achieve greater vitality and dramatization in the show.

Lucia often notes down the characters' intentions, gestures, moods, indifference, or vanity. She also takes advantage of the music. There is no unity of place or time. The action takes place at different times and settings, although always in the bourgeois salon. Sometimes it refers to outdoor locations. The language is that of the everyday life of the petite bourgeoisie. Occasionally, Lucia even uses silence as a powerful resource that causes tension and strangeness.

Flight is a play in three acts. In the first act, as an introduction, the room darkens. Before the curtain rises, you can hear the music of a fugue that gradually descends on the stage. A voice behind-the-scenes says:

Flight... humane resolution of life's conflicts. End of love and death of longing... The themes come and go in a perennial chase. Flight... the evolution of time... escape from the impossible... a foundation of man. Flight... a condition of life... a synthesis of death... flight...

The main characters are:

Olivia, the mother (45 years old) dressed in mourning.
Alfredo, the eldest son (23 years old)
Alicia, the daughter (21 years old)
Gerardo, the youngest son (20 years old)
Max Spencer, Olivia's lover (35 years old)

The play develops a little generational drama. Olivia, who has recently widowed, considers her future and her sons' projects. Alfredo, the eldest, wants to succeed financially and boasts of his audacity and how well he will do in life. Gerardo, his brother, studies philosophy, is an idealist, and longs for his freedom and the pursuit of social justice. His brother Alfredo mocks him by calling him a poet and an anarchist and believes that pragmatism will always be above the chimerical. Alicia, the youngest, wants to be a dancer, but her brother Alfredo also attacks her, telling her that the only good business for a woman is marriage.

The mother, eager to relax all these tensions, announces to her family that she has finally recovered the Los Olmos farm. It was a property that their father had left them as an inheritance. But, until recently, she had not been able to recover it due to some legal obstacles. Then the question of the exploitation and administration of the farm arises. Olivia offers her sons this life in the country, as a new opportunity to re-emerge in business.

However, her sons, one by one, show selfishness and rejection of their mother's offer. Alfredo says he hates farm life. Instead, he wants to succeed in the stock market and not live a life of hardship and privation. He argues that he knows nothing about the country and its workings. His brother, Gerardo, likes urban life and wants to continue his studies. He loves politics and literature and believes that the countryside is for fools or the apathetic. Alicia has dreams in the world of dance.

Olivia, who clings to reality, accuses her sons of being afraid to live. They couldn't cope with the problems and were lazy and cowardly. Considering this situation, the mother has no choice but to hire an administrator. She finds him in Max Spencer, a qualified agronomist. After the loss of her husband, Olivia sees the Los Olmos farm as an Eden for her illusions. It is a place not only to work but to enjoy its flowers, the landscape, the loneliness, the rumors, and the stars. Olivia wants to live her own life, enjoying her new freedom.

At first, it was all jokes. The children agree with the choice of the administrator, which they consider an excellent idea. All are good omens. Olivia gets a loan, and she plans to plant and buy new animals. The siblings in their selfishness want to enjoy the benefits of the farm, but without making any sacrifices. Everything seems to be going well. Yet, little by little, complications arise.

In the second act, the scene takes place in the country house. Four months have passed, and during that time, Max and Olivia have shared many things and fallen in love. They make plans together for a new life. But one day, Olivia receives a letter in which the sons announce their arrival. After the dreams of youth, the sons had failed in their purpose. Alfredo had lost all his money in the stock market and had had to leave his girlfriend, Elisa.

Max insists on Olivia that she must do without her sons and seek her happiness. Her sons only came to her now that things were going well for her. Who remembered you when you were sick? Max tells Olivia. Max reminds her of their love. He puts a lot of pressure on her to tell her sons the truth about their situation. However, Olivia hesitates and asks for time to tell them everything. She can't give up her sons so easily. She doesn't want to make them suffer.

Olivia is afraid of life, of getting old, of the age difference she has with Max. One day I won't attract you! She tells him. Olivia, very unhappy, feels harassed by Max, perceives his presence everywhere, and asks him to leave her alone. Max leaves the house. Before doing so, he kisses and hugs her, reminding her of their great love. He begs her again to find a chance to tell her sons everything.

Two other characters appear on stage, Pedro and Rosa, two servants. The mother is very excited about the early arrival of her sons and orders the servants to clean the house and prepare something to eat. She finds the hat, the cigarette butts, and a photograph of Max and tries to get rid of them quickly while saying to herself: Coward! Coward!

The sons arrive with a certain ironic air. They brag that the house in the countryside wasn't bad. Gerardo, who said the country was for fools, now has new ideas. The somewhat hypocritical sons are invasive: they eat, drink, and explore the house at their leisure. They also meddle and disqualify the administrator. They call him "a cunning and distrustful huaso," while they make their plans.

Ungrateful sons change karma completely. They plan to have a big Christmas dinner, with firecrackers and fireworks. We'll dance and have fun all night long! Alfredo says. Not enough, they remind their mother of the last supper with their father. Olivia is confused. She doesn't know how to deal with Max anymore, or how to announce to her sons that she's fallen in love again.

The third act takes place on the same stage as the previous one, the country house. Max appears joking with Alfredo, with whom he makes plans to buy new animals. There is a jovial atmosphere of joy. Almost everyone is expansive. However, some strains arise. Max, Alfredo, and Olivia accuse Alicia of being bored, strange, and thoughtful. Alicia has tensions with Alfredo.

Before going out with Alfredo to do some business, Max presses Olivia again to tell her sons everything. Alice, somewhat removed from the scene, seems to hate Max. She realizes the nervousness of her mother that she's trying to hide. Then the mother and daughter are left alone, initiating an interesting dialogue between them. Olivia, who finds her strange, asks her about her dance school. She also wants to know about some of the boys she has been dating, entering into her relationship status.

Alicia gets exasperated and irritated, becoming disrespectful to her mother. Alicia tells her to stop the hypocrisy. She is perfectly aware of the comedy she and Max are playing. The young woman has been watching them. She can't stand the passion they both feel, nor Max's looks at her mother. The mother at first denies the situation, but Alicia continues with the reproaches.

She accuses her mother of looking at him in surprise, with her bright eyes, her face transfigured in his presence. Besides, he looks at her as equally captivated.

Then Alicia explodes. She starts sobbing while the desperate mother tries to explain what happened. Alicia covers her ears so she can't hear anything. It's horrible! She says. She doesn't want to hear a confession. Her mother grabs her tightly. So, Olivia accuses Alicia of being in love with Max, but she denies it. They continue with a heated discussion, and Alicia seems very jealous.

Alicia can't stand that Max doesn't notice her. All the attention was for her mother. She accuses her of shadowing her, of making her disappear. The daughter questions her beauty. She's horrified. The mother tries to comfort her, but Alicia pushes her away violently. She thinks her mother has made her miserable and has no right to pity her. Then, full of vanity and with an air of superiority, she makes her mother see how old she was. Her youth was worth more than all her virtues. He punishes her even more by telling her that young people should be with young people.

Olivia is overwhelmed and depressed. Her daughter's reproaches have penetrated her skin like darts. She hides her face and cries, leaning against a wall. Then, Alicia regrets and tries to reconcile with her mother, but she disowns her. Alicia, in desperation, feels she should have died with her secret but recognizes that she could not keep it any longer. Olivia accuses her of being in love with Max. At first, Alicia denies it but finally gives in to the evidence and confesses.

Understanding the complex state of things, the mother sacrifices herself for her daughter. She recognizes that she is no longer so young. She wears herself out with the long walks, the intense emotions, the effort to organize everything, and even the excitement of the sons. Alicia then regrets the damage done and feels sorry for her mother for making her suffer. Olivia prioritizes her daughter's health and well-being, offering her various plans to restore her serenity.

They both want to run away from home for different reasons. One, for not daring to consummate their love, the other for not bearing a grudge. But Alicia, full of resentment, still wants to see Max, to show him all her indifference and contempt. Nervous, mother and daughter finally agree to run away. For the last time, the mother looks at herself in the mirror and says in tears: yes, I'm not so young anymore, but he loved me, it was me he loved...! She takes one last look at the house as if she had forgotten something. Full of tenderness and doubt, she finally leaves with her daughter. The curtain falls as the music of the fugue slowly begins to fade.

This fugue, in its double Spanish meaning of musical piece and escape, shows the audacity of the author to conceive a love without fear. It is an almost forbidden passion in a woman of her time. She dares to control her relationship status after her widowhood and wants to resume her life with new illusions. Despite this courage, social conventions prevail, and the writer, through her characters, represses herself. She chooses eternal mourning, showing her generosity as well, feeling sorry for her sons' pain, not wanting to put her well-being before their suffering.

This play is undoubtedly one of Lucia's best. Here we can see a simultaneous play of opposing interests, a variety of sensations, the power of some emotions, and multiplicity of scenarios. It is also advanced because of the multitude of indications about poses and gestures, moods, silences, intentions, and even presumptions. She also highlights the antagonism of the characters and the intensity of the drama, which, however, is diluted in a conciliatory ending.

The end is not abrupt, but neither is there justice in the solution. As for love, everyone is unhappy, and especially Olivia, who exhibits cowardice. Yet, at least there is peace of mind and filial love. Max's feelings don't matter, and how he might have reacted to the escape is an enigma. Finally, if Alicia, in the first scenes, seemed to be a minor character, she ended up monopolizing the stage. She did it even above her brothers, since the primary purpose of the play, turned out to be the dilemma of love (Richard, 2004).

At the Edge of Dawn

his is one of Lucia's most complex plays, set in the colonial era, which takes place on a winter day in August 1558. The author describes it as a historical fantasy about Don Alonso de Ercilla. In it, she relates fictitious events based on a well-documented factual reality (Richard, 2004).

Lucia Richard Barnard

In the play that could be classified as Spanish classical theatre, there are several planes of time, space, and place, comprising four acts. The first takes place in an inn and has seven scenes; the second in prison and has six scenes; the third also in jail and has three scenes, and finally, the fourth takes place in the Plaza de La Imperial and has only one scene.

The play, which could be described as a drama with a happy ending, is a pure genius worth staging in the best theatres. It embraces many characters and internal tensions, leading to images full of symbolism. Moreover, it brings together motifs from the most acclaimed themes of world literature.

The number of characters in the play is surprising. In addition to the main characters, a plurality of captains, an innkeeper, men and women of the town, Indians, priests, and street vendors enter the scene. It is also remarkable its perfect structure and hierarchy, its dynamism, and the antagonisms in the scene.

Lucia also uses an infinite number of resources such as music, voices, greetings, laughter, the ringing of bells, sounds of all kinds, the murmur of the parties, silence, lights, and shadows. She even indicates the intensity of this music, which is sometimes louder or imperceptible. She also captures very well the intentions of the characters, describes different scenarios and shows feelings, emotions, moods, gestures, and postures.

The language that Lucia uses is equally excellent, developing the colloquialisms of the 16th century. She applies dialogues full of intensity and effect, and even uses interjections. The ideological codes of the century also emerge, such as honor, mysticism, the pre-eminence of lineage, heroism, selfless service to the king, and the ideals of chivalry.

The core of the plot has to do with a quarrel that took place in La Imperial between Don Alonso de Ercilla, the famous author of *La Araucana*, and Don Juan de Pineda. Both were Spanish knights who, at that time, participated in the Arauco War. Apparently, the discussion was about nobility, both drawing their swords. As a result, a small tumult formed.

The riot compromised the governor, Don Garcia Hurtado de Mendoza, an arrogant young man, son of the Viceroy of Peru, who ended up falling off his horse. The governor had his face covered. So the contestants could not recognize him. But he believed it was a conspiracy, so he condemned both of them to be executed at dawn.

Ercilla and Pineda had to spend the night together in jail. There, an exciting dialogue takes place that sums up all the complexities of a tragic and expectant moment. According to the most established tradition, the governor locked himself in his house. Although several captains and soldiers tried to change his mind, he did not alter his severe sentence. In the end, an Indian woman entered through a back window, and after a whole night of pleas, she obtained Don Garcia's pardon.

The main characters are:

The captains:
Don Alonso de Ercilla
Don Juan de Pineda
Don Francisco Irarrázaval
Don Simón Pereira
Don Pedro Olmos de Aguilera

Don Pedro de Portugal, senior lieutenant

Don Francisco de Ortigosa, government secretary and clerk
Cariolano, indian servant of don Alonso

The first act takes place in an inn, and through its various scenes, the narrator introduces the characters and informs about the conflict. Little by little, the dialogues show us the governor as an impulsive young man, who had taken away many privileges from the old captains. He had imposed a new political order that did not recognize the merits made in the period before his arrival.

Among his arbitrariness and outbursts, he took many farms from their former owners. This injustice produced a sense of deep unrest, leaving many soldiers resentful. Besides, he sent the captains Francisco de Villagra and Francisco de Aguirre to prison. The affair had not helped to calm things down.

For many, Chile was a country that enjoyed some freedom. There, judges did not send you to the galleys, and the Inquisition did not yet exist. However, the text emphasizes the tendency to abuse power, fostered by the slowness of communications with the metropolis. This fact allowed the complaints to fade away under the outbreak of new events.

The Indians and the Arauco War also loom up in the first descriptions of the early conquest. This is how the mythical sphere enters the narrative. At that time, the Spanish were thought to be centaurs, expelling rays of fire. Soon Lautaro arrived, who began to understand that those they fought were not gods and that the beasts they rode were only animals.

Under these precedents, Irarrazaval and Pereira arrive at the inn. They are assisting Ercilla, wounded by the terrible blow the governor had given him. The Cariolano Indian, Ercilla's faithful servant, also goes with them. In their talks, they comment on the fall of the governor's horse. This episode connects with one of the most popular themes in literature, "the runaway horse," a symbol of nonsense and madness.

The horse as an allegory of irrationality, we can see, for example, in Picasso's *Guernica*. The runaway horse, of great theatrical efficiency, comes to symbolize the loss of control over instincts. In the present case, it goes from the foolish recklessness of the rivals to the barbaric response of the governor. This fact is a clear sign of his insanity, at least temporarily.

Cariolano offers Ercilla to flee, but he refuses to do so, referring to reasons of honor because this meant taking the blame. Running away would have been cowardly. He had to prove his innocence. He also learns that although Juan de Pineda had taken refuge in a church, the guards took him out of there and finally arrested him.

In an atmosphere of sides, Ortigosa, the scribe, accompanied by the governor's secretary, enters the scene. He comes escorted by many soldiers to arrest Ercilla. He is an evil man, an enemy of Ercilla and his allies, in whom we can see different attitudes towards power. Maintaining parallelism with those sketches by Leonardo da Vinci, in which he portrayed Caesar surrounded by grotesque characters, Ortigosa would be the unscrupulous sycophant who enjoys power.

Ortigosa mocks the prisoners, telling them that just like Villagra and Aguirre, who did not fit into a kingdom, they now had to live in a cell. Ercilla argues that he acted in self-defense and that Pineda was the provocateur. Although he does not admit his guilt, Ercilla does not hold a grudge against him and is willing to forgive Pineda and dismiss the matter. The Araucanian enemy was the real danger. He was the one they had to defeat.

The second act takes place in the cell where Sub-lieutenant Don Pedro de Portugal led Ercilla and Pineda. It is a simple and rustic cell, with a crucifix, a window, a table, and on it, an inkwell, a pen, and a candle. The two characters confined there were once sworn enemies. But now they understand each other because they share the same terrifying experience.

In the despair of their confinement and their inevitable death, the condemned begin an intimate dialogue. In the conversation, they confront two different personalities and various psychological levels. The fatal episode, even the trance, through which Ercilla and Pineda pass is not only the unique experience of some men but a universal idea in which all humanity participates. Sooner than later, we will all be condemned to death, a terrible idea that is very difficult to accept.

It was the tragedy of the human being when humanism gave him a privileged position in the universe. This idea of the end of the century was linked to the baroque deception. That is, the orphaned and defenseless man on earth after having lost his connection with the creator. Lucia enters this debate by contrasting faith and reason. And she does so through a skillful syncretism, or the ability to reconcile different doctrines. Many of these approaches have parallels with *Life is a dream*, a masterpiece by Calderon de la Barca.

In prison, Ercilla and Pineda reconstruct the facts by adopting different attitudes towards their conviction. Pineda, full of terror, refuses to accept the situation. She cries out, madly his innocence, taking refuge in God. On the other hand, Ercilla, at first beside himself, attacks Pineda, making him see the futility of his position. He admits the circumstances and resigns himself to his execution. Ercilla is dejected and skeptical, while Pineda is idealistic and imaginary and is irritated.

There are esoteric forces in the air. What will happen? No one knows. Can we overcome this terrible blow? Can we survive death? The condemned are asking themselves. Human and divine powers come into play in foreshadowing destiny. Fortune and fate are opposed to God's designs. Free will desires to triumph over divine providence or predestination.

In this process of denying reality, the idea of rebelling against an unjust sentence arises. The condemned ask themselves whether it is legitimate to submit to an unfair law. The law is Don Garcia, the governor who subjects the detainees to a summary trial. In his stubbornness, he is not willing to listen even to the church authority. It is corrupt, absolutist, and abusive justice.

Ercilla wonders about the origin of power. Where does it come from? Who has authority over me? Thus, human justice is opposed to moral justice. The theatricality of power brings with it the unconditional adulation of the powerful and the pride of the one who holds it. The corruption of power contradicts the humility of virtue. All this leads to the failure of power to guide men.

Juan de Pineda does not accept his frightful end and shows his rebelliousness and nonconformity. This view contrasts with Ercilla's stance that he resigns himself to his death and his fate as the stoic accepts the meaning of life. For Pineda, if the environment conditions man's freedom, even if others seek to annul the human being, the individual's capacity to rebel can give him back his self.

Then different feelings arise. A range of exalted emotions come to light at the terrifying thought of death, which leads them to sarcasm, disdain for power, panic, even crying of helplessness. Pineda, in his desperation and madness, conceives an uprising. Ercilla believes that the rebellion will come late, without seeing a way out of the situation that is tormenting them. Ercilla, resigned to his fate, appeals to the courage and honor of the Spanish soldier. For him, the rebellion can only be internal.

The coldness of the governor, his inability to show affection, contrasts with the intense emotions of the condemned. But after the storm comes the calm. They had to flee from the anguish by evoking something that would make them forget their situation. So they relive their memories at the court of Philip II, their trip to England and Valladolid, the parties, the ladies of the palace. They could not forget their arrival in Spain on the same ship as the viceroy and their departure shortly afterward together to the New World. They were happy moments of loyalty; of good subjects loved by their king.

Then their friends Francisco de Irarrazaval and Simon Pereira come to the window of their cell. They tell them not to worry because they are working to solve everything. Again, hope arises in Ercilla and Pineda, who cling to that illusion as to their only way out. With that joy, they embrace each other. They want to live, and they want it with a fire-like ardor. But again they have doubts. Could it be that our companions are bringing this news trying to spare us the suffering we are in? Could it be compassion?

Ercilla and Pineda watch from their window cell. They listen to folk music, popular songs, and rustic instruments. Perplexed, they see how the party goes on without them. The universal cycle advances without connection to the concrete man and his vicissitudes. The dismayed prisoners feel great helplessness before the outside party, the music, and the jokes. Life was beautiful, and we wasted it on trifles, they comment. They hear even more sordid noises. In the square, they are digging holes and building scaffolding. Worried, they tell themselves that a nobleman cannot die by hanging. Even in death, they cannot take away our dignity!

In their dismay, the condemned express a duality between culture and life, past and present, materiality and immateriality, theory, and practice. They aspire to eternity even though they know human finitude. They feel the universal desire of every man to transcend his own limitation, even his own death. But at the same time, they perceive the human agony of aspiring to an impossible eternity when they realize that they are a fragile entity. This break is the disjunction between capacity and will: the two intimate forces in a constant struggle in the human being.

At this point, the condemned can only appeal to the three dimensions: the human level, with its desire to overcome limitations; the mythical level, in which man fights for his eternity; and the mystical one, which would be the eternal life of the Christian. It is in the mythical sphere that Don Alonso de Ercilla focuses. It is the third way, the Renaissance celebrity, the literary fame to survive death and reach eternity. Ercilla sings of the Araucanian race and the Spaniards who dared to conquer them and wonders what he would do if he survived death.

Thoughtful, Ercilla struggles to review his past. How many things would I have changed if I had known my destiny? With the little time he has left, he still thinks about finishing his poems. Lucia, in her story, recreates many literary themes. *Carpe diem*, which means taking advantage of the time before old age and death arrive. *Vanitas*, in the world, everything is vanity. *Theatrum Mundi*, the world is a theatre where men stage the role that corresponds to them. Nothing is left out of this fiction. Generous, Ercilla evokes all the brave, praises the enemy in his stanzas, regrets not being able to finish his work, but keeps trying until the last moment.

Ercilla conceives a new hero who, unlike the traditional tragedies, and far from that governor he describes as a "young, impulsive captain," exalts the truth, enhances the dignity of the combatants, the heroism of the people. Pineda, irritated, contrasts death as a malefactor - which he finds detestable - with heroic death. He promotes the glory of the Spanish soldier, the honor in selfless service to his king, the fame, so widespread in symbolic literature, and the books of chivalry.

Both companions languish with the sorrow of those who know themselves deprived of their honor: the highest offense a courtier of his time can suffer. They accept their fate: one commits himself to God, the other to his eternal fame. The embrace of the condemned and their reconciliation means that love is the only thing left in the world when everything ends. Man's only rationality is to do good. In his despair, Ercilla appeals to love by reading some passages of his poetry:

> What can be good without love?
> What verse without love will bring happiness?
> Where has ever been fertile writing if it does
> not have in love its origin?
> We cannot call entire matter what does not have
> in love its ground:
> the happy moments, the tastes, the cares,
> are fake if they are not of love.

The intensity of the torment is increasingly unbearable. When the pain is already intolerable, the initial arrogance and rebellion transmute into acceptance, humility, love. Locked in that dark cell, they guess all night long. They look out the window and see the house of don Garcia lit up. Once again, Lucia introduces symbolism, darkness-distress, pessimism, death versus light-hope, life. But this love may not be that universal redeeming force, a joint engine of energy capable of changing man's destiny. It could be a selfish love, a sensual love. Ercilla speculates that Don Garcia locked himself up with a woman to silence his conscience.

Good and evil are in constant dialogue in the play. An Indian woman had entered the governor's house and spent the night with him. Ercilla tells Pineda that the governor enjoyed himself while they rotted in their dreary confinement. The contrast was too strong. But they still clung to that illusion, that fragile but intense life, even more powerful as it faded away. What if goodness presided over the intentions of that woman, the symbol of life? Love achieves everything. Love is an impulse that can change the world. Could that woman have managed to twist Don Garcia's stubbornness? Could she have succeeded in saving us? They asked themselves.

Like planes spiraling down, the condemned loss in a psychological collapse. The priest gives them absolution. They settle their accounts with the afterlife.

They forgive each other for their grievances, but that does not stop the obsession from continuing, which becomes more and more radical and oppressive ... They harbor bittersweet and bipolar feelings. The condemned cling to life like mollusks to rock, but at the same time, the nightmare of death turns into madness. Let us think of something else, or we will go mad! Ercilla says.

Human, mythical, and sacred times still speak in the drama. Ercilla asks Pineda to pray to God to give them serenity in the face of death. But for a moment, they change their roles. Ercilla talks about God and eternal salvation, while Pineda is merciless. In an endless game of combinations, earthly events embrace spiritual intuition. The symbolic elements and the mystery they contain seize the conscience of the audience like the shadow of a claw extends its threat.

In the distance, they listen to Araucanian music. The inmates feel the rain as a balm that revitalizes their senses. They contemplate the bright stars, and hope emerges again. Through the music, Pineda reaches the patriotism of that same country that has condemned him to death. Ercilla remembers his childhood, his mother, and his siblings. Pineda keeps his eyes fixed on the crucifix. Ercilla sets the table, picks up the pen, and prepares to read and write.

Then he tells Pineda about his arrival on Chiloé Island. There he carved on a giant tree, stanzas of his poetry. Pineda reminds Ercilla of the many times he delighted the soldiers with his verses as they warmed up in the fire. Ercilla had found his way in poetry. The poet had also seen the noblest of human beings in those Mapuches he loved and admired so much. Have you never heard a piece of music that haunts you even in your dreams? Ercilla tells him. So, brutal voices flood my ears, war cries torment me, I see ghosts, and the passages of *La Araucana* recreate in my mind!

Suddenly, Caroliano arrives. The faithful Indian of Ercilla forces the locks and proposes again to his master to flee. He offers him to be a toqui or leader of his people. He is willing to die for him if necessary. Pineda comes to consider it. For a moment, the weakness of the flesh over temptation triumphs, the worldly prevails over the supernatural. But again, Ercilla refuses his offer. To run away is cowardice. A life without honor is no life at all. Ercilla prefers injus-

tice and hanging. At that time, selfless service to the king was part of the decalogue of nobility. Not to do so represented the greatest indignity.

Ercilla is a man of high ideals who can escape again but prefers death. Ercilla's honor and virtue portray him as a faithful follower of the ideals of chivalry
and those of the Spaniards of his time. His character of a man of integrity allows him to triumph morally over the venality or corruption of justice.
Balthasar de Castiglione described in his work *The Courtier*, the difficulties of
men in the labyrinth of the world. Another piece was the *Mirror of the Princes*,
a binding treaty of conduct for the nobility. The value of friendship prevails
over mistrust, fear, and hate.

In the third act, they continue in jail, and little by little, they enter the most
acute phase of the night. The ordeal gets worse as they reach the most transcendent moment of the drama. Then the tricks multiply to forget the horrible
and inescapable end that awaits them. In the thickest part of the night, the
dream confuses with reality, sanity with irrationality, life with death. Everything was true and not a dream, says Ercilla, but the reality appears as a
dream, the dream is reality.

Ercilla reads aloud passages from *La Araucana*. A piece of elegiac music ac-
companies the sad mood of the characters. Ercilla is delirious. He can no
longer distinguish reality from illusion. Sometimes he goes crazy. He can't get
away from the ghosts that haunt him more and more. The voices of Rengo,
Galvarino, Caupolican, Lenomeno continue to enter his head tormenting him.
In desperation, he covers his ears so that he no longer hears those defiant
cries. Ercilla fights like a sleepwalker and moves his arms. I don't have a sword!
He says. In my hands, I have only a quill! Mind overcomes matter; the force of
reason surpasses the reason of force.

It's the theater within the theater. It's fiction inside fiction. Ercilla's self relates to the world and others in different spheres. His self divided into
different people, makes it a little theatre in itself. As in Cervantes with his
Quixote, lucidity is confused with dementia. The value of the individual and his
idealism can overcome the malice of the world. "To be or not to be," says
Shakespeare. The dream of life is equated with death, as in his famous *Hamlet*.
The oscillating flame of the candle produces changing shadows, which over-

dimension reality and the human figure creating specters. As in Goya's sketches: "the dreams of reason produce monsters."

The topic of the sleepwalker continues. Ercilla, at the peak of his hallucination, conceives the birth of a great nation. But the cell manifests itself as a metaphor for the imprisonment of a man who cannot defeat death. Similarly, the darkness represents inaction and impotence, the absence of life, irrationality. The prison is a vault, an existential allegory in the shape of a womb, a coffin. The dream is a narcotic to escape from a reality that is impossible to face. The dream reflects the evidence of the fragility of everything that exists. It confuses the sensitive and intelligible world. It expresses the passage from shadow to self-knowledge.

The anguish of time running out is constant in the play. *Tempus Fugit*; it means that time passes quickly, and we must take advantage of every moment. *Memento mori*; remember that you must die. *Ubi Sunt*; where are those who died? What is beyond death? The prison cell is equated with the allegory of the Platonic Cave. The cavern is the situation in which human beings face with knowledge.

Thus, they are caught between two worlds: the sensitive appreciated through the senses, and the intelligible, only reachable by reason. The myth of the cave represents the passage from shadow to light, the illusion of an idea, the insecurity before reality. It serves as a metaphor to explain knowledge, truth, beauty, and faith. We are all in a cave where one day, there will be no new dawn.

But there is still time for worldly things, for the theatre of life and the marketplace of the world. The malicious Ortigosa approaches the cell. The evil, adulator of power, mocks his enemies once again. He makes them believe in false hopes. He only comes to talk and speculates on incriminating their friends Irrarazaval and Pereira in the alleged conspiracy. Do you want to sour us our last moments? The condemned say. You could have escaped, and you didn't. That will be considered in your favor! Ortigosa says with a half-smile.

There's hardly any music left. Ercilla approaches the window of his cell. Again he contemplates the universe. Alone, in the vastness of the night, he searches the sky with the eyes of the scientist. It is the pagan sky, the sky of the philosopher, the sky of the astronomer, the sky of the poet. A miserable window is all I have to communicate with the universe! He says. The universe appears as a sea of question or an ocean pregnant with esotericism. He gazes at the stars looking for a solution to his situation in the macrocosm.

It contrasts the immobility of his tiny being with the vast potential of the universe. In Ercilla, a tension crystallizes between the earth and the cosmic, between consciousness and the world. The universal and timeless symbol is combined with concrete and material example. How can something be enclosed in a world full of possibilities? How can the greatest of possibilities become the impotence of death? The light of the constellations would be the guide of man in the night of ignorance. As they fade away, Ercilla feels dark and gloomy. The gravity of the cosmos oppresses him. The stars are fading. The silence is more expectant: it is the dawn.

A soft but powerful light illuminates the prison cell like a magical essence of optimism. If darkness was death, light is hope. From a life that is extinguishing, they pass to a life that revives. Light as a symbol of life has a tremendous metaphorical meaning. It involves resurfacing, starting over, reviving. It is the myth of eternal return, rebirth, seeing life as a continuum. Ercilla becomes human by differentiating between truth and right, from darkness and savagery.

The condemned look out the window and enjoy nature. They watch the treetops light up. They participate in a mysterious beauty, that *Locus amoenus*, or ideal landscape where they can find peace surrounded by nature. They momentarily enjoy that *Beatus ille*, which extols life in the village and belittles the court. Ercilla invites Pineda to contemplate the orchestral spectacle of the dawn. Pineda believes that life on Earth no longer has any meaning. Ercilla clings tightly to life and remembers the sunrises in the mountains of Guipuzcoa.

The day promises to be splendid, even if it is the day of our death! Ercilla says. Pineda takes refuge in grace. Beauty is God's radiance. Ercilla is a sinner in love with beautiful things in life. He only learned to write poems and not to pray. What a paradox to die when everything is ready to resurrect! How cruel it is to perish in the spring. Both seek external reality as their last grip on the earth. But perhaps they could take for granted what might not be true.

Once again, Ercilla remembers his childhood, his youth, and his mother. He recalls when his mother told him: Men don't cry, Alonso! So he covers his face to hide his crying. God is with us! We are not alone! Says Pineda. Ercilla feels the joy of the street, which he interprets as a good omen. Will it be a party? The skeptical Pineda says no, they're nailing logs to the ground where they can stick our heads! To which Ercilla replies, they've already put up the scaffolding!

For a moment, they thought the night would never end. But they can no longer bear the situation, and now they want death. Every blow hits me in the heart! Despite my faith in God, I feel weak! Pineda says. Ercilla says the logs have to be too strong to hold their heads of smoke and illusion! Smoke and illusion... smoke and illusion... The ideal, the chimerical, wants to triumph over the perishable. The show has begun. Soon the characters will come to play their roles.

Pineda realizes that the blows have stopped. Suddenly, a bunch of people approaches the cell. This is the end! Ercilla says. The condemned embrace each other. They forgive each other for their offenses. Ercilla asks Pineda to comfort him with his prayers! To which Pineda replies to do the same with his illusions! There are footsteps and murmurs of prayer. The bells are ringing sadly. They hear women's cries, and two religious men enter the cell. There is a scene without words. Only the pathetic reality remains.

The fourth act takes place in the main square of La Imperial. In the center of the plaza, there is a scaffold where the guards bring the condemned. There are several captains, Spanish and Indian women, authorities, street vendors, two old cripples, Yanaconas children, Mapuches, etc. The atmosphere is expectant, and you can hear Araucanian instruments, murmurs of villagers, and bells ringing incessantly. The crowd talks on a conjuration. Women comment under their breath, but soon the soldiers silence them. Older soldiers point out the governor's injustices.

The crowd starts talking in the past tense. So it says: the condemned were brave and kind! The air brings a clamor of protest. A superstitious old man pronounces gloomy omens: There are bad signs. People say the volcanoes are active. The waters of the rivers flow with agitation. Two innocent saints will be killed! Two Christs will be condemned! The people cry out. Unlike Pilate's dilemma before Christ and Barabbas, here, the people rebel against authority in defense of the two convicted.

An older man addresses the mob with a threatening voice: Woe to those who stay, no one will defend God's people! An unjust act would provoke the wrath of God, which would allow the enemy, the Araucanians, to devastate the Spanish and Christian people. The condemned face the executioner who is about to behead them. Even in the last moments, the author stresses the value of friendship. Cariolano insists that he wants to die with his master.

At the last moment, Pedro Portugal arrives and stops the execution. There is a deathly silence as the tension mounts. The music stops, and only the sound of the bells is heard in the distance. The governor has suspended the sentence for limited freedom! Don Pedro says. Pineda takes his hands to his head as he says God of mercy! The people shout miracle, miracle; the apostle Santiago came to save them! Don Pedro and the captains embrace those now released.

Ercilla and Pineda are baffled and don't know how to react. Pineda alludes to the strange ways of the Lord. Ercilla, full of happiness, can't believe the unexpected change. Could it be divine providence? Ercilla believes it was an Araucanian woman who obtained a pardon from the governor. This fact increases his admiration for them and promises a great poem to the Araucanian race.

The people rebel against Ortigosa, blaming him for everything that happened. Ortigosa surreptitiously escapes from the tumult to avoid being lynched. Here we can see many parallels with *Fuenteovejuna*, a famous play by Lope de Vega. Ercilla climbs to a platform and calms the masses. He tells Pineda to fulfill his vows, consecrating himself to God. In turn, Pineda tells Ercilla to write that great poem about Arauco.

Finally, note that the ruthless governor, Don Garcia Hurtado de Mendoza, grumpy and impulsive, shows sanity in his final decision. Although more than goodness, he shows pragmatism in his determination not to stain his biography by executing two captains, very dear to his soldiers. At the end of his term, he would have had to explain his severe sentence to the Crown.

But all this matters very little. What is significant is that the condemned were victorious in the test that life placed upon them, now living intensely with a moral purpose. Optimism and hope overcome death. Sentiment defeats irrationality. Man imposes himself on his milieu, exalting his will and his freedom. Knowledge surpasses ignorance. There is a totalizing idea, an open and positive sense at the end.

Justice triumphs because the need to do good outweigh the need to do evil. Life prevails over time that is running out. It goes from the instinctive and wild to the rational and civilized, from unconsciousness to reflection, from pride to prudence, from the arbitrariness of justice to balance as the only reason in the world. Man has triumphed, at least in this fiction. And if dreams can come true, we must welcome them.

CHAPTER XI

AN ENTHUSIASTIC RADIO SPEAKER

Talking about a Generation

Lucia contributed to the dissemination of national and international culture through radio broadcasts, either with sporadic shows or programs she directed and presented. We know, for example, her *Art Guide, Artistic Report, Art Chronicles, Musical Evenings,* or her *Gone Poets Evocation.* But there are signs that there were others with different names. At that time, there was no television, or it had just been born, so the radio represented one of the most modern means of communication. Sometimes a painter and a musicologist also participated in these programs directed by Lucia.

In these programs, she showed interest in areas as varied as music, theater, history, psychology, architecture, poetry, mysticism, literature, painting... In them, she interspersed beautiful pieces of classical music and sometimes spread the career and achievements of the greatest national artists. Lucia also made known the artistic novelties that came to the country and reported national news. I have already mentioned some of these programs in other parts of this book, looking for the aesthetic sense of her work. Others present the novelty of not being in the *Complete Works,* so its brief commentary will offer us at least a glimpse of her many interests.

Sweet Country of Pablo Neruda. In this radio program, broadcast in 1949, Lucia comments on the recently published book *Sweet Country* by the famous Chilean poet. In it, she plays down the darkness of Neruda, which had a long tradition in Spanish literature. Alluding to Garcia Lorca, the radio announcer points out that poetry required a long initiation. Apart from the fear of the dark or the bold metaphor, she sees great originality in the poet. Nor is the author's political affiliation decisive: circumstances pass, but the poetry remains.

Then Lucia relates many innovations of Neruda as the use of the myth. It was time for poetry to cease cultivating the old classic cliches like Apollo and Venus. Now writers had to praise the legend of the Americas, the impenetrable jungles, the oceanic rivers, the powerful volcanoes, the epic of the conqueror, the tragedy of the aborigines. Although she believes that the ancestry and nobility of some things should be respected, it was time for someone to make this transformation.

Poets could no longer use the Lark, the Nightingale, or the Dove. Now Neruda enhanced in his poetry the native, describing birds like the queltehue, the loica, or the condor. Also, plants appear in his writings as the case of the balsam, boldo, and copihue. Another innovation of his poetry was to mention the conquests of science, modern inventions, mechanization, gunpowder, bullets... Her contemporaries appreciate all this. But she confesses that they have difficulties in adapting to these developments.

To understand this modern poetry, Lucia believes it was necessary to realize that language was something alive and changing. The twists and turns of language were not eternal, and someone had to renew them. Leaving aside some allusions to class struggle, of what she considers very human he would not want to get rid of, she believes that his poetry was high and dignified national glories. Lucia especially remembers the beauty of his poems to Jose Miguel Carrera, San Martin, and Bolivar.

Reading: Neruda's first poems along with some chapters of *Sweet Country*.

Tribute to Gabriela Mistral. April 1949. In this homage to the famous Chilean poet, winner of the Nobel Prize for Literature, Lucia is eager to discover the true reasons for her feelings. Beyond the loneliness of her retirement, her restless pilgrimage around the world, or the prominent figures she had met, the origin of her inspiration and personality was in her childhood home. This place was small and modest, with narrow and vulgar walls, situated in a small town.

In this village, with its vast horizons, without buildings or monuments, she developed all her anguish, her deep and torn emotions. It was in that provincial corner that she shaped her feeling. From then on, she became interested in God, death, childhood, and the earth. Rurality and her love for children stood out in her poetry. Her images recreated themselves in nature and had a taste of biblical and evangelical parable. Her poetry was that of the sad Indian, the old Castilian fed by the common saying and the verses of the early Christian. For all these reasons, Gabriela was palpitating and also bitter, crystalline, and simple, meaningful and sincere

Reading: The main poems of Gabriela Mistral.

Maria Luisa Bombal. In this program, Lucia talks about her work *Sea, Sky, and Earth*, as well as *The Shroud*. Much had been said about her creative fantasy, her immersion in the unconscious. But what impressed Lucia most about this first work was its complete poetic sense. In her opinion, it was an authentic confession, in which the author detached herself from imaginary characters and let her heart speak directly. Lucia reflects on what poetry is and finds poetry in all human manifestations.

In *The Shrouded*, she speaks of a woman caught in her mortuary immobility and yet thinks, remembers, feels, sees. She recalls her life with a voice that goes beyond death. Maria Luisa looks back to those events that left her a vivid impression: the echoes of the small sensations, the unique moments, and the silent gestures. She also evokes the image of the universe blurring in the pond, the twinkling stars, the shadows, and the light.

Reading: Maria Luisa Bombal's *Sea, Sky, and Earth*.

Carlos Pezoa Veliz. Lucia portrays him as an author disenchanted with life, carrying a natural bitterness that corroded his soul. That's why he ended up dying in a hospital at the age of 28. The writer tended toward melancholy and pessimism. In his writings, he gave brushstrokes of malice and saw death as an abrupt end. From romanticism, he took morbid exaggerations. Besides, he became interested in rude authors.

He also examined the Chilean people, but not to praise them, but to describe all their misery, vileness, and great ignorance. In his depictions of peasants, the girls are stained with foul language. In Lucia's opinion, he lacked the portrait of the witty and funny huaso, poor, enthusiastic, and brave, tireless adventurer, who was an essential part of the Chilean soul. The existence of this author languished in a constant struggle between poverty and illness.

He gets a better job, overcomes poverty, buys a house, dresses better, and dreams of being a gentleman. However, in 1906, an earthquake imprisoned him between two walls, mutilating his legs. Then he contracts tuberculosis. He dies in a hospital without seeing his work collected, expressing to the end his pain with his tearful poetry.

Reading. *Evening in the Hospital* by Pezoa.

Manuel Magallanes Moure. This author was born in 1878 in La Serena and died in 1924 in San Bernardo. For Lucia, he belonged to a generation of poet-painters, like Samuel Lillo and Pedro Prado. Passionate about colors, he was also a painter of words. Moved by landscapes, he gave that same height and plasticity to his lyrical expression. The intense brightness and the wide ranges of tones gave perspective and luminosity to his visions.

The writer sang about love, emotion, and nature and knew how to do it with a soft voice and a meditative peace. Magallanes stood out for his lyrical poetry, but he also ventured into the theatre, narration, and essay. Under the pseudonym of Miguel de Avila, he collaborated in several newspapers, doing art criticism and spreading foreign literature. He was also generous enough to provide a site for Tolstoy's colony, where poetry flourished.

He was a great romantic but in a minor way. His gaze focused on the small motifs, which he portrayed with a soft melancholy and a touch of gentle complacency: the cart, the oxen, the pond, the old cats, and above all, love. Like Goethe, he lived among symbols, and in everything, the artist found love. The poet had a hypersensitive heart, and he didn't aspire to great things. He was a self-taught man who acquired knowledge through his own efforts. He wanted to satisfy his appetite for beauty, to unleash his thoughts in an atmosphere of serenity and spiritual peace. The titles of his books were *Shades*, *Facets*, *The Day*, *The House by the Sea*, and *Anthology*. He was an author who lived his existence, dreaming and contemplating.

Reading. Poems by Manuel Magallanes Moure.

Manuel Magallanes Moure. Retrospective Exhibition. Continuing with the same author, Lucia tells about the exhibition of his life and work, which took place at the Renoir Hall of the School of Fine Arts in Santiago de Chile. Through paintings, letters, manuscripts, and illustrations, visitors were able to reconstruct the artist's personality. Those interested in the poet's biography had a good arsenal here: many portraits, traces of his subtle and delicate calligraphy, his private correspondence, and the outline of his first poetic notes. Taking advantage of the occasion, Lucia explores his creative process.

Reading. Verses by Manuel Magallanes Moure.

Claudio Arrau. In this show, Lucia, far from interest herself in the great international pianist he became, focuses on the artist's beginnings, the awakening of his vocation. Therefore, she recounts an episode in which he was about seven years old, the same age as her. One day he showed up at her house, hoping that her father, then a state counselor, would give him a scholarship to study in Europe.

He made a deep impression on her dressed entirely in white, with his curly blond hair, his distinguished air, and the prestige of his genius. He played softly, contemplating the paintings in the room, complex pieces like *Mozart's Fantasy Number I*. But after playing three or four parts, he would go out into the garden to play and eat sweets, like a child he was. When he was only four or five years old, he asked his mother to bring him some sheet music to his bed. Soon after, he played the piano with what he had read.

Master Paoli gave him his first lessons, which terrified him. By then, his only orchestra was his mother, who accompanied him on the piano. However, in his early days, he organized concerts in his own home, inviting his close friends and doing the programs himself. In between, he would offer his guests refreshments and sweets. It also impressed Lucia when she heard the child count in French. These descriptions of Lucia are interesting because they place the future international artist happily playing among his many siblings.

Rosita Renard. May 24, 1949. On the occasion of the recent death of the acclaimed Chilean pianist, Lucia pays a pleasing tribute to the artist. Rosita, under her lens, was a woman of great modesty, a morally upright person, devoid of envy and pettiness. She was always affectionate and sympathetic. Her teacher, Martin Krause, declared that for him, more than a job, it had been a real pleasure to teach the talented and already great pianist, Rosita Renard.

In 1930, the Chilean government hired her to give some courses at the National Conservatory, a mission she fulfilled splendidly. With a generous heart, she was an innate artist who knew how to blend in with Mozart's luminous soul. Abroad, the public applauded her widely, as in her concerts at Carnegie Hall, where she received great praise from New York critics. In Lucia's opinion, history would remember her for her immense kindness, generosity to her fellow men, and simplicity. All this, despite the inexorable law of fate, and the humiliating cold wind of oblivion, which dried up the tears, withered the flowers, erased the epitaphs and names but did not forget the pure beings.

Artistic News. Pedro Prado and Maria Flora Yañez. It was a program of informative character in which Lucia comments, first, the recently awarded National Literature Prize to Pedro Prado. A poet and painter, he exhibited a keen eye for all visual wonders. He was a writer of deep human content, who, in poetry, had cultivated the sonnet. His best-known works were *Flowers of Thistle, The Queen of Rapanui, A Rural Judge, and Alsino*. In the latter, he delved into man's eternal desire to go beyond.

Secondly, she comments on the launch of the second edition of *Ashes*, a charming novel by Maria Flora Yañez. Both in this work and *The Pond* and *Visions of Childhood*, Lucia saw pure poetry. Love for nature gave nobility to her stories. The author was not a local writer. Beyond the peasants and their dialect, she was interested in the horizons, the landscapes of flowers, the sea... She didn't develop a true national sense or geographical feeling. Her eternal characters reflected her interest in the human soul, the beauty, the anguish of man, the passions.

In her writings, a kind of aesthetic complacency emerges, whose scenarios are those of high society. This attitude reveals a fine observer and a sensitive woman who strives to enter into the psychology of her characters. In *The Pond*, she brings to life the fantasies of the subconscious. In *Visions of Childhood*, she portrays her first years of life, without forgetting the world of adolescence. *Ashes* was a psychological novel imagined in a fluid and vibrant style.

In addition, Lucia reports on the upcoming "Porcelain Exhibition" at the Pacific Hall by two women: Ana Lagarrigue, sculptor, and Teresa Leon, writer. She also announces the great concert recently given at the Claudio Arrau Municipal Theatre. She also tells of the future arrival in Chile of internationally renowned violinist Yehudi Menuhin.

Painting News**. **June, 1949. It was a radio program, in which Lucia comments on an exhibition that took place between May 30 and June 14, 1949, at the National Museum of Fine Arts. Organized by the Pan American Union, it was entitled "Exhibition of Works by 32 Artists of the Americas." In her commentary, she praises the initiative of bringing together the different nations of the Americas. But she also denounces the lack of originality of the Chilean pictorial environment. In her opinion, with some honorable exceptions, it revolved for years around neo-impressionism, expressionism, and surrealism.

Lucia claims that international painting went through a period of theatricality, of false positions created to produce sensations, intending to scandalize the bourgeoisie. But the bourgeoisie had entered the snobbery of art and was no longer afraid of anything. She also criticized Salvador Dali's surrealism. He painted furniture on trees or faceless orthopedic mannequins hugging each other. That was the case with the painting of Carra, *Hector, and Andromache*. She is also grateful that this type of painting did not enter the exhibition.

She praises the work by Venezuelan Hector Poleo *Return in The Night*. For her, it was a neoclassical canvas, formal in its drawing, depicting normal human figures, and a balanced arrangement of architectural elements. His work exuded neo-Renaissance intellectualism. Lucia is kind to the Mexican Diego Rivera. He came with his canvas *Girl in a Checkered Dress*, which represented a symbol of the Aztec race. In contrast, she is ironic about the Mexican muralist Clemente Orozco. He had brought his painting *Cemetery* to the exhibition, which she thanks for not including the macabre.

She is sarcastic about the work of the Brazilian Candido Portinari, who participated with the canvas *Return from the Fair*. She describes this piece as a poster. Those who returned were nightmarish beings, disheveled heads, and ghostly figures. They seemed to be returning from a mental hospital. On the other hand, she praises the composition of the Argentine Alfredo Guido, *Dockers Resting*, for its expressive balance, tonal tranquility, vigor in the drawing, and harmony in the colors. All these skills portrayed him as a great engraver.

She also appreciates the work of the American Karl Zerc, *Harlequin*. She describes it as "plastic art without theatrical influences, imaginative reflections, or obsolete literature." Finally, she praises the Chilean artist Israel Roa, for his painting *The Painter's Birthday*. This canvas represented them with dignity. It gathered qualities such as the beauty of its tonalities, the modulation of color, or the spontaneity of execution.

Centenary of the National Conservatory of Music. June 17, 1950. This program includes the interview Lucia had with Rene Amengual. He was a composer and director of the Conservatory, which had its headquarters in Compañía Street. After some historical difficulties of the institution, Lucia focuses on its generational achievements. The Conservatory not only trained soloists or good musicians but also broadened the musical environment of the time. As a result, four categories of musicians emerged from its classrooms: performers, composers, teachers, and amateurs.

Those who stood out for their exceptional skills would be concert soloists or symphony orchestra musicians. The teachers would cover the needs of music education. The fans, well oriented, would maintain the programs of the concerts. The highest importance was given to composition, offering special prizes to the best students. With this impulse, some talents would continue their activities within the Institute of Musical Extension, which was a branch of the Conservatory.

All these achievements, together with the seasonal schools, made one hundred years of prolific work bear splendid fruit. The conservatory offered the world and the country great concert artists, good teachers, and famous composers. Furthermore, Lucia hoped that modern radio and recording media would also broadcast their works.

Talking About Art. Art Chronicles. In this program, Lucia believes that it is a mistake to conceive of art only for the elite or the artists. Not only those who have fortune and time, or consume art as a luxury, can enjoy art. If we want to feel the beauty, it helps to possess some culture and a natural inclination towards higher things. But we can find beauty in many situations. That is the case with exhibitions, charming gardens, open-air shows, statues along public walks, or the contemplation of the mountain range.

For Lucia, truth, beauty, and goodness are the greatest treasures of humanity. The humble people can also access these wonders as long as they know how to contemplate and admire. The small details contribute to form that sense of the sublime. It can be in our house or following our artistic taste. Our minor daily choices refine our sensitivity: the beautification of our abandoned garden, or cleanliness, and order.

It also helps to elevate our artistic taste, the cheerful carpets, the appropriate furniture, a terrace for sunbathing, a comfortable and straightforward style, a plant planted in a beautiful pot, and light and discreet curtain. We can also enrich our soul with love or friendship, in the search for the right word, in the choice of a suitable book, in the placement of beautiful flowers, or the appreciation of works of art.

Window by Wally Ossa. As the title announces, Lucia comments on the work *Window* by Wally Ossa, a neophyte author in his early twenties. Brief and condensed, the book reproduces a complete collection of images that represent the life cycle. After reading it, Lucia felt in all its crudeness the tragedy of existence, as Andrei had shown it in the Municipal Theatre with his *Expressionist Paintings of the Life of Man*. The author, through robust poetic strokes, had offered all the biological and psychological processes of our existence, through powerful words, unparalleled symbols, and daring metaphors.

Music: Ballet *The age of steel by Prokofiev in its parts:* Entrance of the characters, The countrymen, The commissaries, The little sailors, The hammers and final, by the London Symphony Orchestra.

Theater Season. In this program, Lucia reports on the arrival of new plays in Santiago de Chile. She contrasts modern theatre, which she considers to be an anxious, experimental theatre, with traditional, quiet theatre, which she prefers. This is how she talks about the appearance in Santiago of *Montserrat*, a drama set during the Venezuelan War of Independence. Its theme was dramatic, making use of hate, retaliation, and basic instincts of all kinds.

In front of Captain Izquierdo, a bloodthirsty tyrant, and a looting despot, the young hero Montserrat stands out as a fanatic of the new ideas of freedom and patriotism in Latin America. Besides, Lucia sees parallels in this play with existentialism and other disconcerting concepts. For her, the whole plot showed more cruelty than the beasts themselves.

In contrast, Lucia pleases the performance of *Cheerful Mood*, a friendly comedy by the Alvarez Quintero brothers. The core of the play was the joy of living and peace of soul. The young people lived on the fringes of intellectual or social concerns. *Cheerful Mood* was an intermezzo that allowed us to take a break from a theatre full of complications. It invited us to relax from philosophies and realities and let us wander on the mere poetic and sentimental level.

She also reports on the arrival of Bernard Shaw's *Pygmalion*, *Drosselbart's ballet*, *Beggar Prince*, Mozart's music, and Marisa Regules' performance. She was a young Argentinean concert performer who had achieved impressive successes in London, New York, and Buenos Aires.

Musical Evenings. Trap Choir Concert. In her show, Lucia raises the importance of musical evenings within the family. This old tradition existed in homes before the media broke in. The radio or the phonograph had eradicated this beautiful custom. The cinema had killed the theatre. The day before, she attended the concert of the Trap Choir. It was a musical evening with a mother, her five daughters, two sons, and a conductor.

On these evenings, for example, performers played Gregorian chant music by De Lassus, Morley, and Palestrina. This tradition was typical of musicians such as Juan Sebastian Bach. There is a painting that portrays him seated on the harpsichord, with his wife and eldest daughter. All of them are singing in front of other sons.

Reading: Fragments of the *Memoirs of Ana Magdalena Bach*.

Musical Humor. Erik Satie. Lucia comments on her attendance at a concert at the Municipal Theatre. There she heard Claudio Arrau perform Erik Satie's *Sport et Divertisement*. Here Lucia criticizes musical modernism, with its use of humor applied to music. Therefore, she enters the old dispute between the supporters of pure music against those who used descriptions in music. Erik Satie was a musician who wanted to rebel against Debussy's musical impressionism and pure music. Critics criticized him for creating music without forms. He entitled one of his sonatas, *In the Shape of a Pear*.

A painter named Martin had requested some music for his drawings. He asked for Stravinsky's collaboration. Finally, Satie carried out the project creating the play *Sports and Divertissements*. In Lucia's opinion, the fact of applying titles or intentions to compositions prevented them from appreciating them freely. So, this description of the music hindered the power of a piece to arouse imprecise sensations, alien to the intellect. So humor applied to music was a failure.

Comedy was a social necessity, allowing people to deal with moral, aesthetic, or logical issues. Applied to the visual arts, it produced the cartoon. In literature, it created a Molière or a Dickens. Even Shakespeare had cultivated the genre with his *Taming of the Shrew*. Cervantes made his *Quixote* the most grotesque figure. From the sublime to the ridiculous, there was only one step, in her opinion. If it was not ballet or comic opera, the musical humor was in-comprehensible.

Masterly evenings were held at the Municipal Theatre, where the pianists played pieces such as *Beethoven's Sonata 31 opus 110* or *Schumann's musical studies*. But then came these works that spoke of tennis, fishing, hunting, or unappetizing chorales. Finally, *Ravel's Water Games* came to refresh the room from fruitless musical humor.

The Poetry. In this program, Lucia explains the evolution of poetry and its es-sential components. She describes how modern poetry had changed compared to classical. Far behind was the concept of the poet as an artist that imitated nature. It was also outdated that given by the Royal Academy, which defined the verse as a combination of words subject in their number and ca-dence to specific rules. Modern poetry had broken with all these principles: its laws, classifications, and models. Furthermore, its dictionaries of rhyme were no longer critical.

Despite all these transformations, Lucia thinks that some of the essences of the poetry remain unchanged. It is difficult to define: everything great remains indefinable. The inexpressible that exists in poetry oscillates between music, language, the heart, and the brain. For the Greeks, the poet was the one who invented or who did it again. Lucia sees poetry in certain music, in some paint-ings, in serene landscapes, and love. Rhyme would be the ally of music in poetry, a companion that modern poets had abandoned.

When the rhyme betrayed the thought, it used superfluous words and fill-ers, to guarantee the elegance and beauty of the verse. But it did it at the expense of demolishing the main idea. The rhyme was a historical aid to the memory displayed in the most famous sayings and poems. We had to rely more on the rhythm as the original music of the verse. However, the most modern tendencies gave more preference to the depth of thought than to the musicality of the rhyme. For the moderns, the content prevailed over the form, and the assonant rhyme helped all this.

There were examples of free versification that came to prove the success of rhyme-free poetry. We could see this in *The Song of Songs*, Tagore's poems, or Oscar Wilde's *Nightingale and Rose*. In Lucia's opinion, the artist's lack of interest in profit, in applause and even in glory, was the characteristic of the true creator. Examples of anonymous poems would confirm this act of generosity: popular sayings, legends, the *Mio Cid*. The Americas did not have that richness of song. However, the music or folklore was immense.

Reading: *The Sonnet of Anvers, The Ballad of Reading Gaol* by Oscar Wilde.

Argentinian Popular Poetry. In this program, Lucia describes the gaucho as the main hero of the Argentine nation and the highest representative of its popular poetry. In the immensity of the pampas, in the suburbs of the cities, the gaucho sang to the homeland, loved freedom, and prepared for independence. Descended from Spaniards and Arabs with a slight indigenous mix, the gaucho possessed a contemplative and poetic temperament. Warrior and artist, nomad, and singer, his two main cults were personal courage and the guitar.

He could not conceive of music without poetry, and so the singer of popular songs emerged. He was a versifier who, together with his vihuela, created ballads and popular music. Educated writers later collected his songs, giving rank to his message. Without losing their Creole flavor, legends like Santos Vega's were born. His epic struggle with the devil represents the destiny of a race and the synthesis of its poetry. Another example is *Martin Fierro*, a magnificent poem by Jose Hernandez. It is a beautiful and sincere story that tells the misfortunes and adventures of a gaucho.

Reading: *Martin Fierro.*

Rhythm. In this program, Lucia defines rhythm as one of the first expressive manifestations of man, the ancestor of all music, equating it with religious feeling. Rhythm gives solemnity, is a vehicle for religious emotion, and is an integral part of the liturgy of all times. The greatest musicians had written sacred music, and the most famous composers had been fervent believers. That was the case of Bach, Beethoven, Brahms, Haydn, or Mendelssohn. Lucia expresses her admiration for Holy Week when the Church showed all the splendor of its liturgy.

Good Friday was also a time when the bells were silent. The absence of any sound, suspended the soul, as a prelude to the dawn of the resurrection. Recalling her memories of youth, she also expressed her admiration for the ca-cathedral of Milan, an imposing architectural structure with its four thousand statues. St. Mark's in Venice shone in the sunlight. St. Peter's in Rome was the highest expression of art and faith. There, she could imagine those gigantic organs played by Bach or another famous master.

In the cathedral of Florence, the view of *La Cantoria* sculpted in marble by Luca Della Robbia, impressed her. Inspired by the beautiful psalm of David, it reflects the joy, the ecstasy that music provokes. Besides, Lucia tells how she attended the Holy Week ceremonies at St. Peter's in Rome and heard the Sistine Chapel choir. She participated in the emotion and fervor of the moment, with the sound of the bells ringing in the air and the packed crowd. The Pope and his court presided over the magnificent sacred rites. She was also able to admire the works of Michelangelo and other Renaissance artists. All this expressed the cyclopean strength of the Catholic Church and its wonderful synthesis of goodness, truth, and beauty.

Music: Vittoria, *The Response of Holy Wednesday* by the choir of the Julia Chapel.

Earthquake in Cuzco. Lucia informs her listeners about the extent of an earthquake that had devastated the city of Cuzco, burying or damaging its main buildings and artistic treasures. Cuzco was tied to the beginnings of the history of Chile. From this mythical capital, Pedro de Valdivia had departed with his army of soldiers to his famous conquest. Cuzco, the ancient capital of the Incas, kept many traces of that civilization. Formerly a sacred city, it became the main center of Spanish power. It preserved the memory of those times engraved in its churches, its precious ornaments, and monuments, and it embodied a beautiful example of the introduction of plateresque in America.

The Childhood. In this program, Lucia gives a huge compliment to children, pointing out the respect they deserve and the need to channel school failure. It was necessary to fight against the exaggerated severity of parents. It was essential to understand the sensitive soul of the child to avoid failed vocations and diminished characters. The complexes that developed in childhood accompanied us for the rest of our lives. However, the precocious genius, the gifted child, was a miracle of nature.

Examples of great children who showed early virtues were Pascal, Lope de Vega, Murillo, Michelangelo, Chopin, or Mozart. Every sensitive soul was attracted to the child's soul and tried to understand it. This fact happened, especially with susceptible artists. Some periods seemed to forge geniuses. We could see this in Greece of Pericles, the Italy of Leonardo, Raphael, and Michelangelo. The date 1810 had been crucial for art. That year saw the birth of Schumann and Chopin, Liszt a year later, and in 1813, Wagner and Verdi. Between 1820 and 1830 the torrential overflow of romanticism took place with Victor Hugo, Lamartine, Berlioz, Mendelssohn, Musset and George Sand.

Among them was Robert Schumann, an author who fought against madness all his life and yet dedicated unforgettable pages to children. Among those beautiful poems composed by him to children are *Scenes of Children* and *Album for Youth*. His music evokes everyday scenes, children's longings, games and sorrows of the little ones. His *Reverie* is a funny alliance between poetry and music. Only a child or an artist would have been able to abstract himself like this. Some say that he conversed with the angels. Others believed that his memory deteriorated as he recalled past lives, glimpsing passages from unknown worlds.

Music: *Laudate Dominum* by Mozart. Choir with orchestral accompaniment.
Reading: *New Moon,* a book of poems for children by Cristina Menares.

Some Problems of Children. Here Lucia addresses the many problems of children throughout their education and how to overcome these obstacles to achieve prosperity. She denounces cruelty to children as the highest insensitivity someone could commit. Indifference would be our greatest sin. In the poor performance of each student, there would be a lack of cooperation from the parents. The parents would have to make an effort to offer the child an inflexible, constant, and vigilant teaching. But, excessive severity could nullify the child and reduce his chances.

We must never disown a teacher. There are cases where children are partly responsible for poor grades. We must never teach children to be hypocrites or to succeed unfairly. Discipline is necessary if we are to avoid school failure. But it is also crucial to educate with love, understanding, and optimism. Latin America needed daring men, those who risk and fight, suffer, and sacrifice. To be a mother was to be an artist and a teacher. Therefore, the blame for these problems fell on the parents who did not avoid the catastrophe; on the children who neglected their studies and on the cruelty of teachers with the maladjusted children.

Inspiration. ***August 8, 1949***. According to some, the inspiration was a moment of trance that came from the divinity. But this idea does not satisfy Lucia. Others believed that it was reminiscent of previous lives, as is the case with interpreters or mediums who capture strange concepts. However, science could not prove any of these assumptions. For Lucia, it would be much more correct to conceive of inspiration as a liberating force of the subconscious. Like hypnosis, it was an attitude close to that of the lover. In that situation, we sublimate our desires and surrender to the game of our fantasy.

Reading: "Inspiration," a poem by Lucia Richard from her *Sursum Corda* poetry collection. "Portrait," by Antonio Machado.

Psychoanalysis in Art. In this program, Lucia summarizes Dr. Gallinato's talk at the Salon Caveau of the French Bookstore, precisely on this subject and on the psychology of crowds. Gustave Le Bon and Freud also delved into the latter topic. All this showed how an individual of good virtues, dragged by the masses, could become a bloodthirsty person abandoned to his impulses. An example of this return to the cave state we see it in Christ's trial before Caiaphas or in the French Revolution.

The best revolutions were the bloodless ones, like the one defended by the New Deal that saved the US from the worst of its crises, making the creation of the League of Nations possible. Lucia also talks about Dr. Andre Anne and his work on Shakespeare and the complexes. Thus, he described *Hamlet* as being possessed by the Oedipus complex. *Othello* revealed the person with epilepsy.

In *King Lear*, he announced early dementia. Freud had studied Leonardo da Vinci, a natural son separated from his father when he was seven. In his opinion, his mother was the driving force behind all his emotions, producing such mysterious works as the *Mona Lisa*.

Erwin Piscator had worked in the theatre for the crowds. In it, far from showing the complexes or abnormalities of the people, he enhanced the idealized life. Dr. Gallinato referred to child psychology, pointing to the first four years in raising a child as decisive for his later life. As for sociology, Lucia thought that exalting the forces of the spirit, strengthening moral principles, was the only way to achieve peace and understanding between peoples.

St. Peter's Basilica in Rome. In this program, Lucia tells of the enormous fervor around the Basilica. Holy Week was an exciting moment that she witnessed and was able to experience first-hand. In St. Peter's Basilica, people of all races and nationalities gathered to profess their faith and see the pontiff. On that occasion, the Vatican decorated its beautiful gardens and squares. Also impressive were its thousand fountains and the vibrant joy of its bells. If at the Tower of Babel, people gathered to perpetuate their pride, in Rome, citizens of all nations shared their humility, speaking the only language of faith.

Vatican Square represented that great dream of Bernini, which opened in a semicircle as if embracing Christianity. Saint Peter's was the work of three geniuses and three schools: Bramante's, Michelangelo's, and Bernini's. Lucia relates the stages of the construction of the Basilica since Pope Julius II entrusted it to Bramante. During this period, he demolished the primitive church and erected the enormous central dome. After Bramante's death, for a while, the project passed through the hands of St. Gallo and Raphael, without making much progress. After them, Michelangelo gave it the final push.

She also admires the *Pietà* sculpted by Michelangelo. After his death, Bernini finished the work. He added to the Basilica many statues, holy water basins, the papal throne, the large bronze altar, as well as the exterior urbanization. The Baroque made, in turn, some important transformations. In short, the magnificent temple was the most interesting museum in the world. There, she had the privilege of contemplating the Pope and listening to the choirs of the Sistine Chapel. All this was a supreme experience of enthusiasm and faith. All this splendid architectural ensemble had remained unchanged for four centuries, despite the many international ups and downs.

Mystical Literature. In this program, Lucia contrasts two mystical compositions with very different orientations. On the one hand, the sonnet "My God does not Move me to Love You." Despite all the efforts of scholars, it remained anonymous like the authors of romances, cathedrals, or popular songs. This sonnet reveals the pride and arrogance of the Spanish Renaissance poets in speaking to God as an equal. On the other hand, she comments the "Good Friday" poem by Gabriela Mistral, which shows her humble, tender, and pious voice. Here it is the peasant woman, the sister of the farmers, who addresses her closest friends to give them friendly and humane advice.
Lecture: The painter Marta Cuevas spoke about crucifixions and descendances in painting.

The Bible. In this program, Lucia comments on a lecture on the Bible given by Carlos Silva Vildosola at the Pontifical Catholic University. For Lucia, the chronicle of these people has never been so exciting. The Bible brought together the difficulties of the people of Israel, from their birth to their dispersion, dying to history. The people had been held captive in Egypt. They had suffered much but had finally risen victoriously from the hand of Moses. Genesis tells us about the early ages of the world.

But what most impressed Lucia was *The Book of Tobias*. The teaching in the book allowed sustaining the faith of the scattered Jews in a pagan and hostile environment. Paganism had brought relaxing customs, a rude cult, and a materialistic civilization. Tobias, captive among idolaters, represented the image of the Hebrew people, who defended their unique God among the multitude of gods that populated the temples of the earth. They were morally upright amid a terrible corruption. For Lucia, The Bible showed us a spiritual religion, honesty, free people, and a heroic nation.

On Voices of Peace from India. Lucia collects these voices from India, which came like a balm in a world of materialistic disorientation. After the terrible experience of World War II, the scene was that of humanity still riding on its ruins. Even worse, the threat of atomic destruction was on its doorstep. There, in India, were those men who meditated and believed in non-violence. They worked hard to achieve a conquest far more enduring than overwhelming force.

Among them was Rabindranath Tagore, the Bengali poet who won the Nobel Prize for Literature for his work *Gitanjali*. He seduced the world with his mystical-poetic scent. His message was full of a pantheistic philosophy, and of fusion with nature. Mahatma Gandhi, with his peaceful resistance, struggled to conquer the freedom of his country. He achieved national independence only by using patience and persuasion. She also spoke of the death of El Maharishi, India's most famous saint, a symbol of unification, and a great spiritual guide of his country.

Writings of Famous Musicians. In Lucia's opinion, the music lover was not interested in the musical technique but in the total comprehension of the composer and what inspired him to compose his masterful compositions. Among them, Beethoven stood out singing joy with his ecstatic and triumphant notes. Another example would be Dante celebrating light and color with his *Paradise*. Saint Francis of Assisi also knew how to sing of joy despite hardships and suffering. To understand perfect happiness was a gift of the saints and to express it, a privilege of the geniuses.

Reading: *Beethoven's last letter to his brother*.
Music: Beethoven's *Symphony Nº 7.*

French Contemporary Art. According to Lucia, at that time, Santiago's theatres, universities, exhibition halls, and meeting places were full of people eager to learn or to distract themselves. The Municipal Theater had commenced its activities with its Comedy Company. Now it announced the performances of Marisa Regules, a young Argentine pianist of international success, Claudio Arrau with three concerts and the famous Polish violinist

Henryk Szeryng. The experimental theatre had begun with *Montserrat*, the play by Robles. The symphonic concerts also took place.

Until 1950, "Manet's French Art Exhibition" came to Santiago. The Palace of Fine Arts exhibited one hundred and thirty-seven representative works of this style. Impressionism was born almost a hundred years ago, thanks to a painting by Monet entitled *Impressions*, presented by him in 1897 at the Paris Salon. After summarizing the principles of the impressionist school, Lucia tells us about several movements that later emerged such as cubism, the so-called Common Sense, the Abstract, or surrealist art. Cubism was a movement that liberated form and created its own pictorial universe.

Reading: Mihat, *French Contemporary Art.*

Origin of the Waltz. In this program, Lucia explains the development of the Waltz in imperial Vienna. Its obscure origin is debated between Provençal and German. It was born among peasants and from there, it spread to the palaces. It was gradually refined by adapting to the melodies of Weber, Schubert, and Chopin. Finally, imperial Vienna fell. The cataclysm of two wars came, and with it, the catastrophic shaking of the foundations of European culture. But in the dance halls, people continued to dance to the sound of *Strauss' Blue Danube* stanzas, like a smiling echo of that vanished world. Then Sibelius would come with his *Sad Waltz* to throw cemetery lights and ghosts of past lives onto that beautiful lifestyle.

Music: *Chopin's Waltz of Farewell.* Other waltzes by Chopin.

On the Centenary of Chopin. October 17, 1949. In this program, as in the next one dedicated to the preludes, Lucia does a splendid work of synthesis defining the Polish genius. Chopin was not a hero in the proper sense of the word; he was not a man who would have triumphed by force or cunning. However, he had made us dream with his personal and delicate notes, waking up the poet who lives in each one of us.

Chopin emerged between the cathedral of Bach and Beethoven's music, Wagner's storm, and the jubilant bells of Liszt, like a graceful and delicate beam that filtered through the windows. His three axes were misunderstood love, a shattered homeland, and an inexorable disease. Maria Wodzinska would be the young coward who abandoned Chopin, because of the hostility of her relatives and her incomprehension. For her, Chopin wrote his *Farewell Waltz*. George Sand was the woman who dragged him into active life, being indifferent to his personality.

When the musician could not enjoy the elegant and snobbish world around him, George Sand left him. In the same way, he suffered greatly from the estrangement from his homeland and the taking of Warsaw by the Russians. When he found out, he composed his study, *The Revolution.* The disease consumed him while he was still young, leading to his death while living in Paris. His music was immortal because it did not respond to the whims of fashion, and came directly from the heart, penetrating the heart. Schumann said upon learning of his death, "The soul of music has passed through the world."

Reading: Camille Mauclaire, description of Chopin.

Music: *Funeral march, 1st part. Prelude No. 6 op.28. Waltz op.69 nº1. Study nº 12 op. 10 in C minor. Funeral march, whole sonata op.35.*

Preludes of Chopin. It is a magnificent work by Lucia, divided into three radio programs. In them, she analyses all the preludes, using the critiques of the music specialists, together with her beautiful and subtle descriptions. Chopin composed these preludes while having a relationship with George Sand on his famous trip to Mallorca. About these pieces, George Sand said, "they were poems of immense elevation, dramas of unsurpassed energy." For Lucia, "they were perfect and profound works." For Schumann, "they embodied the most remarkable thing about Chopin." James Huneker said, "Wishing to show his genius, Chopin carved these preludes with great delicacy."

In short, these were extremely personal and intimate preludes, in which Chopin poured all his perfectionism. Some were typical of a musical avant-garde, others fatal, others joyful and serene, others cosmic, others powerful, and all of them fascinating. Without a doubt, they all move us, leading us to an inevitable sentimental trance.

Music: All the Chopin's Preludes.

Beethoven and Goethe. Here Lucia discusses the meeting of the two greatest German geniuses of their time: Beethoven and Goethe. While there was mutual admiration in the distance, it faded when the two met face to face. Bee-Beethoven's harsh temperament struck the refined courtier that was Goethe. In turn, the acclaimed musician mocked Goethe's submission to the rulers. However, this fact did not prevent the republican and libertarian Beethoven from using Goethe's *Egmont* to write his *Overture*. He even expected to play music for *Faust*, a project he never carried out.

Haendel. Listening to his famous *Messiah* at the Municipal Theater inspired Lucia to make this program about the outstanding musician. The University Choir conducted by Mario Baeza, accompanied by the Chilean Symphony Orchestra, performed the remarkable piece. Handel was a German musician born in 1685 in Halle, who had considerable prominence in English society and court. There he was especially acclaimed by the public for his oratorios. A precocious genius, at the age of eight, he improvised on the organ. He wrote many operas, but nothing was more revealing than his oratorio *The Messiah*, composed in only twenty-four days. For many years, Handel imposed himself on all sorts of enemies who tried to ruin him.
Music: *Overture and Hallelujah* of the Haendel's oratorio *Messiah,* by the BBC London orchestra conducted by Sir Thomas Beecham.

Richard Strauss. In this program, Lucia pays tribute to Strauss, who died on September 18, 1949, at the age of 85. Like no other musician, he made the fusion between literature and music possible. He commenced his musical life with the Lied. He sought the friendship of poets and philosophers who gave him themes for his works. His *Symphonic Poem* inspired Nietzsche. The poet Hoffmann used his *Electra*.

Riebe relied on the lyrics of his songs and some of his operas. Oscar Wilde took his *Salome*. But one of the most popular plays was his operetta *The Knight of the Rose*, with its charming waltzes and romances based on a legend of old Vienna written by Hoffmann. He was a rather melancholy artist, imbued with Schopenhauer's pessimistic philosophy. He lived his last years in London, composing and exhibiting the gifts of his personality.

Richard Wagner. Famous German musician, born in Leipzig, who revolutionized the music of his time, being a good representative of musical romanticism. Wagner abandoned pure music and used other arts, looking for an artistic synthesis that would translate his aesthetic ideals. In this way, he created musical drama, which earned him violent detractors. Later, he was deified to the point of exaggeration and then was attacked again by the supporters of pure music. Many critics saw in the exaltation of his myths the symbol of the threat of German authoritarianism.

After the irruption in the 19th century of a great gallery of illustrious men, calm arrived. In its place came Wagner, reforming everything, and promoting new ideas for art and society. Wagner, in Lucia's opinion, had been contradictory and Dionysian. On the one hand, he relied on myths and legends to create his musical dramas. On the other hand, he worshipped Catholicism with his *knights of the Middle Ages*, as happened in *Parsifal*. Or he based on dogmatic Protestantism, returning to a pagan and barbaric past as in his *Master Singers*. Lucia labeled him as a man of the future who came to change things; a change that by then had reached the ballet, the cinema, and even the theatre itself.

The Little Chronicle of Ann Magdalene Bach. In this program, Lucia comments on how the last edition of *Pro-Arte* had discredited the charming chronicle. This publication was a weekly newspaper in Santiago that featured news about literature, music, and the visual arts. In this case, it reported many errors in Ana's text. Johann Sebastian Bach's second wife allegedly wrote the book. It soon caused a sensation among educated people in Germany, who bought 125,000 copies.

Researchers later revealed that the author would not have been Anna Magdalena Bach but a contemporary English writer named Esther Meynell. Even knowing of its dubious authenticity, Lucia read it with delight because of the simplicity of her style. She maintains, however, that no mother would ever make a mistake in the name of her children.

Music: *Concert in F minor* for piano and orchestra by J. S. Bach. At the piano Edwin Fischer and his chamber orchestra.

Arcangelo Corelli. In this program, Lucia tells us that Corelli developed in the mid-Renaissance when a vigorous humanism flourished in opposition to or as a complement to theology. He was first and foremost an innovator or a precursor. Monteverdi, Frescobaldi, Boccherini, Vivaldi, and Corelli had been the Italian masters who had paved the way for Bach, Handel, Haydn, and Mozart. When culture had not deviated from the norm, the Italian musician created his own expressive language.

It was a time when religious art declined, and humanist art prevailed. Its innovations had surprised and even scandalized the official talents represented by the prelature. But he claimed that he did not know how to please the critics who had no other knowledge than the fundamentals of composition and modulation. According to Lucia, the norms of beauty changed from century to century, from generation to generation. This is how culture was transmitted. In the end, the Vatican recognized the talent of Arcangelo Corelli. Despite early misunderstandings, the Church contributed to his immortality by burying him with the famous Raphael in Agrippa's Pantheon. His tomb bore the inscription of *Corelli Princeps Musicorum.*

Music: *The Folia* by Archangelo Corelli in an arrangement for violin and piano.

Listz. In his life, people called him *"the magnanimous."* Lucia makes us see how generous this musician had been in reaching out to other artists. This is the case with the protection he gave to Wagner or the dedication and affection he showed to Chopin. Glory had been easy for him, and popularity had followed him to the point of slowing down his creative impulse. He was a man of the world, a sought-after artist and a famous pianist.

Forgetting the piano concerts, the applause, and the fame, the musician locked himself in his workroom to produce his deepest compositions. At the end of his life, he retired to a convent where, at least for a moment, he found that peace to find his music: great, dynamic, and beautiful. In other words, he pursued his divine ecstasies without worldly impositions.

Music: *Liszt Melancholic waltz.*

Contemporary Holland*.* In this program, Lucia pays homage to Holland ten years after the German occupation. Marta Cuevas took part with her, reviewing its history, monuments, and art. Lucia tells us about the enormous sacrifice of a bloody war, the price of occupation and destruction, the considerable damage caused by the dismantling of its industries. The enemy had destroyed all its infrastructures, disrupting the physical and moral health of the new generations. As a country of great artists such as Rembrandt, Puyadael, Vermeer, and many others, the Dutch had to hide their pictorial treasures in underground chambers to preserve them from the occupying forces.

Despite all this destruction, Holland was a nation of hardworking people who had begun the reconstruction, reviving trade and navigation, and re-educating its youth. In spring, a symphony of colors exploded with its grasslands illuminated with tulips, hyacinths, and daffodils. Not only was Holland, the country of canals, mills, and blue villages, but also a paradise for flowers. Holland would resurface full of glory and broad horizons, advancing with confidence towards the future.

Lecture: Marta Cuevas gave a talk about Van Gogh.

Music: *The Submerged Cathedral* by Claude Debussy.

Netherlands. Chronicles of Art. In this excellent program, Lucia expresses her admiration for the Netherlands. She marvels at its majestic cathedrals, paintings, and altarpieces. She is also impressed by the pantheistic dreams of its poets, mines and industries, traditional songs, and bells. Referring to the unified and free Belgium, she tells us about Antwerp. It got the prestige of its elegant buildings and its international music contests, and spa, etc. She also refers to the old and modern Brussels. Leuven exuded science and knowledge. Liège remained eternal and wise, like a living resonance of the ancient.

Lucia also points to the giant figure of Maeterlinck, the sweet and poetic profile of Verhaeren, the realistic chisel of Meunier, and Van der Stappen. She also speaks about Rodenbach's evocative pen, the music of César Frank and Peter Benoit, and James Ensor's visionary palette. Belgium also had a rich past with its great chorales, where Del Monte and Orlando de Lassus became famous with their polyphony. Van Dyck was acclaimed for his beautiful altarpieces like the one in Ghent. Mechlin was celebrated for its lace. Antwerp was one of the most important ports in the world at the time of Charles V. **Music**: Cesar Franck and Orlando di Lasso.

Belgium. Art Chronicles. Returning to the earlier program, here, Lucia speaks about Flanders, which went through different dominations, united or separated from Holland, under the rule of France, Spain, or Austria. She continued with its exciting and active communal life, ennobled by religion, art, patriotic love, and work. In her opinion, it was tough to separate the history of Holland from that of Belgium. Their artists came and went, and their political problems were generally the same. Ghent was important for being the birthplace of Charles V.

From Belgium, Philip II and the Duke of Alba extended their rule. The "Old Thirds" arrived in Holland proud and brave, fighting bloody battles, but returned to Spain, biting the dust of defeat. Rubens and Van Dyck embodied the Baroque in all its glory. Rubens, drunk with light and color, with grace and satisfaction, pursued the young and pearly flesh of Helena Fourment. Humberto and Juan Dick had joined their talents to create a great composition called *The Polyptych of the Mystical Lamb,* which Lucia defines as an apocalyptic, symbolic, and impressive vision. This altarpiece possessed the miracle of its beauty, and brilliant tones: intense reds, radiant blues, almost metallic greens, luminous backgrounds surrounded by a transparent atmosphere.

Reading: Stanza of Charles Baudelaire dedicated to Rubens.

Music: Compilations of ancient songs provided by the Legation of Belgium. *Hymn for the Feast of Ste Cecille.*

Maurice Maeterlinck. In this program, Lucia talks about the great Belgian poet, who died at the age of 88 in his retirement on the Côte d'Azur. He, along with Rodenbach, Picard, and Verhaeren, had formed the chosen group of Belgian writers who burst into French literature in the last century, conquering universal prestige. Among them, the one who had shone most was Maeterlinck with his gifts as a philosopher, playwright, and scientist. He had ventured into the mysteries of the beyond and the secrets of the microcosm. His *Intelligence of the Flowers* and his *Life of the Bees* introduced us to a wonderful universe of minimal beings.

As a poet, he had become a member of the Symbolists, and as a playwright, he conceived original ideas, becoming a father of modern theatre. With the *Blue Bird*, the poet had surpassed both the philosopher and the playwright. He received the Nobel Prize for his beautiful work. He also triumphed as a playwright with plays such as *Princess Maleine*, *The Blind Man*, *Death* and many other pieces full of symbols. The writer also stood out for the composition of *Pélleas and Melisande* on which Debussy based his opera of the same name. For the breath of mystery in his works, he has been compared to Ibsen.

Edward Grieg. In this program, Lucia remembers the famous Norwegian composer, the glory of his homeland. He was a musician who needed solitude to compose. In his youth, he found it in a piano factory, and later in a rustic hut. His constitution was weak and sickly. At first, he became Germanized, but then, when he returned to his country, the musician felt the powerful force of his land. Lucia tells us how "in the depths of those fjords, in those blue coves, music cannot be created by reason alone. There, one dream, one sees visions..." He met Nordraak and Ibsen, and this meeting determined his destiny. He composed popular motifs, his masterpiece being *Peer Gynt* based on Ibsen's drama. Using the words of Jose Enrique Rodo, Uruguayan writer, and politician, Lucia describes *Peer Gynt*.
Music: First suite of *Peer Gynt* with "The Death of Asse," "The Dance of Anitra" and "In the Cave of the King of the Mountain."

Christoph Willibald Gluck. Of the 18th century Austro-German trinity of Mozart, Haydn and Gluck, the latter was the least celebrated but not forgotten. According to Lucia, he was an operatic innovator. He lived at a time when composers were fighting for their emancipation, against businessmen and singers who abused their work. Lucia is surprised that the son of a forest ranger was able to acquire such a vast culture. This knowledge included the secrets of harmony and composition, courtly manners, the ability to amass a large fortune, and even the tenacity to resist his critics. The Knight of the Golden Spur made Rousseau exclaim after listening to his *Orpheus and Eurydice* that "it is worth living after enjoying so much pleasure for two hours." Voltaire in turn said that "Louis XVI and Gluck would create a new century."

Frederick Smetana. He was born in 1824 in Czechoslovakia, and like Gluck, was the son of a ranger. Federico Smetana, in Lucia's opinion, saw the light in that same exuberant nature, full of poetry and mystery. He had a humble background, which did not prevent him from studying with the best teachers, including Proksch and Liszt. At the age of twenty-two, the musician became the conductor of the Gothenburg Orchestra and five years later the musical director of the Prague Theatre, founding a school of music of which he became a teacher. The talented artist composed eight operas, the most famous of which was *Dalibor*, of symbolic significance. He was inspired by ancient legends and customs and by the natural beauty of his homeland. Among his orchestrated plays and symphonic poems are *The Forests and Fields of Bohemia* and *The Vltava*. Smetana's mental equilibrium suffered during the last years of his life, dying insane on May 12, 1884, in a sanatorium in Prague.
Music: *The Moldovan* by Federico Smetana.

Chinese Art. China was a country that had the Great Wall and the Grand Imperial Canal. However, from Marco Polo until today, not even missionaries, explorers, or merchants had mastered or understood this vast empire inaccessible to the Western mind. Great public buildings stood out like the Imperial Palace in Beijing, the Marble Bridge, or the Porcelain Wall. Lucia highlights the avenues of Colossus in the royal tombs of Nankin, of the Ming dynasty. Confucius was a Chinese thinker, who possessed a resigned and speculative morality. Beyond trying to understand the universe, he felt an infinite sympathy for the most humble beings.

The Chinese paintings used to be pictures of an ascetic, who at the foot of a tree looked in ecstasy at the fog that hung over the valley. The common motifs were the simple branch of an almond tree moved by the wind or a bird placed on the stem of a reed. The emperors themselves were sometimes great artists. The monks painted, and even the writing itself had traces of art. The artists of the Far East felt close to the lower beings, the animals, and the plants. The first rule of painting established by Sie'Ho was to express "the spiritual element of life." The second was to "penetrate the interior of natural beings, surprising their soul with gesture and structure through the form."

Lecture: The painter Marta Cuevas gave a talk about a modern Chinese painter.

Music: The opera *Turandot* by Puccini inspired by arguments and Chinese musical motifs. (Richard, 2004).

CHAPTER XII

BLUE SMOKE

Blue Smoke, Chaste and Ethereal

Blue smoke was the title of a collection of poems compiled by Lucia Richard in 1957, in Santiago, which were not published in her lifetime[18]. These are some poems written in her maturity. They reflect in some passages the disenchantment of decadence, which does not prevent many others from reigning in joy. In her prologue, she speaks of the uselessness of fame, when we sought it as an end in itself. Speaking of her style, she defines it as follows:

> "And so I have continued all my life, fleeing from the rigidity of style as one flees from death. I never considered literary schools nor did I have eyes for fads or strange influences. I tried to listen only to the voice of my heart. I sought to capture the emotion of each moment, without this becoming a job. Because, I do believe poetry is a state of the soul, not a profession." (Lucia Richard, 2004, p.177).

---

[18] Existing documents show that in the author's initial project, *Blue Smoke* comprised only 35 poems, including some written in the 1940s. In the *Complete Works* and for practical reasons, others not intended by the author were added. In the first compilations made by her daughter Carmen, she clearly distinguished between *Blue Smoke* and other unpublished poems. These 35 poems were *Blue smoke, Inspiration, Waves, The Voice of Bread, Portrait, Beside the Shore, Evocation, Tiredness, The path, The Mill, Welcome Romance, Melancholy, Laziness, If You Ever Wanted to Listen to Me, The Sleeping Waters, Denial of the Spring, Rain, Leaves, Prodigal Son, The Useless Accent, Simply, New Anthem, Antaeus, Water, Passage of the Air, Fire, Oh Dreadful Night.*

Lucia, as she says, had her own style to which she applied her personality and subjectivity. Although when she studied at the Conservatory of Declamation directed by Vera Zouroff, she followed the neoclassical teachings, and these guided her verses. The neoclassical imitates the classical models, gives predominance to reason and academia, respects the rules of art, writes with metric rigor, and is concerned with formal expression. But we can never fully apply this to Lucia Richard. She never abandoned her emotions, and sought her style, within certain respect for tradition.

By then, two movements were destroying the laws of poetry: modernism and the avant-garde. Although Vera Zouroff taught classicism and considered it superior in technique to other movements, in her projects for anthologies of Spanish-American poets, she also included the modernists. Moreover, in her poetry recitals - in which Lucia Richard also participated - she included many modernist poets such as Jose Santos Chocano, Francisco Villaespesa, Victor Hugo, Guillermo Valencia, Jose Asuncion Silva, and many others. Among them, we cannot forget Federico Garcia Lorca, closer to the avant-garde or surrealism, and Edgar Allan Poe, not strictly modernist but a precursor of modern literature through the use of terror and mystery.

Lucia Richard, as we have said so many times, fled from Gongorism, from darkness and the implausible. But these movements were already installed in the world's poetry and were exerting their influence. Modernism was a reaction to the bourgeois mentality present in realistic creations. It also implied aristocratic isolation, nonconformity, aesthetic refinement, bohemianism, and dandyism.

The modernists distanced themselves from the Spanish literary tradition, except for Becquer, whom they much admired. Romanticism influenced them, especially French writers, close to Parnassianism and Symbolism. From Romanticism, they imported that same uneasiness for life, the uprooting from society, a way of expressing themselves intimately and sentimentally. They also deepened in the passions, in the mysterious, the fantastic, the dreamlike, and in escapism. In their works, the sensitive prevails over the intelligible.

They used colors, sound effects, synesthesia, with exquisite treatment of lexicon and metaphor.

At that time, Ruben Dario was the great patriarch of Spanish-American literature and a great modernist. To say that he influenced Lucia Richard is not to risk too much since he attracted a large part of the Latin American poets. If Becquer was the hero of the Romantics, Ruben Dario was the hero of the modernists. It seems that this aristocratic influence of Dario, of French origin, with his evocation of swans, fountains, abbeys, pages, counts, and marquises, fits in with Lucia's mentality. The poetry of the time experienced some osmosis concerning the Modernist movement, from which it received its influences.

However, with regard to Romanticism, Lucia always advocated "a more serene imagination." If she liked the Classical Antiquity, or if she cultivated the mysterious, she always fled from the extravagant or exaggerated. Her world is that of minimal beings, humble creatures, and simple objects. She seeks the soul of these beings and finds parallels with human feelings. With this, she aligned herself with figures like St. Francis of Assisi, Tagore, Chopin, Maeterlinck, or the Chinese artists. Lucia believes in the sacredness of beauty, in the eternity of art, and in her formal expression, the senses prevail over reason. She imposes aesthetics and charm on the concept.

In this, she was totally opposed to the avant-garde. Lucia did not copy but was inspired by nature. The model for her verses was nature, while the avant-gardes wanted to create their own reality. The avant-gardes broke with any academic position. They practiced irony, defended cynicism as a moral value, despised rhythm, and rhyme. Moreover, they believed in poetry that was pure or devoid of all artifice. The avant-garde movements were based on surrealism, cubism, Dadaism, ultraism, stridentism, futurism, machinism, among others. Breton, Marinetti, and Picasso were their heroes.

Their motives were new. The technique, progress, and modernity attracted them. They rejected the sweet sentimentality and sacredness of art or beauty. Chopin, in their opinion, had to go to the electric chair. They hated Ruben Dario and publicly degraded him. The avant-garde was rebellious, irreverent, and insolent towards tradition and its norms. They made fun of the academy, defended Creoleism or nativism. They despised everything Spanish. They were interested in the native, pre-Columbian, and indigenous aspects. They also distanced themselves from modernism and followed black culture. Emotions did not matter at all, reason prevailed over feeling, and the use of irrationality was omnipresent.

Moreover, the avant-garde was ungodly, fleeing from dogmas and mysticism, and practicing eroticism. Many of them were Marxists who used poetry as a political and even revolutionary tool. Transgression, black humor, the macabre, and the baroque were their hallmarks. They denied the divine powers of the poet. Nor did they believe in the universality of art. What mattered was the now or the future, the past was worthless. Jazz would be their music. Huidobro, with his creationism, used typographical experiments, his well-known calligrams. Speed attracted the avant-garde. They were nihilists. They broke with Aristotelian mimesis, and any recourse was valid as long as it scandalized the bourgeois (*epater le bourgoise*).

All these ideas were totally opposed to the way Lucia Richard perceived things. Although Lucia declared that she did not follow any school, on many occasions she objected to orchestral literature, to Neruda's surrealism, and bizarre verse. The writer also scorned the pointless and torn painting, the macabre, and the musical avant-garde. She was not interested in populism or nationalism. On the contrary, she pursued a certain mysticism and had a markedly sentimental and intimate spirit. The poet deified beauty beyond measure and loved calm. She shared the romantic vision that only through love could one enter the mysteries of life. Lucia was incapable of creating with cold reason: *Omnia Vincit Amor*, love overcomes everything.

In the prologue of *Blue Smoke*, she clearly explains her aesthetic ideology:

> "The first condition a poet must have is sincere admiration. When we get used to a landscape, we stop seeing it. Every time we take up the pen, we must ask ourselves how we would write if it were the first time. True poetry, like pure music, does not begin on paper but in the heart. To admire, understand, and love passionately is art or poetry. The rest is wit, dexterity, brainstorming, fireworks." (Richard, Lucia, 2004, p. 178).

And it is precisely this "cerebral reasoning" on which the avant-garde is based, something from which Lucia fled as if from death. The avant-gardes practiced ugliness and claimed disorder, the storm, the disappointment of melancholy. What interested them was the industrial and mechanized world. They renounced tenderness. They were iconoclastic, heterodox, and marginal. They introduced neologisms and truculent images. They were provocative and attacked established values. However, although Lucia did not support these ideas, she ended up accepting some postulates of this movement. In her first poems, she practiced the consonant rhyme, whether embraced or crossed. But later, she used assonance and free versification, a typical element of the avant-garde.

Although Lucia continued to write sonnets and quartets, she also used this absence of rhyme, getting rid of the musicality of the verse to focus more on the meaning, the concept, even the metaphor. In her final years, the poet leaned more towards content than form. She was more interested in the semantics than the lexicon, more in the meaning than in the aesthetic enjoyment of the poem. Also, skepticism and melancholy emerged in many of her verses, but she never gave up on beauty or authenticity.

We can divide her verses into naturalistic, existential, mystical, and miscellaneous. Her naturalist poems include works such as "Symphony of the Seasons," which, as in *Vivaldi's Four Seasons*, tells us about the metamorphosis of nature, when it is transformed in its various stages. In "Flowering," she describes the emerging energies that spring releases, its vital orchestra, its bacchanal of flowers and laughter, its vivacity of colors, the optimism it awakens in beings. In "Fullness," she talks about the emotions that summer transmits, with its intense colors, sounds, crickets, fruits, and golden reflections.

Birds, insects, and butterflies populate the air. In the landscape, trees, and flowers reign. All compete to form this picture of beauty, an image of God. In "Premonition," she announces the fall, dialoguing with the imprint of a waning world that refuses to die. It is dying but still is warm and latent, ready to dream and love, disposed to nostalgia, and melancholy. Its skies are elusive of stars, and its avenues padded with leaves, are golden tunnels that creak in our path. "Death" is the end of this act of transmutation, in which beings die, leaving behind their trail of cold desolation.

In "Ceremonial of the Dawn," Lucia tells us about the shy smile of light that is drawn on the horizon when morning comes. It is just a faint glow expressing itself imperceptibly. It is also an invisible and virginal anima that suddenly transforms into a torrent of light that illuminates beings, insufflating them with beauty and radiance. In "Little Golden Clouds," she describes with all her feminine sensuality, and her plastic and colorful sensitivity, the fragile beauty shown by the clouds of the first morning. Light, graceful and subtle, full of grace and color, they draw their chaste physiognomy on the surroundings, which, as in Rafael's strokes, reflect all the delicacy of a nature that is a naive expression of art.

In "Joyful Dawn," she shows us the virile power of light, whose splendor illuminates the trees, the streams, the earth, and the sky. Once again, she enters into the incorporeal; what we can only suggest in order to understand it; think to model it; see its manifestations to capture its presence. "Solitary Trees," are proud natural watchtowers dominating the horizon, contemplating the exuberant spectacle of life. Haughty lookouts of the summits, robust star shepherds, they witness the passage of the elements and the changes in the environment.

In "Domains of the Sea," Lucia skillfully explores all the characteristics of the sea: its violence, its majesty, the beauty of the elements that dialogue with it, its flashes of light. In "Sleeping Waters," she bases herself on a painting by Lucien Peri, a French painter of Corsican origin (1880-1948). He was a remarkable landscaper, gifted with a subtle vision of transparency and clarity, and a great colorist. As a sensitive artist, he could recreate the beauty of the sea, the imposing mountains, and the best moments.

Lucia, in a different tone, speaks to us of sadness and mystery, of water with a personality that reflects the subconscious, and holds the beautiful. It remains motionless like a mirror of the universe and sleep. Facing the impetuosity of the sea or the agitated movement of life, the sleeping waters, in eternal rest, collect the visions of the sad poets; reflect the lights of the sky. The sleeping waters evoke human consciousness itself. In the form of static figures, they are the embryo that does not undergo metamorphosis. They remain inert, silent, as perennial witnesses to the merciless passage of time.

"The Denial of Spring" from 1942 is strange poetry, very different from Lucia's jubilant style. Here, she denounces the absurdity of the renewing power of spring, when one lives in a world of annihilation and war, devastated by death and destruction. There is nothing to celebrate in a grieving world. Spring and its healing power would be like sacrilege on a stage desecrated to beauty.

"Rain" would be a poem endowed with a certain speed. It combines the exaltation of the marvelous with some acrimony and ghostly silhouettes with explosions of light. In the background, she discusses the inexorable passage of time, the destructive violence of nature when it manifests its strangeness. These are murky scenarios that evoke abandonment, loneliness, melancholy, or the longing for a mysterious past, burdened with a broken charm. And so, she feels vertigo before a silent world that has already disappeared.

In "Leaves," she deals with the melancholic laxity of autumn and the groaning of the leaves when the wind blows. They suffer as souls their destruction when the agonizing tree detaches itself from its once precious garment. The wind is killing the beings with its invisible dagger.

In "Water," she sings to the liquid element, especially the free-flowing, wild, and crystalline one. She compares seawater to a shred of eternity. It is a star that has sunk into the abyss, evoking the very process of the formation of the earth. It is also a hydra: a mythological animal with several heads that hit the rocks. In rivers, the waters are light. They are beautiful in the backwaters. In the small drop, it transforms into precious stones and a reflection of the heavens. The water is beautiful in the fountains and an enigmatic murmur at night. It is interesting to consider the lake as a placid pupil, for all that it absorbs and all that it reflects.

In "Steps of the Air," the poet strives to describe the intangible and ineffable. The wind, with its ability to make the universe vibrate, is a dreamt universe that dissolves the weight of matter. Lucia goes in search of an ungraspable beauty, of the intuited, disembodied, fleeting, and transparent poetic emotion. Defining what we can't see is like setting human personality reflected in things. Mystery and curiosity, fearful anxiety turned into uncontrolled truculence.

And so we come to her poem "Fire." In it, Lucia continues her search for the ethereal, for lyrical and unattainable beauty, where spirit and matter forge. In that place, the signifier meets its meaning; reality finds its ideal. Interspersed between the mythical and the ancestral, the cave, and the universal, Lucia defines the concept of the concept, the nothing that burns, the invisible power of what we barely see. In "Dawn," she expresses with all her feminine sensuality, the magnificent spectacle of the dawn, the beauty longed for and felt. The poet finally reaches that realm, or rather a state of the soul. There she experiences the fecundity of the world in its lights and colors. She contemplates the radiance of its throne while listening to its bacchanal of echoes and sounds.

In "The Aromo and the Summer," she describes the powerful resonance of the aromo. The aromatic myrrh-tree acts as a harbinger of spring, with its wonderful blonde hair and halo of light. It conveys hope and illusion and announces life as a song of resurrection. All this dynamic resurgence ends with the slow rest of summer, with its warm presence of precious beings and its wonders of beauty.

In "Austral Winter," she portrays the lack of life in desolate landscapes, expressing her despair in the face of a barren world. In passages full of lyricism, she describes all the pain of nature, when it contracts lethargically and inertly, devoid of all its strength and beauty. In all these poems, the author often uses prosopopoeia. It is a figure that consists of attributing to inanimate or abstract beings characteristic of animate beings. And so, the spring, the wind, the light, the water, the leaves, and the sea have personality. They think or manifest themselves in their environment. They disturb or uplift the atmosphere.

Continuing with the second cycle of poetry, "the existential ones," the work begins with the poem entitled "Blue Smoke." In the same line as Quevedo when he wrote: "I will be dust but dust in love," the blue smoke, the color of melancholy, would be what remains after a passionate life that ends in ashes. Eros, the god of fertility, is annihilated. But when matter and spirit merge on its sacred altar, the dying man is renewed in blue smoke, chaste and ethereal.

Here, the poet suggests the survival of the soul in the face of the transience of matter.

An interesting metaphor is "The Crystal Fishbowl." Here Lucia compares the restless life of some goldfish locked in their glass bowl to the life of men trapped in their banality. And like those who believe in their freedom, men live a life of arrogance and vanity. They do not realize the futility of all their purposes or the absurdity of their trifles. These selfish individuals lead a life of appearance, in the service of a world of materiality. Precious life, fleeting life, wasted in a useless posture, of empty beings. They are tied to their alleged superiority. With their oblique and reptilian glances, they try to tame those who are different from them: those endowed with vision and goodness.

In "The Windmill," Lucia, imbued with a sad mood, creates a parallel between a simple object, embodied in an old mill, and a human being. And like the human, the mill grows old. It does so beaten at the mercy of the wind, of fate, of some blades that squeak like moans. Its suffering is a widespread clamor. Like human beings, its skeletal, aching arms ask for shelter when they tire. As a regret or a song, windmills make us spin, without an end, just like a vain existence.

"The Path" is a beautiful poem in which Lucia walks and walks. Abstracted and out of her temporal space, she wanders as if she were in a desert. Going through an invisible trajectory, she looks for something indefinable and strange. The poet is alone and obsessed, deaf to the world, unaware of herself, and without direction. She walks as she suffers a shower of glances that surround her like darts. Under the rhythm of uniform and constant steps, steps without footprints, Lucia continues to walk with indifference. In the woods, a star spies on her. This poetry symbolizes the disenchantment of a woman who has lost her horizon in life, living secluded in her solitude. She transits by inertia, floating on the sensitive world, detached from people and things.

"Fatigue" reinforces the discouraging feeling we've seen before. Here, Lucia portrays pictures of an idyllic mansion, the one chosen by the author to spend her last hours. These are the restless hours when she would like to die, but she would not. It is a country house, in which humble and simple objects coexist. They lie in perennial tranquility, of detained time, of inviolate beauty, watched over by a sleepy and friendly mastiff. That enclosure of rustic silence, lost abbey, has a smiling bell that warns when the wicked stranger tries to desecrate that indolent peace. In that place, nobody can disrupt those pure and pleasant thinking.

In "Sadly Alone," she continues to talk about loneliness, in a world where nothing could make her vain. She has lost interest in earthly things and even believes that her loved ones would stop loving her. Only the love she felt was hers, like the song of the bird or the murmur of the river. Abandoned without a purpose, she remained with her sad thoughts and strange silences. That alone was hers in a world that never knew how to grasp or understand her.

In her poem, "I Built a Tower of Silence," Lucia tells us how she built a fantastic tower. It was a tower of privacy where she lived her own world, ideal and imaginary, disembodied, and unworldly. There the poet felt the night full of mysteries, suggestions, and languages. The air was blowing signs and rumors. Suddenly, she saw a shower of stars that ignited her soul and dilated her pupils. She also perceived the anguish of the waters as they produced shadows in the night. Fear distorted reality and created strange figures. The pines projected black silhouettes around them, and the dark mountain outlined a tragic profile.

But then the first-morning ray burst into the sky, illuminating the stream and the road. There, in her tower, in a somewhat telepathic experience, and surrounded by a magical atmosphere, she had presumptions of presences. She captured the intensity of the glances and felt the energy of the passing thoughts. She understood the hidden forces that produced the smiles and screams. Her tower of silence was her accepted and desired prison. From there, she could see the world in the distance, and its ills could not harm her.

In "Melancholy," the author sketches with an impressionist stroke, a blurred path of naked trees. In it, some lovers kiss each other without the shadows hiding the brightness of the day. But she, with a diffuse brushstroke, in the manner of Delacroix or Fortuny, continues to paint her melancholy, her path of frozen leaves. She can't glimpse the stars, and the moon hides lost. There Lucia finds herself trapped in that gloomy and romantic world. In her lines, one can sense an atmosphere of fog, a faded day, a pale and unlit after-noon, and gray dawn. The night is deep and insane, and life tires her out like a painful burden, like a blind remora. A world without light is a world without hope. It is a place of sorrow populated by unfortunate thoughts, where death lurks unmoved.

In "The Rebellion of Suffering," Lucia continues in a melancholic tone, now even more intense. Suffering is rebellious because it imposes itself on our will to tame it. Once again the author is interested in the invisible things that have consequences in the physical world. How much does sadness weigh? Can we quantify it, measure it, or materialize it? We do not glorify crying, nor do we exalt grief. Strength, domination, attracts us, and we make fun of the weak in circus shows.

Sadness becomes anguish, settles in our throat, and squeezes so hard that even talking torments us. Silence drowns us, and its pain is as sharp as a tight rope knot. Melancholy grows and grows so profusely, like a mist that it turns to darkness, that when it settles, it is the night that has come.

In "Sloth," Lucia, with ascetic humor, claims the contemplative life, quiet-ism, the value of serenity. For her, that laziness is half sensuality, half melancholy. She looks for an ancestral sense to her laxity and finds it in a Moorish past, of love and dreams. She feels laziness before the sun, when she scrutinizes the stars, or when she sees a sunrise. The indolence, the suspen-sion of the senses, attracts her to the point that he would like to be a stone or a quiet lake. The poet compares laziness to a liquor that rises to her head and intoxicates her pagan body.

In a similar way, we find her charming poem, "The Useless Theme." She seeks this motif or emphasis, that blue note that disarms us, those vital epi-sodes that apparently do not transcend the calculated architecture of life. It can be a subtle moment, a sublime image, an evocative word, or an irresistible fragrance. It can also be a subjective silhouette, a brush-stroke of Monet, slowly emerging from the water to the rhythm of Satie's music, smiling at us and suddenly fading away.

It can be the sun contemplating us timidly as it passes between two clouds that embrace each other. It can be the foam that walks between two waves, which suddenly bursts its rainbow into the environment in slow motion. It can be a lonely flower clinging to life on a stony path. It can be a warm and unexpected wind that suddenly revitalizes our senses.

Our heart is like a sanctuary, a sleeping lake, which lies without expression, subjected to the routine of the days. It waits patiently for the arrival of these signs, which bring splendor to our life. The useless theme is that divinely gentle one that does not count in the tyrannical geometry of life. Lucia's ear extends, embracing the world in search of its echo.

In "Joy," Lucia shares an almost lustful feeling, her desire to achieve supreme happiness. The poet seeks a vibrant and turbulent emotion, a lively symphony, a crazy fantasy, a triumphant, and attractive agitation. It would be like an orgy of exciting sensations coming out of her mouth until she drowns in that unbridled rage of joy and laughter. She would want all this as a way to forget the eternal pain, the unfulfilled love, the anguish of death, the weariness of life, and the things she loved but lost. She would not want to hear anything sad or unattainable dreams.

If Lucia usually expresses tranquility in her poetry, her poem "Disorder" appeals to chaos, as the germ from which the beauty of life is born. The disorder of the seas, the upheavals of revolutions, the trees shaking their foliage: all this leads to harmony. The cold swirl of leaves in autumn, or the stars that emerge grouping in constellations, create, in the end, a sweet balance of the world.

But "Disorder" is also a love letter between the author and her anonymous reader, whom she seduces and makes him feel as if her words address only to him. She realizes that at last, her message will reach its recipient. In the end, she will release and share her emotions. The more she perceives the arrival of this person, blessed by nature with the capacity to understand, the more her heart races in a crazy beat. The longer this encounter delays, the more she feels dying because she knows that without her absence, this meeting would not be complete.

She verbalizes her story with the shared tone of the first person plural, incorporating the reader into her feeling. Thus she invites him to listen to the waves and to vibrate with the groaning of the storms. The poet also summons him to feel the hoarse singing of the wind or to sense the heroic voices of the landscape. Lucia wonders if, when she has to lie in the cold, narrow, and icy grave, she will not be nostalgic for her restless body. She does not know how she would get used to living in the ether.

Pagan life, changing and unstable, is beautiful as it is. In the unpredictability of life, she finds the joy of existence. Discovering a new mystery, uncertain and ineffable, is like tasting an unexpected sweetness on the same lips we kissed yesterday. She declares her affection for us. The poet believes that by reading and re-reading her work, we will discover her each time with a different facet. Then her love will be the rebirth of another love. With her usual generosity, she takes us by the hand. Lucia invites us to an agitated race in search of joy, to delight in the restlessness of love. With this, we can distill a little bit of infinity and escape from the routine that hurts human existence so much.

In "Inspiration," she tells us in a few lines what the creative process is for her, whether in poetry, music, or painting. She compares it to the flame of a moment. It can also be a commanding voice that cries out to us or an insatiable longing that the soul agitates. All this transports and torments us, allowing us to see the world.

In "The Voice of Bread," Lucia describes in a sonnet of consonant and embraced rhyme, the experience of having heard the music of a violin in her garden. From other sources, we know that it was Bach's music that provoked her profound rapture. Affected by synaesthesia, her stanzas became musical. She still believed she could hear the resonance of its echoes. They transformed the roses into sounds and the fragrances into cadences. As imaginary characters of a great story, the fuchsias, jasmines, and palm trees were the protagonists of this chorus of fantasy. It showed, along with the music, her singing voice of beauty and brotherhood.

Also interesting is her poem "Portrait," in which she traces the main features of her personality. These are not physical traits. On one occasion, she said she wanted to be remembered with the enigmatic smile of the Mona Lisa, half melancholic, half cheerful. Lucia considered herself peaceful and, at the same time, restless, tender and serene in her way of loving. But above all, the artist felt proud and fortunate to be a romantic and a poet. But she also considered herself mystical, serious and curious, frivolous and flirtatious. That is, she was fervent and demure, but this did not impede her from being also profane, carnal and worldly; from loving herself and things of the earth.

She always longed for beauty and knew how to face life's misfortunes. She lamented being an anchorite, an introverted person. But this was the source of her adoration for vague fantasy, for lyricism. She didn't mind lying if she found poetry in things. Or to put it another way, her extreme search for beauty might lead her to prefer fiction to reality. Sometimes she enjoyed the fact that she existed. When that happened, her joy overflowed into her verses, exalting her feeling.

"Evocation" is a tribute to her father, whom she remembers with great reverence and respect, shrouded in a Franciscan robe. She evokes him always close to her and at the same time distant. She did so in peace or bitterness, restlessness or tranquility, generosity or tenderness. The image of her father accompanied her as if it were her shadow, and it would close her eyes when she died.

In the poem "If You Ever Wanted to Listen to Me," Lucia raises a sad voice. She laments, in a tone of otherness, that she cannot reach her audience, that her message is not understood. It seems she had reached a threshold where the illusion of her life, her survival, was fading as her literary career declined. And so the poet feels like a forgotten statue, like something inert that transmits life beyond physical death, but is no longer aware of itself. To be heard, she would like to erase the universe and its ghosts, to remain in the solitude of the extinct stars, to stop their flight without wings.

"Dreadful Night" is an extraordinary poetry. In it, she tells us of her astonishment at the experience of contemplating the vast universe. It is a trance from which all sorts of confusing feelings arise. First, she speaks us of her weakness in communicating with this superhuman entity. Lucia faces it, shrunken and overwhelmed by its immense power. With this being, she dialogues while receiving its effluvium and particles. This distant reality sends its messages. The poet tries to interpret its invisible stars and its luminous signs.

She attempts to understand the sidereal mysteries of this infinite cosmos. But she shudders at its shadows. In that eagerness of study, she feels dread and the poet connects with the deepest part of human consciousness: its Stone Age. She compares space to the sea: a deep ocean into which she is irresistibly drawn. There, alone, she enters another dimension. The poet experiences a growing fear when confronted with that powerful colossus, a pagan universe.

She appeals to the priestess of the mystery, who, in her oracle, makes predictions to discover hidden things. Then she asks her if she is the one who steals our shadows or if she turns our bodies into shadows. That is, Lucia asks her about the enigma of the beyond. The poet wants to know if she is the one who takes possession of our souls, or if she transforms our bodies into nothing. Then Lucia declares her orphanhood. She feels an immense loneliness. The possibility of losing the connection with the creator causes her anguish. Abandoned, the writer perceives an untranslatable suffering. All human miseries come to take refuge in her breast.

After crossing this threshold of insanity, she speaks of mysticism. Souls pass by and specters come out of their tombs. Also she talks of esotericism, intuition and premonition. And so the night birds launch their moans of the day of the final judgment. They bring to the environment their strange symbolism. Here the pantheistic power of the poem reveals. The poet denies the possibility of an afterlife.

Absorbed and silent, she contemplates a dark space and suffers a cosmic terror. She thinks of the insignificance of human life, of how little it is worth. In her opinion, we are just a dead cocoon adrift, something that blossomed to wither. We are only a substance floating in the current of time. It is something that flows and is cyclic, that comes and goes eternally. Faces pass, but the process doesn't stop. Personalities and experiences overlap over the years. But they do not retain the meaning of a single life.

She lives this communion under the night, beneath this starry ceiling, as if she were a Roman priestess, a fortune-teller who makes her omens. She foresees human misery and feels cosmic anguish, uncertainty, and fatal loneliness. She has an irrational fear of being alone with her soul. There may be no hereafter, and death may be inevitable and definitive. The Sphinx could tell its secrets and reveal the tragic sense of human life.

As we scrutinize this dreadful night, she says, we come to the madness, to a heartrending night, touched by the aesthetics of romanticism. It is a night that we try to detach ourselves from so as not to fall into its madness. That's why we look for the past. We struggle to stop philosophizing. We try to hold on to the things of the earth, to listen to its beats, to avoid being alone with fear. Memories are a deception with which to avoid severe thoughts. They are allies to fight against this disturbing thought that imprisons and annihilates us. But it is useless because the overwhelmed soul is still in contact with this terrifying infinity. We cannot stop looking at the night. As ecstatic lovers, we continue to feel its abysses of mystery.

The next step in our classification comprises her mystical poetry. They are few in comparison with those included in her early books of poetry. There the mystical theme or allusion was more abundant. These poems begin with the series entitled "Jacob's Ladder." In general, Jacob's Ladder is considered the connection between Heaven and Earth. It symbolizes the hope of humans to reach eternal paradise by climbing it, as shown in many works of art. In secular contexts, it represents the ascent, progress, from darkness to light. It is a passage from the material to the spiritual and also from ignorance to knowledge.

In "The Last Supper," Lucia describes the main features of Christ's personality. She talks about his journey to Jerusalem and his relationship with the apostles. In particular, she refers to his entry into the city as a king. The magnates covered under golden canopies received him. But this did not prevent Jesus from approaching the humble, the beggars, the disinherited, and the sad. In Lucia's opinion, when the holiness of God reaches man through the Eucharist, a supreme miracle takes place. From this wonder are born sacred words that strengthen the bond between humanity and its creator.

More personal and less historical is "A Vision of Toledo." In this poetry set in the cathedral of Toledo, Lucia expresses severe and fatal thoughts. She is a woman who has lost her faith. Ghostly birds surround the poet, drawing fateful circles in the sky. But beyond that, these mysterious creatures portend misfortunes. They pursue her with their black wings and their dense shadows.

For her, there is no present, no past, and no future. Above, she sees only vultures; ahead, thick fog and behind, only pain.

Around her, she sees people carrying the same heavy cross on their shoulders. The road is winding, and she stumbles and gropes for the light. In this Dantean hell, she is lost. Everywhere the poet perceives hatred, injustice, selfishness, anxiety. She wonders how this can happen after centuries of triumphant Christianity. Where is the new world announced by the Redeemer? Where is the Promised Land? How long must we wait for the kingdom of God? She wonders if Christ's sacrifice was useless. She sees so much sterile suffering, so much love thrown in the furrow, so much hope planted that did not seem to flourish.

Amid that despair, sobbing, she screamed into the night. Her anguished voice tore up the atmosphere. Lucia felt like a castaway confined to her grave. Her instinct rebelled against a death that could not be postponed. With this restlessness, this tormented feeling, she entered the shadow. There the poet saw a phantasmagorical cathedral emerging before her. She arrived shaking at its threshold. The colossal temple remained solitary and silent, possessed by a mysterious darkness. Painfully, she continued groping until she reached the altar.

There she fell prostrate and mute, unable to pray. Trembling and fearful, she looked up, hoping to find some sign of welcome. Through the crystals, a soothing light filtered through. Its igneous rays shone with gold and blue. It was a sacred and powerful light that kissed the capitals and caressed the golden crafts. It comforted the wide pointed ceiling until it illuminated the altar. Suddenly, the silence ceased, and a vague rumor took hold of the vaults. Then the bells invaded the temple with their incessant clamor. The organ spread its beautiful harmonies, its songs and melodies.

The whole cathedral shook with its powerful notes, reviving the saints and virgins. Armed knights, monks, and cardinals stirred in their tombs. Then angels and demons appeared and organized a violent fight in the holy precinct. She heard the voice of Patmos. The Apocalypse and the Seven Golden Trumpets resounded calling the Final Judgment. Among these angelic voices and lightning, she saw waters that fell like a storm. The bells sounded. A priest placed the censer and the dense veil of Zion. Then, the people knelt, humbled, and trembling saw the presence of God.

In "Ask and you shall receive," Lucia speaks to us about the mystery of the Eucharist. That silent world is full of meaning. The reincarnation of Christ takes place through the Host and the consecrated Wine. No phenomenon of nature was, in her opinion, as transcendent as this prodigy. As she explains, the fact that the bread becomes a body speaks to tired believers, to sad people, and mourners. And so, Jesus Christ enters into consciences and speaks of truth and grace. Centuries will pass, but Christ will remain a prisoner in the tabernacle. He will forever be offering his blood to attain eternal life.

Among her miscellaneous poems, we find the series *Heroic Deed of Man*. She entitled her first poem, "Song to Primitive Man." Here Lucia highlights the audacity of those ignored men. Argonauts of the seas, they arrived at the coasts of Chile when there was still no history. They were strong men who faced thousands of hardships. With their tenacity, they conquered through the seas and rivers the different places of the coast.

They were bold fishermen, modest without history, sailors who rowed and paddled. Searching the sidereal signs, they came to Chile to find their Promised Land. There they procreated, built, left their mark. It was a world without borders, full of rituals, and poetry. Myth and reality merged between wild winds and impenetrable jungles. Lucia wondered what remained of those first men in us. What was left of their adventurous blood through the centuries? Those mysterious eyes, those high cheekbones, spoke for themselves. The poet was anxious to know what they were telling us about their ancient world full of ancestral traditions.

In "Presence of Chile," the author is enthusiastic about the description of her homeland. She introduces abstract concepts, beautiful ideas when she talks about a hidden seed. It fermented the fertile soil of the centuries, imprisoned between the seas and a gigantic alabaster wall. Then she comments on the narrowness of Chile, which she compares to a thin spike or a slender lily. This land is remote, punished by avalanches, lashed by waves, shaken by tremors, volcanoes, wind, and rain.

She praises its millenary forests, its wealth of metals, the dark faces that came and forged its race. It is a desert land in the north, warm and fertile in the center and rainy in the south. It is a land of peaks, of a vibrant sea, of thousands of contrasts and beauties. Greedy, it hides its treasure in the farthest place in the world.

In "Crowd," Lucia focuses on the group's strength to transform the world. She compares the crowd to a mass caught in invisible networks, working in unison. This swarm can act like a raging sea or a frightened troop. It can feel pain and make it even bigger or gather joy, fervor, and mysticism. In its image, the innumerable and opaque corpuscles of the sands were created. Like drops, it gets confused by water or rain. Fleeing from the void and silence, men huddle one beside the other, like trees in the forest.

Its appearance resembles that of the infinite stars. This crowd is comparable to a giant horse, which rides animatedly with its voided wills. It is like a beast that advances or restrains in response to the whip or bridle of history. Its trait is the seed that will one day be a bud and a plant. When something stirs it, with pain, an epoch is born. Its misery is immense, as is its hope. The lonely man sometimes withdraws in fear, sad, and alone. But when he becomes part of the multitude, he shines brightly like the light of the dawn that throbs in a new morning.

"Terror" is a criticism of the evil power of the atom. It is a fear embedded in man, comparable to the dread of primitive man. This irrational concern has led men to fight each other. They break laws, knockdown idols without mercy, and destroy everything with madness. There is certain anxiety in man inherited from the times of the caves. A response activates against danger. The first eclipse or flood caused horror to our ancestors. Other examples are lightning, fire, and flood. The Atlanteans shuddered when they were buried. Also, we can mention the panic of men of the first millennium before the end of the world. In the face of this imminent threat, they did not hesitate to destroy themselves.

In this terror the frightened consciences hid. That is the case of scientists who released the atom and destroyed life. What difference does it make? Some will say. Is not the world already doomed? In some, there is cowardly hypocrisy, and in others, cynicism. Several suffer from hysteria and regurgitate their crazy laughter, most, hidden sobs. Terror is for Lucia like an unhealthy tumor. It gnaws at the entrails, devours beings, like the fateful ghost of the atom.

In "The Sky So Blue," we see as on other occasions, the search for an idealized reality. She seeks the intangible beauty of the landscape, and also certain pessimism. The author wonders what travel is and whether life should not be a continuous journey. Our existence should be a driving force of exploration and enthusiasm. Only through the capture of the beautiful things in life can we find meaning. However, all effort is futile. Life escapes us. We follow in our footsteps, carrying miserable pains, and our future is them.

Like the previous poem, "By the Shore" is a short sonnet. In it, she compares the human soul to a boat. Once again, she gives life to things, in theory, inanimate. They dazzle under the filter of her thought. The shore lies ecstatic and asleep, and in it, a fragile boat waits. It is anxious to set sail. Its soul is divided among all the places in the world that it has traveled before.

One pleasant afternoon the boat will depart, along the blue route of the chimera. An invisible captain will decide: the sensual dialogue of things begins. Like the ship, the soul also longs to free from its moorings. It wants to conquer its destiny, to release its ideal self, hindered by the prosaism of everyday life. No matter what obstacles life surprises us with, for the patient, there will always be a port. There will always be a chance to find that balsamic sense. Like a spell, it beautifies everything, and opens infinite doors, giving us the key to all the secrets.

In her poetry "Waves," the author observes this hypnotic phenomenon, full of lyricism. In it, she finds similarities with human life. The waves shine; they carry the roar, the confusion of the foams, and the slide in their retreat. Suddenly, they interrupt their infinite swaying, tired of their monotony. They raise a bright dome, which later collapses in a cataclysm. Such is human life. It is just a brief boast, a somber scene in which we try to impose our voices. Up there, high above, the gods of Olympus, with their prisms of titans, look at us with mockery. Poor humans, brief, tiny beings, ants of their time, busy in their miseries and selfishness! They live trying to hide their insecurities, entangled in their vile machinations!

For Lucia, the waves are like crowds that arrive and threaten. But soon they retreat in disorder, like fugitive troops in defeat. As essences, they continue in an infinite turn of history, little else. Like winged butterflies of the seas, the waves continue to dance their endless dance. They represent an eternal rhythm, a cyclic look of the inexhaustible time. They are a satyr that deprives us of meaning. They are beings that confuse us in the perpetual amalgam of forgotten purposes.

In "Welcome Romance," she talks about a house decorated to receive a child about to be born. With supreme sensitivity, her delicate spirit outlines this world of beauty. The poet depicts simple and pure characters. They offer their gentle emotions to beautify this house. She describes furtive images, like that of a sparrow spying through a shutter. It hits the window with its beak. The linden trees are proud, and the red cardinals are on guard in front of the place.

In the acacia tree, the thrush forms its nest. This will be the first singing school of the little tender thrushes. Lucia continues to give free rein to her emotion blessed by nature. Finches, doves, orioles, blackbirds, and woodpeckers populate her dream world. Trees also have a personality. The old willow tree smiles. It is tender and a little conceited and has the grimaces of a grandfather. Wildflowers conquer the cracks in the road. The moss peeks shyly through the brownish roof. The clouds, the sun, and the clear skies announce the spring.

In "The Prodigal Son," she talks about that crazy desire we all have to escape from reality and expand. We aspire to be ourselves and not what others or circumstances impose on us. We all have those frantic moments of feverish delirium. They are episodes of physical and mental ecstasy. It is a time when we turn like the blades of a mill in search of our destiny. We want to run away, to flee at all costs, like the *Two Women Running on the Beach* by Picasso. They run full of joy, with their arms outstretched and anxious steps. They embrace what life offers them, even the effluvium of the cosmos.

For Lucia, it is like riding winged steeds, while ascending in a dream into space. Like smoke, she breaks free from her material prison. The poet becomes ether, formless, lazy, capricious, and volatile. She refuses to be an insensible, immobile, rigid, cold, and eternal statue. Her life is made of music, of vibrant melodies, of endless variation and movement. She wants to be like shining waters that flow vertiginously through the valleys. She likes to have young blood, which she compares with cordial liquor.

Lucia wants to run through the fields with an abundant supply of dreams. She rushes with her soul detached from things, and her sandals fitted to her light feet. She wants to leave happily to conquer the open horizons, pushed by the winds of nostalgia. The poet continues her path thinking that the dream will not end, with no purpose in mind.

"Simply" would be the counter-figure to the previous poetry. Here Lucia is sad and melancholic. She faces the attitude of every writer: words could be just words and not meanings. Therefore, we can shape them and even distort them. She is tired of so many anxieties and can no longer ruminate on her sadness. She cannot stand anymore to go after words and chimeras. Why condense emotion and then give it away as embalmed perfume?

She wonders if she is not caught in a vicious circle. Her message could well be a fountain of fake transparencies. It could vanish into thin air without leaving a bright flash, a result, or a consequence. It could be lost forever without being heard by an attentive audience. She wonders if it all comes down to a juggling of the image or a firework of the idea. She asks herself if her words were just beautiful dry butterflies arranged on a cork. Lucia searches for authenticity. To achieve this, it is even necessary to leave the words aside. Sometimes, they become redundant and an obstacle to expression.

That is why she sees in simplicity the highest seal of purity, of genuine ingenuity. She wants to get rid of all the false clothes that veil us, leaving us eclipsed and confined in a spurious world. She wants to go carelessly to the mountain, without lies and serene. Lucia demands that you listen to her when she says "star" or "light" or speaks of silence or sadness. She asks you to understand her almost with a gesture, without any more words or adjectives.

A very different outlook has her poetry "New Hymn" from 1944. In it, she evokes the damage caused by the then unfinished Second World War. After the horror of shrapnel, madness, and the ravages of a useless war, Lucia writes her new hymn with deep love and tears. In it, she remembers the children who died without caresses, hugs, or games. The writer also recalls the kind and tough peasant, who was forced to cut down lives as if he were going to harvest the wheat. She also evokes the humble teacher who had to abandon his message of love and innocence. She even pays homage to the torn mothers who lost their children.

Summoning everyone, Lucia asks that the smiles resound. People must hear the motherly songs again. Hope must return. Contestants must abandon their rifles. They must embrace others. She implores the politicians to let the world of the simple exist, that of humble souls and lily-livered hearts. Leave in peace those who believe, those who love their land, the peasant, she says. He also prays that the illusion of the poet may thrive like the sweet naivety of the child. In the name of the devastated land, she pleads for peace. In the name of the dead, she begs for a new life in a world with hopeful dawn.

To heal the devastated regions, Lucia longs for the snow to fall and put on a mantle of forgetfulness. Spring will bloom, and in the trees, birds will return to nest. To wash away the bloody earth, she wishes for the lake to overflow. Then the green and the illusion will grow, where before there was only hatred. We must unite our voices in a song of hope. A new hymn of bells will rise above our heads redeeming the wounded world.

Finally, closing this cycle of *Blue Smoke*, we find the poetry "Antaeus." It is a criticism of modern man, locked up in the big city. Antaeus was a giant of Greek mythology, who challenged and killed all those who crossed his domain. He always won in his attacks, because his mother, Gaea, or the Earth, continuously revived his forces. In the same way, modern man had lost the connection with the land. He had stripped himself of his roots with nature and hence his current weakness.

Contemporary man glorifies his apparent freedom. He boasts of his omnipotent will. But deep down, he does nothing but lives locked up in his cabin, confined in his anguish and tiredness. This man cannot contemplate beauty.

His daily life absorbs him. The sun shining on the fields does not move him. He spends all his time in his lair, and there, death surprises him.

Nor does he listen to the harmony of the world. He only pays attention to the incoherent murmur and stridency of the big city. This human being cuts his ties with infinity. Of course, deep thought does not concern him. The afterlife is of no importance. He moves away from the field, and with a blind impulse, enjoys the neon lights. And so, he becomes a prisoner of the new concrete cities. Lucia believes that these modern cities are a den of anguish, a Babel of perdition, and punishment. This new man created by the Industrial Revolution lives happily in this microcosm. This person is like a leaf thrown into the stream, or a bird lost in exile.

Lucia believes that this man lives in chains. He has succumbed to the attraction of this city, the product of artifice, and all that is false. That is why she implores this tired and weak man to leave his prison. For his safety, he must get out of the cell in which he has confined himself. Leaving behind his illusory Eden, like Anteo, he can purify his spirit and invigorate his body. The poet feels sorry for this sad man who lives in anguish and discontent. She pities him for being incapable of appreciating beauty.

He, who was born a nomad, now lived locked up in his cave. He was a humble miser, a slave of his need. Lucia wonders if this man realizes the joy of creating something of his own with his own hands. The fact that this man is indifferent to spring or autumn disturbs her. This man does not value the peace that a pool of clear water offers. How can he not see poetry at a bend in the path? How can he not feel the warmth that the sun gives us when it looks at us through a hole in the clouds?

He doesn't even feel the emotion of understanding how the night expresses itself. When the enigmatic moon shows its brightness, it means nothing to him. Its benevolent rays fall like rain in the peaceful countryside, but it does not interest him. In short, Lucia exhorts this modern man, tired and weak, to kill his old, old-fashioned and sterile self. He must renew himself. She asks him to tear out those eyes that do not see. He must move his arms freely and adhere to the earth to live passionately again (Richard, 2004).

INSIGHTFUL ESSAYS

Marina Ortiz de Gaete

Around 1947, after having published *The Enigma*, Lucia Richard undertook a new challenge. The Zig-Zag publishing house had announced a biographical contest in which she became fully involved. After long research sessions at the National Library, Lucia sent a new essay to the contest. It was based on the historical figure of Martina Ortiz de Gaete, wife of the conqueror Pedro de Valdivia. In her work, she showed great psychological introspection. The writer also stood out for her great capacity for research and her ability to relate different aspects of colonial society[19].

---

[19] Although the family considers that Lucia wrote this work in the early 1950s and probably in 1955, Vera Zouroff in her book *The Cenacle of Poetry to its Poets: 19 Poets of the Poetry Cenacle* dating from 1947, (cited above), already referred to this work that qualified as a biographical essay. Note that Guillermo Gonzalez Echenique acknowledged receipt of the work and replied to the author on July 12, 1949. There-fore, she must have written the piece before this date (*Obras completas*, ob Cit, p. 368). On the other hand, the author herself said that the idea for the essay came about in 1941, on the occasion of the commemoration of the fourth centenary of the foundation of Santiago (*Obras completas*, ob Cit, p. 268). However, everything indi-cates that it came up later than *The Enigma*. Vera Zouroff, in her book *19 Poets of the Poetry Cenacle* published in 1947, stated that Lucia *"had an essay ready for the press-es."* But, if it was a biographical essay (she referred to complete some passages with her fantasy), the author would have superimposed her personality and her judgments on this pile of information. For this reason, even if she went through difficult historical

With this new literary project, Lucia was trying to broaden her intellectual horizons. By publishing more serious works, she was fighting for her survival as a writer. She chose a pseudonym *"Eleerre,"* a clear allusion to "L.R." (Lucia Richard). The reason for this pseudonym is not easy to know, but we can guess several reasons behind it. Lucia likely wanted to give a new impulse to her literary career. Therefore, she did not want to be "typecast" as a poet. Perhaps she did not want the jury to prejudge her for being a woman, or for belonging to a particular social group. A third possibility is that the use of the pseudonym was mandatory by the rules of the contest.

In any case, the work was discarded. Otherwise, the editor would have published it, which did not happen. This rejection must have been a big blow to the author's career. From that moment on, she did not publish anything else. Yet, Lucia overcame this setback with intense social work. The fostering of culture, women, youth, and children were some of her priorities. Later she dedicated herself to her role as a columnist and radio broadcaster. With all these initiatives, the writer developed a great work as a promoter of knowledge.

On July 12, 1949, Guillermo Gonzalez Echenique, received a copy of her essay. After examining the book, he responded to the author in commendable terms. Then, summarizing the main aspects of the work, he told her the following:

> "Let me suggest an idea. Print your work. And who will read this book? You will ask me. I cannot assure you of great public success, in these times of crime novels and film dramas. But rest assured that there will always be people who stop to pick a rose. And they will admire the perfect elegance of its petals and the vivacity of its colors. As long as there are people who bless the Lord and his creation, your book will have readers." (Richard, 2004, pp. 368-369).

---

research, she did not have to follow a system of sources. Although by including historical documents, it would have been more appropriate to mention them. Everything indicates that the work is of a hybrid genre.

Mr. Gonzalez Echenique's response was friendly and courteous. But perhaps he did not understand the real reasons that led Lucia to become interested in this character. We usually perceive history through a male lens, the result of battles and more battles, names, and dates. It is the chronicle of the victors, the powerful, the rich, and the strong. It is the account of the madmen, who oppressed the peoples and subjugated the weak. Later, the writers bribed by the victors praised them. There was nothing left for the humble, the poor, or the women. In general, women have not been the protagonists of history. They are mere shadows of shadows, ashes.

Something similar expressed Lucia in her poem "Medal." With great elegance and without cataclysms she wrote:

Observe

Sculpted with the bronzes of glory and fame / the medal of life, exhibiting goes on its obverse:

The brave winners of battles, / in proud and perfect reliefs, / those who triumphed in the jousts of the sciences, / those who overcame in the fights of money. / For them the pleasant looks,/ the laudatory smiles, for them.

Reverse

And on the reverse, with simpler, more faded profiles, / go the long caravans of oppressed, / which to the cunning of the fittest succumbed; / the heroic precursors fought, / the dreamy and bohemian poets; / Go the Christs betrayed by the Judas, / go the timid, the good / and the anguish of the miserable plebes / of a hundred peoples / who through different latitudes / is the same humanity that is suffering (Richard, 2004, page 103).

In 1936, Jorge Gustavo Silva, Lucia's partner in the Cenacle of Poetry, had already written these ideas with some nuances. In his work *The Leftists in History*, he dared to attack Chileans for their love of genealogies and heraldic shields. The work cataloged as progressive was a gallery of Fathers of the Church, freedmen, reformers, martyrs, and rebels. In it, he revived heretics of all ages, illustrious or obscure forerunners, and all those who protested against something or someone. He also focused on those who suffered oppression and exile or opposed the constituted powers. History can never tell everything. It is a selection. Made by the winners, it has selected those who won.

Lucia Richard never got that far. Her interest was in the heart, not in politics. With this biographical essay, she wanted to dignify a woman who had been vexed and forgotten by history. It would have been much easier to extol the figure of a hero of great and remarkable acts. Yet, Lucia was concerned about an almost anonymous woman. Surrounded by bitterness and failure, the conqueror's wife was an anti-hero. Her figure represents the antinomy to any colossus in history. This aspect is what awakened Lucia's interest. It was a brave choice, perhaps not well understood by her editorial jury.

The work can be described as slow with a lack of speed in some passages. Besides, it has a lack of virulence, or dynamism and is more oriented towards serenity. But above all, defect or virtue, we could speak of the absence of dramatic sense. These are attributes that define Lucia Richard's personality. With a mastery of adjectives, Lucia drew up an entertaining and well-constructed story. The concatenation of the characters and the historical events are well shown. But for Lucia, this was just an excuse, a pretext, to focus on what she was most interested in. And that was, to enhance the dignity of an ignored woman, who by the injustices of fate saw her life completely cut short.

It all starts in Castuera. There Marina married Pedro de Valdivia, the future conqueror of Chile. However, happiness is ephemeral. The great man goes to the Conquest, and his wife remains in Extremadura, abandoned in a long wait. There was no time to enjoy the pleasures of sex. There was no time to have children to remind her of her husband. The days pass and pass without a break. Marina has to face the mocking smiles. Then there is the suspicion of infidelity.

Finally, there is hope. Alderete brings good news to Castuera. Pedro de Valdivia is now the new governor of Chile. Excited, she embarks on a long journey abroad to join her husband. But upon arrival, she receives the news of his death. After enthusiasm, it comes desolation. The Indians have destroyed the city of Concepcion. And what is worse, her husband's lands were there. The new governor recognizes her right to inherit her husband's plots. But later some in the court conspire to strip her of her property.

She manages to impose herself on those who encourage intrigue, but it doesn't matter anymore. Her life is a desert, which no longer has any purpose. She does not feel at ease with her husband's mistress, the sanguine Ines de Suarez. A kind of American Joan of Arc, she is brave and vital. Unlike her, Marina is a dignified and shy woman. As a perfect wife, the faithful woman continues to mourn her husband. She lives many years, sees many of her relatives die, and dissipates in time in slow anonymity. Despite her husband's love affairs, she still has comfort. She still believes that he respected and loved her.

A whole life lost, truncated to love, condemned without sentence. History ignored her, leaving her sunk in an indescribable moral stagnation. Finally, she is imprisoned in the jail of her unjust destiny. And it is to this woman that Lucia, in a bold way, tried to dignify. She dedicated to her dozens of study sessions in the National Library. She played a secondary role in history, being the shadow of the hero. They were the Romeo and Juliet of Arauco, deceived by a wild and cruel world. They paid with their lives the price that the Conquest imposed on its heroes.

DANIEL PIEDRABUENA RUIZ-TAGLE

The Disturbing Question:
Synthesis of a History Review

n the last years of her life, Lucia wrote her essay, *The Disturbing Question*. This writing was not included in the *Complete Works*. It has a skeptical tone in clear contrast to the sweetness of her youthful writings. But despite that, it is by far the most advanced writing of her literary career and for many reasons. There we find a mature woman in the last years of her existence. She knew that she would not publish anymore and that she had nothing to lose. It is a piece that she directed directly to her offspring. For the first time in her life, she freed herself from worldly ties. At the end of her career, the author expressed herself through political-ideological positions. To ignore it is to denaturalize her true message.

After a lifetime of reflection, Lucia wondered what the truth was. Based on her knowledge and experiences, she reviewed the journey of man, coming to some interesting conclusions:

> "At the root of all religious feeling beats the desire to know the truth. Man, unable to discover it for himself, takes refuge in revelation. And so, he asks help from supernatural powers to find it." (Richard, ca 1965, page 6).

Another of the themes that Lucia shows is the anachronism of life. Things that were important at another time today are ridiculous. Scientific discoveries that represented a milestone in an era are today sad antiquities. Solid ways of thinking that were the pillars of other societies are now meaningless. Fashions, the search for a canon of beauty, and literary styles of the past dissolve into the dust of time. For Lucia, everything is vanity, superfluous objectives, banality. Neither imaginary heroes nor false leaders of the people help in the search for this truth. They embody the collective trampling that made paranoid people the undisputed leaders of the nation.

Lucia denounces many vehemences of history. She criticizes the announcement of the end of the world or the regime of terror in the French

Revolution. The madness of totalitarian regimes and episodes of mystical exaltation also pain her. That is the case of the crusades to Jerusalem.

> "In many cases, ignorance, superstition, or lack of vision of leaders, were the causes of regrettable events in the past." (Richard, ca 1965, page 8).

Lucia considers that what happened in Alexandria was an aberration. The Caliph Omar ordered there the destruction of the best books of classical antiquity. Another example was the burning by order of Cardinal Cisneros of all the Jewish-Moorish wisdom after the conquest of Granada. The fanaticism of Savonarola also stands out. He was a Florentine monk who destroyed the works of Renaissance art in great pyres. About the latter, she wrote:

> "Savoranola, the Renaissance monk, is an example of the man who wanted to twist the arm of history. It was a century of joyful paganism, in which man discovered his value and felt curiosity and desire to live. Savonarola wanted to go back in time and impose the asceticism and penance of other times. His thunderous voice moved his followers for a while. The temples resounded with his words of a threatening prophet. But in the end, he died as in medieval times, in the trial by fire. Some few years later, the festivity of the divine paganism that was the Renaissance resumed." (Richard, ca 1965, page 16).

Many of the driving forces of the past, when looked back, now become absurd mistakes. In the long run, the crucified man defeated the Roman Empire. Jerusalem was destroyed. Joan of Arc perished at the stake. The Church forced Galileo to retract his discoveries. Most European courts despised Columbus. Consequently, the average man is prone to be conservative. When new advances in science or conquests of civilization appear, they attack them as if they were evil spirits. These men do not go deeper into the search for a better explanation of things.

Leaping to our present time, Lucia exposes the deification and sudden decline of leaders such as Hitler, Mussolini, Stalin, or Peron. Genocide and anti-Jewish phobia, she says, are one of the most tragic mistakes of the 20th century. Chile would be like Saturn devouring its children. This annihilation took place with great liberators such as O'Higgins, Rodriguez, Portales, or Balmaceda. All these shifts in politics, philosophy, or thought disrupt her. And so she concludes that only humility could be the fundamental principle on which all wisdom is based.

In the face with the fragility of changing history, she realizes there are eternal and immutable laws. One of them is the human heart. Its eagerness for conservation, creative restlessness, and progress makes it endure. People's idiosyncrasy is circumstantial. Physical peculiarities, climate, geographical position, and beliefs, condition it. That is why the responsibility of the historian is enormous. He must have a multifaceted personality close to the humanist of yesteryear. He must detach himself from the present time to contemplate history with perspective. Only with independence of criteria can he scrutinize with certainty the facts of the past.

There is no point in clinging to absolute truths. The mentality of men changes depending on their origin, country, century, belief, or ideology. Terms like "heresy," "democracy," "freedom," have completely changed their meaning over time. Today they are completely unrecognizable. There are great contradictions in history. The ideals embodied in words like "equality, liberty, and fraternity" were betrayed in their time. They do not fit with the savage campaigns of terror carried out in France to impose those terms.

Many times this lack of vision appears in the actions of rulers. The aim of the conquest of America was the search for a shorter route to the East or rapid enrichment. But proud Spain did not see then the immense potential of that virgin land. On the contrary, it spared no resources to prolong an absurd war in the Netherlands.

The poet believes that in this search for truth, we must free ourselves from prejudice and preconceived ideas. We must tear down the false idols we have built within ourselves and those who worship them. Often, out of laziness, we admit the beliefs imposed on us. A paradigmatic case would be modern propaganda. Even if it harbors a positive facet, it often exaggerates and deforms events, exalting mediocrities. Radio and television cooperate in this invasion of privacy. Spaces of rest and silence define the charm of a country. Certainly, propaganda affects the aesthetics of cities. Besides, it attacks our nerves with its silly messages.

Lucia is like an ascetic. She abhors all this abuse, the crowds, and the barrage of propaganda into our lives and our minds. All this publicity deifies mediocrities, causing collective hysteria. It does so especially among teenagers, the naive and the ignorant. In short, our artist denounces the manipulation of people through information. The distortion of culture for selfish purposes is something she cannot tolerate. Behind this control would be the desire to benefit the commercial houses. These brothels are home to anemic and extravagant writers or pseudo-wise painters.

The ills of Latin America also interested the writer. It was time to get out of this inferiority complex. The plundering vision that other nations had had on our continent was feeding this weakness. We had to get rid of this lack of confidence. We had to believe in the vitality of our own culture and stop reflecting on the achievements of others. Starting from an economic, sociological, and geographical base, she analyzes the problem of underdevelopment. Another problem was the difficulty of uniting diverse cultures, languages, and unexplored territories. The issue of endemic warfare and poverty implied political subversion. This situation gave rise to a spirit of rebellion and discontent in the people who suffered from it. In the end, it triggered strikes, guerrillas, etc.

It is interesting how she exposes the exuberance of the Latin American landscape. She also emphasizes the way in which intellectuals perceive all this grandeur:

"... The Latin American man knows the great distances. He experiences the arduous task of mastering the forces of nature. But this also makes him love his vernacular landscape. That paradisiacal vision was built more by spaces than realities, more by desires and legends than by looks to the future. The writers of Latin America, the great poets of this century, had set their eyes on Europe and the West. They sang these virgin forces with a vigorous brio like that of stone and red metal. They explored its nature and its primitive men, songs, and rhythms. Its dazzling colors shine in these times. Even archaeology helps to reconstruct a past influenced by the same powerful telluric force." (Richard, ca 1965, page 28).

Another burden for Latin America was the lack of personal and cultural integration of the indigenous race. The mistake of the colonizers and the heroes of independence had been to despise these peoples. In the end, from this fusion of forces of foreign and native elements, racial mixtures were born. As she put it:

"Our leaders fought on the battlefields to throw off the European yoke. But once they achieved that goal, they acted only with their eyes on their former oppressors. The new rulers copied their culture, lifestyle, and ideologies." (Richard, ca 1965, page 30).

But it wasn't just the history that was contaminated. Literature, a true mirror of the people, also looked at the West and its Greek or Eastern roots. Ultimately, Lucia stresses the need to revive the riches, art, and culture of indigenous peoples. Above all, she advocates the elimination of social classes. This was the origin of the division of Latin America and one of the greatest evils that plagued the entire continent.

Another thing that worries the author is the irruption of the atomic bomb. Using passages from the Apocalypse of Saint John, she sees in this new weapon an unprecedented threat. Its devastating effects could not be limited to a specific area. Without any kind of containment, it would spread like radioactive fallout across all countries. It was the time of Kennedy and Kruchov, the exhibitions of force, and improvised pacts. But it was also the time of panic with the coming of this new curse of humanity.

In front of this, she contemplates the positive forces of nuclear energy. The thinker urges those responsible for its use to take advantage of it as a tool for progress. Other threats to humanity were racial struggles. Lucia believes that the era of white hegemony had passed with the end of colonialism and protectorates. It was a fact that the white race led by the United States was in control of advanced technique and culture. But this did not prevent the emergence of other races from a growing boom. In her view, the yellow race was changing the face of the earth.

Chinese nationalism, with its new leaders like Mao, posed a new threat to the Western world. Proof of this was its political and military interventions in several countries and its nuclear programs. China, with communism and demographic proliferation, had awakened its millennial dream. It had acquired pride, haughtiness, and self-confidence. The Far East, in its yearning for expansion, would not forgive its former oppressors.

With similar reasoning, she reflects on the problems faced by the black race. Black people were a race historically abused and forcibly grafted into various parts of the world. This fact had caused many tensions in different societies. The era of colonialism and shameful slavery had passed. But even today, there were many black minorities in the U.S. and elsewhere. They lived oppressed by a white majority, fighting for their civil rights, which was a great source of conflict.

In front of Martin Luther King and his program of non-violence, it opposed the racial bigotry of the Ku Klux Klan. Against this, the Black Power supported violence. No less, we could see countries like South Africa, with a black majority ruled by a white minority. There were also newly independent countries like the Congo. All these antagonisms were at the origin of many disorders.

Therefore, in Lucia's opinion, strength and muscle were no longer valid. The new leaders had to devise new measures to achieve effective racial integration. These policies were to avoid these conflicts and the resentment of the old despots. Lucia explains it this way:

> "White leaders must seek the very root of evil. They need to solve these issues through education, adequate livelihoods, and housing. These rulers must respect the dignity of man regardless of the color of his skin." (Richard, ca 1965, page 43).

Consecuently, the problems of the world had only one path to redemption. And that was the total racial integration of the human family. In a show of democratic spirit, Lucia puts the Christian religion on the same level as Islam. Many different races profess both. She refers to the freedom of belief, a right now enshrined in many constitutions. This right implies the possibility of believing in one religion or a different one. It also includes following a philosophical system or not believing in anything. Let us shape the future! - She tells us - as she speaks of equality and respect:

"The second great revolution in history, the French one, proclaimed equality as an intrinsic good of man. In our times, the Charter of the United Nations also expresses it. It declares its faith in fundamental human rights and the dignity and value of the human person. The equality of men and women is essential in nations large and small." (Richard, ca 1965, page 44).

In the following paragraphs, she is thoroughly reaffirmed in these ideas:

"We must look for a deeper and more radical solution: to erase the concept of race and to make prevail the much nobler and true concept of Man."

"A true racial integration is one that does not place restrictions on family and blood unions. Thus, the world of the future will be one great nation. It will enjoy the same technique and uphold the same ideals. This society will taste the advantages of progress and will speak a common language understood by the majority of peoples." (Richard, ca 1965, page. 45).

The author realizes that she is on the verge of utopia, wondering:

Why can't the spirit of man progress as much as physical and mathematical knowledge does? (Richard, ca 1965, page 45).

Ethnocentrism is, in fact, a very intense instinct. It is a complex issue. We tend to cluster around our race, culture, and social status. Total racial integration sounds like a difficult idea to realize. But at least there should be social integration. Respect for the dignity of the different races in the human family is a central idea. We must avoid any kind of discrimination.

Lucia believes that this integration is perfectly possible. We don't have to do more than analyze history. Latin America was the result of a large number of intersections of different peoples. In successive waves of migration, they came to the continent. The same happened in Sicily, which was occupied by an amalgamation of different races. The various campaigns of conquest caused this fusion in all European countries.

Archaeological remains show surprising similarities between different civilizations in terms, myths, and customs. The language draws a varied collection of words from diverse origins. The extermination of the Indians was never complete in colonial Spain despite some bloody struggles. The Spanish merged with the indigenous population. The different features of the races were a product of the adaptation of the individuals to the climate. All these environmental factors produced a type of skin pigmentation, hair color, etc.

She also highlights the fact that racial discrimination is relatively recent. In the Middle Ages, Jews were persecuted because of their religion, not their race. Slaves from Roman conquests could be white or black. North Africa was a center of high culture. The Carthaginians made Rome tremble. That is, with these ideas, Lucia shows us the relativization of the concept of racial supremacy.

The emergence of a race at a certain time does not imply its hegemony in another different time. Unfortunately, today, says Lucia, the world tends to differentiate between different ethnic origins. Yet, she sees the creation of the UN as a formidable tool. Its integration of races, cultures, and different languages cooperates in universal understanding.

By changing her discourse, but not her goal, Lucia enters the problems of the Middle East. The Arab-Israeli war was a three-thousand-year-old conflict. The Bible alludes to the protagonists and places of this struggle. The hatred that divides the two peoples is deep and ancestral. Lucia explains it:

> "Huge deserts and oil under the sands. Asian pomp and misery. Monstrous regimes, with princes educated in Europe and illiterate, ignorant, and superstitious people. Societies with slaves in this century, ruled by socialist governments, and absolute autocracies. All this under the common denominator of lack of water and suffocating heat." (Richard, ca 1965, page 48).

Then she analyses all Nasser's political errors. The writer wonders if some day Isaac and Ishmael will be reconciled in the bosom of Father Abraham.

A new threat to humanity would come with the population explosion. Hunger would be followed by the lack of living space for human beings. In Latin America, governments encouraged increased birth rates and immigration through various programs. And the health system depended on population growth. The authorities saw this as a sign of progress. But soon, politicians had a sudden awakening. Following Malthus, they realized that the population was increasing exponentially. But food production remained stationary or did not grow at the pace of the people.

The lack of resources and the problem of hunger were later combated with birth control campaigns. The paradox is that developed countries with a white majority exercised this control. But the Asian and African countries, many of them immersed in poverty, continued to increase their populations. In Chile or in other countries, this uncontrolled population increase created (and is creating) various problems of housing, transportation, infrastructure, employment, health, and education. It also causes competition from scarce resources such as water, crops, and industry.

The different physical geography of nations had not made possible a homogeneous solution of the problem. Trying to face all these threats, FAO and other international organizations had proposed to increase the food in the world. In short, the man trusted in his technique, taking advantage of sun rays, tidal forces, and nuclear energy. The peoples devised a more rational way of redistributing and producing the land. This responsible production has been called Agrarian Reform.

American technicians introduced all this creative impulse with their Brain Trust plan. This program improved the production of the land, allowing better living conditions. The development continued thanks to important advances in machines, biology, education, and sociology. All these new ideas became a determining factor of progress. In Lucia's words:

> "It would be the dictatorship of the technique. The submission to the machine would imply a total conviction and faith in its mandates." (Richard, ca 1965, page 53).

All this machinism, industrialization, and rational use of resources tormented her. So she recalls the past with nostalgia. It would be the time of the great conquerors and navigators, explorers of the desert, and ice. She prefers these pioneers, with their sense of honor and search for glory, over the desire for material goods. Concluding this passage, she reflects:

> "One day, we will master science, technology, and energy quality. That day people will put aside their petty passions, rivalries, and ideological arguments. In this foreseeable future, we will renounce resolving conflicts through weapons." (Richard, ca 1965, page 54).

Lucia sees all these threats to humanity as a form of apocalypse. She wonders whether, in the face of all this material revolution, a spiritual one might not also be necessary:

> "More than the Americans' Brain Trust, she believes in Teilhard de Chardin's Noosphere. This ring of spiritual forces must surround us to join the future world, in its new stage of evolution. We must meet the kingdom of God on earth before the final destruction." (Richard, ca 1965, page 54).

Humanity was going through many dilemmas. Despite this, Lucia praises *Homo sapiens* as a versatile creature capable of adapting to the most hostile environments. He could produce great innovations to make life easier. The man had successfully tackled the conquest of energy and put an end to colonialism. He had overcome the disease. Now came one of the most exciting revolutions in human history. And it was the development of technology.

It was a new world, a world of science fiction. Everything had begun with a patriarchal society. From there, we moved on to the concept of community. Then we introduced the State. All these advances had brought war, slavery, and other evils. The first science, the fundamental science, was the one that explained natural phenomena.

The Romans, with their strength and organizational capacity, extended their conquests. They civilized the defeated by assimilating them and not annihilating them. It was a world of materialism and paganism. The spiritual revolution of Christ prevailed against it. Love, renunciation, and absence of selfishness were central in his doctrine. These ideas eventually undermined the very foundations of the Roman Empire.

But then the barbarians arrived. They brought down the old empire. With it, the Greek wisdom vanished, and the long night of the Middle Ages began. Knowledge was only preserved in monasteries. But one day, the printing press arrived with its rapid exchange of books and ideas. This innovation led to an era of travel, exploration, conquest, and discovery. The fall of Byzantium extended its scholars throughout Europe. This humanistic exchange favored that great phenomenon that was the Renaissance. Valuable manuscripts appeared again: the crucible of philosophy, thought, and literature of Greece. It was a time when man achieved great advances. This is how Lucia tells it:

> "As man became aware of his intellectual capacity, he seemed to discover himself. He was no longer bound by religious dogmas, traditional ideas, or institutions. This new individual threw himself boldly into the adventure of research." (Richard, ca 1965, 56).

New nations and rulers emerged. They imposed over old feudal powers and their religious influences. But as a result of all this rebellion came the French Revolution. It symbolized the epitome of this new faith in the capacity of man to seek his rights. And so, step by step, modern science, technology, the motor, and industry developed. And so we embraced the Agrarian Revolution and the Industrial Revolution. The village declined in favor of the city.

It is a new, bigger, and more sophisticated city that requires specialized workers. A new union organization gave rise to the strike as a form of demand and the masses as an entity. Art, customs, and religion changed their physiognomy. The elitist art died. It was a type of art from which only princes and the rich benefited in the restricted cenacles. Now art is standardized, becomes popular, and reaches the general public. Precious paintings that were once kept in palaces are now exhibited in museums. The same is true of books now collected in large libraries. People can also listen to music through new media.

The written word was complemented by image and sound. The theater was meticulous and handcrafted, aimed at an aristocratic audience. This approach changed radically with the advent of the cinema. Now the new method of reproducing moving images was ubiquitous and aimed at anyone. Lucia even anticipated the Internet by imagining a large screen in the classroom. This modern tool would house the rudiments of reading, writing, and mathematics. It could also be used to teach moral and religious principles, history, and geography.

In Lucia's thinking, the modern era has fallen into demerit, has lost its value. Now the realm of the ordinary prevails. The human being has renounced to his uniqueness by dissolving himself in a vast ocean of anonymity. The industrial age has brought the ease with which we receive the goods of progress. But also it has brought mediocrity of products and superficiality. We had lost the ability to appreciate the effort. Everything came to us, simplified for easy consumption.

Lucia contemplates with nostalgia the past times, the era of the cart, and the plow. She also evokes with charm the spindle for the homemade manufacture, the loom, the diligence, and the long-awaited letter. Those were times when life had a different rhythm. The man was capable of creating admirable works that defied the centuries. With time, they became works of polishing and perfection, worthy of admiration and joy. Where is the ancient craftsman who carved the stones of the cathedrals? Where is the one who forged irons and made stained glass windows? Where is the monk who illuminated books or painted fabrics? She asks herself.

The small effort to survive would amaze the man of the past. Lucia feels much more identified with this ancient world than with the busy world of today. We must experience and feel great enterprises. Only in this way can the meaning of effort and sacrifice penetrate our consciences. It is amazing the commitment of the organizers of the concerts of the past compared to the cold transmitter of our times.

Passionate comedians brought joy to the stage. They knew with their skills how to cheer people up. Then the stuffed images of the cinema replaced all this enthusiasm. We had lost the sense of community and communication between people. For Lucia, knowledge and even work must be felt. It must penetrate our emotions, pulsating within us. If not, they are merely an exercise in reasoning. They do not transcend the totality of being. They have no meaning for us. This is how she expresses it:

> "Knowledge that is not acquired gradually by a discipline of the mind, but is the result of imposed memorization, is not knowledge. The school that fills us with dates and details takes away the pleasure of experience. It is as oppressive as factory work, which by specialization deprives the worker of the satisfaction of creating." (Richard, ca 1965, p. 59).

The demands of the market, and the pressing needs of society, had brought us mass production. There was a rush to produce more, lower costs, and reduce commercial competition. All this entailed a lack of quality in the products launched. This haste to mortgage the future brought us the mediocre, damaging, in the end, the perfection. Substitutes, imitations, and copies arrived with the irruption of the factory. Lucia again claimed a slower pace of life, seeking authenticity and fullness. The divine halo and underlying beauty in things are essential elements for her. And so she denounces a world tainted with falsehoods, tinsel, and adulterations.

The invasion of technology and culture reached all layers of society. It was the wonderful Industrial Revolution. But it brought a consequence, a side effect, which was the agglomeration of men in cities. Radio and TV had spread the image of an idealized city. Under their irresistible seduction, men from the country arrived. They came in hordes seeking to improve their living conditions and salaries. The possibilities of entertainment also attracted people. This is how Lucia expresses it:

> "This is how this phenomenon of the 20th century appeared: those immense and complicated monsters that are the modern cities." (Richard, ca 1965, 61).

For Lucia, the city was the representation of anarchy. It comprised a disorderly set of buildings, narrow streets, and monuments spreading everywhere.

The superimposed houses had lost their proportion and perspective, growing in great confusion. Very different was a city, the epitome of chaos, of a forest, the most natural representation of harmony. The difficulty of moving from the periphery to the workplaces had brought us hasty meals. We left the house for too many hours. As a result, we had lost the conquests of technique, causing the dismemberment of families.

The human being had adapted from archaic times to all kinds of natural environments. But now, he was forced to live trapped in niches or beehives, enduring all the harmful effects of the big city. He had to face the dense and unbreathable atmosphere and disorders. The bright lights of the advertisements often hit him with their irregular and stupid rhythm. The high volume of the speakers disturbed his nerves. Radio and television programs entertained people instead of educating them, bringing disturbance into the house. Painkillers appeared in an endless sequence. The same causes produced the same effects.

The smog and mist of cities like London or New York had brought asphyxiation, cancer, and lung diseases. Other aspects of those cities were nervousness, mental illness, suicides, and even crime. Lucia dedicated her entire life to glorifying nature, life in the countryside, streams, and seasons. The authenticity of the life of other centuries was for her a model of a peaceful environment. The modern city, with all its confusion, overwhelmed her. Lucia felt very much out of place, in that collective madness and its restless atmosphere.

All her life, she pleaded for harmony, beauty, tranquility, and purity. Disorder, evil, madness, and vileness has no place in her mind. The city represents for the author a cacophony comparable to cubist art. The modern city, with its invading noises, and all its social outrages, invades privacy. The collective irrationality breaks with individual rationality. Lucia denounces the disorders of power cuts and car accidents. She even thinks that cities serve as targets for enemy bombing. But above all, she reflects on the feeling of loneliness caused by big cities:

"It is worthy of study by psychiatrists, the feeling of loneliness, that oppresses the inhabitant of the big cities. Frustration, anguish, and incomprehension are common among people. We never feel more alone than when we try to make our way through an unfamiliar crowd. Even the immensity of the ocean does not produce this feeling of loneliness." (Richard, ca 1965, page 62).

From the general, she goes to the particular. From the city, she descends to the street and then to the square. The Greek Agora was the point where the concerns of the citizens converged. It had a nobility halo since the solemn and consecrating moments took place there. But for Lucia, the real danger was in the street. It had replaced the courtyard of the house and the grapevine of the modest houses.

Lucia again perceives this violation of individual privacy by the community. Previously, the family home was an enclosed area that was difficult for a stranger to reach. Now, not only did people take to the streets more. Media such as radio, television, and telephone invaded their own space. The window was an imperceptible limit between the house and the street. But even through it, the community impacted us.

Life went on outside. When children were separated from their mothers, they risked all kinds of influences. Parents guarded the border between harmless and harmful. They exercised their authority and limited the children's time outside the home. When the child could not find what he or she needed at home, he or she would start looking for it on the street. This fact created a rebellious or maladjusted youth. They threw themselves into the race of delinquency, the search for the absurd and antisocial behavior.

But if the street was a danger to the young man, the city offered other benefits. These were, for example, the proximity to the centers of education and work. In the city, the young person found more possibilities to complete his education. He could visit museums and libraries. And in Lucia's opinion, he could live under a greater religious influence, with more temples and priests. This young man had better medical care and more possibilities to practice sports.

In contrast to this, the writer saw in the homes the seed of rebellion and the maladjustment of youth. The disorientation of a changing world and bad education contributed to this situation. But so did the nervousness and disorder of the homes. This generation would be the one of unconsciousness, collective anger, and debauchery. What was the origin of this rebellion? Lucia asked herself.

It was not only due to inadequate education but also to other circumstances. Heredity and the environment also played a role. The consequences of the war were terrible. After the bombings, the rulers erected the buildings again. However, the psychic personality was much more difficult to rebuild. The subconscious maintained for a long time the damage it had received. The horror of a nuclear war was not a good omen for a serene and hopeful generation.

The disintegration of the homes did not help these young people. Factors such as alcoholism, family quarrels, and child abandonment contributed to their failure. Parents' indifference to their children's problems or indecent speaking before them led to their destruction. He also referred to sexual excesses and pornography as harmful factors. Failed parents instilled false heroism in their children.

They extolled the possession of money as the first virtue. They also sought the scholastic success of their offspring to satisfy their own vanity. Faced with the self-sufficiency of young people, Lucia felt that values were necessary to guide them. Otherwise, they would become disrespectful and conceited. The accumulation of erroneous knowledge would turn the young person into a pedant who would despise his elders.

In addition to the problems on the streets and the home, Lucia was very critical of the young people:

"They judge lightly that the past is worthless, laughing at old age. They even reject the traditions of the homeland. Young people feel they own the world because they belong to this age of the atom and technology. In their ignorance, it seems to them that it has begun with them."

"In their eagerness to protest at everything, they wear flashy clothes and strange hairstyles. They do not know the good manners that in ancient societies made existence more pleasant." (Richard, ca 1965, page 68).

In short, they were young people who despised the union of the family. They ignored the classic values of art and culture. They had become the new vandals who took to the streets to disrupt the life of the citizens. But change does not always mean error, says Lucia:

"In the future we will all lead a more natural, less hypocritical and more courageous life." (Richard, ca 1965, page 68).

Fortunately for humanity, young misfits were a minority. Life itself would bring them back into the fold. Instead, there was an enterprising youth. They researched in laboratories and universities and aspired to succeed in life. In current events, there were immense changes. But these turned out to be not just the product of science or technology. New changes developed in customs, laws, economics, or the pace of time use. All these changes created an international conjuncture, dissolving the isolation of nations or nationalism. New trends in the economy led us to a world without borders:

"The world is going to its integration. As Teilhard de Chardin said, the era of civilizations is over, and the era of civilization has arrived." (Richard, ca 1965, 71).

The leisure of the upper classes was a sign of distinction in other times. But in her thinking, it cannot exist anymore. This liberal thought has many derivations. The suppression of the birthright diminished the power of the aristocracy. Kings can no longer lead absolute monarchies. A world of meritocracy reduced the laxity of the elites. Pluralization of surnames is a fact. Lucia also believed that the classification between noble and vulgar professions had disappeared. Hundreds of new specialties competed for the attention of the youth.

Let's think that in the Baroque, manual occupations were badly considered. The literature of the time is full of parodies that make fun of the impoverished nobleman. He clung to his ancestry, preferring to live in misery than to descend into the world of the unnamed. The new youth had to face the forces that were pressing the world. These tendencies were the dictatorship of technology and the masses. Many factual powers limited governments when they ruled. These could be scientific, military, or trade union cryptocracies. Besides, Lucia relativized the importance of materialism and mercantilism. She also questioned the self-sufficiency of science as the only rational explanation for the mystery of life:

> "We need to give the seemingly useless the value it really has. We must respect the spirit in all its manifestations. Let's say religious feeling, philosophy, art, and poetry. Pragmatism made us give too much importance to the usefulness of things. But many times we ignore their intrinsic value." (Richard, ca 1965, page 71).

Here she approached Unamuno, a complex and sometimes contradictory man. He moved from religious fervor to non-Catholic views. At times, he condemned the intransigence and dominance of the Church's thought. But the intellectual also criticized the new deification of science. For him, it was a new tyranny as lacerating as the previous one. He was a regenerationist thinker who sought the modernization of Spain. However, he feared the public whom he called the beast of many mouths. He went from being a practicing Catholic to raising the banner of the secular religion of freedom.

He believed that any ideology that became a sectarian faith generated new idols. This doctrine became a new form of latent inquisition. He believed that scientism worked as a new positivist faith. Intellectualism questioned the great questions of human destiny. Skepticism could become fanatical. Progressivism was a new religion that awakened critical consciousness. All this has much to do with Lucia Richard. She sought consensus by advocating a more ethereal individual. The material was of little importance to her. Consequently, she saw it as another great tyranny of the 20th century.

In the next paragraph of this *Disturbing Question*, she establishes a true synthesis of her thought:

"Today's youth should not let themselves be swept away by all that is new. They must defend the good of the past, the core of tradition, worshipping eternal values. These are Greek thought, biblical Decalogue, and Chris-Christian love. They are also classical art, the sense of love of country, duty, loyalty, and friendship." (Richard, ca 1965, p 71).

The strength of Lucia's personality lay in her extraordinary ability to express beauty. Yet, she limited herself to nature, for which she had true devotion. This predilection distanced her from other possible motifs in her verses. She especially did not mention the feelings of the Chilean people. The most important note of her thought is "eclecticism." She tried to unite faith and reason, pantheism, and Christian fervor. The writer equated paganism, classical art, and Greek thought with an incorruptible faith. Sometimes she questioned certain dogmatic aspects. However, the poet also defended them as a sign of a people's identity.

In her thinking, there are outbreaks of elitism, exclusivity, contempt for the vulgar. She combines all this with an amalgam of liberal ideas and the condemnation of social divisions. She believes in the uniqueness of certain races or beauty as a source of vigor of the races. But in other passages of her work, she openly advocated racial integration. The writer was a feminist and praised meritocracy. She made many statements in favor of women's emancipation. Still, as a married woman, she sometimes avoided exposing herself to the level of her partners. Instead, she harbored a class consciousness.

We can also portray her as a woman who was inclined to preserve the most enriching traditions. But she also advocated progress and change: *"To change is to be human; to stagnate is to make a caricature of God."* -she says. She was able to glimpse the significant advantages that science and technology provided. But she also considered that the worship of these new gods could lead us to a world suffocating with materialism. The cult of the spirit is for Lucia much more than Christian devotion. She equates art, philosophy, and poetry with religious feeling.

The thinker identifies the danger of erecting new idols as a way of confusing the community. The deification operated by the masses was a new form of tyranny. It attempted against individual identity. She also asks herself: Can tradition be more than a pedestal on which to place the statue of a new God? This new God is for Lucia a multifaceted concept and, of course, a polysemic threat. It invaded many spheres and embodied various forms of oppression. These menaces were not necessarily ideological. But they always worked to the detriment of human freedom.

Life followed a crazy pace, with concrete cities and silly messages. The lack of joy in experiencing knowledge was omnipresent. All kinds of invasions of privacy would have led man to a process of denaturalization. New conquests of the modern world had been achieved. But they had been imposed at the expense of reducing spirituality to the human being. Materialism and indifference were everywhere. Lucia claims for the beauty of the ancient world. It was a slower, more genuine world, more in contact with nature. She also favors a purer mind, which develops through a more extensive rhythm of time.

Lucia was not only close to Paul Claudel, but also Pierre Teilhard de Chardin. She mentioned him several times in her work and had read his writings. Teilhard de Chardin was a kind of Darwin of the Church. A philosopher, scientist, and Jesuit, he was one of the great thinkers of the 20th century. As such, he tried to reconcile Christian dogmas with modern advances in science. A traveler, mystic, and geologist, his thought powerfully influenced the Second Vatican Council. He was also a paleontologist, naturalist, and visionary. With this background, he contributed to the dialogue between Christians and materialists.

The distinguished Jesuit was a convinced Democrat and Republican. He held positions close to socialism. For that reason, he was a victim of the intolerance of the ecclesiastical authorities. From a very young age, Chardin dedicated himself to scientific work. He visited the Altamira caves in Santander. In 1922, he earned a degree in Natural Sciences. Later, the priest worked as a professor at the Catholic Institute in Paris. For some time he lived in Mongolia and in Beijing, where he worked in paleontology. Later, in 1950, the Academy of Sciences of Paris elected him as a member. Due to the censorship of his scientific work, he went into exile in the United States. There he died in an accident in 1955.

His view of the world starts from a debate about nature. This interpenetration of phenomena led him to a monism. Reality is shown as a unitary whole. Under these premises, he spreads optimistic progressivism. He also speaks of plurality, unity, and energy. Man is a living matter that comes in a slow progression toward spirit and consciousness. His essays are long and complex to explain here. In essence, he was a man who tried to reconcile science and religion, biology, and spirit. Chardin did all this under the criteria of evolutionary anthropology. In this sense, he had a dissident thought of the Church that brought him many criticisms. But in brief, he had an eclectic thought. The same thought that we can trace in Lucia Richard.

After describing the many advances of the modern world, Lucia states:

> "We live in a paradisiacal or Dantesque era of humanity. This world will only be sustainable if young people understand their enormous responsibilities. They cannot be seduced by technology alone. As they advance in science, they must defend moral values. These young people must fight for the development of spiritual forces." (Richard, ca 1965, page 72).

To conclude this *Disturbing Question*, Lucia offers the young people a series of tips. She achieves that by picking up on the most positive aspects of tradition and progress. And so, she mediates between two groups in conflict: the young and old. Finally, the thinker conceives history as a cyclical journey, in which young people are a link in a universal chain.

The Psychoanalysis' Debate

n another vein, Lucia believes that the greatness of art lies in its eternal permanence. Its main seal of nobility would be the lack of interest in its creation, its apparent uselessness. The artist's major driving force is not profit. Lack of selfishness opens the way for him to build an imperishable work. Work alienates modern man, without him being able to perceive the fruits of it. Therefore, only art can redeem man from his materialism. This disinterest is what allows him to develop a complete sense of his personality. Lucia also tells us:

> "Art, with its school of disinterest, is a kind of religion. It penetrates areas where another form of spiritualism could not have reached. This discipline or disposition imposed by art, far from suffocating the imagination, gives it amplitude. Every work of the artist is a struggle between the habitual and inspiration. Where are Dr. Bergler's abnormal, the lazy, manic, and selfish people who do so much harm to humanity?" (Richard, 1956).

To be more precise in our understanding of mania in the creative process of art, we must read other opinions. These are more authoritative or scientific if you will. They allow us to know to what extent there was exaggeration in Dr. Bergler's statements. They also let us know whether Lucia's argument was rational and her words were full of sense.

To understand this dilemma, we must follow Carlos Humeres Solar. He was a contemporary of Lucia Richard and a relative of mine. He devoted much of his life to study and promote art in all its manifestations. Mr. Humeres was a professor of Aesthetics at the University of Chile and director of the Faculty of Fine Arts. He was also secretary of the National Conservatory of Music, being passionate about these subjects. In 1935, as editor of the *Art Magazine* of the Faculty of Fine Arts, the professor published an article entitled "Art and Psychoanalysis." This article fits perfectly with our purposes.

In that article, Carlos Humeres combines everything gathered by science and philosophy of his time. The subject of the debate is the interpretation of artistic creation. The aesthete puts special emphasis on the highest representatives of psychoanalysis. Among them were Freud, Adler, Jung, Baudoin, Abraham, and Rank.

He begins his presentation by pointing out the most controversial aspect of psychoanalysis concerning art. And this was the fact that it was a therapeutic method. It was used with greater or lesser results in the treatment of certain nervous diseases. He continues to emphasize that the central object of the new science was the study of the subconscious or the unconscious. The romantic philosophers had already theorized about this. They argued that psychic life was not reduced to reason alone. This was something that the rationalists also believed in. Instead, it occupied a small part of the vast nebula of the unconscious.

Carlos Gustavo Carus, in his 1846 work *Psyche*, had been the first to talk about this. He stated that the soul had an extension much greater than consciousness. These ideas influenced Eduard von Hartmann. He wrote similar reflections in his *Philosophy of the Unconscious*. The theosophical movement, based on oriental mysticism, also explored the new frontier. Yogism was one of the greatest exponents of this new conquest. Authors such as Myers in his work *Human Psychology* and William James in *The Varieties of Religious Experience* were also pioneers. They showed a consciousness surrounded by an unfathomable ocean of unconsciousness. They considered this unconsciousness as irrational or suprarational.

In turn, psychoanalysis took up the theme again. Its originality lay in trying to create a morphology of the unconscious. The new science believed that it was subject to laws such as those that order organic evolution. Thus, the individual unconscious would be determined by hereditary factors and by experience. Both were the source from which the impulses came. Sometimes they could arise with high virulence, typical of the vital instincts.

Psychoanalysis also distinguished between the primary instincts, common to the animal species. And it also spoke of the higher instincts. The latter were those that made the human being capable of having sociable, altruistic, moral, or religious feelings. In an intermediate zone between the two would be the complexes. Baudoin defined them as feelings that came from unconscious roots. Moreover, the complexes had a dynamic character, constituting tangled networks of tendencies. They represented ways of psychological reaction.

The complex would be a phenomenon of accommodation between the lower nature of man and his rational and superior behavior. The instinct and selfishness of man had to be balanced with conscious imperatives of the social environment in which he lived. The man was forced to sublimate his instincts or to transmute them to a higher order. If he did not do it, he could provoke neuropathic conflicts. Psychoanalysis also spoke of the primordial instinctive forces that constituted the root of psychic evolution. They were the libido, or sexual instinct, according to Freud, and the instinct of dominance or will power, according to Adler.

So sublimation is interpreted from antiquity as the satisfaction of sensual pleasure. It is also believed to be an external purpose of intellectual origin. The genetic psychology defended by psychoanalysis found its greatest support in Aristotle. He baptized it with the name of *Katharsis*, being the role of art as purifier of passions. Schopenhauer would be more explicit. In his work, *The World as Will and Representation*, he writes that *"every will comes from a need."* In other words, it comes from deprivation or suffering. Therefore, the satisfaction of desire would come to redeem that torment derived from a lack.

Another interesting aspect of psychoanalysis is its inductive research methods. The similarity between dreams and works of art has been observed. The dream is the main way that puts us in communication with the unconscious. Dreams are interpreted as symbols. They are disguised as expressions of unconscious impulses that the consciousness has censored. They remain in a latent state hidden in the form of complexes.

Therefore, these impulses do not find adequate expression through real action or sublimation. By not doing so, they originate disorders of affection and personality. So, psychoanalysis tries to cure them with its unique methods. Under this point of view, the work of art emerges from the unconscious, similar to dreams. Baudoin went even further by saying that the work of art is a dream or a crystallized dream.

In short, man needs to free himself from these emotions. Under pressure in the subconscious, they demand an escape valve. Finally, they release their energy into artistic creation. Until now, humanity considered art as one of the most sublime manifestations of human spirituality. But after this explanation, it found itself in an equivocal and unstable position. It was the result of a mere compensatory process close to neurosis with which it shared many similarities. Rank defined art as a state of balance between neurosis and perversion.

This is what until now science, especially psychoanalysis, had explained about artistic creation. However, not all of its followers agreed with its postulates. Carlos Humeres himself recognized its merits. The new science explained the processes of development of the soul. But he also believed that its statements were mere hypotheses. It had some doses of fantasy. The new theory was full of risky assumptions, shocking puerility, and other nonsense.

The artistic catharsis did not explain the external or internal circumstances that lead the artist to create a work of art. Carlos Humeres recognized that psychoanalysis provided some satisfactory explanations. But he also believed that it was insufficient in many respects. The driving forces of art were the same conflicts that led some individuals to neurosis. Yet, it was another thing to establish where the creative power of the artist came from. For him, it was a dilemma that remained outside the realm of psychology. Matter, life, and spirit - he concluded - were fundamental phenomena. But their essence still escaped both the analysis of the wise and the ambitious speculation of the metaphysicist (Humeres Solar, Year I, 1935).

That said, we must understand that when Lucia attacked psychoanalysis, she did not do so out of malice. She did not pursue universal truths or academic statements. She fought it for reasons that were very solid for her. The poet opposed the petulance of a language that sought to seize the truth about the gestation of art. That was something that hurt her deepest feelings. It also made her very angry.

Lucia felt upset by the contempt for art and its creators. She could not remain indifferent to seeing the art defenestrated by the psychoanalysts. They had taken away its most precious virtues and its authentic seal of nobility. Psychoanalysis, with the coldness of a surgeon, had tried to seize the most sacred mystery of art. Without any blush, it had stolen the source of its inspiration. The only thing that she claimed was the dignity of the artist and the greatness of his committed and sincere work. His transcendence in time, immortality, universality, and generosity were superior efforts. It was a task that could not be equated with the category of nervous diseases.

Art as a purge, beauty as defecation of a disturbed mind, is an irreverence to its deepest excellence. Art, like great deeds, nourishes by the ideal it serves and finds its ennoblement in the golden layer of which it is impregnated. Art has an unfading crown of glory. It wears a laurel of grandeur for its conquest of a world without frontiers. It exists for the benefit of all mankind.

The version of psychoanalysis does not contribute to the beauty of the generous act that is art. Despite its scientific pragmatism, it does not answer all the questions. It cannot be the only rational explanation for the phenomenon of the gestation of art. Lucia, like the best athletes of Olympia, carries here the baton of the eternal flame, its most precious treasure, the Holy Grail of art. And that is the secret of its most sublime and hidden meaning. The poet is herself, by a mysterious innate quality, one of its most sincere representatives. Art in Lucia is a corpuscle of light, a transit towards divinity, whose vehicle is inspiration or numen. Since ancient times, this word has had infinite resonances. It communicates the poet or artist in his intimate dialogue with the gods.

Psychoanalysis not only refers to the individual unconscious but also to the collective. Lucia Richard, in her radio program *Psychoanalysis in Art*, mentioned Gustavo Le Bon. In his *Psychology of the Crowds*, he had been the first, before Freud, to study the masses. History was full of examples showing how the individual transformed before a crowd. He lost his personality, dragged along by the influx of the masses. But when he was alone, he could harbor the most beautiful virtues. But influenced by his surroundings, he became a bloodthirsty being. In that situation, he surrendered to his impulses.

Lucia gives many examples of all this uncontrolled irrationality. Christ in front of Caiaphas, and the French Revolution with its popular courts, are some of them. The man returns to his cave-like state when a momentary passion of the masses drags him into its current. Sociologists explain this fact. By joining a crowd, the man loses his sense of responsibility. Everything that civilization has imposed on him disappears. His impulses dominate him.

Finally, she mentions that the great revolutions are the ones without blood. Constructive revolutions are those that take place in the sphere of ideas. They are those that imply changes for humanity. As an example, she talks about a doctrine supported by her colleagues: the New Deal. It was a doctrine that saved the United States from the worst of its crises. It established a closed system of capitalism. It also created the American policy of solidarity and good neighborliness, a precursor to the League of Nations (Richard, 2004, page 608).

Lucia Richard and the Masses: Comparison with the Thought of Jose Ortega y Gasset

n Lucia's thinking, we can find many references that show her detachment from the masses. We can trace these ideas in some of her poems, articles, and radio programs. They also appear in her essay *The Disturbing Question*. She described them well in the title "Characteristics of the Modern Era." In this essay, she expressed many ideas that coincide with the thinking of Ortega y Gasset (1883-1955) in his essay *The Rebellion of the Masses* (Ortega y Gasset, 2010). If Lucia did not read this writing, then she developed a very personal thought, generated by the driving forces of her time. In any case, this shows that she had an acute capacity for observation of social reality.

Curiously, the Spanish Falange stole many premises from Ortega's ideology. In the face of this, Ortega reacted with stupor since he did not feel identified with that political program. For the intellectual, the so-called Mass-man is an individual product of the Industrial Revolution. But above all, he is a politically neutral man who can be both conservative and radical. This concept does not exclude the worker, but neither does it intend to refer to a specific social class. It is rather a way of being a man, which occurs in all social classes. This man represents our era and belongs to the stratum of the bourgeoisie, the great winner of our time.

Lucia feels an abomination for this Mass-man. She can identify him as either an ignorant young man or an arrogant disrespectful for tradition and social norms. The vulgar, the snob, or the bourgeois snob also represents him. She defines him as *"a standard and repellent type"* (Richard, 1955). Therefore, when Lucia speaks of the masses, she does not at any time refer to the working masses but does not rule them out. Rather, the thinker refers to an average man, calling him mediocre, average, vulgar, common, or regular. He belongs to a new caste, a superb and iconoclastic lineage, who boasts of his self-sufficiency. This man can be both upper and lower class. His greatest defect is his influenceable character, his materialism, and his ability to overthrow everything that opposes him.

For Ortega, the mass is the set of people not specially qualified. It is a man that does not differ from other men; he is a pattern that repeats a generic type. The mass is anyone who does not value himself, but feels like all the others and yet does not care. He feels comfortable knowing that he is identical to others.

To the mass belongs the individual who does not demand anything special from himself. He is like a buoy that drifts. The characteristic of the present moment is the vulgar soul. Knowing he is an ordinary being, this man has the arrogance to assert his right to vulgarity by imposing it everywhere. The mass runs over everything different, eminent, unique, qualified and select. Whoever is not like everyone, who does not think like everyone else, runs the risk of being eliminated.

In both Lucia's and Ortega's thinking, this new caste comes from a demographic boom. It is the product of an extraordinary increase in population in all countries. The Industrial Revolution and the improvement of living and sanitary conditions favored its appearance. The achievements of science, technology, medicine, advances in the field of health, economy, or social rights, also contribute to creating it.

This modern world would have brought us globalization and the leveling of continents. This fact implies the equalization of fortunes, social classes, and culture. People now pursue common interests. It is the world of agglomerations, traffic jams, and the invasion of all spaces by the multitude. Lucia denounces how lonely she feels walking through this undifferentiated crowd.

Lucia tells us that now everything comes too easily to us. Both agree that there is an overabundance of means. Ortega believes that it has created this new social spawn, a relaxed and haughty individual. Not only does he laugh at the select minorities, but he supplants them. For Ortega, the great conquests of human life have always taken place because there was an imbalance between social needs and the means to satisfy them. But now man lives in a sea of sufficiency that will inevitably lead him to degeneration.

In the thoughts of both of them, we live in a fast-paced world. It is full of disturbing invasions, annihilating noises, neon lights, pollution, road killings. The city is a conquest of civilization, which has brought with it the boundary.

First came the agora, that is, the square; then the street, then the buildings, and finally the city. The city exists to the extent that it has destroyed nature. That is precisely what Lucia most appreciates: the authenticity of the natural environment.

The Mass-man would be the creature of the modern city, invader of the natural environment. The author vindicates the past times when the pace of life was slower. In her imagination, she can contemplate the joy of the artisan who dialogues with his work that can last for years. The poet also visualizes the anxiety of the lover who awaits a widely desired letter. She also enjoys the idea of an old wagon moving peacefully through the countryside.

Ortega considers that the rhythm with which things go today, their impetus and energy, afflict archaic man. This anguish measures the difference between the sense of his world and the pace of our time. This man respected the past, the classical times. They were something wider, richer, more perfect, and challenging than the life of his time. Modern man, on the other hand, makes fun of ancient times. The Renaissance seems to him a provincial episode, very narrow. He aims to wipe out any classicism. This new man believes that he is potentially unlimited. Nothing is compulsory for him, and he does not recognize barriers to his expansion. Moreover, he does not perceive the value of past events.

Lucia, as we know, longs for a "golden age," a state of fullness, perfection, and enhancement that she finds in wise Greece and Rome. That is why Lucia treasures a classical spirit. She vindicates the nostalgia of a better era, that zenithal moment in which the solid pillars of civilization were built. The author suffers in the city, in the modern world, and takes refuge in that classic ideal. Chimera or not, it means for her an enclosure of comfort and stimulus to expand her thinking.

The masses terrorize Lucia. They are ignorant who destroy all civilization with their barbarism and uncontrolled violence. Lucia contrasts the reason of force with the force of reason. The originality of the artist, and his most precious personality values, are opposed to the puerility of an illiterate, anonymous, and irresponsible mass. She defends order against chaos. The poet despises the vulgar, people incapable of delving into the meaning and beauty of things. They are shallow, epidermal, and empty people. This is how Lucia defines this man in her essay *The Disturbing Question*:

> "The werewolf of the early days, or the eagle-man of the Middle Ages who lived in his lofty castle, has been replaced by the ant-man. He lives his life in haste without reasoning about his destiny. This man does not try to differentiate himself from the other components of the anthill." (Richard, ca 1965, page 63).

Ortega described this man on many occasions as an insect, a bee. He lives in the world as if suspended from a hive. The philosopher considers that the masses have become rebellious towards the minorities. They do not obey, follow, or respect them: they put them aside and supplant them. Today, hyper-democracy triumphs through a mass that acts upon de facto pressures. This mass ignores the law, imposing its aspirations and tastes.

The collapse of the Roman Empire had much to do with the emergence of masses that absorbed the ruling minorities, taking their place. In our time, it is the masses who decide. One cannot govern without taking into account public opinion. This means that behind the new social power there is a representative of the masses. They are so powerful that they have overthrown all possible opposition.

In Ortega's opinion, society is aristocratic and always will be. So now a new caste has arrived: the masses, who do not listen to reason and do not want to be right. They push to impose their opinions and often are in favor of direct action. This new caste is as insolent as it is overwhelming. Ortega refers to them as "the empire of the masses." They brought us unionism, fascism, and Bolshevism: movements all dangerous to human coexistence. Furthermore, he considers that the masses vegetate fictitiously suspended in space. Their lives have no weight or roots. They do not care about their destiny, being dragged along by the slightest current.

Thus, all nationalist or totalitarian adventures would be typical movements of mass-men. They are led by extemporaneous and mediocre men, who lack historical consciousness. That is, life is essentially anachronistic. Therefore, Ortega understands that every revolution devours its own children. Everything begins with a moderate party, which becomes extreme. From then on, it goes back to restoration and starts all over again. Both fascism and Bolshevism were not up to the times. They did not take into account the enriching lesson of the past. So, they were doomed to failure and oblivion.

Ortega speaks of the Mass-man as a primitive being that has crawled behind the scenes of civilization. He is a nihilistic, devastating, and iconoclastic individual. Therefore, he speaks of "the vertical invasion of the barbarians." He finds a simile with the figure of the "cynic" of the Hellenistic era, who never created or did anything. His role was to undo, to practice nihilism, to deny. He would be the parasite of civilization. The masses did not come into the world to act on their own. They always needed to be guided, influenced, or represented by excellent minorities.

When they act for themselves, they rebel against their own destiny. And because that's what they did in the 1930s, Ortega spoke of "the rebellion of the masses." The masses lynched and triumphed through violence. On the contrary, liberalism would have been the most extraordinary and unnatural political invention of humanity. Liberalism represented supreme generosity. Although those who govern believe themselves to be omnipotent, their power is limited to welcoming minorities into their midst. Those who do not feel or think the same are also heard.

Its greatest proclamation is to live with the enemy, with the weak enemy. Here there is tenderness, solidarity, and philanthropy. But this does not mean that it is not an unnatural construction. According to Ortega, it is an invention too complicated to be consolidated on earth. In his opinion, the masses do not want to live with the enemy. They do not desire to rule with the opposition or cohabit with what they are not. They hate to death discrepancy and dissidence.

Lucia, in her essay *The Disturbing Question*, told us many things. She made us see the need to make a consensus between the best of tradition and the new contributions that youth brings to us. She taught us that one could not live in a materialistic world. It is also necessary to preserve the spiritual side of life. We must respect the way each one contemplates this spiritual experience. She also made us see the need to overthrow false idols. We had to put a veto on the intrusion of others, rebelling against the greatest attack on thought: propaganda.

She sees a real threat in the alienating commercial propaganda. With its messages, it seeks to invade ideological or political fields. The masses are easily influenced, volatile, and inflammable. Furthermore, Lucia indicates their main character trait: they are not guided by reason but by their feelings. Thus, the intellectual denounces all these paralyzing collective movements of the citizen's will. Let us listen to her words:

> "We have witnessed dictatorships that have applied hypnosis to the masses instead of coercive means. Among them, the most powerful was the German Nazism. In its beginnings, it used, like all totalitarianism, personal propaganda, slogans, and nonsense. Then, once the ground was prepared, a gesture, a word, a phrase, was enough to ignite the spark that made people vibrate and obey. The invisible influence that the orator had on his audience had never been more palpable. Those who led this totalitarian movement made propaganda a true science. They adopted fixed laws based on the psychology and character of the masses." (Richard, ca 1965, page 22).

For Lucia, supposedly legal democratic governments practice other types of oppression. When governments operate as covert dictatorships, they also use propaganda. The single party controls the media. Then the citizenry oscillates between official lies and private insidiousness. This is how corruption, pamphleteering, political manipulation, demagoguery, and distortion of facts appear.

The most representative phenomenon of the totalitarian era was the "brainwashing" of the masses. Especially sensitive were the young. Through persuasive means, these regimes sought to shackle the will and ignite the rage. They tried to bring out hatred and violence, enthusiasm, and applause. She agrees with Ortega about the danger of these movements and the means they employ. She gives as an example the Hitler Youth and Mao Tse Tung's Red Guards.

Exaggerated propaganda promotes nationalism, fosters chauvinist passions, and becomes a precursor to war. It is the way unscrupulous dictators skillfully excite the people to distract them from domestic problems. For Lucia, this mutual connection between the megalomaniac leader and his worshippers has a dual direction. On the one hand, there are flammable people. At any moment, they can be disappointed, burning what they had previously idolized. On the other, the demagogue or leader fears losing the support of the crowd. In his despair, he resorts to all kinds of methods to achieve its attachment. This paradox is what Lucia calls "double slavery."

Ortega agrees that the common people of old have always lived dependent on their lord. They subsisted in a state of oppression, in a horizon of limitations. Now the new Mass-man claims his role as lord and wears expensive clothes. He struts around the world, not recognizing anyone superior to him. There are no "states" or "castes." No one has civil privileges. The average man learns that all citizens are equal before the law. When there are no limitations, this man can quickly abandon himself.

Nothing is impossible or dangerous, there is no instance superior to him, and he is satisfied. Unlike the latter, the exclusive man demands and obliges himself, appeals to a norm higher than him. A Mass-man demands nothing. A nobleman is he who is worthy of fame, excellent and worker, and stands out over the anonymous mass. In the present state of things, it is the select individual, and not the mass, who lives in servitude. And this is an incredible paradox that subverts ancient times.

One of the psychological traits of this new Mass-man would be his conviction about the ease of life. His existence is wide, without tragic limitations, which gives him a sense of domination and triumph. Also, he considers his moral and intellectual judgments valid and complete. He is closed to listening, does not question his opinions, and does not count on others. Furthermore, he intervenes in everything by imposing his vulgar point of view without being asked. Sometimes he does it through direct action.

Games and sports are the main interests of this person. He trains his body, takes care of his hygiene, and the excellence of his attire. But he has forgotten the troubadour romanticism towards women. He has vulgarized love. Ortega believes that three innovations have made possible the appearance of this new man. These are liberal democracy, scientific experimentation, and industrialism. As a substitute for the last two, the technique has emerged. In short, this Mass-man lives with many means and does not get anguished.

He has never solved his economic problem as he does now. His repertoire of possibilities is unlimited. This man believes that he lives in a time superior to any known historically. He has at his disposal modern tools, advanced medicines, social security, and many rights. All this has led to the appearance of what Ortega calls "the satisfied gentleman." In his opinion, by the very inertia of things, since life is a pulse and a sacrifice, he is condemned to degeneration. He is an individual who, despite his possibilities, has no plans and does not build anything.

Lucia shows us the great achievements of science, the power, but also the danger of nuclear energy. She also praises the eradication of many diseases and the development of technology. In this new world, the concept of community is much broader than that of family, clan, or group. Religious dogmas no longer restrain the man that emerged from these wonders. He got rid of the moralizing structures of the past, demolishing the traditional ideas of respect for institutions. This man threw himself into the great adventure of research with a youthful spirit. Nations and their rulers emerged in a new mosaic of power, destroying the feudal organization. They created secularized political and social organizations, freeing themselves from religious influences.

It is a world of the effervescence of science and advances in technology. The engine was invented, multiplying the forces of the industry. The age of the muscle was over, and the age of the machine began. The Agrarian Revolution and the Industrial Revolution arrived. According to Lucia, this new order required the appearance of specialized workers. These men ended up leaving the fields and villages. The big cities, trade unionism, and the masses were born. Through the strike, the masses conquered their rights, improving their living conditions. They beat the governments of the old order, forcing them to listen.

Lucia also agrees that in this world there is an influx of livelihoods, defining "ease" as the keyword of our time. The least effort to move from one place to another, to get and prepare food, or to get dressed, would amaze the men of the past. The same would be true of our ability to communicate, to overcome disease, or to survive. Besides, she also evokes the dangers of mass production, which leads to the mediocrity of the products launched on the market.

It is a world that has damaged the craft creation of yesteryear. The old days were lavish with industriousness and perfection, with selfless commitment. Moreover, the new form of manufacture suppresses human participation. Now low-quality products prevail, born from an impersonal, rational, and dehumanized process. It is a system that banishes the genuine. Factories introduce substitutes, imitations, copies, and tinsel.

All these advances of science, and the benefits of civilization, had remedied many shortcomings of man. But they had also caused a series of side effects. Among them, we must refer to the agglomeration in cities, with its consequent smog, riots, advertising invasion, and artificial lights. From this overcrowding, collective conflicts, whether emotional or ideological, had emerged. These conflicts did not exist before in the cities or the small towns. In Lucia's work *The Disturbing Question*, we can find other reflections of her that have many parallels with Ortega's ideas.

"It is in the city, where psychic rape occurs due to propaganda. Collective hysteria turns the defenseless man into a delirious mob. Even if the group offers him protection, this average man is easily influenced. He expands on the street, at the parade, or sporting events. It is only in the group that he feels important, unlike the upper-class man who has the means to stand out in the salons, universities, or professions." (Richard, ca 1965, page 62).

Ortega spoke to us of an exclusive man, not necessarily of an upper class, but as opposed to a politically neutral mass. Lucia sometimes identifies the masses with an inferior social class. She polarizes the mass, going beyond the concept Ortega wanted to give it. In other cases, she refers to it as a generic entity. However, the Orteguian construction of a mass, different from all known classes and belonging to all of them, is as complicated as the generosity and tenderness of liberalism. But apparently it is not impossible.

Lucia also tells us the following:

"The agglomeration of the city influences the standard man. He is prone to follow his leaders blindly. In his ignorance, he makes them his heroes and easily becomes dominated by terror or exaltation." (Richard, ca 1965, 62).

In another passage, she adds:

"This contemporary anguish has been a favorite theme of the theater, the cinema, and the novel. It is a problem that concerns doctors, psychiatrists, or sociologists. It paralyzes the will and impoverishes the personality. This utilitarian civilization reduces everything to statistics and has not yet grasped the loss of the big city." (Richard, ca 1965, 63).

As we see, Ortega studies this Mass-mann from a sociological, philosophical, or political perspective. Lucia, instead, delves into the existential question. She focuses on the deterioration of the human personality and the suffering of men in cities. For Lucia, this Mass-man is not only a transgressor. He is not even an individual who subverts the values of society with the support of the community. He is also a being who suffers the consequences of the world he has created. It is a much more sentimental vision, less abstract or theoretical. She sympathizes with the emotions of that mass, with those lost individuals, as the human beings that they are.

The education or culture of these masses was also a special concern for Ortega. For the philosopher, modern man has a much healthier and stronger soul, but also much simpler. Schools teach this man technique of contemporary life but have not succeeded in educating him. They have given him tools to live better, but they have not instilled in him the sensitivity of the great historical duties. Educators have hastily inoculated him with the pride and power of the nation, but nothing spiritual. Ortega describes this man as a primitive being that has emerged unexpectedly in our time.

He is an airtight man who feels perfect, fulfilled, mentally complete. He is unable to discover his insufficiency or to compare himself with other beings. His mediocre soul denies transmigrations, the supreme sport. Ortega qualifies this subject as a "fool," a "dumb," who rejoices in his self-sufficiency. The questions about life and destiny do not interest him. It is impossible to get him out of his stupidity. It does not mean that this individual is not intelligent. Nor does it mean that he has no more intellectual capacity than other people of antiquity. But all this is worthless. The mere fact of possessing it only serves to enclosure him more in himself and not to use it.

Ortega adds that ordinary people from other centuries never had "ideas" about things. They had beliefs, traditions, experiences, proverbs, but not theoretical opinions. They were not allowed to decide about public activities. Although modern man now has a superior culture, he has no ideas per se, nor is he educated. These individuals are not interested in the fundamental values of society. They learn them but do not use them. They do not guide by them.

The scholar criticizes today's man of science, who has become a specialist, narrowing his field of vision. He is a reductionist who despises the ancient encyclopedic man of other centuries. He has divided science into small segments, but only dominates his little corner of the universe. He is not properly ignorant, but neither is he a sage. Even so, he judges and decides in our time.

In Lucia's essay, the theme of culture acquires other nuances, in which she coincides with the philosopher. Lucia says:

> "We must achieve things through effort and sacrifice. Otherwise, they do not penetrate deeply into our consciousness. The knowledge that is not acquired step by step through the constant discipline of the mind is not true knowledge. That which is nothing but the product of memorization, in the long run, it is useless. We must flee from a school that fills us with dates and details, moving away from the pleasure of experimenting. This school is as oppressive as factory work. Specialization deprives the worker of the satisfaction of creating."

> "Young people love books and the technique seduces them. But, amid this indigestion of texts, they do not have a true philosophy, like the one that life gives." (Richard, ca 1965, page 59).

This reasoning is very similar to what Ortega said about the inoculation of modern technology. This fact would have deprived the present man of the historical sensibility. This education was utilitarian, stereotyped, cloned, and cold. It created equal subjects, mass-men. Lucia believes that the data received becomes part of a process of personal enrichment. This learning can only be authentic when you feel it. The matter must penetrate our pores through our emotions. An impersonal education creates rational machines, not passionate men. Besides, it produces a standardization of society but does not extract the best essence of the human being. That may be practical and effective but it robs us of the intimate beauty of things.

A society thus built can easily fall into darkness, into a world of ordinariness, or into communal thinking. It is the autocracy of technique that leaves less and less room for the uniqueness of man. Could there be a greater uniqueness than that of a poet who seeks his world of beauty and goodness? That freedom is what Lucia claims. We must avoid closed classrooms, imprisoned children or teachers enervated by exhausting effort - says Lucia. The artist imagined education as a place of enjoyment, as a recreational activity:

> "In the classroom, there will be a big screen. With it, educators will explain reading and writing, math, and good speech. They will also teach moral and religious principles, history, and geography." (Richard, ca 1965, page 57).

On another level, Lucia explained how much the relationship between man and culture had changed. Solitary art restricted to the cenacle of princes, and destined for the enjoyment of a few, had died. Now the modern media used recordings or radio broadcasts, and music reached all social classes. Paintings had left the palaces. Now they were exhibited in museums, and everyone could see them.

Books were once the treasure of the bibliophile. They adorned the aristocratic libraries, but now they had become the heritage of all. Then came the cheap summaries, pamphlets, and paperbacks. Publishers published illustrated stories and frivolous magazines to kill time on public transportation. They added image and sound to the written word. The meticulous preparation of the old theater came to an end. Now the profusion of cinema and the abundance of television programs appeared. The culture had become vulgarized, lowering its quality in favor of the majority.

Lucia is a woman who loves the Renaissance, and as such, believes in the elitism of culture. Culture cannot be spread at any price, and even less so if in doing so it becomes superficial. She rebels against positivism at all costs. Materialism and scientism are not the only reality of life. So she thinks that we cannot base progress only on economic terms. Raising the standard of living is an honorable goal. But it is also vital to increase culture through the deployment of spiritual forces.

In Lucia's vision, there is a struggle between quantity and quality. One cannot pretend to elevate the masses at all costs. When we achieve this by inhibiting the select spirits, it is at the cost of reducing the value of culture. Once again, she expresses her distrust of the masses. With their widespread ignorance, they ruin the uniqueness of the creative genius:

> "The great sin of these times would be to flatter the ignorant, making them believe that the only valid artistic manifestations are their own. Yielding to the tastes of the majority, we deny other immortal expressions of art. Folklore is important and valuable, but it does not represent all music. Neither the clay pots are all the plastic, nor the melodic singing or the dislocated rhythms are the only manifestations of musicality." (Richard, ca 1965, page 60).

It seems that Lucia in this passage prefers Beethoven to Violeta Parra. She has her reasons and they must be understood. She seeks perfection and sublime beauty. Popular art, on the other hand, with its lack of polish and study, carries a burden of ignorance, rudeness, and improvisation. It also has a connection with the feelings of the masses, which the author abhors without dissimulation. It is an arriviste vision of culture that would clash directly with Nerudian thought.

Those figureheads that Neruda carefully collected are actually a metaphor. They represent for Lucia the guiding principle of art and by extension of culture. But for her, they cannot be anything other than perfection and beauty. Lucia's high social origin gave a degree of refinement to her work. But this fact also prevented her from reaching a wider audience. This exclusive sense of culture was a widespread thought in ancient times when most of the population was illiterate. But today, in advanced societies, it is empty of content, it is meaningless.

As an epilogue, Ortega glimpses this mass-man as a giant of our time, and as a cosmic question mark. He has installed himself in our world to shake up our civilization. Our thinker predicts a bleak future. He equates this new caste, this "mobocracy" with the aristocracy. Worse still, this new class dominates our time by living in a relaxed way as did the nobility. It lulls itself into a superabundance of material means, relying on its sufficiency.

It suffers the internal process that leads all the hereditary aristocracy to its irremediable degeneration. This excessive overestimation of itself inevitably drives it to vice, laxity, and total ruin. It is a mistake to think that the excess of means favors life, quite the opposite. A world full of possibilities produces serious disorders and leads to decay. A clear example of how society destroys itself from within would be the collapse of the Roman Empire.

The huge gap between social force and public power made the revolution possible. Through it, the bourgeoisie took public power and applied its virtues to the state. As a result, a powerful state emerged. The mass-man sees in the state an anonymous power like himself. And that is why he considers it to belong to him. The greatest danger threatening our civilization today is the dominance of life by the State. It is the interventionism of the State and the absorption of all social spontaneity by the State. It functions as a colossal and overwhelming machine that tries to crush all the creative minorities that oppose it.

In the new era, a new God appeared: the State. It establishes modern slavery, imposing its hegemony as a superpower. It rises as an absolute power over the individual, who languishes entangled in the tentacles of bureaucracy. Ortega finds it frightening to hear Mussolini say: "Everything for the State; nothing outside or against the State." He sees in fascism a typical movement of mass-men. Moreover, Mussolini's state has its roots in a liberal democracy. Paradoxically, these were the ideas he was fighting. Therefore, he believes that there is reason to fear. The "empire of the masses" would end up crushing the independence of the individual, destroying the future.

Compared to Ortega's thoughts, Lucia built a much more hopeful future. The artist was afraid of the shrinking of the natural environment. The city would be the epitome of this new invasion. The city was erected as an artificial construction that corrupts the authenticity of the human being. This adulterated society would have brought us all kinds of degradations. Psychic violations of the individual were omnipresent. The creature of this artificial world was the mass, transgressive, iconoclastic, and disrespectful.

Therefore, Lucia fears the homogenizing power of the masses and the intrusion of others. She cannot stand their invasion of privacy. This community imposes its outrage on the individual. For this reason, she denounces the behavior of some young people. They display themselves on the streets with their flashy clothes and extravagant hairstyles. They do not know the good manners with which the old society made existence more pleasant. These people ignore the traditional values of art and culture. In short, they are the new vandals who throw themselves into the streets to disrupt civic life.

Some disguise themselves as patriots, like Mao's Red Guards, and destroy the basis of the country's culture and traditions. They do not respect the nationality and the ancient values enshrined in it. It is a new youth, a product of the disorientation of our time. They are the children of a world war, of neurosis and bewilderment. Furthermore, they go out to the streets without knowing why they are ruining monuments, breaking gardens, turning over cars, or breaking windows. These young people show discontent that they cannot specify.

Despite all this, she believes in the power of youth. The new generations must respect the finest of the past, the traditions, and the right habits. But these young people must also know how to conquer the future. They must reach a consensus between material and spiritual forces, between religion and Greek wisdom, between the reasons of the old and the passions of the young.

As an example of that hopeful future, she spreads the message of the great musician Pablo Casals. He had revealed the difficult relationships between parents and children. They had different opinions that prevented communication between them and increased silence. But he also considers it a transitory phenomenon. That youth was the reflection of an agitated society. However, passion and feeling had prevailed over reflective and serene reasons.

Likewise, she believes that young people are capable of investigating the elementary, simple, and unfathomable truths of Creation. The poet, in turn, points out the beauty that lies in the generosity of young people. The eloquence of great gestures hypnotizes them. The young person is bold. He sacrifices the beauty of his passion for the truth.

The young person should stop seeking self-affirmation by copying everything around him. He must abandon the habit of fashion, imitating the costumes of others. Heroes cannot be his unique models. Neither should he blindly follow schools, hobbies, literary movements in art or literature. In his opinion, this will lead to the creation of a standardized, dull, and undesirable subject: a snob. He needs to know how to escape from routine, from relaxation, and to be able to hear his own voices.

In Lucia, there is a bridge, a parallel between the contempt she feels for the masses and the aversion she professes to the snob. This feeling is stronger when it comes to the snobby woman. That woman had a lack of elevation, a superficial spirit, a propensity for charlatanism, and banality.

There is evidence that Lucia Richard was involved in feminist aspirations since 1925. However, never before 1956 had she spoken so boldly on this subject in public. This freedom shows how much Santiago society had changed by then. In an article entitled "The Black Keys," published in *El Mercurio* on June 3, 1956, Lucia confronted the representatives of her sex. There she described women as: *"the great conservatives of the human species."*

Women had fought hard to gain their political rights. But having achieved them, they did not opt for positions of popular election. Nor were they able to organize politically. Meanwhile, they continued to support all kinds of laws against their rights. Rhetoric and more rhetoric, but it seems that women did not want to change. She succeeded individually but failed collectively.

She analyzes this failure in three classes: the lower class, the middle class, and the upper class. What she once silenced in her article "Aunt Eulalia," she now clearly denounces. The woman of the village was almost illiterate. Her lack of knowledge had not allowed her to reach civic maturity. Her difficulty in having resources did not make it easy for her to devote time to culture. The woman stoically bore the burden of the children. These kids were often natural or abandoned by drunken husbands.

A struggling, hard-working woman emerged from the almost narrow middle class. These women went to university, practiced professions, engaged in commerce, excelled in art, and teaching. But in this frenetic activity, there was no time left for organization or culture.

Her criticism of the upper class is quite harsh. The women of this stratum were elegant, full of innate good taste. But they worried about many banalities and spent too much on superfluous things. They set their sights abroad; not to acquire culture, but to dress well. They had a poor education and lived comfortably in their environment. That's why they didn't understand the profound change that was taking place in Chilean society.

Some began to react: they worked, they pursue an education, they acted... But there was still the "Bibelot de luxe's group." That is, those who went through life looking like a vase of flowers. These women were only interested in fashion and in appearing in the newspapers in the columns of social life. They enjoyed a comfortable life and laughed at women's political rights.

As an epilogue to this passage, Lucia believes that the elegant and superficial woman did not represent the true soul of the Chilean woman. We should be proud, she says, of the intelligence and spirit of sacrifice of the Chilean woman. Many had excelled both in Chile and abroad. Times, according to Lucia, had changed. People were no longer hired for their last names, but their skills. To get social justice, one had to fight for it. Finally, she urges all Chilean women to change their mentality to transform the country.

In this trilogy of the Chilean woman, we can contemplate *"le monde à l'envers"*; that is, the world upside down. As in many other cases, Lucia claims "order against chaos," sacrifice and virtue in the face of laziness and indifference. The first representative in this taxonomy of the Chilean woman would be the woman of high class. She could be bourgeois or aristocratic, wealthy, or oligarch. This woman was the only one who had the means to make a profound transformation in Chilean society. However, her most common attributes were idleness and her accommodation in the dominant sexist order. Her hedonism, banality, and snobbery also identified her.

She is a woman who lives only to follow the dictates of fashion. That superficial woman does not go deep into her true needs. Her fulfillment is not in her priorities. She uses her sensuality to hunt for men who will solve her life. This behavior ensures her survival but does not dignify her figure or put her on intellectual parity with men. She is a gossiping woman who laughs at women's political rights. She is the only one who can make the change, but she is not interested.

Lucia's Democratic heritage is her great praise for middle-class women. Yet, she wonders if such a class exists in Chile. This class would be the backbone of progress in a new world of meritocracy, full of self-sacrificing, professional women. They fought to move the country and their family forward. But they were so immersed in their activities that they did not have the time or the means to organize themselves. Despite these obstacles, she argues that some women from the bourgeois class had begun to react.

Finally, we see how compassion arises in Lucia towards the village woman. Due to her lack of culture, her illiteracy, and her total absence of economic means, she passed through life as a soul in pain. Even worse, she dragged behind her a legion of illegitimate children, abandoned for drunken men. This woman had no choice of political representation. She was neither subject nor object of history.

In summary, here is a definitive recipe for the progress of Chilean women. It is the same -differences aside- that caused the French Revolution. But this is a silent revolution, a revolution of the intellect. In other words, it is a bloodless social struggle: that of the spirit. This metamorphosis could only be achieved through sincere commitment, dedication, and sacrifice. *"Le monde à l'envers,"* is that those who could make the change did not want it or did not need it. And those who wanted to achieve their goals did not have the means to do so.

ANNEXED DOCUMENTS

Articles, Biographical Excerpts
and Letters, Not Included in
Lucia Richard's Complete Works

1- "For Gabriela Mistral." April 16, 1922. National Library of Chile.

First of all, forgive me for writing to you because I do so by giving in to my first impulse, which is very spontaneous and sincere. You have come with your *Lullabies* to fill a need. You have brought a scent of the garden and a glow of stars to the child's little bed. So far, to fall asleep, he has heard nothing but nonsense words coming from the sweet and tender voice of his friendly mother.

I have written your poems in an album in which I write down the advances and memories of my "baby." I did it so that they would penetrate his soul and record in his ears. So that when he reaches the age where you only live from memories, he can repeat them. And I hope he does it with the same emotion that men sometimes remember the first Hail Mary. The one they learned to recite curled up in their mothers' arms.

For that I thank you, countless times, on behalf of the children and on behalf of the mothers. You have been the first to be able to translate their emotions. You have transmitted to us all that poetry that emerges spontaneously from childhood.

Lucia Richard de Piedrabuena (1922)

2- Lucia Richard, "The Women of Quixote," *Revista de la Sociedad de Escritores de Chile*, **SECH, 1946, vol. II, nº 6/7, pags. 36-38.**

When Cervantes wrote his *Quixote*, he included in his palette the full range of women in Spain. Among them, he described the famous Maritornes "with a wide face, flat neck, blunt nose, one eye, and not very healthy." He also talked about the Duchess, "funny, and friend of the ridiculous." He marked so sharply the contrasts of the characters and situations, like El Greco the light-dark of his visions. Authors of the same period seemed to like both the exaggeration and the strong nuances. They used them to express the total synthesis of an epoch or the subject.

There is a contradiction in Cervantes' characters. Dreams and reality are confused in Don Quixote and Sancho. And these, in turn, are evoked in the female characters of the novel. This is the case of the imaginary and dehumanized Dulcinea del Toboso and the human and earthly Teresa Panza. In them, we see the same parallelism of reality and repeated fantasy, of what we see and what really is. Madness and senselessness are the parallels that harmonize without ever colliding. The appetites of the flesh and the urges of the spirit mark the reason for the unreason of the Castilian soul.

One facet, the imaginary, shows us the visionary fever and exaltation that agitated many in those days. The other, the real one, is a human document of permanent interest that contains unsurpassed life lessons. Consequently, the Quixotes and their Dulcineas set out to conquer the world or heaven. The Sanchos and their wives continue to pour their innate wisdom into the unparalleled grace of their sayings. And they do so wherever the Spanish language is spoken.

That whole episode of the squire's kind wife and the naive and thoughtful Teresa Panza is of unparalleled freshness. She is as simple as her husband. But she is not gullible, but suspicious and distrustful. No promise of Sancho makes her lose her temper as to the wellbeing of her daughter. That discreet and amusing talk between Sancho Panza and his wife Teresa Panza -as Cervantes says announcing his chapter V of the second part- is of a naive and delicious truth.

It is also worth noting the couple's concern about Sanchica's fate. The Father wants to see her become a countess, to give him grandchildren. In this way, he would be called by the common people, Lord. But, the mother insists on not altering her marital status. As she says: "one good thing would be to marry our Mary to a count or a gentleman who when he wanted to, would disqualify her, calling her a villain, the daughter of a clodhopper and a poor spinner."

Time passes, and the governorship that Sancho dreamed of has become a reality. The duke had achieved everything thanks to his mocking spirit. Then the Duchess writes to Teresa Panza, informing her of the event, sending her a cord of corals with golden points. This news was too much for the naive peasant. Shortly after, Teresa left the house with the letter and the cord around her neck. She was playing with the letters as if they were a tambourine. Suddenly, she met the priest and Samson Carrasco, and began to dance and say, "Now there are no poor relatives, we have a governor."

Wasn't it wonderful to see the gifts and courtesies of the Duchess? Then she thinks of the humiliations she had received from the well-dressed noblewomen of the village. "Honor and rank above all," she says and dreams of riding in a horse-drawn carriage to the governorship. There she would see her daughter carried in carriages and litters by a large number of servants.

Why should we admire the credulity of the kind Teresa? The island of Barataria was no more inaccessible than the empire of the Incas or the Aztecs, conquered by other Sanchos' of Extremadura or Castile.

In this episode, as in all the others, Cervantes proved to have written what he had seen and lived. We must admire how his constant misfortunes did not drown out his festive mood or overshadow his vision of things. And so we must agree with El Greco when he placed the luminous clouds beside the mourning knights (1946).

3- "Who is Gonzalez Vera?" Lucia Richard. *La Hora*, June 19, 1950

This title, which seems like a detective story, answers a question that at this moment arises from many lips. The public does not know the writer who has received the National Literature Award. We must ask ourselves the reasons why his work has not transcended the mass of readers. We even have to guess why so many who closely follow our literary production have ignored him.

Who is Gonzalez Vera, and why is his work unknown? To answer these questions, I would like to use the words of the writer Ernesto Montenegro. He was one of the members of the jury that awarded him the prize. Montenegro says it so clearly that any other argument seems redundant:

> "The work of Gonzalez Vera stands out in Chilean literature for its originality, representing the Chilean genius at its best. We find in him a direct vision of people and things. His style embodies literature without literature. His narrative is sober to the point of asceticism, expressing himself with humility and sincerity. We see in his texts a reflecting mind, which points to a true vocation as a writer."

These words synthesize the best qualities of Gonzalez Vera. The writer has overcome the stage of struggle with technique. Without a doubt, he has his own. But it is so well mastered, and hidden among the qualities of his thought, that we do not notice it. For him, words do not work in isolation with a musical or eloquent purpose. He uses them to achieve a direct vision of the things he wants to represent. Thus, he limits all exuberance, expressing himself in voluntary poverty. Yet, he enriches this sobriety of style with his poetic brushstrokes and his subtle humor, which in the end, compensates for the surrounding aridity.

I randomly copy a paragraph from "El Conventillo", one of the stories in his work *Minimum Lives*:

"At dusk, I went to a neighbor's yard and I took a rose. It was a little pink rose, very perfect in its simplicity. When I cut it, I thought about her and left it in a glass until she would arrive.

Already at nightfall, my friend came. My mother had not yet returned. I received her in my room, and we talked about simple things. At that moment, my little girl arrived in a terrible mood. I wanted to joke, but she began to say many impertinent things. Despite that, I offered her the rose. Then, without taking it, she said with disdain: The cemetery is full of that garbage."

What we have seen is a whole poem among brambles or a flower on a rock. His style depicts a direct vision of nature, a real evocation of life. He has a fine grace, an emotional tenderness, through which he channels his personality. The subjective and objective elements move in a rhythmic, balanced, and harmonic game. To get these results, he needs neither erudition nor artifice. He looks around him and becomes aware of himself. Nothing else. He describes with simplicity the human types, the characters, expressing what he feels for them. And so, with his precise and emotional look, he transmits a high-quality poetic language. Amid his apparent reticence and triviality, his finished and perfect productions come to light.

Another consideration about his style is that Gonzalez Vera never abandons the mocking look that disarms. His Volterian smile and light humor are always present in his writings. They are not born from dryness of heart, from bitterness, but human understanding. That is why his humor never hurts. It does not ridicule; it does not punish: it paralyzes.

We have yet to clarify the reason why his works, although popular and easy to read, are not known by the public. The reason must be sought in his irritating withdrawal and his disregard for publication. He distanced himself from literary societies and publishing circles. Only through people who knew him personally was it possible to make him known to the general public. These readers do not look for new talent but receive what the market gives them: facts for easy digestion (1950).

4- "The Book of Hours." Lucia Richard. *El Mercurio* 1/1/1957

The delicate medieval artists painted images to depict different months of the year. They bordered these sacred books with allegorical garlands. They also added gracious and detailed paintings of the customs and tasks of the period they wanted to illustrate. These Books of Hours, as they called them, followed step by step the development of the seasons and the most important events of the year. As these artists understood, each month has its own physiognomy. We associate them in our imagination with our minor occupations or with the most serious problems.

Always before our eyes hangs, visible or invisible, an inexorable calendar. We cannot do without it from the moment we have had to accept the imposition of the clock, deadlines, and punctuality. The modern order helps and destroys our lives. The beginning of each month has a particular story written on it: each one indicates a path to follow, or warns us of a task or a challenge.

Over time these ideas associated with the calendar vary. It is no longer March the month for quince candy or January for swimming in the sea, as we thought in childhood. In any case, we remember some months as full of charm, along with other arduous ones that overwhelm us with their difficulties. December's Last Judgment is softened by the sweet images of the feast of the Immaculate Conception and Christmas.

School exams, bank balances, or looking back on the past year are difficult things. They often bring some compliments or indulge vanities. But, above all, they leave us with a bitter taste of the harsh reality of life, which is rarely a pleasant image.

I cannot imagine what goes on in a man's heart when the New Year comes around, without experiencing any excitement. That means starting one day like another three hundred and sixty times and finishing it another three hundred and sixty times. All year long, this man comes home overwhelmed and tired. Beginning a new year without ending such a routine is a superhuman endeavor that would be impossible for me.

Saint Francis of Assisi was the first to understand the beauty and emotion produced by this celebration of the birth of the Divine Child. Since then, every year, the bells of the earth have rung. Children smile with hope. And men free themselves for a moment from the burden of their duties. All live that happy midnight destined to men of goodwill.

For some, Christmas comes among snowflakes and hooded pines. For others, it arrives among green fields, golden wheat, and early fruits. We are fortunate to have such a flowery Christmas. It has entered so deeply into our hearts that it has left a profound impact on folklore and popular art. The mangers, now relegated to churches, were a small world in miniature. The Christmas carols kept all the flavor of the musical and poetic sense of our city. The clay figures represented the Divine Mystery. To relive all this spectacle, the peasants would gather in the church to attend the blessed Midnight Mass. They were reminders of the fervent joy of the people when they were not preoccupied with complex reasoning, but with liberating their feelings.

That was a Christmas like ours and the one we must defend. The other is a worldly celebration, an imported performance, and a joyless bustle. This holiday can never move us with its false joy. That is because it does not bring its sources from the past.

It seems a contradiction to talk about these things when every day there are others so urgent that they rob us of our peace of mind. World events alter and excite us. We live in an orb without borders. Modern science has transformed all men into citizens of the world, like microscopic particles of a universal entity.

But each man needs to preserve his individuality and each people his physiognomy. To get rid of them is to go against the human heart. When a man does not fall into evil, he explodes magnificently at every stage of history. And thus, he shows that he can live without material satisfaction, but not without freedom for his beliefs, customs, and traditions.

On our invisible calendar, next to the sheet for this end of December, let's put a happy ending. It is a parenthesis, a break between the routines of life, a soothing and refreshing energy drink. This celebration is the genuine expression of the Chilean way of life that erases the differences between classes and ages. It makes us feel like children, sharing that simplicity, generosity, and illusion (1957).

5- *La Opinión newspaper*, **"A Question to Six Writers," December 25, 1946. Interview to Lucia Richard**

"An appropriate book for children is one in which the author places himself at their level by taking the life of children as his subject. All classic works of children's literature have a child as their main hero. That's the case of *Heart of Amicis*, *Alice in Wonderland*, *Oliver Twist*, *Three Years of Vacation*, etc. The influence of these early readings is enormous. They are the first window that opens to the outside world. Even before being able to read, the child can build his own universe with these books.

After that age, he leaves his rich inner life and takes his first steps in the outer world. He will never forget the heroes of his books as the first companions of his life. For this reason, we must be very careful in choosing these companions. The books they need are those about the lives of famous children. Thus, he places himself from the beginning in the company of these select beings who will become his models and teachers.

In our own country, we have the exemplary lives of those who have forged our nationality. It would be interesting to publish stories of the childhoods of O'Higgins, Perez Rosales, Blanco, Arias, Plaza, Alfredo Lobos, Gabriela Mistral, etc. We could add to these stories, novels about figures of America and supporters of humanity. This book awaits the Chilean child and not only the Chilean. When we talk about childhood, we cannot speak of nationality. In those first years of life, there are no racial or social differences. All the children are like an immense jungle to discover." (Richard, 1946).

6- Omer Emeth (Emilio Vaisse). Literary Movement. *Sursum Corda*, poems by Lucia Richard de Piedrabuena, illustrations by J.Delano, Santiago, Impr. Universo, 1925, bibliographic chronicle of *El Mercurio* of Monday, December 25, 1925, p. 3. Catalog No. 1878 of the articles published by the author.

LITERARY MOVEMENT BY OMER EMETH

SURSUM CORDA. Poems by Lucia Richard de Piedrabuena. Illustrations by J. Delano. Santiago. Universo Publisher, 1925.

When opening this book, we notice from the first poem that we enter in a garden of delights where a fresh breeze blows, and everything speaks of health, vigor, hope, and joy of life. Even if the verses were bad (and I hasten to say they are not), the author of *Sursum Corda* would deserve my most sincere congratulations and all my gratitude for that breeze and that joy...

I do not know if, in this, my readers share my way of feeling. Still, I confess: I am tired of reading pessimistic verses that seem written in prison, in a hospital, in a land that in no case is a happy copy of Eden and where life has become purgatory or hell.

It disgusts me as much for the lack of art as for the absence of sincerity. Some of those tearful poets whose laments distill so much sadness are, in fact, cheerful people who take good advantage of their youth. "The rest is literature," as one French poet used to say.

Mrs. Lucia Richard of Piedrabuena confesses her happiness and sings it:

Up hearts! / Life is joy! / Who dares to cry / when the sun smiles? / Look, it has come out / and the day is radiant / without winds and without rains / or clouds or glow.

Let us not think, however, the author of this stanza is incapable of perceiving the melancholy of certain landscapes at special hours:

I adore the imprecise landscapes / that are sketched in the light of the afternoon / when everything is mystery and gloom / in the sad environment.

I seek the quiet solitudes / where vague melodies are heard / and the quiet voices of things / evoke memories.

And the quiet and gloomy woods / where some fountain murmurs uneasy / and through the thick foliage / I discern the stars.

But these moments of melancholy are very brief: the joy of living overcomes even to the point of engendering scruples. And so the poet, feeling too happy, asks God for forgiveness:

Forgive me, Lord, if I love the earth / and put my loves in things, / You sowed my way with flowers, / of fragrant flowers.

I have felt perfume on the path / and I have seen the light of the day behind the mountain / I wait it dawns and I look for flowers... / Lord, you send them!

Forgive me, Lord, if sometimes I look / at the earth with affection and tenderness / here, you created it and well you know it! / There are also pure things!

For the first time in twenty years, I stumble upon a poet who confesses being happy. This is one of those days that the Roman poet marked with white stone... Praise God! (Omer, 1925).

7- Sara Guerin de Elgueta, *Sursum Corda*, 1928. Guerin de Elgueta, Sara, *Women's Activities in Chile*: work published on the occasion of the fiftieth anniversary of the decree that granted women the right to validate their secondary examinations (data until December 1927). Santiago, printing and lithography, *La Ilustración*, 1928, págs. 721 and 728.

"Without great patrons, a volume of poetry by Mrs. Lucia Richard de Piedrabuena, entitled *Sursum Corda*, recently came to light.

Her subjects are tender, absolutely poetic, so to speak, because the author does not versify but delicate and spiritual motives. We can see this in her way of feeling and interpreting nature, as in "Country Quietude." It is also visible in the simple and sweet expression of her maternal love, and her Christian piety, as in her "Prayer to the Nazarene." All these features predispose from the first moment in her favor.

She is inspired, correct, and her well-formed phrase springs up easily. Making no effort to gain a place in the ranks of the women who write, Mrs. Richard de Piedrabuena stands out among our best poets. The reader can judge our claim by reading some stanzas of her most beautiful poem "Prayer," which we cannot resist transcribing." (The text continues with the most representative passages of "Prayer"). (1928).

8- Stefan Zweig, lecture given by Lucia Richard, Bulletin of the Cenacle of Poetry nº 3, 1942, p.6.

Stefan Sweig

"On the personality of this wonderful Jewish writer, there was a brilliant lecture given by the writer and poetess, Mrs. Lucia Richard de Piedrabuena, in the Cenacle of Poetry.

The speaker is a prominent figure of the Chilean feminine intelligentsia, who treated the subject with extreme ease and amenity. The ill-fated suicidal writer revived in the speech of the cultured lady. She depicted him with all the outstanding lines of his intellectual silhouette.

The select audience that filled the Auditorium listened in fervent recollection to the enlightened words of Lucia Richard de Piedrabuena, who was much applauded and congratulated, being forced, by the demands of her admirers to recite some of her original poems." (Zenteno de León E 1942, page 6).

9- Marta Elba Miranda, "El Enigma," *Revista de la Sociedad de Escritores de Chile* / SECH, 1946: II, (7/8): 44/45.

The Enigma, short stories by Lucia Richard, Tegualda Publisher.

"With a set of ten stories, united under the name of *The Enigma*, Lucia Richard has launched her first prose work. In these stories, facts or scenes, she paints the simple and anonymous life of beings who live, act and suffer, lost in the main events of everyday life. The author handles the dialogue well, which gives interest and movement to the development of the arguments. She does not extend herself in vain analysis or annoying disquisitions, nor does she detail her characters. It is enough for her to point out a gesture to underline an aspect to show the intention and the psychological strength of the subject.

"When Bernard marries, you will give him the bronze cot," says the letter the mother gives to the priest. She gives it to him so that he understands why she is resisting the marriage of his son to the woman he loves. This sentence summarizes the intensity of the conflict that the protagonist has. She is caught between the duty of fulfilling the will of the husband, who orders her to give their son the bronze cot on his wedding day, and the pain of getting rid of her precious wedding gift.

This story, perhaps the best of the volume, shows the creative capacity of Lucia Richard. She is a subtle observer of those small tragedies that afflict humble souls. Peter, the boy who earns his living at the cemetery gate by offering 'water for flowers' in exchange for some coins, is another example. These inconsequential characters who suffer and struggle amid simple conflicts, also resolve them.

How about we make the cake he likes so much? Says Cristine, the spinster, at the end of a bitter dispute with her widowed sister, mother of a smallboy about to return from school. The love for the child is the bondage, the yoke -as the author calls it- that makes them live together. This bond makes them endure their dissimilar temperaments, which sometimes lead to fights full of hurtful words, bitter reproaches, as in this case where the spinster invites the mother to prepare the child "the cake he loves so much." Lucia Richard joins the many Chilean families of storytellers with a serious and valuable credential. Her storybook is fine."(Elba Miranda, 1946).

9- Review of Lucia Richard by Vera Zouroff. Vera Zouroff, *The Cenacle of Poetry to its Poets*, 1st series, Santiago, Nascimento, 1947.

"I have said on another occasion that in Lucy Richard there is something transparent, like those images where the light is turned on.

Transparent!

She has exquisite femininity and the distinction of a great lady. These traits show the intense personality of a strong woman, as described in the Gospel. Yet, this temperament fades into the pale and sweet softness of her somewhat pearly face. These are the crystals in which reflect the many changes of light of the internal flame. Her poetic taste oscillates at the call of the outbursts of her artistic restlessness. To fulfill this need, she is always studying, going on a perpetual pilgrimage along the paths of art. Born in an aristocratic home, educated according to her lineage, she shaped her literary tastes in the ancient European culture. There, she acquired the impeccable classical correctness of her elegant style. She also developed a serene eclecticism to look at the things of life from the height of her thoughts.

Travels and readings have enriched her mind, which reflects in her writings. She has published several poems and prose. She has given many lectures and talks on the radio and has an essay on the way. Her verses and stanzas are richly carved gems. In them, we can see the spirit of the Christian woman, the tender mother, the lady, and the artist of boundless inspiration." (Zenteno de León E., 1947)

10- Emilio González López, *The Enigma*, Revista Hispánica Moderna, 1950, vol. 16, page. 145.

"These exciting stories of Lucia Richard have a common thread that binds them together. They are all small events that suddenly reveal themselves as a shot at close range. In the development of the story, there is always something that ruins the protagonist's illusions. The writer looks for a trivial detail, which produces consequences for the person who suffers it. The title of the first story, "The Enigma" (which is the story of a poor widower who searches the desk where his wife kept her personal belongings, discovering that she was unfaithful), could serve as the title of her other stories. In each of them, Lucia Richard finds many mysteries of the enigma of life." (Gónzalez López, 1950).

11- Virgilio Figueroa, review of Lucia Richard. *Biographical and Bibliographic Historical Dictionary*, Nendeln, Liechtenstein: Kraus Reprint, 1974, volume V, p. 678.

Virgilio Figueroa:

Omer Emeth was very selfish in his criticism of authors, except when it came to French intellectual hegemony. But when he referred to *Sursum Corda*, a collection of poetry by Mrs. Lucia Richard that appeared in 1925, he thought otherwise. For the first time in twenty years, he had met a poet who confessed to being happy. And to prove it, he transcribed some verses, imbued with the honey of sweetness and the elixir of happiness.

Omer Emeth:

Few disciples of Apollo sing psalms of joy and offer on the altar of conformity. Almost all of them cross the valleys full of tears and distill the juice of their sorrows, which are fictitious and imaginary most of the time. In *Sursum Corda*, Mrs. Richard ignores the pathetic voices and sings joyful songs. In "Dim Light," unlike the legion of the sad, she does not seek the pain or sorrow of the gray days. In "Forgive Me, O Lord," she admits to being happy and asks for forgiveness. (Figueroa V., 1974)

12- Facsimile copy of a letter from Esmeralda Zenteno de León (Vera Zouroff) addressed to Gabriela Mistral on September 8, 1954, who on behalf of the Steering Committee of the House of America, welcomed her on her return to Chile. National Library of Chile (Zouroff, 1954).

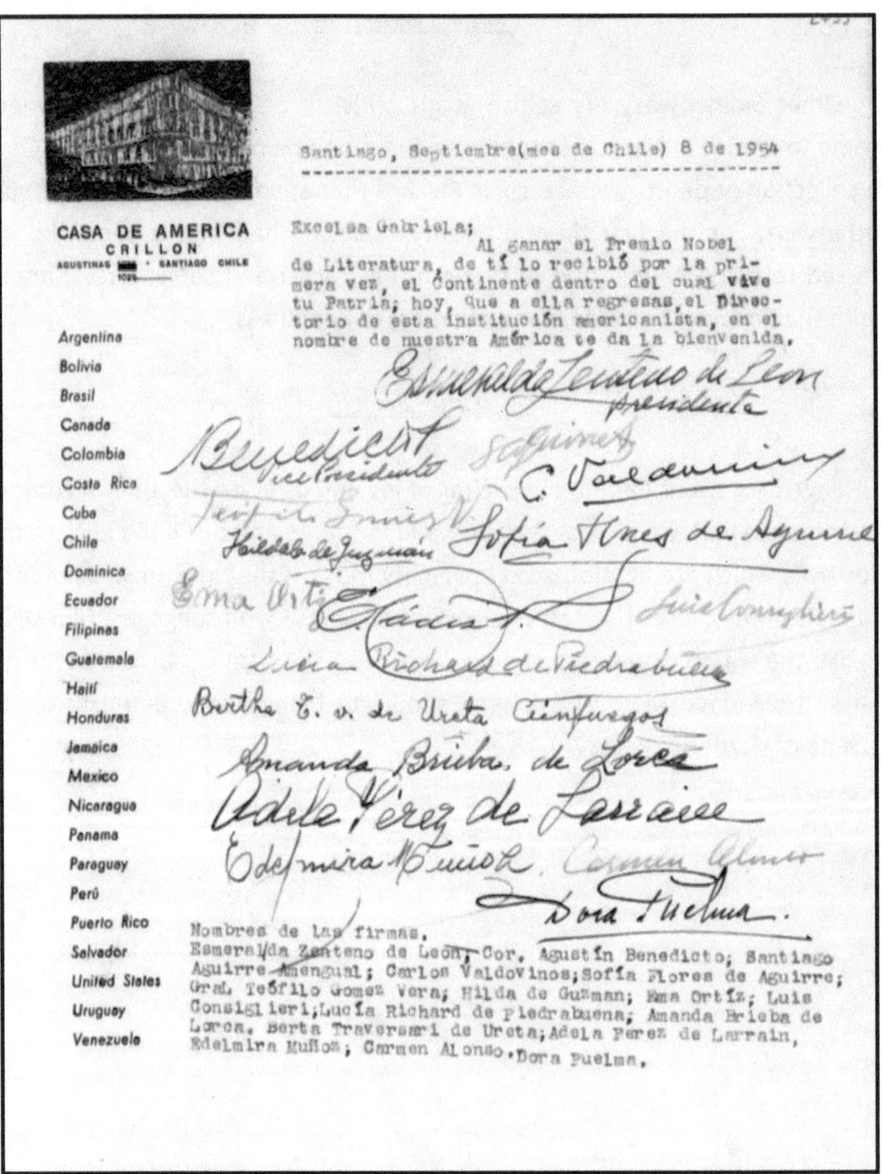

412

Bibliography

Amunátegui Johnson, M. (enero-febrero de 1949). El congreso de Chile concede a las mujeres los derechos políticos. *Mujeres de América: "Manos Unidas, Corazones Fuertes"* (9), págs. p.1-2.

Andonie Dracos, C. (30 de Diciembre de 2004). La escritora que transgredió los cánones sin romperlos. *El Mercurio*, P C12.

Andrade Coello, A. (1939). *Perifonemas: programas de Radio Cuba.* Quito, Ecuador: Imprenta Ecuador.

Arabena Williams, H. (1950). *Enrique Nercasseau y Morán (1854-1925).* Santiago: Editorial Universitaria.

Arabena Williams, H. (1986). *Ensayos de exégesis literaria* (Vol. I). Santiago, Chile: Editorial Nascimento.

Araneda Bravo, F. (12 de julio de 1978). En la muerte de Patricia Morgan. *La Prensa Austral*, pág. p.2.

Besoaín Armijo, R. (1997). René Amengual, un enamorado de la música. *Tiempo Nuevo*, pp.87.

Brieba de Aldunate, M. (septiembre-octubre de 1949). Contribuyamos a la rehabilitación histórica de la mujer. *Mujeres de América: "Manos Unidas, Corazones Fuertes"* (13), pág. p.1.

Brieba de Aldunate, M., & Guiller, E. (14 de septiembre de 1949). Carta de Mimi Brieba de Aldunate y Elena Guiller a Gabriela Mistral, residente en Santa Bárbara, Estados Unidos. (B. N. Chile, Recopilador) Santiago, Chile.

Calderón, A. (31 de enero de 1991). *La Nación*, pág. p.14.

Casa de América. (junio de 1951). *Boletín Anual de la Casa de América.* (B. H. Madrid, Recopilador) Santiago, Chile: Casa de América.

Díez Aljaro, F. (martes 20 de mayo de 1997). El sacerdote Bernardino Abarzúa Troncoso. *El Heraldo*.

Donoso, A., & Wilson, E. (1910). *El parnaso chileno/ Compilado por Armando Donoso: aumentado en una segunda serie por la baronesa Wilson.* Barcelona, España: Maucci.

Elba Miranda, M. (1946). El Enigma. *Revista de la Sociedad de Escritores de Chile, II* (7/8), pp.44-45.

Fernández Richard, J. (ca 2000). *Surcos en la Arena.* Santiago, Chile.

Figueroa, P. (1900). *Diccionario biográfico de extranjeros en Chile.* Santiago, Chile: Imprenta Moderna.

Figueroa, V. (1930). *Diccionario histórico biográfico y bibliográfico de Chile* (Vol. V). Santiago, Chile: Imprenta y Litrografía La Ilustración.

Figueroa, V. (1974). *Diccionario histórico, biográfico y bibliográfico* (Vol. V).
Nendeln, Liechtenstein: Kraus Reprint.

García y García, E. (enero-febrero de 1949). Salvemos a los niños. *Mujeres de América: "Manos Unidas, Corazones Fuertes"* (9), pág. p.3.

González Cerda, R., & Casanova, M. (1913). *Corona funebre a la memoria de Enrique Richard Fontecilla/sus amigos.* Santiago, Chile: Soc. Imp. Lit. Universo.

Gónzalez López, E. (1950). El Enigma. *Revista Hispánica Moderna, 16*, p.145.

Gónzalez López, E. (1950). El Enigma. *Revista Hispánica Moderna* (16), 145.

Guerín de Elgueta, S. (1928). *Actividades femeninas en Chile: obra publicada con motivo del cincuentenario del decreto que concedió a la mujer el derecho de validar sus exámenes secundarios (datos hasta diciembre de 1927).* Santiago, Chile: Imprenta y Litografía La Ilustración.

Guerrero, P. (7 de junio de 2015). Rescatando a Lucía Richard. *El Mercurio: Sección Artes y Letras, Revista de Libros*, pág. p.12.

Hooper, F., & Yust, W. (1948). Two collections of short stories, El Enigma by Lucía Richard and Melodías de antaño by Victoria Orjikh. *Britanica book of the year. Enciclopedia Britanica*, p.62.

Hübner, S. (1919). Charlas. *Sucesos* (1-897).

Huidobro, V. (marzo de año XI, 1956). Oposición al surrealismo. *Caballo de Fuego* (8), p.1.

Humeres Solar, C. (Año I, 1935). Arte y psicoanálisis. *Revista de Arte* (6).

Huneuus, G. (18 de octubre de 1951). Carta de Gabriela Huneuus a Gabriela Mistral. (B. N. Chile, Recopilador) Santiago, Chile.

Huneuus, G. (26 de enero de 1955). Carta de Gabriela Huneuus a Gabriela Mistral. (B. N. Chile, Recopilador) Santiago, Chile.

Jarpa Gana de Lazo, S. (mayo-junio de 1948). Absurdo coloniaje en América ¿América para los americanos? *Mujeres de América "Manos Unidas Corazones Fuertes"* (5), pág. p.3.

La Opinión. (25 de diciembre de 1946). Una pregunta a seis escritores. *La opinión.*

La Torre, M. (31 de marzo de 1926). *Revista Atenea*, 69.

Larco Herrera, R. (1952). *La última carta de la democracia: América en la encrucijada roja.* Lima, Perú: Editora Médica Peruana.

Lillo, S. (1947). *Espejo del pasado.* Santiago, Chile: Nascimento.

Lillo, S. (1952). *La literatura chilena.* Santiago, Chile: Nascimento.

Mariategui Oliva, R. (1953). *Visión de Chile.* Lima, Perú: Editorial Ausonia.

Mayer de Zulen, D. (enero-febrero de 1949). La primera etapa de las mujeres de América. *Mujeres de América: "Manos Unidas, Corazones Fuertes"* (9), pág. p.3.

Minchero Vilasaro, A. (1957). *Diccionario universal de escritores* (Vol. 2). San Sebastián, España: Edidhe.

Muñoz, E. (junio de 1950). Carta de Edelmira Muñoz a Gabriela Mistral. (B. N. Chile, Recopilador) Santiago, Chile.

Nachrichten. (18 de noviembre de 1829). *Allgemeine Musikalische Zeitung,* p.758.

Nómez, N. (1996-2000). *Antología crítica de la poesía chilena/selección, introducción, notas y bibliografía de Naín Nómez* (Vol. I). Santiago, Chile: Lom Ediciones.

Oliveira de Núñez, I. (1 de octubre de 1950). Carta de Inés Oliveira de Núñez a Gabriela Mistral, residente en Jalapa, Veracruz, México. (B. N. Chile, Recopilador) Santiago, Chile.

Omer, E. (lunes 25 de diciembre de 1925). Sursum Corda, poesías de Lucía Richard de Piedrabuena, ilustraciones de Jorge Delano. Santiago, Impr. Universo, 1925. *El Mercurio. Crónica bibliográfica de Movimiento Literario*, pág. p. 3.

Ortega y Gasset, J. (2010). *La rebelión de las masas*. Madrid: Espasa.

Parker, W. (1967). *Chileans of today*. New York, Estados Unidos: Kraus Reprint Corporation.

Piedrabuena Richard, C. (1995). Recuerdos de Conchalí. *I*. Santiago, Chile.

René Correa, C. (1944). *Poetas chilenos (1557-1944)*. Santiago, Chile: Editorial La Salle.

Richard, L. (16 de 04 de 1922). A Gabriela Mistral. Santiago, Chile.

Richard, L. (1925). *Sursum Corda: poesías /Lucía Richard de Piedrabuena; ilustraciones de Jorge Delano*. Santiago, Chile: Sociedad Imprenta y Litografía Universo.

Richard, L. (1934). *Recuerdos de viaje*. Santiago, Chile: Imprenta La Bandera.

Richard, L. (1938). *Poesías*. Santiago, Chile: Imprenta Nascimento.

Richard, L. (1945). El Rescate. *Revista Atenea, 80* (239), p.113.

Richard, L. (1946). Las mujeres del Quijote. *Revista de la Sociedad de Escritores de Chile, SECH, II* (6/7), pp.36-38.

Richard, L. (25 de diciembre de 1946). Una pregunta a seis escritores. *La opinión*.

Richard, L. (1947). *El enigma*. Santiago, Chile: Editorial Tegualda.

Richard, L. (19 de junio de 1950). ¿Quién es González Vera? *La Hora*.

Richard, L. (2 de julio de 1950). Neruda y los poetas chilenos. *La Hora*.

Richard, L. (18 de diciembre de 1955). Juventud rebelde. *El Mercurio*.

Richard, L. (18 de marzo de 1956). Divagaciones sobre el arte. *El Mercurio*.

Richard, L. (3 de junio de 1956). Las teclas negras. *El Mercurio* .

Richard, L. (23 de septiembre de 1956). Vida, pasión y muerte del retrato. *El Mercurio*.

Richard, L. (1 de enero de 1957). El libro de las horas. *El Mercurio*.

Richard, L. (28 de febrero de 1964). En el cuarto centenario de Miguel Ángel. *El Mercurio*.

Richard, L. (7 de junio de 1964). Tagore, Gandhi y Nehru, los gigantes de la India. *El Mercuio*.

Richard, L. (2004). *Obras completas de Lucía Richard* (1 ed.). (G. P. Richard, Ed.) Santiago, Chile: Editorial Andrés Bello.

Richard, L. (ca 1950). Holanda contemporánea. *Radio Chilena. Crónicas de Arte*. Santiago, Chile.

Richard, L. (ca 1950). Crónicas de arte. Holanda contemporánea. *Radio Chilena*. Santiago, Chile.

Richard, L. (ca 1950). Crónicas de arte: Franz Liszt. Santiago, Chile.

Richard, L. (ca 1950). Crónicas de arte: Preludios de Chopin. *Radio Chilena*. Santiago, Chile.

Richard, L. (ca 1950). Crónicas de arte: Preludios de Chopin, programa de Radio Chilena. Santiago, Chile.

Richard, L. (ca 1950). Temporada teatral. *Radio Chilena*. Santiago, Chile.

Richard, L. (ca 1960). Defensas del hombre. Ensayo, Santiago, Chile.

Richard, L. (ca 1965). La pregunta inquietante. Ensayo, 75 págs. Santiago, Chile.

Richard, L. (ca. 1950). Bélgica. *Crónicas de Arte. Radio Chilena*. Santiago, Chile.

Rocuant, M. (1902). *Brumas / Miguel Luis Rocuant: prólogo de Marcial Cabrera Guerra: ilustraciones de Santiago Pulgar*. Santiago, Chile: Imprenta y Litrografía Francho-Chilena.

Romero, G. (ca 2006). Revolucionarias très chic. *Caras*, pp. 43-44.

Rubio, P. (1994-1999). *Escritoras chilenas, novela y cuento.* (Vol. III). Santiago, Chile: Editorial Cuarto Propio.

Sainz de Robles, F. (1953). *Ensayo de un diccionario de la literatura* (2 ed., Vol. 2. Escritores españoles e hispanoamericanos). Madrid, España: Aguilar.

Santa Cruz, L., Pereira, T., & Zegers-Valeria Maino, I. (1978). *Tres ensayos sobre la mujer chilena.* Santiago, Chile: Editorial Universitaria.

Santivan, F. (ca. 1920). Crónica periodística sobre Sarah Hübner. p.7. (B. N. Chile, Recopilador) Valdivia, Chile.

Santiván, F. (ca. 1930). Sara Hübner Bezanilla. (B. N. Chile, Recopilador) Valdivia, Chile.

Silva Castro, R. (1961). *Panorama literario de Chile.* Santiago, Chile: Editorial Universitaria.

Silva, J. (20 de julio de 1947). Carta de Jorge Gustavo Silva a Gabriela Mistral. (B. N. Chile, Recopilador) Llolleo, Chile.

Simpson, A. (9 de julio de 1978). Patricia de Chile, *El Mercurio de Valparaíso*, pág. p.2.

Sudermann, M. (1918). Diario íntimo de Magda Sudermann. *Revista de Artes y Letras*.

Sux, A. (1911). *La juventud intelectual de la América hispana/ por Alejandro Sux; prólogo Ruben Darío.* Barcelona : Presa Hermanos.

Ugarte, M. (1908). *Las nuevas tendencias literarias.* Valencia: F. Sempere.

Vergara, M. (1962). *Memorias de una mujer irreverente.* Santiago: Zig-Zag.

Wilde, O. (1996). *The complete Oscar Wilde.* Londres, Reino Unido: Michael O'Mara Books.

Yutronic Cruz, M. (Año CXIII, tercer trimestre de 1955). Presencia de Omer Ometh en la literatura chilena y su magisterio crítico. *Anales de la Universidad de Chile* (99), pp. 13-24.

Zenteno de León, E.(29 de noviembre de 1940b). Gran Festival Poético en la Sala Cervantes. (B. L. U. Texas Austin, Recopilador) Santiago, Chile.

Zenteno de León, E. (1941). *Boletín del Cenáculo de Poesía (2)*. Santiago, Chile: Imprenta y Litrografía Leblanc.

Zenteno de León, E.(30 de octubre de 1941). Gran Festival Poético en la Sala Cervantes. (U. T. Benson Latin American Collection, Recopilador) Santiago, Chile.

Zenteno de León, E. (1942). *Boletín del Cenáculo de Poesía (3)*. Santiago, Chile: Imprenta y Litografía Leblanc.

Zenteno de León, E. (24 de agosto de 1942). Recital poético en la Sala Cervantes. (T. A. University, Recopilador) Santiago, Chile.

Zenteno de León, E. (1943). *Boletín del Cenáculo de Poesía (4)*. Santiago, Chile: Imprenta y Litrografía Leblanc.

Zenteno de León, E. (30 de septiembre de 1943). Recital poético en la Sala Cervantes. (U. T. Austin, Recopilador) Santiago, Chile.

Zenteno de León, E. (1944). *Boletín del Cenáculo de Poesía del Conservatorio de Declamación (5)*. Santiago, Chile: Imprenta y Litrografía Leblanc.

Zenteno de León, E. (1945). *El arte de la declamación y la enseñanza práctica de este arte.* Santiago, Chile: Nascimento.

Zenteno de León, E. (1948-1951). *Mujeres de América.* (B. N. Chile, Recopilador) Santiago, Chile.

Zenteno de León, E. (1948-1951). Mujeres de América. (B. N. Chile, Recopilador) Santiago, Chile.

Zenteno de León, E. (septiembre-octubre de 1950). Alessandri. *Mujeres de América: "Manos Unidas, Corazones Fuertes"* (19), pág. p.1.

Zenteno de León, E. (ca 1944). Recital de poesía en la Sala Cervantes. (T. A. University, Recopilador) Santiago, Chile.

Zenteno de León, E. (1940a). Cenáculo de Poesía del Conservatorio de Declamación. *Boletín del Cenáculo de Poseía,* 1-6.

Zenteno de León, E. (29 de noviembre de 1940b). Gran Festival Poético en la Sala Cervantes. (B. L. U. Texas Austin, Recopilador) Santiago, Chile.

Zenteno de León, E. (1941a). *Boletín del Cenáculo de Poesía(2)*. Santiago, Chile: Imprenta y Litrografía Leblanc.

Zenteno de León, E. (30 de octubre de 1941b). Gran Festival Poético en la Sala Cervantes. (U. T. Benson Latin American Collection, Recopilador) Santiago, Chile.

Zenteno de León, E. (1942a). *Boletín del Cenáculo de Poesía(3)*. Santiago, Chile: Imprenta y Litografía Leblanc.

Zenteno de León, E. (24 de agosto de 1942b). Recital poético en la Sala Cervantes. (T. A. University, Recopilador) Santiago, Chile.

Zenteno de León, E. (1943a). *Boletín del Cenáculo de Poesía (4)*. Santiago, Chile: Imprenta y Litrografía Leblanc.

Zenteno de León, E. (30 de septiembre de 1943b). Recital poético en la Sala Cervantes. (U. T. Austin, Recopilador) Santiago, Chile.

Zenteno de León, E. (1944). *Boletín del Cenáculo de Poesía del Conservatorio de Declamación(5)*. Santiago, Chile: Imprenta y Litrografía Leblanc.

Zenteno de León, E. (1945). *El arte de la declamación y la enseñanza práctica de este arte.* Santiago, Chile: Nascimento.

Zenteno de León, E. (1947). *El Cenáculo de Poesía a sus poetas: 19 poetas del Cenáculo de Poesía* (1 ed.). Santiago, Chile: Talleres de la Editorial Nascimento.

Zenteno de León, E. (septiembre-octubre de 1950). Alessandri. *Mujeres de América: "Manos Unidas, Corazones Fuertes"* (19), pág. p.1.

Zenteno de León, E. (ca 1944). Recital de poesía en la Sala Cervantes. (T. A. University, Recopilador) Santiago, Chile.

Zenteno de León, E., C. de Guzman, H., Decarett Jaar, L., Jarpa G. de Lazo, S., & Mayer de Zulen, D. (mayo-junio de 1948). Dora Puelma. *Mujeres de América: "Manos Unidas Corazones Fuertes"* (5), pág. p.4.

Zenteno de León, E., C. de Guzman, H., Deccarett Jaar, L., Jarga Gana de Lazo, S., & Mayer de Zulen, D. (mayo-junio de 1948). Nuestra directora recibe distinción honorífica por su labor americanista (Homenaje a Vera Zouroff). *Mujeres de América "Manos Unidas Corazones Fuertes"* (5), pág. p.1.

Zenteno de León, E., C. de Guzman, H., Deccarett Jaar, L., Jarpa Gana de Lazo, S., & Mayer de Zulen, D. (mayo-junio de 1948). Mujeres en la diplomacia. *Mujeres de América: "Manos Unidas Corazones Fuertes"* (5), pág. p.2.

Zenteno de León, E., Enríquez , G., Puelma, D., Bose Méndez, B., Deccarett Jaar, L., Jarpa Gana de Lazo, S., y otros. (julio-agosto de 1948). Bolivar, 27 de julio de 1703. *Mujeres de América: " Manos Unidas Corazones Fuertes"* (6), pág. p.3.

Zenteno de León, E., Enríquez, G., Puelma, D., Bose Méndez, B., Decarett Jaar, L., Jarpa, S., y otros. (julio-agosto de 1948). Mujeres en la diplomacia. *Mujeres de América: "Manos Unidas Corazones Fuertes"* (6), pág. p.2.

Zenteno de León, E., Enríquez, G., Puelma, D., Bose Méndez, B., Deccarett Jaar, L., Jarpa Gana de Lazo, S., y otros. (julio-agosto de 1948). Problemas sociales. *Mujeres de América: "Manos Unidas Corazones Fuertes"* (6), pág. p.1.

Zenteno de León, E., Jarpa Gana de Lazo, S., Aguirre Cavada, R., Deccarett Jaar, L., Mayer de Zulen, D., Sosa Mendy, B., y otros. (enero-febrero de 1949). Unidad política continental. *Mujeres de América: "Manos Unidas, Corazones Fuertes"* (9), pág. p.3.

Zenteno de León, E., Jarpa Gana de Lazo, S., Mayer de Zulen, D., A.Bailey, A., de Lara, G., & de Marin , M. (mayo-junio de 1949). Marta Herrera de Warnken (Patricia Morgan). *Mujeres de América: "Manos Unidas, Corazones Fuertes"* (11), pág. p.1.

Zenteno de León, E., Jarpa Gana de Lazo, S., Mayer de Zulen, D., García, E., Daccaret Jaar, L., & Urivi, A. (julio- agosto de 1949). Dora Mayer de Zulen. *Mujeres de América: "Manos Unidas, Corazones Fuertes"* (12), pág. p.4.

Zenteno de León, E., Jarpa Gana de Lazo, S., Mayer de Zulen, D., Garía , E., Daccarett Jaar, L., & Urivi, A. (julio-agosto de 1949). Obra cultural realizada en Brasil por la poetisa chilena señora Gabriela Huneeus de Izquierdo. *Mujeres de América: "Manos Unidas, Corazones Fuertes"* (12), págs. p-1.

Zenteno de León, E., Jarpa, S., Aguirre Cavada, R., Deccarett Jaar, L., Mayer de Zulen, D., Sosa Mendy, B., y otros. (enero-febrero de 1949). A las mujeres de América de la Mesa Redonda Panamericana de Chile.

Mujeres de América: "Manos Unidas, Corazones Fuertes" (9), pág. p.1.

Zenteno de León, E., Mayer de Zulen, D., & Huerta Oliveira, M. (noviembre-diciembre de 1950). Actividades de la Casa de América. *Mujeres de América: "Manos Unidas, Corazones Fuertes"* (20), pág. p.1.

Zenteno de León, E., Mayer de Zulen, D., De Miranda, D., & Sosa Mendy, B. (septiembre-octubre de 1950). Homenaje a O´higgins en la Casa de América. *Mujeres de América: "Manos Unidas, Corazones Fuertes"* (19), pág. p.2.

Zenteno de León, E., Mayer de Zulen, D., Huerta Oliveira, M., & Silva de Santolalla, I. (enero-febrero de 1951). Estatutos y objetivos de la Casa de América-Chile. *Mujéres de América: "Manos Unidas, Corazones Fuertes"* (21), págs. p.1-2.

Zenteno de León, E., Mayer de Zulen, D., Vilchis Baz, C., & Huertas Oliveira, M. (julio-agosto de 1950). Actividades de la Mesa Redonda Panamericana de Mujeres de Chile. *Mujeres de América: "Manos Unidas, Corazones Fuertes"* (18), pág. p.1.

Zenteno de León, E., Mayer de Zulen, D., Vilchis Baz, C., & Huertas Oliveira, M. (julio-agosto de 1950). En Santiago de Chile se funda la Casa de América. *Mujeres de América: "Manos Unidas, Corazones Fuertes"* (18), pág. p.1.

Zenteno de León, E., Mayer de Zulen, D., Vilchis Baz, C., & Huertas Oliveira, M. O. (julio- agosto de 1950). Acta de fundación de la Casa de América. *Mujéres de América: "Manos Unidas, Corazones Fuertes"* (18), pág. p.2.

Zenteno de León, E., Mayer de Zulen, D., Vilchis de Baz, C., & Huertas Oliveira, M. (julio- agosto de 1950). Generoso gesto de Gabriela Mistral. *Mujeres de América: "Manos Unidas, Corazones Fuertes"* (18), pág. p.2.

Zouroff, V. (6 de octubre de 1949). Carta dirigida por Vera Zouroff a Gabriela Mistal. (B. N. Chile, Recopilador) Santiago, Chile.

Zouroff, V. (8 de septiembre de 1954). Carta de Vera Zouroff a Gabriela Mistral. (B. N. Chile, Recopilador) Santiago, Chile.

About the author

Daniel Piedrabuena Ruiz-Tagle (1964). He was born and lived his first nine years of life in Santiago, Chile. Later, he moved to Spain where he has been living for more than forty years, mainly in Madrid. He has a degree in Law (Uned), a degree in Business and Tourist Activities (Uned), and a degree in Advertising (Spanish Center for New Professions). For seventeen years (1994-2012) he was a researcher at the Spanish National Library, the Royal Academy of History, the National Archive, the Army Archive, the Navy Archive, the Hispanic Library, the Tavera Foundation, the German Foundation of Göerres, and many other archives and libraries.

He has also researched several regional archives, making a total of six trips around Spain: three to Malaga, where he has examined the Provincial Historical Archive, the Municipal Archive, and the Cathedral Archive; two to Seville, where he has researched the General Archive of the Indies and the Casa de Pilatos; and one to Granada, where he has explored the documents of the Royal Chancellery. As a result of this enormous research effort, he has written a series entitled *Los protegidos del César*, which is divided into two volumes; the first, *El conquistador alemán Pedro Lisperguer Wittemberg*; and the second, *Los Lisperguer Wittemberg: una familia alemana en el corazón de la cultura chilena*.

A great admirer of his grandmother's work, the author has also written another work entitled *Impresiones de Lucía Richard,* in which he not only devotes himself as a researcher but also masterfully relates the main literary and feminist movements of the 1940s and 1950s. He has also recently written *Concesión de la Cruz de la Orden de Franz Joseph a Carlos Boríes, Gobernador de Magallanes (1898-1904).* This is a small work, but very significant, due to the few Hispanic-American personalities who have received the award from the Kaiser of Austria.

The intellectual vocation of the author and his love for the American land that saw him born has led him to continue studying and reading about the literature and history of Latin America and Spain. He is now working on a new and inspiring book focused on 18th century Spain.

Author of the book: *El conquistador alemán Pedro Lísperguer Wittemberg: las vivencias europeas de un intrépido cortesano*

Author of the book: *Los Lisperguer Wittemberg: una familia alemana en el corazón de la cultura chilena*

Author of the book: *Impresiones de Lucia Richard*

Author of the book: Concesión de la Cruz de la Orden de Franz Joseph a Carlos Boríes, Gobernador de Magallanes (1898-1904).

Author of the article: Los Lísperguer Wittemberg: Luces y sombras de una singular familia alemana presente en la historia de España y Chile

Administrator of the Blog: Los Lísperguer Wittemberg

Visit his site on Facebook: El conquistador alemán Pedro Lísperguer Wittemberg

Visit his web site on Wordpress: Booksideals

If you want to comment on any aspect of this work you can do it through the following email address: booksideals@gmail.com. If this research has captivated you, It has interested you; if you think this topic has advanced, or if it has simply been useful to you, please feel free to comment on the platform where you bought the book.

Thank you!